Shrines and Pilgrimage in the Modern World
New Itineraries into the Sacred

Shrines and Pilgrimage in the Modern World
New Itineraries into the Sacred

Edited by Peter Jan Margry

Amsterdam University Press

Cover: Kok Korpershoek, Amsterdam

Illustration: based on Christ giving his blessing by Hans Memling, ca 1478

Lay-out: ProGrafici, Goes

ISBN 978 90 8964 0 116

NUR 728 / 741

Contents

III The Sports Realm

IV The Realm of Life, Spirituality and Death

On the Authors

Marijana Belaj (1970) is Assistant Professor at the Department of Ethnology and Cultural Anthropology, University of Zagreb, Croatia, where she defended her PhD thesis in 2006 on the veneration of saints in Croatian popular religion. Her research interests are contemporary pilgrimages, non-institutional processes of the sacralization of places and religious pluralism. Her list of publications includes articles in edited volumes and national and international journals. She is currently developing a research project on Medjugorje (Bosnia-Herzegovina).

marijana@belaj.com

Marion Bowman (1955) is Senior Lecturer in Religious Studies, and Co-director of the Belief Beyond Boundaries Research Group, the Open University, UK. She is currently President of the British Association for the Study of Religions and Vice-President of the Folklore Society. Her research interests include vernacular religion, contemporary Celtic spirituality, pilgrimage, material culture, and 'integrative' spirituality. She has conducted long-term research on Glastonbury, and her publications include 'Drawn to Glastonbury' in *Pilgrimage in Popular Culture*, edited by Ian Reader and Tony Walter in 1993 and most recently 'Arthur and Bridget in Avalon: Celtic Myth, Vernacular Religion and Contemporary Spirituality in Glastonbury' in *Fabula, Journal of Folktale Studies* (2007). She co-edited (with Steven Sutcliffe) the volume *Beyond New Age: Exploring Alternative Spirituality* (Edinburgh University Press 2000).

M.I.Bowman@open.ac.uk

Huub de Jonge (1946) is Senior Lecturer in Economic Anthropology at the Department of Cultural Anthropology and Development Studies, Radboud University Nijmegen, the Netherlands. He was awarded a PhD from the same university in 1984 with a dissertation on commercialization and Islamization on the island of Madura, Indonesia. His main fields of interest are economy and culture, lifestyles and identity, and entrepreneurship and ethnicity. In 1991 he co-edited (with Willy Jansen) a volume on Islamic pilgrimages. He is also co-editor (with Nico Kaptein) of *Transcending Borders: Arabs, Politics, Trade, and Islam in Southeast Asia* (Leiden 2002) and (with Frans Hüsken) of *Violence and Vengeance: Discontent and Conflict in New Order Indonesia* (Saarbrücken 2002) and of *Schemerzones en schaduwzijden. Opstellen over ambiguïteit in samenlevingen* (Nijmegen 2005).

h.dejonge@maw.ru.nl

Erika Doss holds a PhD from the University of Minnesota. She is Professor and Chair of the Department of American Studies at the University of Notre Dame, Indiana, USA. Her research interests are American and contemporary art history, material culture, visual culture, and critical theories of art history. Her recent books are *Twentieth-Century American Art* (Oxford University Press 2002); *Elvis Culture: Fans, Faith, and Image* (University Press of Kansas 1999); *Spirit Poles and Flying Pigs: Public Art and Cultural Democracy in American Communities* (Smithsonian Institution Press 1995). Her current research project is 'Memorial Mania: Self, Nation, and the Culture of Commemoration in Contemporary America.'

doss.2@nd.edu

Jill Dubisch holds a PhD from the University of Chicago (1972). She is Regents' Professor of Anthropology at Northern Arizona University, USA. Her research interests include religion and ritual, pilgrimage, 'New Age' healing and spiritual practices, and gender. She has carried out research in Greece, other parts of Europe and the United States. Her published works include *Gender and Power in Rural Greece* (Princeton 1986), *In a Different Place: Pilgrimage, Gender and Politics at a Greek Island Shrine* (Princeton 1995), *Run for the Wall: Remembering Vietnam on a Motorcycle Pilgrimage* (with Raymond Michalowski, 2001) and *Pilgrimage and Healing* (co-edited with Michael Winkelman, 2005).

Jill.Dubisch@NAU.EDU

Peter Jan Margry (1956), ethnologist, studied history at the University of Amsterdam, the Netherlands. He was awarded his PhD by the University of Tilburg (2000) for his dissertation on the religious culture war in the nineteenth-century Netherlands. He became Director of the Department of Ethnology at the Meertens Institute, a research center of the Royal Netherlands Academy of Arts and Sciences in Amsterdam. As a senior researcher at the institute, his current focus is on nineteenth-century and contemporary religious cultures in the Netherlands and Europe. He has published many books and articles in these fields, including the four-volume standard work on the pilgrimage culture in the Netherlands: *Bedevaartplaatsen in Nederland* (1997-2004). He co-edited (with H. Roodenburg) *Reframing Dutch Culture. Between Otherness and Authenticity* (Ashgate 2007).

peter.jan.margry@meertens.knaw.nl

Paul G.J. Post (1953) is Professor of Liturgy and Sacramental Theology and Director of the Liturgical Institute, University of Tilburg, the Netherlands. His current interests include pilgrimage and rituals. His major publications are (with J. Pieper and M. van Uden), *The Modern Pilgrim. Multidisciplinary explorations of Christian pilgrimage* (Peeters 1998); as co-editor *Christian Feast and Festival. The Dynamics of Western Liturgy and Culture* (Peeters 2001) and a *Cloud of Witnesses: The Cult of Saints in Past and Present* (Peeters 2005).

p.g.j.Post@uvt.nl

István Povedák (1976) studied history, ethnography and religious studies at the University of Szeged, Hungary. He is currently writing his PhD at the ELTE University of Budapest on celebrity culture in Hungary. His academic interests lie in the field of neofolklorization, civil religion theory and celebrity culture in Hungary. He teaches at the Department of Ethnology and Cultural Anthropology and the Department of Religious Studies at the University of Szeged.

povedak@yahoo.com

Deborah Puccio-Den (1968) is an anthropologist and a research fellow at the CNRS (French National Centre for Scientific Research) who works at the Marcel Mauss Institute-GSPM (Groupe de Sociologie Politique et Morale), of the Ecole des Hautes Etudes en Sciences Sociales (EHESS) in Paris. She is the author of *Masques et dévoilements* (CNRS Editions 2002); she edited a special issue of *Pensée de Midi* (Actes Sud 2002) entitled 'Retrouver Palerme' and has written many articles on the Sicilian mafia, including 'L'ethnologue et le juge. L'enquête de Giovanni Falcone sur la mafia en Sicile' in *Ethnologie française* (2001). In her recent work, she analyzes the connections between religion and politics within the anti-Mafia movement: 'De la sainte pèlerine au juge saint: les parcours de l'antimafia en Sicile' in *Politix* (2007) and explores relations between the state and violence: 'Mafia: stato di violenza o violenza dello stato?' in Tommaso Vitale (ed.), *Alla prova della violenza. Introduzione alla sociologia pragmatica dello stato* (Editori Riuniti 2007).
puccio@neuf.fr

Daniel Wojcik (1955) is Associate Professor of Folklore and English, and Director of the Folklore Studies Program at the University of Oregon, USA. He was awarded his PhD in Folklore and Mythology from the University of California (Los Angeles) in 1991. He is the author of *The End of the World As We Know It* (New York University Press 1997) and *Punk and Neo-Tribal Body Art* (University Press of Mississippi 1995), and has published 'Polaroids from Heaven: Photography, Folk Religion, and the Miraculous Image Tradition at a Marian Apparition Site' in the *Journal of American Folklore* 109 (1996), as well as numerous articles on apocalyptic beliefs and millenarian movements, vernacular religion and folk belief, self-taught visionary artists, and subcultures and youth cultures.
dwojcik@uoregon.edu

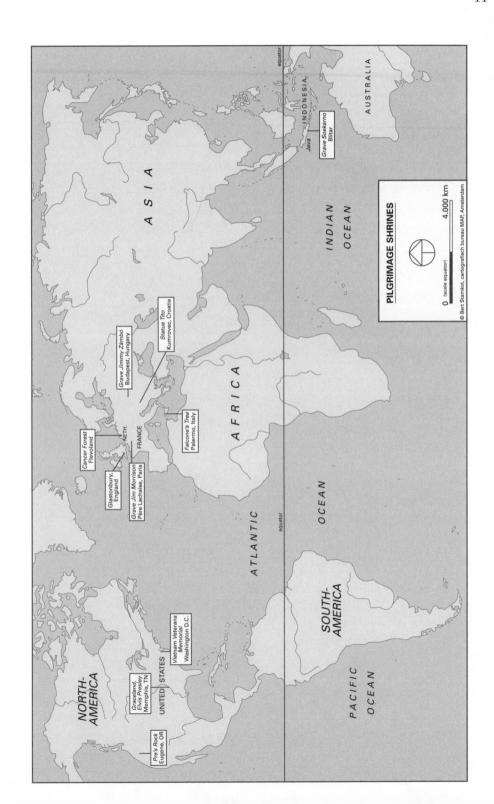

PILGRIMAGE SHRINES

0 (scale equator)   4.000 km

© Bert Stamkot, cartografisch bureau MAP, Amsterdam

NORTH-
AMERICA

Pre's Rock
Eugene, OR

Graceland,
Elvis Presley
Memphis, TN

UNITED STATES

Vietnam Veterans
Memorial
Washington D.C.

SOUTH-
AMERICA

PACIFIC
OCEAN

ATLANTIC
OCEAN

Cancer Forest
Flevoland

NETH.

Glastonbury,
England

FRANCE

Grave Jim Morrison
Père Lachaise, Paris

Grave Jimmy Zámbó
Budapest, Hungary

Statue Tito
Kumrovec, Croatia

Falcone's Tree
Palermo, Italy

AFRICA

A S I A

equator

INDONESIA

Java

Grave Soekarno
Blitar

AUSTRALIA

INDIAN
OCEAN

equator

Chapter 1

Secular Pilgrimage: A Contradiction in Terms?[1]

Peter Jan Margry

The definition of the term 'pilgrimage' is in need of re-evaluation. This does not imply that there have been no previous re-evaluations – quite the opposite, in fact. The phenomenon of the pilgrimage has been a focus of special attention in various areas of academic research for several decades. As a result, a broad corpus of ethnographic, comparative and analytic studies and reference books has become available, and the pilgrimage has been 'regained,' 'localized,' 're-invented,' 'contested,' 'deconstructed,' 'explored,' 'intersected,' 'reframed,' etc. from a variety of academic perspectives.[2] However, the results of all these different approaches have certainly not led to a fully crystallized academic picture of the pilgrimage phenomenon. There are still plenty of open questions, and distinct perspectives and schools of thought still exist.

This volume is based on a symposium held in Amsterdam in 2004 which was dedicated to the phenomenon of 'non-confessional pilgrimage' and the issue of religious pilgrimage versus non-religious or secular pilgrimage.[3] By both widening and narrowing the scope, the differences between 'traditional' pilgrimage and 'secular' pilgrimage were discussed, and in particular to what extent secular pilgrimage is a useful concept.[4] However, it is not up to the outsider to distinguish between the two concepts in advance. In this context, the evaluation will depend on the behavior and customs of the visitors to these modern shrines. Therefore, the authors in this volume would like to make a new contribution to the pilgrimage debate by focusing their attention on contemporary special locations and the memorial sites and graves of special individuals in order to determine whether apparently secular visits to these sites and adoration or veneration of them has a religious dimension or may even be religiously motivated, and – if this is the case – whether it is in fact appropriate to refer to these visits as pilgrimages. This book sets out to analyze manifestations of pilgrimage which parallel or conflict with mainstream pilgrimage culture in the modern world and at the same time to define the distinction between secular and religious pilgrimage more precisely. Although it is often difficult or impossible to make a distinction of this kind, it is contra-productive to use the concept of pilgrimage as a combination term for both secular and religious phenomena, thereby turning it into much too broad a concept. The term secular pilgrimage which is bandied about so much today actually contains two contradictory concepts and is therefore an oxymoron or contradiction in terms.

An important factor in the large amount of academic interest focused on pilgrimage is the personal fascination of researchers, but an even more im-portant factor is perhaps the awareness, shared by many, of the great socio-cultural and politico-strategic significance of this religious phenomenon. After all, the pilgrimage, a complex of behaviors and rituals in the domain of the sacred and the transcendent, is a global phenomenon, in which religion and *a fortiori* religious people often manifest themselves in the most powerful, col-lective and performative way.

Insights into the great significance of shrines and cults in relation to pro-cesses of desecularization and 're-enchantment' in the modern world have in themselves also reinforced the pilgrimage phenomenon (cf. Luckmann 1990; Berger 1999, 2002; Wuthnow 1992). The growing importance of religion in its social, cultural and political context has only increased the significance of the pilgrimage. For example, over the past few decades an informal fundamental-ist Catholic network, active on a global scale, has apparently succeeded in strengthening the conservative movement within the Catholic church with the help of the relative autonomy of contestative Marian shrines (Zimdars-Swartz 1991; Margry 2004a+b). The best-known and most important example is the Marian shrine at Medjugorje (Bosnia-Herzogovina). It is important not only because of its spiritual and liturgical influence but also – and above all – because of the ecclesiastical and political conflicts it has led to (Bax 1995). But the growing social and political role of Islam in the world has also strong-ly enhanced the significance of the hajj, the pilgrimage to Mecca, which is one of the five sacred obligations of Islam, in strengthening identity in the Islamic community (Abdurrahman 2000; Bianchi 2004). This significance in terms of identity formation is not only manifested on a global scale as in the case of the *hajj*; the symbolism and identity-forming powers of shrines have also increased greatly at the local, regional and national levels. In general, the considerable attention devoted to religion and rituals in the modern world has also indirectly enhanced ethnic/religious identities (Van der Veer 1994; cf. Guth 1995). Partly as a consequence of this, pilgrimage sites have also become involved in the strategies of military conflicts; the deliberate destruction of pilgrimage sites and shrines has evolved into an effective tactic for the purpose of harming national or religious identities or as a rationale for provoking conflicts, as in the case of the Sikhs' golden temple at Amritsar (India 1984) or the Shiites' golden mosque at Samarra (Iraq 2006, 2007).

However, because of its significance in relation to identity, the 'rediscovered' pilgrimage has also once again become a pastoral instrument in the secularized West, used to help control the crises in the institutional churches – in particular the Catholic church – in Western society, and to propagate the religious messages of the church more emphatically (Antier 1979; Congregazione 2002: 235-244). Apparently, shrines and pilgrimages have characteristics which enable them to generate, stimulate or revitalize religious devotion and religious identity (cf. Frijhoff 2002: 235-273). These dynamics are reminiscent of the situation in the nineteenth century, when the Catholic church used the pilgrimage on a large scale as an instrument to fend off enlightenment, rationalism and apostasy with the help of the church-going population; and in the twentieth century, after the Russian revolution and during the Cold War, pilgrimages and veneration of the Blessed Virgin were again used as a social and political instrument against atheistic political ideologies and secularization. Precisely in the Western world, especially in Europe with its anomalous secularization process (see Davie 2002), people who no longer had any ties with the institutional churches acquired a framework for new forms of religiosity and spirituality and for the alternative shrines and pilgrimages that went with them.

Research into change

Eventually, due to the ecclesiastical innovations in the Western world in the 1960s, the Catholic church also began to have reservations toward popular religion and to oppose some elements of it. The catholic Church's view that religion and church needed to be modernized even led to a temporary removal from the church's pastoral and ritual repertoire of practices such as pilgrimages and the veneration of saints, which were now seen as relic phenomena. Paradoxically, this process and the wide media coverage it led to brought the theme of the contemporary Western pilgrimage very much into the limelight, and it was partly because of this that it made it onto the research agenda of academics. Until then, the pilgrimage had been more or less the exclusive domain of ethnographers, church historians and theologians, who had been analyzing the phenomenon since the nineteenth century, mainly at the local level (Margry and Post 1998: 64-74). In terms of analytic comparison, pilgrimage in Europe had been relatively poorly studied, until the interest of cultural historians and cultural anthropologists was aroused. It was scholars such as Alphonse Dupront and Victor Turner who opened the theoretical debate about the significance of pilgrimage from the 1960s on.[5] The most important themes of that debate will be briefly evaluated below.

How 'clandestine' and little known and thus poorly studied the phenomenon of pilgrimage could be was revealed – for example – in the Netherlands. The stereotypical image of this small Western European country is of a Calvinist nation. Lengthy Protestant domination of the country had made the significant Catholic minority (35-40%) 'invisible' in the public domain. Nevertheless, it turned out that the Dutch Catholics had a large and finely meshed network of pilgrimage sites and pilgrimages, which was not widely known, even in the Netherlands itself. It was due to historical factors – the rigid political and social segmentization of the country into ideological 'pillars' and the constitutional restrictions imposed on the public manifestation of Catholicism – that the pilgrimage had been reduced to a more or less clandestine phenomenon ever since the Reformation. A large-scale ethnographic and historical study in the 1990s resulted in a sizeable body of data about no fewer than 660 *Dutch pilgrimage* sites, of which about 250 are still active today.[6] The amount of material which emerged from this effort to catch up made it possible to analyze the functions and meanings of Dutch pilgrimages in greater detail. From a broad anthropological perspective it became clear that the pilgrimage is becoming less and less an exclusively Catholic phenomenon and that more and more inter-religious and other forms of pilgrimage can be distinguished.[7] This is why at the conclusion of this research project, during the symposium referred to above, attention was drawn to various new forms of pilgrimage which had acquired a place in the world in connection with the changes in society, culture and religion in the second half of the twentieth century and are usually categorized as 'secular pilgrimages,' and implicitly opposed to 'religious pilgrimage.' To distinguish the two concepts and to analyze them in relation to each other, I would like to define religion (and *a fortiori* religiosity) as follows: all notions and ideas that human beings have regarding their experience of the sacred or the supernatural in order to give meaning to life and to have access to transformative powers that may influence their existential condition. Seen in this context I take 'pilgrimage' to mean a journey based on religious or spiritual inspiration, undertaken by individuals or groups, to a place that is regarded as more sacred or salutary than the environment of everyday life, to seek a transcendental encounter with a specific cult object for the purpose of acquiring spiritual, emotional or physical healing or benefit. I will come back to these two definitions later.

Particularly because of its frequent use in the media since the 1980s, the concept of pilgrimage has become embedded in common parlance, all the more because the massive 'subjective turn' in Western society meant that basically everyone could decide for themselves what they regarded as a pilgrimage destination, and sanctity or sacrality could be attributed to anyone or anything.[8] To an increasing extent the media themselves rediscovered pilgrimage and pilgrimage sites as interesting focus areas. These concepts, with their suggestive connotations and significances, could also be applied in a society where mass culture and personality cults such as those associated with film and rock stars, sports celebrities and royalty took on an increasingly important role, and media coverage followed the trend (cf. Couldry 2003: 75-94). Any place where people met occasionally or en masse to pay their respects to a special deceased person soon came to be referred to as a 'place of pilgrimage,' although it was not clear what this actually meant. Although the religious realm in the postmodern 'Disneyesque' environment is changing, it is questionable whether visitors to or participants in such diverse destinations and occasions as the house where Shakespeare was born, the military Yser Pilgrimage in Flanders, a papal Mass in Rome, the D-Day beaches in Normandy, the Abbey Road zebra crossing, the WorldYouth Days, personal journeys, Disney World, or shopping malls can really be categorized as pilgrims (Reader and Walter 1993: 5-10; Clift and Clift 1996: 88-112; Lyon 2000; Pahl 2003).

Occasionally, a certain link with religion may be found, as in the case of the 'civil religion' element in commemorations of war victims and monuments and in visits to the houses or graves of national heroes or famous battlefields (Zelinsky 1990). Even in the early twentieth century, visits to war cemeteries were referred to in newspapers as pilgrimages.[9] A form of religion also often seems to be involved in these visits. In this context Lloyd wrote that the presence of the memory of the war in private lives 'transformed these sites [battlegrounds/cemeteries] into places of pilgrimage' (Lloyd 1998: 217). It is more or less clear that religion frequently plays a role (Walter 1993; Lloyd 1998). However, Lloyd also takes the 'pilgrimage' concept for granted in his study, without operationalizing it or giving it any further empirical basis. His conclusion is that 'Pilgrims distinguished themselves from tourists in order to stress their special links with the fallen and the war experience' (Lloyd 1998: 220). A short, generalizing statement like this is rather unsatisfactory, especially because Lloyd draws attention to the individual and emotive experiences of mourning, coping with grief, and the role of traditional religion in visiting war cemeteries, elements on which he could probably have based a more explicit evaluation of the status of the visits as 'pilgrimages.'

It was mainly pop music and the rise of fan culture which stimulated their own culture of visits to the graves of rock stars and icons. Particularly in rock culture, where stars relatively often die young in dramatic ways, new forms sprang up in which the adoration and veneration of the deceased heroes and idols came together. Graceland is the most famous and most spectacular example (Doss 1999). However, it is certainly not clear how attributions of holiness to the last resting places of music stars in general should be interpreted (Frijhoff 2004). A striking feature of Reed and Miller's visual reportage is that practically all the musicians' graves seem to be associated with rituals, consisting for example of placing flowers, objects and texts by the graves (Reed and Miller 2005). Accessorizing graves with objects relates back to age-old commemorative practices, and although these rituals associated with (western) rock legends are influenced by Christian culture, they are actually shared across many religions. This does not mean that the secular pilgrimages do in fact convert the sites into pilgrimage sites; nevertheless, the visual and material culture associated with these graves does in fact seem to connect them with cults and pilgrimage. But is this really the case? Is it a matter of individuals visiting a grave or have the locations acquired lasting and universal sacred significance?

At most of the sites the meanings attributed by the visitors to the individual and that individual's grave are confused or contradictory. Asking them does not always produce helpful results either, because the language used among fans is itself influenced by the media and therefore often consists of idiomatic narratives. Because the concept of the pilgrimage has been stretched, the word has acquired a new semantic dimension, so that more and more frequently visitors themselves refer to profane practices and events as pilgrimages, partly because fans themselves are often aware of parallels between traditional Christian religion and their own (Cavicchi 1998: 51-57). Fans of rock singer Bruce Springsteen said that they regarded going to one of his concerts as 'going to a church and having a religious experience' and visits to places where he had lived and places mentioned in his songs as 'pilgrimages' (Cavicchi 1998: 186). In her description of Graceland, Christine King – unlike Doss in her later study – used so many Christian terms with so little discrimination that it became a self-fulfilling academic prophecy and – without any substantial empirical justification – the place was proclaimed a pilgrimage site in the universal sense (King 1993). What meanings are concealed behind these terms, and how can the religious factor be identified and interpreted?

To an increasing extent, not only the media but also researchers characterize tourism and other transitory phenomena metaphorically as 'pilgrimages' (cf. Reader and Walter 1993; Kaur 1985; Basu 2004; Hodge 2006; cf. Chide-ster 2005). In his book *Sacred Journeys*, anthropologist Alan Morinis ascribes an explicit place to the allegorical or metaphorical pilgrimage, namely the pilgrimage 'that seeks out a place not located in the geographical sphere' and says that 'one who journeys to a place of importance to himself alone may also be a pilgrim' (Morinis 1992:4). No matter how titillating it may be to thought processes and the imagination to combine these apparently similar phenome-na, constantly linking them to each other does not seem to have provided any essentially deeper insights into the 'traditional' pilgrimage; in fact, its main re-sult has been to increase the confusion surrounding the concept. For example, as Jennifer Porter wrote: 'By broadening the boundaries of pilgrimage to en-compass such secular journeys [= Star Trek Conventions], pilgrimage scholars can perhaps go where they've never gone before.' Expanding on Morinis's work, Porter goes on to say (merely on the basis of external analogies and without further substantiation): '…then *Star Trek* convention attendance truly does constitute pilgrimage in a secular context' (Porter 2004: 172; cf. Chidester 2005: 33).

Be that as it may, in recent decades the question of what the term pilgrima-ge means exactly and what should be regarded as the criteria for a pilgrimage has only become more complicated. This applies even more strongly to what is referred to as 'secular pilgrimage' – a term consisting of two concepts which are troublesome to define and difficult to unite. In order to define pilgrimage as a religious phenomenon more exactly and to deconstruct secular pilgri-mage as a concept, we need to evaluate the main academic research themes relating to the constitutive elements of pilgrimage.

Communitas vs individuality

One of these themes is the relationship between the individual and the group and possible interference between these two social categories during a pil-grimage. An initial theoretical debate on this issue arose as early as the 1960s when a dispute broke out in German ethnographic circles about whether pil-grimage could be regarded as an individual affair at all (Kriss 1963; Dünninger

1963). According to some ethnographers, the fact that group pilgrimages were universal in the German cultural area excluded individual pilgrimages. They therefore only regarded a sacred place as a 'pilgrimage site' if pilgrimages to the site were undertaken by groups or in a processional way. The problem was that this view only took the public manifestation of pilgrimage and its performative character into account, and not its motives and the social relationships involved. Due to this functionalistic approach, the pilgrimage was regarded as an extension or confirmation of the everyday social structure – a view which was based only on a specific regional *praxis* and was therefore eventually rejected as a theoretical concept (Brückner 1970).[10]

The first to approach the Christian pilgrimage as a phenomenon with the intention of forming a new theory was the American anthropologist Victor Turner. Because of the inter-related dynamic social processes involved, he thought that he could see a special kind of group formation during pilgrimages, and on this basis he developed what was to become a leading theory in cultural anthropology. Proceeding from the notions of Van Gennep, Turner drew up a theoretical framework for pilgrimage as a rite of passage (cf. Van Gennep 1909). Turner saw pilgrimage not as a phenomenon which confirmed the existing social structure with its status and hierarchies, but precisely as an alternative structure – therefore termed 'antistructural' – because of the development of a new community of pilgrims. In his opinion, pilgrimage was a temporary antithesis of the ordinary, everyday community to which the pilgrim normally belonged (Turner and Turner 1978; Turner 1986). The liminal and transitional character of pilgrimage temporarily eliminates the pilgrim's normal situation and status, and in consequence spontaneous, egalitarian ties are created which Turner refers to as the group experience or 'communitas.' Turner also drew attention to a certain tension between the journey and the location, and in connection with this, to the necessity of 'liminoid' behavior on the part of the pilgrim.

Although Turner's postulate that 'anti-structure' and 'communitas' are created during a pilgrimage is regarded as the only significant theory regarding pilgrimage and was decisive for the debate for a long time, the theory has been falsified over and over again on the basis of ethnographic case studies (cf. Eade and Sallnow 2000: 4-5; Reader and Walter 1993: 10-15; Badone and Roseman: 3-5). In response, critics such as Eade and Sallnow called on researchers to collect much more ethnographic material.[11] Whatever the case may be, in practice researchers always encountered a wide variety of behaviors and experience, and to an ever-increasing extent the theory was abandoned (Sallnow 1981: 163-183; Morinis 1992: 8). The strongest formulation of this rejection was by Coleman and Eade, who regard Turner's notions on pilgrimage as a 'theoretical cul-de-sac' (Coleman and Eade 2004: 3). They also rightly question whether pilgrimage is in fact as exceptional as it is presented as being in the world of anthropology and in environments where the research focus is on the biggest shrines or on exceptional shrines.

But if there is no *communitas*, what is there then? Undeniably, during a pilgrimage there are various important group connections and forms of sociability. For instance, in Huub de Jonge's article in this book about Soekarno's grave, he identifies a metaform of *communitas* which develops on the basis of shared ideas about national and religious unity, while Marion Bowman describes a loose kind of sociability – an 'intermittent co-presence' – among individual pilgrims in Glastonbury. The wide revival of the 'traditional' group pilgrimage on foot in the Western world is also a clear example of new forms of sociability. The other side of the coin is that within Christian culture a lack of or aversion to the group process can be ascertained. While it is true that in Christian culture pilgrimage has collective elements which are identity-forming or demonstrative in character, in essence it is much more individual than is often thought. Alan Morinis has already asserted that pilgrimage, in spite of external manifestations such as group pilgrimages, penitential journeys and processions, is regarded in the first instance as an individual, personal affair rather than a social one (Morinis 1992). Although collective actions at or around shrines are the most obvious, fieldwork is showing more and more frequently that in the mainstream Western pilgrimage culture, pilgrimage is partly separated from the formal rituality and liturgy of the location. To an increasing extent it is a personal journey, which is undertaken collectively mainly when there is no alternative. Those who set off for a shrine in a group are often 'compelled' to do so because of physical injuries or practical financial constraints. This applies even more strongly if the pilgrimage site is a long way away and the journey thus more arduous, more expensive or more complicated to organize. People prefer to conduct an activity which is so personal as a pilgrimage with a certain measure of privacy: with few other pilgrims present, without being constrained by collective rituals, and if possible using their own cars, perhaps accompanied by close family members or a good friend. Pilgrimages are personal visits, with strictly personal intentions directed toward the cult object. Pilgrims are generally not keen to talk about the religious dimensions and find it difficult to do so; this is also true of the pilgrims who feature in this book.[12] In fact, it may apply to them even more strongly, because on the face of it their motive has no right to exist in this environment which is so secular in other respects. For privacy reasons, this dimension is scarcely expressed in writing at all, with the exception of intention books with their anonymous messages. This characteristic individuality is also found in the pilgrimages discussed here. For example, it turned out that the close in-crowd fans around Jim Morrison's grave who did actually seem to have a form of *communitas* were not among those who had a religious motivation for their visit. Such a motivation was found mainly in individual visitors to the grave. If individualization is a sign of the times, then this is also reflected in pilgrimage.

Movement and travel vs sanctuary and locality

Movement is an inherent part of pilgrimage. As a result, throughout history the performance of the phenomenon has been visible as spatial movement. But at the same time the pilgrimage site is fixed in space (Coleman and Elsner 1995: 2002), and the holy place or shrine is the 'very *raison d'être* of pilgrimage' (Eade and Sallnow 1991/2000: 6) or as *Dupront* put it: 'Il n'y a pas de pèlerinage sans lieu [sacré]' ('There is no pilgrimage without a [sacred] place') (1987: 371). This is why it is important for the theoretical discussion about the primary aspect of pilgrimage to continue: should the focus be on location and locality, with the sacred site as the ultimate goal, or should it be on the journey and being on the way? As far as Christian pilgrimage was concerned, it was possible to choose between the two (namely, the destination was the most important), but because of changes in pilgrimage culture over the past decades this choice is no longer feasible.

I would like to stress that in principle the core or rationale of the Christian pilgrimage lay within the physical boundaries of the shrine. In a process of placemaking, the presence of a cult object associated with a specific location gives shape to the sacred, both physically and intangibly. Sanctity is attributed to that object and *a fortiori* to its environment, a space where the pilgrim expects salvation, healing and solace, or hopes to effect a cure. Dubisch and Winkelman formulate this as follows: 'Pilgrimage sites shape the pilgrimage and nature and history shape its power' (Dubisch and Winkelman 2005: xviii). At any rate, this statement applies or has applied to virtually all Christian pilgrimage sites. The fact that things have changed is due to a development in which the pilgrimage journey has also become an end in itself.[13] The most important catalyst in this process and its most powerful reflection is the modern pilgrimage to Santiago de Compostela. Whereas before the mid-twentieth century the cathedral of Santiago was the pilgrimage destination in the classical sense, it is now largely the other way around: the pilgrimage in the sense of a spiritual journey has become the rationale. Santiago has been discovered and reinvented by spiritual seekers and lovers of cultural history and tranquility. For many walkers the journey along the *camino*, the 'transit' as I would call it, has become an individual rite of passage or 'a pilgrimage to one's self' (Eberhart 2006: 160). The media and politics have also played a stimulating role in this development.[14] Without the lengthy and wide media coverage of this ancient pilgrimage and the cultural politics of Spain, the transition from a destination-oriented pilgrimage to seeing the journey as a pilgrimage in itself would not have been so universal. It was due to this process that 'transit' pilgrimage made its appearance in the west. Transit pilgrimage does not really have a beginning or an end, or at any rate they are not relevant. Moving, walking, the accessibility and freedom of the ritual, being in nature, and tranquility are all elements which have contributed to its success. As a transit pilgrimage, the Santiago pilgrimage is sometimes even spread across several years or vacations, with one stage of the whole journey being completed at a time.

For many walkers the shrine in Compostela is now so far removed from their new experiential worlds that when they arrive there they are disillusioned.[15] All kinds of pilgrimage routes and walking tracks can now be found all over Europe. This major innovation in pilgrimage culture is not restricted to Christian pilgrimages; this volume reveals that there are also transit pilgrimages like this around Glastonbury, and that the motorcycle pilgrimages undertaken by Vietnam veterans across the United States are similar in character.

Whereas in the first half of the twentieth century Santiago only functioned as a place of pilgrimage to a limited extent, it was initially an interest – with medieval overtones – in Romanesque heritage along the formerly French pilgrimage routes leading there which put the pilgrimage site and its access routes back on the map. This was stimulated by the strong focus on the three big pilgrimage locations (Jerusalem, Rome, Santiago de Compostela) of the Christian Middle Ages, which dominated historical pilgrimage literature for a long time. Since then, new editions of a guide to the pilgrimage to the shrine of St James in Santiago passed down in the twelfth-century *Codex Calixtinus* and the great interest shown by art historians in architecture and art objects along the route have converted the pilgrimage paths to Santiago into a constructed and invented heritage concept which could be widely appropriated in European society. Moreover, romantic images of pilgrimage as being strenuous, hazardous, and a constant form of penance were added to the picture: 'The journey was to be arduous and dangerous' (Swatos and Tomasi 2002: 207).[16] It is partly due to this dominant element in the literature that the major shrines like Santiago and Rome (Holy Years), which appeal to the imagination, are constantly used as examples in research. While there is nothing wrong with this in itself, it should be borne in mind that these two places are not representative; in fact, they are anomalies.

The view that the journey is the most definitive aspect of pilgrimage was backed up by the results of the conference titled 'Sacred Journeys' which Morinis organized in 1981. In the volume of the same name which appeared later, he characterized the phenomenon of pilgrimage as 'a human quest' (Morinis 1992: ix, 4; cf. Dupront 1987: 413). With this approach he made a connection with the idea of the early Christian *peregrinatio* as formulated by St Augustine

(Bitton-Ashkelony 2005: 110-115) – a quest and a long-distance pilgrimage.[17] Morinis narrowed down the research perspective, stating that 'a true typology of pilgrimages focuses on the pilgrims' journey and motivations, not on the destination shrines' (Morinis 1992: ix, 10).[18] He proposed a major classification based on pilgrims' motivation perspectives, but paid little attention to the contextuality of pilgrimage and the placemaking process that results in a sacred pilgrimage site.[19] However, no matter how clear it may be that pilgrimage research should not be limited to the location and that the journey is also such an important component of a pilgrimage that it must always be taken into account in the entire pilgrimage culture, there is no justification for reducing the phenomenon primarily to the journey element.

By now, the wide interest in pilgrimage routes and the decisive role attributed to the pilgrimage paths to Santiago, Rome and later also Glastonbury and other places has extended beyond the domains of cultural heritage and the New Age movement. Since the 1970s, in the Catholic church itself there has also come to be a stronger focus on the journey than on the cult object. Whereas formerly the journey was a necessary evil, nowadays it is seen as 'tradition' or as pilgrimage heritage, and more and more frequently a pilgrimage is only seen as a 'real' pilgrimage if it is completed on foot. While this is not the invention of a tradition, it is a reinvention of the meaning of a tradition. Nowadays, this kind of 'active' pilgrimage is used as a 'new' pastoral instrument to revive interest in religion, particularly among young people. The emphasis is on the group experience and the spiritual and healing elements of the journey – which often takes place in the evening or at night (Albers 2007). These journeys are successful because, as a rule, young people are much less interested in cult objects and the associated healing aspects than in the great questions of life and the meaning of religion. The pilgrimage formula is not restricted to young people. Various organizations offer people from a variety of denominations international, national, and regional opportunities to undertake reflective and spiritual journeys.[20]

It was due to this development in particular that Coleman and Eade drew inspiration from the idea of physical motion for their book *Reframing Pilgrimage*. Following on from Hervieu-Léger's *La religion en mouvement* (1999), they see pilgrimages as 'cultures in motion.' By focusing on this aspect, like Morinis they relegate the place-centered approach to the background and concentrate on the sanctifying effect of forms of movement toward and at shrines. To a large extent, Coleman and Eade's reason for doing this was that they were convinced by the many testimonies of the spiritual and physical transformation effected by the journey to Santiago and the combination of 'travel, pilgrimage and tourism' on the *camino*. The fact that their concept is based mainly on practices associated with the pilgrimage to Santiago is surprising, since as has already been mentioned this pilgrimage is not representative of mainstream pilgrimage culture (Coleman and Eade 2004: 11). Its existence confirms that there is not just one kind of Christian pilgrimage. It is therefore questionable whether, on the basis of this specific case, motion can be assumed to be the primary constitutive element of the pilgrimage as a universal phenomenon. It may be true that no pilgrimage can take place without some distance being covered, but even this notion is now open to question. In the twentieth century the development of hundreds of 'branches' of the pilgrimage sites of Lourdes and Fatima all over the world had already made a huge difference in the distance to be covered, and now, in the twenty-first century, the Internet brings the virtual shrine right into people's homes (Macwilliams 2002, 2004). Moreover, no satisfactory answer has been given to questions about the relationship and distinction between pilgrimage and the local veneration of saints or cult objects.[21]

Because of the sacrality, rituality and exceptional material culture attributed to pilgrimage shrines, they are more or less dissociated from everyday life. This means that a pilgrim must consciously 'extricate' himself or herself from everyday life in order to set off for the sacred place. This is what Turner calls 'separation.' Because it requires going beyond the physical and mental boundaries of ordinary life, pilgrimage is a liminal activity. This crossing of boundaries is a constant element of pilgrimage. In the narrower sense, parish, village, or municipal boundaries must also be regarded as geographic boundaries. During the Dutch pilgrimage research project a somewhat ragged dividing line emerged according to which a cultus within the visitor's own parish is not regarded as a pilgrimage, and a visit to a holy place in the immediate vicinity of the individual's everyday life is seen as local saint veneration. On the other hand, this does not mean that a pilgrimage necessarily entails long-distance travel. This became clear in the dominantly Catholic regions in the south of the Netherlands, where the lower limit for a pilgrimage turned out to be about five kilometers from the pilgrim's home. As a distance for a pilgrimage this seems very short, but apparently it applies at least throughout the rest of Europe as well. This suggests a much greater density of the network of places of pilgrimage and pilgrimages than has previously been assumed.[22] However, as a rule, definitions associated with pilgrimage are still based on data relating to a few major shrines and not to the smaller ones which are probably more representative of destination-oriented pilgrimage because there are so many of them and thus provide a different perspective on Christian pilgrimage culture.

Tourism and Pilgrimage

In the wake of movement and travel, the concept of tourism also entered pilgrimage research. It was thought that tourism, because of its similar characteristics, would generate new insights into the operation of pilgrimage. After the French anthropologist Alphonse Dupront first put this theme on the research agenda in the context of collective psychology (Dupront 1969), Badone and Roseman tried to reconcile the conceptual dichotomy between religious travel and tourism as secular journeying. They write: 'Rigid dichotomies between pilgrimage and tourism, or pilgrims and tourists, no longer seem tenable in the shifting world of postmodern travel' (Badone and Roseman 2004: 2; cf. Timothy and Olsen 2006). However, this seems rather self-evident, since the element of tourism is 'rediscovered' on a regular basis (cf. Macioti 2002: 89). Throughout the centuries the repertoire of pilgrims' secondary motives has always been wide, and has included 'tourism.' It started more or less with the *curiositas* and the *missio* of the early Christian *peregrinatio* referred to earlier and has always played a role ever since. In the past few decades a few modern pilgrimages – to Amsterdam, Lourdes and Wittem (Netherlands) – have been the subject of sociological research based on multiple-choice questionnaires aimed at collecting data on motive repertoires (Post, Pieper and Van Uden 1998: 19-48, 173-203). One reason for choosing this non-qualitative method was that, as a rule, pilgrims find it quite difficult to formulate their motives (cf. Reader and Walter 1993: 237-238). The wide variety of motives mentioned by the pilgrims is striking, but even more so is their sheer number. Sometimes the number of motives was as high as 20, and the tourist and social components of the journey were certainly included. However, they are secondary motives to the main objective, namely the religious reason for going on a pilgrimage (Post, Pieper and Van Uden 1998: 157-242).[23]

The Turners' much quoted observation that 'a tourist is half a pilgrim, if a pilgrim is half a tourist' (1978: 20; cf. Swatos and Tomasi 2002: 208), which is often cited as 'proof' of the secular element of pilgrimage, is above all suggestive. Again, the fact is that the main goals are the sacred, the religious, the cultus object; without them there is no pilgrimage. Of course most pilgrims have one or more secondary motives: the beauty of the scenery, tourist aspects, the sociability of the collective journey, etc. But if that is all there is, then there is no question of pilgrimage; the journey is for tourism or other motives. Obviously, this does not alter the fact that sometimes individuals – tourists, passers-by, etc. – visit shrines without any religious motivation, but are in fact affected by the sacred place once they are there. This is part of what Badone and Roseman call 'intersecting journeys.' The concept does not imply that tourism and pilgrimage are interchangeable. Intersections between the two only come to the fore when tourists allow themselves to be carried away – intentionally or unintentionally – by the sacred experiences of the shrine or the pilgrimage. Tourism is also explicitly discussed in this volume. The grave locations of Elvis Presley and Jim Morrison are both tourist attractions where mass tourism is manifestly present. However, apparently visits to Graceland and Père Lachaise are stratified and contested. Erika Doss makes it clear that for a specific group of fans, the religious factor is in fact present, and that narratives employed by these fans during their visits are distinct from those of the tourist masses.

The Secular and the Religious

Pilgrimage is a product of the social environment, just as religion is a human, cultural activity. Activities of this sort are subject to change, and this also applies to pilgrimage. No matter how complex and stratified pilgrimage may be, not all phenomena related to travel and veneration can simply be included in the concept, as Reader tries to do, without distinguishing between different behaviors (Reader and Walter 1993: 2-3).

Not surprisingly, use of the oxymoronic concept of 'secular religion' leads to constant epistemological confusion. Practically all studies which work with this concept fail to reveal what they actually mean by it. Moreover, because of its vagueness, it stimulates over-interpretation, tending either toward the secular or toward the religious (Piette 2003: 93). Although the term secular religion is often used, the internal contradiction persists, and as such is rarely solved or explained in the studies in question. This obfuscating effect becomes even stronger if the concept is also used in a metaphorical sense. The problem is similar to the central question of Knott's book: how to locate religion in everyday life, in order to distinguish it from the secular (Knott 2005). If one assumes that the religious dimension or motivation is a constitutive element of pilgrimage, then the next question is whether the 'secular,' modern and non-confessional shrines and pilgrimages, outside the traditional (Christian) pilgrimage culture, do in fact have a religious dimension. To answer this question, the visits to special places and their associated veneration examined in this volume have been approached as much as possible on their own terms, quite apart from institutionalized religions, and authors have tried to ascertain whether forms of religious devotion could be found at these places, so that the epithet 'secular' could be omitted with respect to the components in question (cf. Glock 1962, 1974; Piette 2003: 96).

It is in fact not the first time that researchers have devoted attention to this topic. Ian Reader and Tony Walter more or less acted as pioneers when they edited *Pilgrimage in Popular Culture*, a book that was the result of an Implicit Religion Conference organized by Edward Bailey. Reader argued in favor of a further secularization of the notion of pilgrimage (Reader and Walter 1993: 221-222). Hopgood's more recent book, *The Making of Saints*, also sees 'commonalities and convergence of forms' and common characteristics of pilgrimages and generic saints as a possible approach (Hopgood 2005b: xvi).[24] Hopgood examined 'processes of deification of secular personages' and in this context compared James Dean with El Niño Fidencio of Mexico, as representatives of secular religion and devotion and folk Catholicism, respectively. The research analysis compares many elements of the two cultures, but not the religious dimension which distinguishes a saint *a priori* from a hero, an icon or an idol. In cases like this, it is also unsatisfactory if the conclusion is more or less that in both cases T-shirts with images of the individuals in question are on sale (Hopgood 2005c: 140). Hopgood tries to explain the growth of the 'new sainthood' among celebrities – icons – mainly in terms of communication technology. He sees a blending of styles and narratives developing in this area due to the influence of modern technology and mediatization. However, the research practice is overly focused on external characteristics, on the adoption of styles and narratives, and on analogies of form and representation, while the differences in function and meaning are overlooked.[25]

By contrast, the editors of the journal *Etnofoor* (Van Ede 1999: 3) have studied this problem in greater depth. In a special issue of the journal titled *Personality Cults*, they write that cults of this kind show an 'intriguing mix of the sacred and the secular.' And they ask: 'Is the likening of a political leader to a present-day saint mere trope, or can the anthropological understanding of saints as mediators between the mundane and the heavenly help explain the worship that he engenders?' They go on to state – quite rightly – that the boundaries between the religious and the secular are highly artificial and permeable. Nevertheless, in my opinion we still have to make the distinction, because otherwise their view that 'notwithstanding their secular content, personality cults are religious phenomena in the sense that they aim at rendering the world a meaningful place' (Van Ede 1999: 3) still does not define the relationship between the secular and the religious, not even when they write that 'personality cults around secular figures may be read as attempts to bridge the experiential world of the individual devotee with some larger system of meaning,' since such systems of meaning are not necessarily religious. In short, the existing view that the sacred and the profane are not two separate worlds but are closely connected with each other has led mainly to further blurring of the boundaries. In order to determine whether the apparently profane or secular truly has sacred or religious characteristics, we have attempted in this volume to make a more precise distinction between the secular and the religious in relation to pilgrimage on the basis of ethnographic research (cf. Greil and Bromley 2003: 3-18).

Ethnography and Analysis

In their external appearances, visits to graves, shrines and special places display parallels in rituality, materiality or (religious) vocabulary, but these say little about their religious meaning. Piette has already stressed the importance of ethnographic fieldwork in determining the '*fait religieux*' in speech and writing in everyday life (Piette 2003: 101-108). He noticed an almost complete lack of such fieldwork relating to the monotheistic religions.[26] As religious experiences or impressions are difficult to pin down, how can religiosity – the condition of being religious – be identified? How does it manifest itself, and what exactly does religiosity consist of?[27] Is it purely a belief in supernatural powers or a transcendental reality? As religion is seen here as a human, culturally determined activity, it makes sense to reflect on what people may possibly expect from religion. Here we must consider elements such as finding meaning in life, membership of a living community and identification with its deceased members, safety and security, strength and support, comfort and hope, and healing and resolution, but also the expression of gratitude and possibly the expectation or hope of salvation and eternal life after death. I defined religion earlier in this article as all notions and ideas that human beings have regarding their experience of the sacred or the supernatural in order to give meaning to life and to have access to transformative powers that may influence their existential condition. But within the cognitive domain, religiosity is not only about having certain ideas, expectations, motives, or feelings inside one's head; it is also about the articulation of actions and practices. It is in behaviors and rituals and through the attribution of meaning to material culture that religion can manifest itself most clearly, while as a rule its most precise expression is through oral or written communication or information about its content. Both methodological approaches have been utilized in this study.

However, in practice it still proves difficult to identify the religious element unequivocally in the course of research. There are often several religious narratives that unfold simultaneously or are intertwined with each other. Especially in the Western world, which was partly created and missionarized by Christianity, almost all incarnations of religiosity are influenced by the continent's religious history. New expressions of religiosity and secular devotions in particular are frequently characterized by cultural hybridity. As such, the public perception of these cults is determined both by cultural heritage and the influence of the media and academics.

As has already been stressed, the analysis of motives and the reasoning on which it is based are of great importance to the analysis in this study. Previously published research has shown more and more clearly that the existential insecurity of individuals holds the central position in the contemporary motive repertoire of pilgrimage (Post et al. 1998; Margry 2004; Margry and Caspers 1997-2004). In the first instance visitors are seeking contact with the holy, the sacred, or with a god in order to gain support, protection, or eternal salvation. Empirical underpinning for this can be found in the texts written by pilgrims in intention books at the sacred sites,[28] but also in interviews with pilgrims themselves, in which the prevailing motives seem to be connected with the *condition humaine*, with problems of sickness, insecurity, levels of happiness and the meaning of life. Although in practice pilgrimage is often performed within a social context, the pilgrimage itself is primarily an individual exercise. In short, pilgrimage expresses the efforts the individual has to make to give meaning and direction to his or her personal existence.

The central place given to rationalism and the success of science and medicine in Western culture has changed the perception of pilgrimage to some extent, but it has not led to its disappearance. While some diseases have been conquered and people no longer need to go on pilgrimages to seek healing for them, new ailments have taken their place. Not only medical and social insecurity, but also a fundamental lack of confidence in social and political systems is a persistent problem. This is confirmed in the study by Dubisch and Winkelman based on the concepts of suffering and healing. They attribute major significance to a pilgrimage site as far as existential difficulties and healing are concerned (Dubisch and Winkelman 2005). Several case studies in this book confirm their findings. In relation to existential insecurity, Marijana Belaj has written as follows about people visiting the Tito statue in Kumrovec: 'The visitors connect the creative and prosperous period of their lives with their then leader,"the greatest son of these lands,"' in the hope that in their current troubled times Tito can do something for them again. Visitors to the small shrine of long-distance runner Prefontaine also see their cult object as an intercessor and as someone who can bestow blessings when a person badly needs support, just as Jim Morrison is expected to provide support for dealing with drug problems because of his own drug-related past.

Where the traditional religious contexts are no longer present or functioning, or are barely so, significant existential insecurities can develop, and people will look for alternatives. Several values surveys have indicated that the subjectivation of life and an increasing feeling of insecurity are widely occurring processes in contemporary Western society (Halman et al. 2005: 60-73). This concurs with what Hervieu-Léger (1999) states in her book about pilgrims, namely that due to major insecurities, the meaning systems which enable individuals to give personal meaning to their lives have been destabilized. The fact that people are led less by an external truth, as was the case in the traditional churches, can be seen in the places that have institutionally separated themselves as fundamentalist or secessionist movements and where the work of salvation can be seen as a pluriform process that can be mobilized for various groups and individuals, as described in the case studies in this book. It is precisely in these places that a desire for existential support and guidance in personal life is more emphatically present. New paths of religiosity are responses to the insecurity which has resulted from letting go of the churches; individuals have started to seek new forms of spirituality or new itineraries into the sacred.

People's dissatisfaction regarding the unreliability of politics and government or the inability of politics to solve the central problems of modern multicultural societies may also lead to unexpected forms of religiosity or personalized attributions of sacredness. The assassination of the charismatic politician Pim Fortuyn, who was able to gain the support of a large part of the Dutch electorate in a short period of time, suddenly stirred up all sorts of terms associated with saintliness, as though people hoped that even from beyond the grave, like a sort of Messiah, Fortuyn would be able to provide solutions for their existential insecurities (Margry 2003: 118-122; cf. Colombijn 2007). Huub de Jonge observed something similar among the visitors to Soekarno's grave. They direct both personal requests and appeals to improve the situation at a national level to him, or as one pilgrim described Soekarno: 'He is able to revive the lives of those who are still alive.' The Soekarno cultus differs from other Indonesian pilgrimages in that it deals with both personal goals in prayer and thought and with national issues. Hope for a change for the better in their own situations is linked to a desire for improvement at the national level, something that can also be found among visitors to the Falcone tree in Italy.

Such forms of religiosity or spirituality cannot simply be lumped together under the heading of what is generally called 'New Age' or a 'holistic milieu' in the West, or as an element of the 'spiritual revolution.' With the exception of Glastonbury, there is no direct connection with the cults listed in this book. They should be seen as independent religious expressions reflecting the same massive subjective turn of modern culture (cf. Heelas and Woodhead 2005: 129-130).

Because of the falsification or inadequacy of pilgrimage concepts, the understanding that pilgrimage has different meanings for different pilgrims and the necessity of an interdisciplinary approach to the phenomenon, it remains difficult to formulate a general definition of the term 'pilgrimage.' The currently held theories are primarily based on post-modern conceptualization, and that most commonly used at present is John Eade and Michael Sallnow's theoretically open concept, according to which pilgrimage can be described as an 'arena of competing religious and secular discourses' (Eade and Sallnow 1991/2000: 2, 5; cf. Kruse 2003: 156).

In this book, we assume that pilgrimage is in the first place transitional. This implies movement, but not as a central focus as it is for Coleman and Eade. The distance traveled is relatively unimportant; for pilgrims the essence of a pilgrimage is to approach the sacred, to enter it, to experience, to draw near, to touch, to make it their own, and if possible to hold onto it for their everyday lives. To avoid qualifying every location visited by many people or every cultus associated with a local saint as a pilgrimage site, a few criteria for pilgrimage sites were drawn up for the Dutch researchers involved in the pilgrimage project.[29] Pilgrimage was defined in advance as a journey undertaken by individuals or groups, based on a religious or spiritual inspiration, to a place that is regarded as more sacred or salutary than the environment of everyday life, to seek a transcendental encounter with a specific cult object, for the purpose of acquiring spiritual, emotional or physical healing or benefit. A pilgrimage must therefore entail interaction between the sacred or the religious, an element of personal transition and the existence of a cult object. Without these elements, there is no pilgrimage; there is thus an essential distinction between pilgrimage and 'secular pilgrimage' (such as recreational travel, etc.) in that pilgrimage has a transformative potential to give meaning to life, healing, etc.

Against this background and on the basis of ethnographic fieldwork, the authors of this volume have examined ten case studies relating to the theme of 'secular' pilgrimage. The authors come from various research disciplines, primarily anthropology, ethnology, and folklore studies, and from a wide range of research traditions. They have reflected upon the religious dimensions of the sites where a secular person is remembered, admired, or venerated. The geographical distribution of the sites was primarily determined by the limited availability of researchers who are actively studying this phenomenon.[30] Almost all contributions deal with shrines and pilgrimages in Western culture and the former 'Eastern Europe.' One contribution, the cultus associated with the former Indonesian President Soekarno, is located outside the European-American hemisphere and shows that 'secular' pilgrimages are not just a 'Western' phenomenon.

Based on the various subjects and the results of the study, the articles can be sorted into four categories: pilgrimages that occur in political, musical, or athletic (sports) contexts; and pilgrimages that can be placed under the heading of 'Life, Spirituality and Death.' The contributions are classified in this way because in modern society it is in the first three contexts in particular – three clearly distinct social categories – that veneration, glorification and idolization of secular individuals takes place. It is precisely in these three realms that mediatization is an important element and where the relationship between the secular and the sacred or religious is not clear. There have always been cults associated with individuals from the fields of state and politics, popular music and sports, but in the past few decades this element, accompanied by attributions of sacrality and sanctity, has increased exponentially. This was why it was important to conduct ethnographic research on the right themes.

Another factor is that the spectrum of pilgrimage has widened further. Due to processes of change in religious culture and in social and cultural areas, a new genre of pilgrimage has arisen in which the focus is on the communal or, more correctly, on the individual and the personal within the collective. The domain of 'Life, Spirituality and Death' has therefore become somewhat more diffuse. In this categorical context the pilgrims do not focus on one specific cult object, but seek meaning, support, comfort and healing in collectivity, in places of shared spirituality or shared suffering.

The contributions grouped under the heading of the political realm deal with the religious dimensions of the worship of 'political' individuals: statesmen, politicians and officials, in cases where veneration is based on grassroots practice rather than on state-organized pilgrimages. In this context, a truly living monument – a tree – for the assassinated Italian anti-Mafia judge Giovanni Falcone has become a central point of reference for opponents and victims of the Mafia. Deborah Puccio-Den makes clear that the texts placed there and the commemorations held at the location constitute a large-scale protest against both the Mafia and the government. At the same time, the martyr Falcone has become a symbol of persistence and self-sacrifice, acquiring the iconic dimensions of a saint in Italy. Puccio-Den has not studied the sacralization of anti-Mafia judges as a process of memorialization, but as a praxis in which a religious dimension is attributed to a civil act.

A comparable practice can be observed in the Croatian village of Kumrovec, where in addition to the usual traditional buildings in the open-air museum, the house where the former Yugoslavian president Tito was born and a statue of the man are situated. The area around his statue is seen as a stage on which conflicts between different collective memories take place, especially during the annual celebration of the Day of Youth in Kumrovec, organized by the Josip Broz Tito Society in Zagreb. While it was not the society's intention to create a personality cult, Marijana Belaj observed that there were groups of women who circled around the statue touching it, while some would simply touch it and cross themselves. Some spoke or sang to the statue or simply saluted it. Many lit candles at the foot of the pedestal. A major aspect of the attraction is Tito's background of poverty and his struggle for humanity during his presidency. As one of his biographers wrote, his was the 'story of an ordinary man with an extraordinary life.' In the first part of this narrative, many visitors can identify with him and project their hope and need for support onto him. The site is thus converted into a pilgrimage shrine, particularly for visitors who come to make close contact with Josip Broz. It is somewhat remarkable that this happens only at the statue, whereas his actual tomb, located in a triumphant memorial park in the former capital Belgrade, hardly attracts any visitors and can certainly not be regarded as a pilgrimage site.

Like Belaj, Huub de Jonge studied a former head of state who managed to forge unity in an ethnically divided country for a long period of time. His account of visits to the grave of former Indonesian president Soekarno depicts the only non-Western pilgrimage of this volume. Although the grave is visited by people who simply want to commemorate Soekarno, there are also many who worship him in a religious manner. De Jonge follows Eade and Sallnow in their theoretical approach, according to which a pilgrimage consists of an arena of competing discourses and has 'accommodating power.' He shows clearly that both elements are powerfully present in Blitar. Although Indonesia currently suffers from internal divisions, De Jong sees a form of national *communitas* taking shape at the grave and at the same time the realization of religious tolerance. He asserts that although the space and materiality of the shrine have been changed to fit in better with Indonesian Islamic culture, it still brings believers from different religious denominations together, and the pilgrimage appears to consolidate and reinforce feelings of being Indonesian, highlighting the country's aspiration toward unity in diversity.

Nationalism and social cohesion like that manifested around the grave of Soekarno can also be found within the realm of popular music and its stars, for instance around the grave of the Hungarian pop singer Jimmy Zámbó. Íst-van Povedák focuses on the stereotypical plot elements in Zámbó's life, which as it were predestined him for the role of a hero and idol who – in contrast to the leap that post-communist Hungary made into Western mass culture and the attendant media hypes – is cherished as an icon of anti-globalization. With his romantic repertoire, he was also a national identity-creating factor for the Hungarians and evoked a certain nostalgia for the past, elements which also played a role in the adulation of Tito in Kumrovec. Although his secular worship and adoration has assumed massive proportions, for a small minority of his fans his intrinsic significance extends beyond his music and the nation. In the context of secularization and individualization processes, they see Zámbó as an 'Apostle of Love' who can provide a new religious and transcendental dimension for those seeking support in the everyday problems resulting from the arrival of modern capitalism. According to Povedák, this can be explained by the fact that with his music and his autobiographically-tinged lyrics, Zám-bó was able to forge a strong link between his own difficult life and the lives and social circumstances of many of his fans.

Whereas Zámbó owes his special position primarily to his nationalistic and anti-globalist views, Erika Doss analyzes someone who stands for the mass culture of capitalist society: Elvis Presley. Doss has already described the meanings of Graceland (Doss 1999); here she deals specifically with the religious dimensions of Graceland, concentrating on three elements: ritual, religiosity and race. For her, Elvis consists of different conflicting images, many relating to his ethnicity (the 'All-White Elvis') and the social circumstances in which he lived, full of suffering and pain and loneliness. As the fieldwork showed, this is why he can function for visitors to his grave as a mediator between God and ordinary human beings. These specific fans regard him as a fellow sufferer. Some of them believe that Elvis has been resurrected or reincarnated, and similar ideas are also to be found in the Morrison cult. But, Doss asks, do ritual practices and revered images constitute the making of a religion or the creation of a saint-mediator? She sees parallels with other sacred sites as regards devotional practices, material culture and commercialism, but are these sites actually linked to a transcendent reality? Graceland or going to Graceland are not religious in themselves, but they may become religious. The Elvis Week with the Candlelight Vigil in mid-August is the most obvious example; many gifts are offered to ask for Elvis's intervention in all kinds of personal circumstances. Doss goes on to show that Graceland is dominated by white people and that both visits and pilgrimages are imbued with an oppressive ideology of racial essentialism that completely disregards the original 'interracial' Elvis.

Despite the fact that, like Graceland, Jim Morrison's grave is also visited largely by white Westerners, the contrast could not be greater. Whereas Graceland seems to have grown to Disney-like proportions, Morrison's grave at Père Lachaise cemetery is hard to find and as modest as can be. In his contribution, Peter Jan Margry shows that within the mass of visitors, there are clearly discernible groups of visitors who follow different narratives, practices, rituals, and expectations and make the site a multiply contested space. Quite apart from the large stream of tourists, the 'real' Morrison fans are also emphatically present around his grave. In addition to a more general group of fans, there is a close-knit tribe in which sociability is very important. Another clear category of more-or-less individual fans are those who visit Morrison's grave in order to seek help and support for their existential problems from 'their Jim.' Based on Charles Glock's theoretical model, Margry determines the religious dimensions in this case. For the last group – the pilgrims – the espace Morrison is a sacred site, and Morrison himself functions as an independent cult object.

Pilgrimage in a sports context is represented here by Daniel Wojcik's study of the famous American long-distance runner Steve Prefontaine, an all-American folk hero and an icon and idol of American sports.[31] When Prefontaine died unexpectedly in 1975, a 'spontaneous' memorial – Pre's Rock – was erected for him in Eugene, Oregon. As with the statue of Tito, this is a sacred place with a pilgrimage linked to an individual whose actual grave is located elsewhere. Wojcik places the erection of Pre's Rock in the context of spontaneous shrines and the theoretical pilgrimage debate. This small roadside shrine also appears to provide people with a new way of dealing with traumatic loss.

However, the success of the shrine has changed it into a monumental site and a place of pilgrimage for contemplation with 'a deeply religious experience.' Wojcik contends that because of the legends and lore surrounding Prefontaine and the way the media have depicted him, his fans go there to find a tangible connection, an 'authentic' encounter with their hero, in a setting that does not seem to have been commercialized or mass-mediated. At this peaceful place on the side of the road, Prefontaine's memory is maintained and nurtured through the desires of those who admire him. The visitors have transformed this place of death and mourning into a place of life, a dynamic ritual space where they can interact with him in some way.

We also find transformations of this kind under the heading 'Life, Spirituality and Death.' This section discusses research into pilgrimages which are more explicitly associated with life and the existential itself, with spiritual beliefs about life, with nature and the supernatural, and with the end of life. These three contributions are about one very ancient and two very modern sacred spaces within which pilgrimages are given shape. In all three cases there is no cult object, personal grave, or direct connection with the physically deceased individual. The pilgrims seek meaning, support, comfort, and healing in collectivity, at recently created locations where suffering and spirituality can be shared.

Marion Bowman opens this section. Her starting point is her extensive research on Glastonbury, but she presents new perspectives on the many journeys, quests and traditional and new pilgrimages she found there, provided by individuals, groups and both institutional and non-institutional religious movements. These are all framed in different paradigms of religion. Again, we often find the word pilgrimage used here as a 'container concept.' However, Glastonbury's position is different from that of the other shrines in this book, mainly because the town, with its pseudo-historical connection with Avalon, is seen almost by definition as sacred, as a sanctuary. People who feel drawn to Glastonbury regard it as a sacred place and perceive a journey there as a pilgrimage. Using Urry's theoretical framework of three bases of co-presence and against the background of the traditional pilgrimages to Glastonbury, Bowman shows how various New Age pilgrimages have found a place there and how they function. Admittedly, it is not always clear who the pilgrims are and how a pilgrimage is undertaken. Bowman sees the experiential aspect of visiting Glastonbury as varied and complex and gives a detailed account of it. It turns out that in many cases, the journey to Glastonbury is itself secondary to the journey within Glastonbury. She finds several separate paradigms of religion there, built up over time. The latest, the amalgam known as New Age, has links to a multitude of sacred traditions: Pagan, Druid, Goddess-oriented and Christian. Bowman concludes that the visitors are all pilgrims and 'going with the flow.' There appears to be a growing consensus that regardless of the stated reason or focus of the pilgrimage, underlying the whole pilgrimage phenomenon is a motive on a larger scale: the timeless, universal pull of earth energies.

The Cancer Forest in Flevoland, on the other hand, has no historical roots or sacred myths at all. It was only planted in 2000, in a province of the Nether-lands reclaimed from the sea. The 'Trees for Life Day' which is held there an-nually for cancer victims and their family and friends shows how individual grief management can develop into a public and collective manifestation of grief. In Paul Post's contribution he shows that the associated rituals have both public and individual dimensions. In this context he does not distinguish between classic religious pilgrimage and a newly emerging location-specific ritual like the Trees for Life Day. Instead, he focuses on the ritual in this par-ticular case, employing what he calls the 'pilgrimage reference' as a heuristic instrument for comparative analysis. He does not specifically discuss whether the Trees for Life Day is a form of non-confessional or post-modern pilgrima-ge, but sets out to describe, analyze and interpret the ritual itself on the basis of this 'pilgrimage reference.' During his fieldwork he was confronted with many narratives about the lives and deaths of cancer victims, and over and over again these narratives suggested an unarticulated yearning for a broader context for those lives and deaths, and ultimately for support and hope. The visitors gain this support and hope by taking part in the ritual, through the idyllic setting of the living forest, and through the solidarity of the temporary community in the forest. According to Post these people, who have different religious backgrounds, find a functional ritual expression in this event.

The Vietnam Veterans Memorial in Washington DC is not the only focus of the commemoration of American soldiers who died in Vietnam, as Jill Dubisch's contribution makes clear. There is also a special event associated with Vietnam veterans: a 3,000-mile journey across the United States on motorbikes – the Run for the Wall – which is claimed to be a pilgrimage. Dubisch, herself a participating biker (but not a vet), shows that the significance of the event lies in overcoming the traumas of the war and its later consequences, as the Vietnam veterans have to contend with above average social, mental, and physical problems and existential crises. On the one hand, the Run draws attention to their situation and gives them an opportunity to protest against the lack of adequate recognition of their problems; on the other hand, the journey is a ritual of resolution for them, and in that sense is comparable with the pilgrimage on foot to Santiago de Compostela, in which for most participants the journey rather than the destination has become the definitive element of the pilgrimage. Dubisch sees the Run as more than a political movement or a commemoration of war victims; according to her it is a profoundly spiritual journey with Christian and Native American connotations. Participants are swept up in the transcendent nature of the journey and its rituals, and are transformed into pilgrims searching for healing and a way to shake off their pain and grief.

Whereas in the following chapters themes relating to the secular and the sacred will be examined and analyzed on the basis of ethnographic fieldwork, in the final essay the main points which have emerged in the various contributions and the differences and similarities between them will be subjected to a synthesizing analysis. Obviously this does not mean that there is no more to say on these matters. Human beings constantly create new itineraries into the sacred, and research can only follow at a suitable distance.

Notes

1 With thanks to Marion Bowman, Arnoud-Jan Bijsterveldt, Charles Caspers and Willem Frijhoff for their comments.

2 These are some of the major concepts and approaches used in the following studies: Turner and Turner 1978; Antier 1979; Rinschede and Bhardwaj 1990; Eade and Sallnow 1991/2000; Morinis 1992; Post, Pieper and Van Uden 1998; Badone and Roseman 2004; Coleman and Eade 2004.

3 The symposium 'Non-Confessional Pilgrimage: New Itineraries into the Sacred in Contemporary Europe' was held at the Meertens Institute (KNAW) in Amsterdam on 28 June 2004.

4 It is important to realize that the meaning of the word 'pilgrimage' in English is not as precise as its equivalents in some other languages. It is possibly due to the focus in English-language pilgrimage studies on travelling and the early medieval *peregrinatio* idea that the wandering, travelling, tourism element has remained so strong in the pilgrimage concept; in contrast, in the Germanic languages concepts with clear semantic differences have developed, such as *Wallfahrt and Pilgerfahrt* in German and *bedevaart* and *pelgrimage* in Dutch. See Berbeé 1987.

5 Turner 1969; Dupront 1967, 1987: 366-415, cf. on the latter Frijhoff 2002: 282-284.

6 The key publication of this project is a four-volume lexicon (in Dutch) by Margry and Caspers (1997-2004). This entire work can now also be consulted online and is kept up to date: www. meertens.knaw.nl/bedevaart/. For the project's theoretical approach and its boundaries see Margry and Post 1998 and Caspers and Margry 2003.

7 For reasons of practical feasibility, it was decided that no attention would be paid in the Dutch project to the veneration of rock stars and other secular individuals or of monuments, etc. In the first instance another reason for not involving them in the project was that it seemed that the religious dimension would play only a very limited role in these cases or would not be an essential part of them. (Margry and Caspers 1997: 17).

8 Actually, views like this also existed in the past, but then they were regarded – for instance – as superstition.

9 The best-known is the Yser Pilgrimage to Diksmuide in Flanders where the Flemish victims of World War I have been commemorated since the mid-1920s.

10 A few years ago this issue was revived and brought up for discussion again. See Hänel 2004: 112.

11 This is actually only partly true, since in their research they rarely consult the large body of fieldwork carried out in Volkskunde or Folklore Studies. Also relevant in this context is the large-scale Dutch pilgrimage project, in which again no evidence was found of the development of communitas (Margry and Caspers 1996-2004).

12 As far as the modern 'new' pilgrimages on foot are concerned, the opposite is true. These pilgrims are eager to publish their experiences online or in book form (cf. Frey 1998; Post et al. 1998: 221-242). See also further on in the introduction.

13 Here I am disregarding theologians such as St John of the Cross who, building on the idea of the *peregrinatio*, have held similar views, mainly in the theological sense, ever since the Middle Ages.

14 In 1987 the Council of Europe declared the *camino* a symbol of European unity and identity, and the route network was designated a 'European Cultural Itinerary.'

15 This phenomenon is reflected clearly in the notes in pilgrim's books, a new genre of reflective journal which has arisen as a result of these changes. Most pilgrims keep these journals and if possible have them published later (Frey 1998; Post, Pieper and Van Uden 1998: 205-242; cf. Coleman and Elsner 2003).

16 Another romantic topos often found in pilgrimage literature is that shrines are located in places that are extremely difficult to reach: 'Marian shrines are often situated in inaccessible places'

(Swatos and Tomasi 2002: 207).

17 Cf. note 4.

18 To supplement the existing travel perspective, in addition to the standard 'exterior' pilgrimage Michael York also distinguished an 'interior' pilgrimage, which he characterizes as 'an individual's transformation from a spiritless or degrading position to one held in relatively high esteem according to the religious framework involved.' The 'revelatory experience and spiritual awareness' then become 'purely internal or mental journeys' (York 2002: 138). This notion did not appear from thin air; apart from the geographic pilgrimage, it also has a connection with the old *peregrinatio* idea. In late antiquity there was not yet any clear concept of what is now referred to as pilgrimage (Bitton-Ashkelony 2005: 17-19). According to Bitton-Ashkelony, between the fourth and six centuries St. Augustine's notion of *peregrinatio* became associated with the sacred topography, so that a sacred mobility arose, which was focused on personal rituality and attribution of meaning to local shrines (Bitton-Ashkelony 2005: 204-206).

19 Later Eberhart more or less repeated this suggestion among German-language ethnographers with the aim of shifting the research focus in the German-speaking areas as well from the shrine to the pilgrim (Eberhart 2005).

20 Apart from these functions, pilgrimages – and processions as well – are also important as opportunities for the participants to publicly disseminate their own religion in the community on the basis of the identity-forming power and demonstrative effect of these events (Margry 2000: 419-421; Hänel 2004: 118).

21 The distinction between local veneration of saints and pilgrimage cults is extremely important, but it is seldom evaluated or examined in detail in pilgrimage research. Especially in view of the rise of Internet shrines, this is a topic which should now be given priority on the research agenda.

22 This sheds a completely different light on quantitative studies by researchers such as the Nolans, which will need to be revised (Nolan and Nolan 1989). Just to compare – at that time Nolan and Nolan (1989: 34) arrived at a figure of 48 obvious Dutch pilgrimage sites, whereas the Dutch pilgrimage project (Margry and Caspers 1997-2004) ultimately included 660 bigger and smaller sites.

23 It should be noted in connection with this outcome that the system of multiple-choice questions has strong steering effects and more easily leads to checking off many motives than a system of open questions.

24 For this theme see also Korff 1997 and Frijhoff 1998, 2004.

25 Passariello's analysis with respect to Che Guevara in the same volume does not get much further than the observation that on the basis of external similarities, Che was 'like a saint' (Passariello 2005: 89).

26 Eade and Sallnow have posited a similar diagnosis regarding the Christian pilgrimage (1991/2000: 26-27).

27 For an approach and definition based on the psychology of religion, see Hill and Hood 1999.

28 We find few or no miracles in the traditional sense, but many supplications for support and help, often in an emotional sense, as well as thanksgiving for support and help received, cf. Ponisch 2003.

29 In short, the criteria consist of the following points: (1) there must be a specific cult object present; (2) this cult object is linked to a more-or-less permanent sacred cult site or space; (3) the site has not been visited only once or for a short time – in other words it must be rooted in both time and space; (4) the visit or pilgrimage must be an international phenomenon: visitors must travel some distance between their daily living environment and the pilgrimage site; (5) the cult site or object must be considered more beneficial than other sites or objects; (6) there must be some sort of religiously inspired pattern of action or expectation, cf. Margry and Caspers 1997: 15-16.

30 The somewhat declining interest in Princess Diana's grave in Althorp Park may explain why no researcher could provide a contribution dealing with this obvious example; by contrast, the spontaneous shrines raised for Diana immediately after her death were researched and immediately and also questionably considered pilgrimage sites, cf. Rowbottom 2002: 35

31 For the phenomenon of sports' idols and idolatry, see Vanreusel 2003.

I The Political Realm

Chapter 2

The Anti-Mafia Movement as Religion?
The Pilgrimage to Falcone's Tree

Deborah Puccio-Den

Immediately after the 'Capaci massacre' on May 23, 1992 – which cost the lives of Judge Giovanni Falcone, his wife Judge Francesca Morvillo, and three of their bodyguards – the tree planted in front of the assassinated judges' apartment became an object of strange devotion. The citizens of Palermo spontaneously gathered in front of it and decorated it with garlands of flowers, letters, and photos. In photos of the time, we see Palermians looking at this tree – which was immediately baptized *l'Albero Falcone* ('the Falcone tree') – in a state of rapture, gathered in a pious attitude, their hands joined, their eyes lifted heavenwards.[1] Such gestures continued long after the moment of intense emotion elicited by the violent death of the most popular anti-Mafia investigating judge, giving rise to practices characterized as religious by the local population. 'Citizens learned to treat this *Ficus magnolia* with the same devotion reserved for the sanctuary on Monte Pellegrino [Mount Pilgrim],' affirms the author of Giovanni Falcone's posthumous biography (La Licata 2002: 67), linking the tree where people pay homage to the judge's memory to the sanctuary dedicated to the patron saint of Palermo, Saint Rosalia.

What processes and mechanisms have transformed a flower bed in the center of Palermo into an altar, and a secular judge into a saint? Unusual regimes of action and new registers of enunciation, combining political involvement and religious faith, have been deployed within the anti-Mafia movement, which traditionally leans to the left. Anti-Mafia activists themselves have noted strange behavior occurring around this tree: 'I saw a bride getting out of her car and donating her bouquet (...). I saw two young girls kneeling down: they prayed in silence and, before leaving, offered up their jewellery: a gold chain and a ring containing a precious stone,' notes Sandra Armuri, journalist for the Communist Party daily (Armuri 1992: 16).[2]

This type of act, triggered by a shock, an incident, or an extraordinary oc-currence (Bensa and Fassin 2002: 8), is nonetheless completely consistent with the Catholic devotional repertoire[3] and recalls, in particular, the cult practices in honor of Saint Rosalia of Palermo: Her reliquary is festooned with jewels, and the walls of her sanctuary are covered in letters. While the Palermians who go on pilgrimage to Monte Pellegrino[4] (the final resting place of the twelfth-cen-tury hermit saint) place their 'notes' on the walls of the cave, citizens who visit l'Albero Falcone attach their written messages to the tree trunk. These gifts of writing, which fade and disintegrate over the years, become more abundant on the anniversary of their deaths: September 4 for the patron saint, and May 23 for the judge. In the same way that the Saint Rosalia cult is administered by a congregation, Giovanni Falcone's memory is nurtured by a foundation created by relatives of the two assassinated judges: the Fondazione Giovanni e Francesca Falcone. The secretary of this foundation regularly removes the notes from the Falcone tree and archives them. On the anniversary of Gio-vanni Falcone's death, these written offerings are framed in a commemorative ceremony. Those who attend this ceremony, whether from areas surrounding Palermo or from other towns in Italy, say they are going on a 'pilgrimage.' This article takes the participants' experience as its starting point and considers the meaning they confer upon their actions at face value or as valid statements.[5] This involves reconstructing their contexts of interpretation and situating this shift to a religious register within the wider framework of the anti-Mafia struggle and the forms it assumes.

The Capaci massacre, an attack of unprecedented violence that destabi-lized established perceptions of Mafia acts and ways of reacting to this phe-nomenon, was intensified by a 'literacy event.'[6] Once the wave of emotion had passed, however, the writing fever that had gripped Palermians in the first few days following the catastrophe did not subside. Adorning the Falcone tree with written messages, drawings, flowers, and photographs has become a lasting practice. For fifteen years now, the citizens of Palermo and elsewhere have continued to express their anger, bitterness, hopes, and sorrow through letters, poems, and drawings, in black-and-white or color, using the widest range of materials and media. Through these gestures, they tear writing away from the intimate sphere and inscribe it in the public arena, forcing it into the register of action. This writing is thus a legitimate object of study for the social sciences. One of the aims of this article, which is based on these motley writings and drawings, viewing them as vehicles for political expression, is to show that these little bits of paper and minuscule acts have contributed widely to establishing the anti-Mafia movement as a cause and a group organization.[7] I shall look at how, and attempt to explain why, this organization is modeled on religious groups of Christian origin.

Giovanni's two sisters and Francesca's brother and sister, ministers of the Falcone tree cult, have gathered these transient testimonies that are already partly faded by time. Thanks to their efforts to keep the judges' memory alive, I was able to view these messages in a book entitled *L'Albero Falcone*, which contains the 1992 writings. Some of them are transcriptions, while others, even more interesting for the ethnologist, can be seen in their original form, such as creations that combine drawing, writing, photography, and/or news-

Judge Giovanni Falcone's tree in via Notarbartolo in Palermo, 2006.
Photo: D. Puccio-Den.

paper cuttings. At this stage of my research, and for the purposes of this particular article, my analysis focuses on the contents of this writing and on the visual impact of these images that highlight the cult practices devoted to Judge
Falcone, shifting them into the religious sphere. When all the letters from the
year of the drama occurred are put together, one realizes how, right from the
start, this collective creation structured by writing has emulated certain iconographic models specific to Christianity. One of the recurring motifs in Christian iconography is that of the tree as the foundation of a religious community
(Donadieu-Rigaut 2005). By using this form, in multifarious ways, the Capaci
massacre, a major event in the history of the anti-Mafia struggle, this 'strange
fold [in time] from which point nothing was ever the same again' (Bensa and
Fassin 2002: 11), calls to mind the founding act of the new Christian era: the
death of Christ (Agamben 2000).

The Tree Form

Why did the magnolia tree situated in front of Giovanni Falcone's house become the rallying point for anti-mafia activists immediately after Falcone's
death, and what are the consequences of this tree being adopted as the symbol of the anti-Mafia cause? At first glance, it is nothing more than a resurgence of 'Palermo spring' rhetoric. This period of political and moral renewal
was inaugurated at the end of the 1980s by the anti-Mafia mayor of Palermo,
Leoluca Orlando[8], and ended with her withdrawal from the Palermo political
scene. The prevailing electoral legislation did not allow Orlando to stand for
re-election in the 2000 municipal elections, as she had already served two
consecutive terms. A representative of Forza Italia, Silvio Berlusconi's party,
was elected mayor of Palermo, which saw large numbers of the former ruling
class return to local government. This marked the end of the Palermo spring.

We have to go back in time to understand the political context in which the
Capaci massacre was perpetrated. When Orlando was elected mayor for the
first time in 1989, she tried an experiment that was totally new to Italy: a coali-
tion between the Christian Democrats and the Communist Party. This political
season – the Palermo spring – was as fleeting as its name suggests. In 1990,

under pressure from the Christian Democrats, the municipal government fell. The mayor then decided to resign and establish her own movement: La Rete ('The Net'). This party, which covered a broad political spectrum, brought Leoluca Orlando to power in 1993 with 75% of the votes. In its program, it used the language of spring to talk about the regeneration of the political system. For the anti-Mafia party, the Falcone tree, watered with the blood of the judge assassinated in 1992, was a place where it could take permanent root, and thus become the focal point of its perpetuation.

The victims' relatives entrusted the perennial leaves of this ficus with the task of perpetuating the 'dreams' the two judges had believed in: 'Justice, State, duty to the point of sacrifice' (Armuri 1992: 13). Young people promise, in writing, to perpetuate this message: 'We shall fulfill your dreams!' writes Loredana, a young girl of 18 (Armuri 1992: 71). It is their way of showing their commitment to the anti-Mafia movement. With the Falcone tree, the Palermo spring – this ephemeral season – is reinforced, institutionalized, and firmly implanted in the very heart of the city. 'You can crush a flower but you can't prevent spring,' writes Simon (Armuri 1992: 46). Regenerated by the judge's 'sacrifice' – a term constantly present in the vocabulary of anti-Mafia activists – the tree would give rise to a new Palermo spring. Its first fruits were demonstrations, meetings, committees, associations, foundations, and the exploration of new forms of protesting, like the very feminine one of hanging a white sheet from one's window. Its pinnacle was Leoluca Orlando's creation of La Rete on 21 April 1993, the first day of a new spring.

With these two powerful propagation metaphors – the tree and the net – the anti-Mafia movement, formed along the lines of the first Christian groups, seemed destined for limitless expansion. The Falcone tree filled the gaping hole left by the explosion that blew up a section of the highway linking Palermo to Punta Raisi airport. Another explosion sounded in response to the Mafia bombs: 'Here [by the tree], you have left your miracle. Would you like to know what that is? The desire to defeat the Mafia has exploded,' writes Rino (Armuri 1992: 76). The anti-Mafia cause imitates the religious expansionism of the early Christians. Orlando's 'net' endlessly extends the full branches of what we can now call the 'anti-Mafia tree.' The sacrificial death of the judges

A schoolchild's drawing of Falcone's tree, May 2003.
Photo: D. Puccio-Den.

and their bodyguards added not only a political dimension to the Palermo spring – weaving the anti-Mafia web to rebuild the social fabric after the catastrophe and ensnare the Mafia 'octopus'– but also an eschatological one. As Anna's message confirms: 'With you, now, we speak more than before / and there will not be a night when / through you, a prayer does not rise up / to God, so we can bring the longed-for Spring to our land'[9] (Armuri 1992: 51).

Those who attended the first meetings, the first witnesses of the murder of the two judges and their bodyguards, people from the left and far-left who very often declared themselves to be atheists, used religious grammar, and not just any such grammar. In the Christian religion, the death of Christ is the founding point of a community whose expansion throughout the world, with a view to spreading the word of the Lord, finds a special significance in the tree.[10] The group assembled at the foot of the Falcone tree recalls other spiritual families that are well documented in Christianity. In the Middle Ages, the tree-order that springs forth from the insides of the founder of the monastic order represents religious communities and their attachment to the source as well as their capacity for expansion.[11] By associating the memory of Judge Falcone to this plant symbol, the anti-Mafia supporters place him in the register initiated by the Passion of Christ and used by saints, martyrs, and the founders of monastic orders (Donadieu-Rigaut 2005: 205). This assimilation can easily occur in a society like Sicily where even non-believers are profoundly steeped in a religious culture of Christian origin.

In other forms of writing, more elaborate than those that spontaneously spring up around the Falcone tree, this Christian symbolism is more explicitly present. The suffering of Giovanni Falcone in an unjust land is the thread that runs through his posthumous biography (La Licata 2002). His 'sacrificial' death following 'betrayal' by his friends, to use the terms employed by his biographer, ties in perfectly with the Christly theme introduced by l'Albero Falcone. This tree recalls the cross. Its verticality and upward reaching branches direct the gaze of anti-Mafia supporters upwards. Like Christ, the judge never really died. Rather, in death, he seems to have attained a new life: 'Falcone lives' (La Licata 2002: 43) claim the students who gather, like apostles, at the feet of the *Ficus magnolia*. Like Christ, the judge is not where his body lies. Honoring him elsewhere than at his grave indicates a desire to remove him from the usual mourning procedures.

In the final resting place his followers have assigned him, the judge is not alone: 'In this strong, thriving trunk which reaches up into the sky, everyone continues to see Giovanni and Francesca, as in the legend of Philemon and Baucis where Ovid recounts that the gods allowed this husband and wife who loved one another dearly to die together, turning into a single tree: united in death as in life' (La Licata 2002: 16). In the same way, Giovanni and Francesca have become a legend. Like members of a religious community unable to conceive their offspring like the rest of humanity and refusing carnal reproduction, the two judges voluntarily did not have children: 'We didn't want to create orphans,' apologized the judge. After their assassination, the two judges became the imaginary ancestors of a community that chose them: 'You didn't want any children. I would like you to be my dad,' Luisa from Naples writes in pencil. How is this relationship established?

The theme of the tree is omnipresent in the posters and drawings produced in schools as part of the 'legality education' programs instigated by the Fondazione Giovanni e Francesca Falcone. In many representations of the Falcone tree, the pieces of paper bearing words blend in with the magnolia leaves; the branches form the links between the anti-Mafia supporters and their founder, the judge, embodied in the tree trunk. A genealogical link is introduced through this writing and the posters, drawings, etc. In the posters created in schools, the Falcone tree has become a kind of anti-Mafia family tree. Sweeping aside the temporal order, Giovanni Falcone is displayed as the ancestor in a line that includes all those who have died for justice: from the trade unionist Salvatore Carnevale († 1955) to the far-left activist Giuseppe Impastato († 1978), the carabinieri captain Emanuele Basile († 1980), and General Carlo Alberto Dalla Chiesa († 1982). Falcone's death marks the beginning of an ideal line that proceeds from his 'sacrifice,' like monastic families take root directly in the insides of their dead founder (Donadieu-Rigaut 2005: 239).[12] These religious communities exist or existed only to spread the word of their founder, a 'martyr,' a 'witness' who died to affirm the absolute value of his religion. Can the same be said of the anti-Mafia movement?

The Pilgrimage as Bearing Witness

On July 7, 1992, just three months after the Capaci massacre, Paolo Borsellino – the judge who had taken over from Giovanni Falcone – was a victim of a new Mafia attack: the 'Via d'Amelio massacre,' in which five agents in his escort also died. These two incidents overlap, like the faces of the two judges side-by-side in the same photo attached to the Falcone tree. The Falcone and Borsellino murders heralded a new era for the anti-Mafia movement. It became a national movement when numerous Italians began to realize that they could no longer remain indifferent to aggression on such a scale, considering the Mafia as a local phenomenon. With these two figures of sacrifice for the public good, the State took on an absolute value, in a country and particularly in a region from which it had been absent until then.[13] Far from undermining the judges' aura, revealing their mortal nature and their failure, this attack on their bodies made them martyrs for the country. The nation, which had been tarnished by the experience of fascism, was once more considered sacred.

Falcone and Borsellino are 'martyrs' primarily in the etymological sense of the Greek term *martyr*, 'witness (of God),' one who experiences in his flesh the ordeal of the Christly sacrifice. Bearing witness means affirming the value of something through one's actions and words. The two anti-Mafia judges faced an ordeal of fire through a lifetime dedicated to promoting justice. A statement made by Giovanni Falcone has become his moral testimony: 'To this city [Palermo], I would like to say: men perish; ideas endure. What endures are their moral ideals which continue to walk on the legs of other men' (Armuri, 1992: 30). This sentence is often seen on the banners that are paraded at the numerous public demonstrations engendered by the deaths of the two judges. Demonstrating is another commonly accepted meaning of 'to bear witness.' As the demonstrators marched, they brandished life-size photos of the torsos of Falcone and Borsellino. Their banners bore the words: 'We will be the legs that will carry your ideas of justice' (Armuri, 1992: 104). If, as Paul Ricoeur says (2000: 201-208), 'the event, in its most primitive sense, is that about which one bears witness,' the people who came from all corners of Italy to attend Falcone's funeral (over fifteen thousand) became witnesses of his martyrdom. In that case, do the messages they left at the Falcone tree at the time not become a kind of 'evidence'?

The need to leave one's mark is a distinguishing characteristic of a pilgrimage. This is seen in certain very old practices, such as the way pilgrims in the Middle Ages traced their hands and footprints on the walls of the churches they visited (Spera 1977: 238). These new pilgrims also seem very keen to leave a mark of their visit to the Falcone tree. This explains the importance attributed to the signature at the bottom of all the messages, despite their apparently informal nature, drawing on its power to 'serve as a sign of validation' (Fraenkel 1992: 18). 'Thank you, judges FALCONE and / BORSELLINO for having / taught us that simple and honest / men can defeat the / mafia and for having encouraged us to / carry out a lifetime pilgrimage of hope and ACTION,' writes Vincenza, who came to Palermo from the town of Cosenza in Calabria to pin her small piece of paper to the Falcone tree (Armuri 1992:

Commemoration of Falcone's death on 23 May 2003.
Photo: Fondazione Giovanni e Francesca Falcone.

117). Is it because, since May 23, 1992, the young have shown their political commitment there that the 'legality journeys' – as schools call the trips
they organize to follow in the footsteps of the 'martyrs of the Mafia' – are
called 'pilgrimages'? This also reveals the political nature of the pilgrimage, as
an experience that implies a personal commitment to a regime of action, and
its legal nature, as evidence that authenticates a saintly life through a personal
ordeal.[14] This writing is endowed with other powers: it commits an individual
to a regime of action, through a written and signed contract, and brings writing out of the intimate sphere. 'Falcone: / Today, nearly one month since the
/ Capaci massacre, I find myself in / Palermo, you know, I felt the need to
write these few lines / and to pin them to the tree below / your home, to testify that / your memory, and that of your wife / and bodyguards, is still alive
in me,' writes Giuseppe (Armuri 1992: 120). For this activist, his testimony
is a memorial. Through these messages, and despite the transient nature of
the media they are written on, which is compensated for by their abundance

and repetition, the judge's memory is now indestructible. The old order can no longer be restored. This sudden absence[15] is a break from the past, introducing a new time, the timeless time of memory, guaranteed by the messenger-writers, who act as 'witnesses' of the past. Rising up like a tombstone, decorated, like those in the south of Italy (Faeta 1993), with photographs of the bodyguards and the two judges, the magnolia displays the classic signs of a funeral monument: 'In eternal memory of all those who have died in the struggle against the Mafia' (Armuri 1992: 28). The writing becomes an epitaph aimed at communicating with the deceased. It attracts the gaze of passers-by, encourages meditation, strives to move them, and above all reminds them of the victims' tragic fate. These fluttering bits of paper that, at first sight, appear so fragile sum up two essential functions of public writing: making people think and making people remember (Corbier 2006).[16] Angelo identifies the tree as the judge's grave: 'I wrote you this poem with all my heart and I hope that, when you bring flowers to your brother, you will read it to him,' writes a student of the judge's sister, a secondary school teacher (Armuri 1992: 33). Some of these letters are read out loud, and thus become a means of praying to the judge. Every year, May 23 – the day on which the Capaci massacre is commemorated – presents an opportunity to perform these acts collectively, thereby renewing the vow to remember. 'Not to forget' is an obligation for Falcone's heirs, the anti-Mafia supporters, a community of remembrance based on writing.

The intrinsic characteristic of bearing witness is that something is passed on, hence the common Italian expression *passere il testimone* (passing the baton) (*testimone* also means 'witness' or 'testimony'). For these pilgrims, witnesses, and potential martyrs, this involves following the indicated path: 'I will never have peace / until the work that you have started / and which it is our duty to continue / is accomplished,' writes Giuseppe, whose signature is preceded by the words 'WITH DUTY' (Armuri 1992: 120). The duty of remembering; the duty of justice. The death of the two judges led to a pact with the people, encouraging new vocations to the profession of judge. Gaetano Paci,[17] DIA (Italian Anti-Mafia Division) deputy prosecutor for the Anti-Mafia District[18] of Palermo, chose the day of Falcone's funeral to wear his robes for the first time. That day, he also carried his teacher's coffin on his shoulders. Many law students from cities all over Italy and Sicily came to Palermo for this State funeral, showing that they were willing to take the place of the assassinated judge. The messages they left around the Falcone tree reveal that these future judges identify with this model of professional excellence: 'I'm studying law in Florence with the intention of carrying out my future profession as judge or lawyer as you did...,' writes L. (Armuri 1992: 24). The feeling of emulation elicited by the murders of Falcone and Borsellino extended far beyond their particular profession: 'I want to fight, GIOVANNI, for you and for PAOLO [...] Your example has made me a better person. You didn't die for nothing, because you have won, you have defeated the cowardice that is part of man, the fear of being alone in death,' writes Cristiana (Armuri 1992: 126), who declares without ado: 'Now, you are heroes for me.' Between hero and saint, there is but one small step.

An arbitrator of justice while he was alive, in death Giovanni Falcone has become a figure of intercession between heaven and earth, like Saint Rosalia, who has been known as the 'advocate of Palermo' since the seventeenth century. The tree, which spreads its branches heavenwards and sinks its roots into the earth, is the vector of this two-way communication: 'Your brother [Giovanni was the brother of Maria Falcone, to whom this letter is addressed] is looking down at us from above, he urges us on, smiles at us and encourages us' (Armuri 1992: 33). In Mariangela's letter, Giovanni Falcone, already elevated to the realm of saint, becomes a channel of communication between heaven and earth. 'Now, I think of you in peace and very close to the heavenly throne, from which God's smile came down and, thanks to you, touched us poor mortals too. You are my saint. Pray for us!' (Armuri 1992: 65). The step has been taken. The letters that citizens continue to place at the foot of the tree or to send to the address 'L'Albero Falcone, Palermo'[19], as though the judge could read them from up in heaven, demonstrates the persistence of this symbolism linking this martyr of justice to the prototype of all Christian martyrs: the Passion of Christ.

Imago Christi

As stated, the tree form introduces a similarity between Falcone and Jesus Christ. The judge's body is one with the magnolia, like the son of God is inseparable from the cross – a cross that, as all Christians know, is made of wood.[20] Whether written, whispered, or thought, the 'prayers' addressed to the judge are prompted by the Falcone tree, like invocations of Christ are inspired by the sight of the crucifix: 'I am here, in front of your tree, which makes me think more and more of your honesty and courage,' writes Roberta (Armuri 1992: 33). Public-spirited, virtuous, and religious thoughts. Verses from the Bible are often quoted in letters placed at the foot of l'Albero Falcone: 'Happy are the persecuted for the cause of justice: for they shall enter the kingdom of heaven!' (Armuri 1992: 33). Did God abandon Giovanni to his fate on May 23, 1992, like he delivered his son Jesus to his fate on the day of his crucifixion? 'And you, merciful God, where were you?' asks Germana (Armuri 1992: 110). A child's drawing shows three crosses on Golgotha: one of them is Christ's, his heart bleeding and situated in a dominant position compared to the other two 'martyrs' at his feet, Giovanni Falcone and the carabinieri captain Emmanuele Basile. The prayer written on the other side of the same piece of quad-ruled paper from a schoolchild's exercise book is addressed to the Mafiosi. Ezia, a 5th grader at elementary school, asks them to think about their sins (Armuri 1992: 138-139).

The theme of sin and forgiveness is present in other messages: 'SEE YOU IN HEAVEN! / Maybe if your assassins repent / through the divine purifying blood of our / SAVIOR JESUS CHRIST, they will be there too!! / I'm sure that you would forgive them / with a handshake' (Armuri 1992: 113). Just like Christ, Falcone forgives his persecutors.[21] In Alba's prayer, Justice is the Word of the judge: 'I hope that, from where you are / in heaven, you will make these people understand / that they are men and not / animals, try to make them understand / that the justice you wanted may be / their word of life now too / I believe in your word "JUSTICE"' (Armuri 1992: 115). The book *L'Albero Falcone* itself ends on a kind of appeal that is intended to be hung on the tree and read by visitors. It is an appeal to Man, the definition of which remains closely tied to that of the Christian:

Man
Why do you create discord?
Why do you like violence?
Why do you not see in others
your brother?
Man-God
who forgives from the Cross
'Father, forgive them
for they know not what they do'

To understand these texts, one must go back not only to the practices that drive them, but also to the context in which they were produced: The transformation of the anti-Mafia struggle into a religious battle.[22] Called upon in the 1980s to reform society, to set it right and amend its morals, the judges became the representatives of a humanist credo that by getting men to turn away from egotism, encouraged them to devote themselves to others and to sacrifice themselves in the name of an ideal of Justice presented as a higher principle. It is useful to compare these unpretentious, apparently disparate writings to the construction of a true literary genre that flourished in the 1990s and that continues to bear fruit: the biography of anti-Mafia protagonists. This literature also focuses on the theme of sacrificing one's private life for the sake of public good, highlighting the exceptional firmness of the anti-Mafia people in the face of the mortal dangers they are exposed to on a daily basis. Their extraordinary courage sets them apart from ordinary mortals. They lead solitary, if not hermitic, lives. Their conduct surpasses human limits. This effacement of the self, this ability to withstand an unbearable pace of work for whomever, sometimes without even eating, often without sleeping, this capacity to overcome the constraints of their material and corporeal being and their possibility to cut themselves off from the world, once again make the judges heroic figures. When their 'sacrifice' is sealed by death, these heroes turn into 'martyrs.'

The theme of the 'martyr' creeps surreptitiously into *The Story of Giovanni Falcone* by Francesco La Licata. The biographer, a journalist who works for the center-left daily *La Stampa*, cannot avoid mentioning that on the day of the judge's birth, 'the calendar showed the feast day of St. Venanzio the martyr.' It is the same with Falcone's sister Maria, who participated in putting this commemorative work together. She cannot help but mention a detail: 'When Giovanni was born, a white dove entered the house. It came in through the window and didn't want to leave. It wasn't wounded. It stayed in the room and we fed it: it never flew away, even though the window remained open all the time.' In the Christian tradition, which is very present in Giovanni Falcone's extremely pious family environment, the dove is the Holy Spirit. Its appearance at little Giovanni's birth – a time when, in Mediterranean societies, omens are predicted – clearly announces his fate as a sacrificial Christ.

In the same biography, the fate predicted by his sister is echoed in that fashioned by his mother: 'I remember Mum, when she spoke of her dead brother (...). He died at eighteen on the Carso, where he had gone to fight as a volunteer. He was a model for my mother, this hero brother whose memory she celebrated unceasingly (...). The memory and example of her brother never left her. So much so that when her son Giovanni was born, she was happy and gave him the second name of Salvatore' (Armuri 1992: 26). With this name – Savior, which recalls Christ once more – Giovanni received as a gift and heritage the fate of a heroic and sacrificial death. But more than his death, it is the judge's life that, in its ascetic austerity, recalls that of a saint. 'The capacity to suffer, to endure much more than others, without ever giving up' (Armuri 1992: 19) is one of the principal qualities Giovanni Falcone was acknowledged to have had. 'At night, he slept on the floor to stop himself from sleeping and lowering his vigilance' (Armuri 1992: 113). Accustomed to this iconography, the Palermian reader immediately thinks of the restless nights of Saint Rosalia, the hermit saint depicted in her cave, lying on the ground, alert to all dangers (wild beasts, the temptations of the devil that assail her, etc.).

Saint Rosalia is an *imago Christi* (Puccio-Den 2007c). As the judge's life neared its end, it became a way of the cross. His biographer tells how his betrayal manifested itself during a 'farewell drinks party.' The Last Supper comes to mind. The judge spoke of the difficulty of his struggle, his professional solitude, the gap that widened painfully between himself and the others. Nobody reacted. As he was leaving his colleagues, one of them broke away from the others: 'And he, Giammanco, without batting an eyelid, slapped him on the shoulder and kissed him twice on the cheeks: like Judas' (La Licata 2002: 126). This kind of comparison appears not only in literary writing. In a speech he gave shortly before the Capaci massacre, Claudio Martelli (then Minister of the Interior) mentions the 'Judases' who, out of jealousy, obstruct the judge's projects (La Licata 2002: 179). 'What saddened Falcone the most was the hostility of those he had felt, ideologically and politically, to be the closest to him' (La Licata 2002: 155). Beyond any literary rhetoric, the judge advocated this position: 'One must do one's duty to the end, no matter what the sacrifice to be endured' (La Licata 2002: 20). Far from any metaphor, we know that this sacrifice was extreme and literal.

To complete this picture, it must be mentioned that well before the publication and distribution of these hagiographic biographies, an anti-Mafia iconography had arisen, modeled on the Passion. Photographs taken between 1978 and 1992 by Letizia Battaglia and Franco Zecchin, two activists in the anti-Mafia movement, were arranged in a particular order and developed according to a very specific visual code. In the light of everything that has come before, one is less surprised by the rhythm of certain works such as *Passion, Justice, Liberté* (Battaglia 1999) and *Chroniques siciliennes* (Battaglia and Zecchin 1989), which intersperse photographs of judges killed in Mafia attacks with scenes from Holy Week processions in Sicily. One is no longer surprised by other works such as *La Conta*[23], this black book of 'Mafia victims'[24], whose cover shows the photograph of an assassinated judge, arranged to resemble the aesthetic model of the dead Christ taken down from the cross. These works, today classified as art books, circulated and continue to circulate in Palermo, helping to spread a religious interpretation of the scenes of daily violence. The meaning, if not always explicitly outlined, is suggested by the dialectic established between image and text, by the ways these photographs are displayed in the street, and by the form of their presentation in local journals and newspapers.

These writings and images that transfigure the political sacrifice also accompany the institutionalization process of some of these figures, as 'martyrs,' leading us to the heart of the issue of the anti-Mafia movement as a 'religion.'

People gather at the tree near the house of Judge Falcone immediately after the announcement of his assassination, 1992. Photo: Franco Zecchin.

'Martyrs of the Law'

To complete the picture and understand the devotional practices surrounding judges Falcone and Borsellino in a wider context, a new category must be taken into account. This category takes to the extreme the heroization of those who are prepared to sacrifice their lives for an ideal of justice: Actual 'martyrs,' that is, the figures of sacrifice for whom the Vatican has initiated a beatification process. July 15, 1997, saw the traditional celebration of Palermo's patron saint, Saint Rosalia. After a procession had carried her urn through the streets, Cardinal Salvatore di Giorgi announced the start of a *super martyrium* process for Padre Puglisi, the priest who had been assassinated on September 15, 1993, by mafiosi in Brancaccio, the district of Palermo in which the priest had been born and, later, had preached. 'The first step in order for the supreme authority of the Church to recognize the martyrdom of this servant of God killed by the Mafia.'[25] This is a historic reversal by the Church with regard to the Mafia. Until the fall of the Berlin Wall, Mafia members were the backbone of the Christian Democrats' power in Sicily, the Catholic religion's bulwark against the Communists. A whole range of possibilities now opened up. When Pope Jean-Paul II visited Sicily just after the murder of Padre Puglisi, he defined Rosario Livatino as 'a martyr of the law and, indirectly, also of the faith,' considering this judge from Canicatti (a town in the province of Agrigente) who had been assassinated by the Mafia to be among those who 'to assert the ideals of justice and legality, paid with their lives the struggle they led against the violent forces of evil' (Di Lorenzo 2000: 87). This speech marked the start of the judge's beatification process.

Since the Bishop of Agrigente, Carmelo Ferraro, started investigative proceedings and set up a commission of enquiry, numerous biographies have been written on this 'judge who believed in the religion of duty and in the law' (Di Lorenzo 2000: 87). It is only through 'witnesses' certifying that he led a saintly life, along the lines of Christ's apostles, that the judge's sacrifice for the city can become an edifying example. Bishop Ferraro entrusted a secondary school teacher with the task of collecting 'testimonies' for the *super martyrium* process: 'Ida Abbate devoted herself body and soul to Rosario Livatino's cause.' Its testimony was passed on to her, so to speak, in reference to the above-mentioned Italian expression *passare il testimone* (Di Lorenzo 2000: 85). The man she 'testifies' for – who, without a doubt, is her life model for this 'missionary of remembrance' (and is author of several books on the Canicatti judge) – is described as 'reserved ... allergic to the limelight,' just like his biographers describe her 'little judge.' Is it because of the identification produced by this itinerary that the journey the teacher undertook in Italy in order to make her former student's experience known is described as an 'extraordinary, moving pilgrimage' (Di Lorenzo 2000: 85)?

Other witnesses are also on the move. In Canicatti, the 'pilgrimage' of friends, relatives, and acquaintances of Rosario Livatino began immediately after his death (Di Lorenzo 2000: 81). The increasing number of 'pilgrims,' who at first met in his house, gathered around his grave. The gestures performed in front of his gravestone ('simply inscribed with JUDGE in capital letters') closely resemble the pious acts carried out in front of the Falcone tree, so characteristic of Catholic devotion to the saints. The expression used is once more that of the eyewitness (Dulong 1998): 'I saw many strangers from all over Italy, kneeling in front of his grave and praying. I saw a mother lift up her child so that he could kiss the little judge.' On this funereal altar, we once again find written offerings. 'Among the flowers, there are many messages and letters: short, moving testimonies written mainly by young people. They are the ones who mostly go on pilgrimage to his grave (...). From this grave, [Livatino] is still able to speak to the conscience and hearts of the men and women of the Third Millennium,' declares the assassinated judge's biographer (Di Lorenzo 2000: 90-91). It is thanks to his testimony that: 'The whole of Italy has discovered in Rosario Livatino's sacrifice the anonymous heroism lived daily by a young Christian servant of the State' (Di Lorenzo 2000: 82).

Besides all this praise written after their death, one might ask how the judges interpreted their experience whilst they were alive. In a speech given on April 7, 1984, entitled 'The role of the judge in a changing society,' Rosario Livatino spoke of the relationship between action in the public and private spheres: 'The claim whereby... the judge can do what he wants in his private life, just like any other citizen must be dismissed (....). A judge's independence lies in his morality, in the transparency of his moral conduct including outside

the office (...). Only if a judge fulfills these conditions himself can society accept that he has such great power over its members' (Abate 1997: 61-74). In
other words, to judge men, one must be above society, and to be above society,
one must be outside of it. In the daily exercise of a profession that is unlike all
others, this is therefore what links justice and religion.

In the rich corpus of writing and images about the patron saint of Palermo,
which was republished in a monumental work at the time of the Palermo
spring (Gerbino 1991), the hagiographic and iconographic model clearly
emerges, informing the way in which the judge was transformed into a saint.
The writers of the Falcone tree messages, playing on the perfect homonymy
between the judge's surname and the name of a bird that flies high in the
sky, assume the judge to have the same piercing vision as Saint Rosalia, the
solitary hermit who, in paintings and engravings, looks down on the city from
the top of Monte Pellegrino: 'Like a large falcon [*falcone* in Italian], Falcone
peers down from on high' (Gerbino 1991: 128). In certain paintings, Rosalia is
one with the 'sacred mountain'[26] guarding her remains, which owes its name
– 'Pilgrim' – to the isolated position it occupies among the other mountains in
the Gulf of Palermo. 'Giovanni Falcone, isolated from all the others'[27] found
himself in the same solitary position as the patron saint overlooking the city
from the top of Monte Pellegrino (Gerbino 1991: 128). In one of the drawings
pinned to the Falcone tree, the judge's head is placed in the position occupied
by the 'Palermo virgin' in the Rosalian iconography: between the mountain
and the city. From the piece of paper scribbled on by the twenty-first-century
student to the paintings commissioned from masters since the sixteenth century, the same structure is involved, reactivated by the Capaci massacre. But
what new things has this event constructed?

Conclusion

Saint Rosalia's hermetic experience was the very condition that enabled her
to intervene in public affairs. This beneficial intercession transformed her into
the 'advocate of Palermo' and enabled her, according to the hagiographic legend, to free the city from the plague that struck it in 1624 (Puccio-Den 2007a).

Rosario Livatino, Giovanni Falcone, and Rosalia Sinibaldi are sacrificial figures for the city. In order to implement their salutary project, the saint and the judges must live an ascetic life. Their commitment to the world requires them to be detached from it, to renounce worldly goods. Ascetic and public-spirited aspects coexist in the judiciary, revealing the intrinsically religious nature of judicial administration. This explains why eminently religious practices, like pilgrimages, are directed at the judges.

The 'martyr judge,' a paradigmatic figure of the complex ties that the law maintains with religion, makes the pilgrimage the emblematic experience of personal trial and sacrifice. This sacrifice must be experienced by everybody and form part of everyone's lives so that they, in turn, may become a 'witness.' From this moment on, each 'pilgrim' is caught up in an 'evidence' process, where writing holds a central position. This is why I have afforded such importance to the little pieces of paper stuck to the Falcone tree: they testify to a cause and form the framework of a community that is situated, like the pilgrimage for which they are the medium, at the crossroads between the individual and the collective. This anti-Mafia community is perhaps the most enduring fruit of the Falcone tree and its transient writings.

Notes

1 I refer to photographs by Franco Zecchin, who photographed events concerning the anti-Mafia struggle between 1978 and 1992, see for example p. 65. Many of these photographs have been published (Battaglia and Zecchin 1989; Battaglia 1999; Battaglia and Zecchin 2006). Some of them are part of Zecchin's personal archive, which I was able to view in Paris in May 2006.
2 Sandra Armuri is a journalist for l'Unità, a daily founded by Antonio Gramsci in 1922 and the mouthpiece of the Italian Communist Party until 1991, when it was disbanded. The quote is taken from L'Albero Falcone, which she edited.
3 Written forms of communication with the saints are witnessed all over Catholic Europe. On votive writings to the Black Madonna of La Daurade (Toulouse, France) and in the chapel dedicated to Saint Rita in the Parisian district of Pigalle, see Albert-Llorca 1993.
4 On this pilgrimage and cult, see Puccio-Den 2006.
5 This approach is in line with the epistemological rupture adopted by Luc Boltanski and Laurent Thévenot (1991).
6 Béatrice Fraenkel (2002) refers to this concept when speaking of the altars, decorated with letters, flowers, and candles, which were created around ground zero in New York after 9/11.
7 On the constitution of the anti-Mafia struggle as a national moral cause, see Puccio-Den 2007b.

8 For a review of this political period, drawn up by its protagonists: Fabre, Puccio (Ed.) 2002.

9 I have kept the spelling (upper or lower case, capital letters, etc.) chosen by the authors of these messages.

10 See Jean-Claude Schmitt's introduction to the book by Donadieu-Rigaut (2005).

11 A rich corpus of images of the tree-order is shown in the work by Donadieu-Rigaut (2005).

12 The prototype of these representations, Jesse's tree, which shows the lineage of Christ, indicates him as a new David (Ibid: 245).

13 The role of the Mafia and the anti-Mafia struggle in the emergence of the Italian state is analyzed in Puccio-Den 2007b: in press.

14 These themes are examined in Puccio-Den 2007a.

15 On the place of the 'absent body' in the institution of Christianity: De Certeau 1982.

16 I owe this reference to Béatrice Fraenkel who presented Mr. Corbier's work (2006) at a conference at the Ecole des Hautes Etudes en Sciences Sociales: 'Actes d'écriture en milieu urbain, la ville et ses scripteurs' ('Acts of writing in urban environments, the city and its public writers') (June 5, 2007). I hereby express my indebtedness to this annual conference, which enabled me to enrich an earlier version of this current analysis.

17 I interviewed him in October 2006.

18 Shortly before he was assassinated, Giovanni Falcone created a centralised institution, the Italian Anti-Mafia Division (DIA), with headquarters in Rome, charged with coordinating anti-Mafia investigations throughout Italy. Each city with a court of appeal has its own anti-Mafia division (DDA). The anti-Mafia division in Palermo is the largest in Italy. It has twenty-two judges who deal only with Mafia trials.

19 I also consulted the archives kept by the Fondazione Giovanni e Francesca Falcone.

20 On the cult connotations of wood in the Middle Ages, see Pastoureau 1993.

21 In this regard, it bears recalling that Mafia repentance, the cooperation with the law in which Giovanni Falcone played a major role (Puccio 2001), is very often described as an act of conversion by those who repent. This is how Leonardo Vitale ended his confession: 'These are the words, the words which I was a victim of, I, Leonardo Vitale, reborn in God's true faith' (Lupo 1999: 312).

22 The close ties between politics and religion within the anti-Mafia movement led by the mayor of Palermo, Leoluca Orlando, is one of the main themes in *Guerres et conversions – Wars and Conversions*: Puccio-Den 2008 (to be published).

23 The title of this book which Franco Zecchin wrote at the time of Judge Gaetano Costa's death († 1980) refers to a children's game which takes on a macabre twist here: who's next?

24 On the slow development of this category: Puccio-Den 2007b.

25 I was present at this homily. This sentence is taken from the recording I made of it.

26 On the sacred nature of the Monte Pellegrino, see Giunta in Gerbino 1991: 21.

27 Elsewhere in Sicily, 'Falcone' is the name given to the highest summits in a chain of mountains. Monte Falcone, to take but one example, is the highest mountain in Marettimo, the island forming part of the Egadi archipelago, off the coast of Trapani.

Chapter 3

'I'm not religious, but Tito is a God': Tito, Kumrovec, and the New Pilgrims

Marijana Belaj

'Are we witnessing a rejuvenation of imagery from Dracula, as the seeming dead arise from the grave, some for the severalth time?' (Verdery 1999: 21)

Kumrovec, a small village in northwestern Croatia, is a real and visible place, in part politically marked, and with its own linear history; it is not therefore a mythical space. In recent times, however, due to the presence of the statue of Josip Broz Tito and related historical objects, it has been designated a kind of sacred place, primarily by those participating in the lively celebration of the *Day of Youth*.

The Day of Youth, celebrated on May 25, was a state holiday in former Yugoslavia and served officially to commemorate Tito's birthday (although V. Dedijer, Tito's biographer, claims that his actual birthday was May 7). The last time this holiday was officially celebrated in Yugoslavia was in 1988. With the subsequent break-up of Yugoslavia and the change of regime in 1991, the holiday was abolished in Croatia, although only officially. Admirers of Tito still gather in Kumrovec to celebrate the Day of Youth. Therefore, there is no doubt that in today's political climate, Kumrovec has been imbued with new meanings which define it as a place of pilgrimage for the approximately 10,000 people from all over former Yugoslavia who come to visit it on that day. Since the persona of Josip Broz Tito is the focal point of these events, my research centers on the events surrounding his statue, in an attempt to grasp at least some of the new meanings. By heeding the assertion 'to go to things as they are and to the places in order to see how nature and the material influence people's ideas and actions much more than what they themselves are able to project into them' (Frykman and Gilje 2003: 14), I was interested in observing what was happening around the statue, and how it influenced those *using* it.

Kumrovec

Kumrovec is the birthplace of Josip Broz Tito (1892-1980), president of the
Socialist Federal Republic of Yugoslavia between 1953 and 1980. For this reason, the place was given special protection and meaning, thereby becoming a
resource for the production of social memory. In the period before World War
Two and for the next 30 years, the old village center of Kumrovec was filled
with new buildings and old, restored houses from other areas. These buildings
had a dual meaning. One group, the monuments, was designed to function
as a resource for the dissemination of socialist principles and programs, based
on the idea of following the path of Tito's life and work. These monuments
were Villa Kumrovec (Tito's former residence), the Political School, the Home
of Fighters and Youth, and the Museum of the Revolution. The second group,
mainly historical and traditional houses and barns, was arranged around Tito's
birth house to show the rural way of life from the late 19th/early 20th centuries,
and 'to serve (…) only and exclusively as a representation of that ambience,
the basis of which is in its main and central object, which is the Birth House
of Marshal Tito,[1]' the building which also exhibits in part the process in which
Tito became an international statesman. The latter group of houses is at the
same time an open air museum, the first of its type in former Yugoslavia, created along the lines of the Scandinavian *skansen*. Judging by the documentation that has been preserved, this museum, which opened in 1953, was the
result of a skilful manipulation of the political climate; it was an exceptionally
ambitious project for the time. Marija Gušić, the project architect, made use
of the prevailing socialist rhetoric to systematically present Kumrovec as an
important political place (Kristić 2006: 103-105, 115-117). In this specific case,
it is the rhetoric about the burdensome life of a peasant who rebels, leaving
his poor home in order to find a more just and happier future: 'One of these
poletarac [a person just starting in life, a career, etc.] has succeeded in standing
at the head of the world struggle for peace, for the future of humanity.'[2]

This combined program turned Kumrovec primarily into a political and
educational but also a tourist destination, a character that it retained until
the end of the 1980s. Since then, the strong political and ideological turmoil
and change in this part of Europe has been marked, amongst other things, by

processes in which some of the factors making up the Yugoslavian idea of na-
tion-building have been deliberately forgotten. Celebrations, holidays, heroes
and other monuments of the Yugoslav era were systematically erased from the
collective memory and replaced by the symbols of the new system, as is the
case whenever political systems change (cf. Connerton 1989). As the result of
these processes, the buildings in Kumrovec, once erected as breeding grounds
for socialist ideas and socialist generations, have become silent witnesses to
that period (cf. Mathiesen Hjemdahl 2006: 53-55), and the Museum of Kumrovec shifted the focus of its presentation exclusively to the monuments relating to rural life. In this process of forgetting, making taboo and concealing,
Kumrovec was erased from the political map.

However, in spite of all attempts to remove traces of Yugoslavian nation-
building symbolism which had been sedimenting for years, once a year Kumrovec turns into a destination for several thousand Tito admirers from all over
former Yugoslavia, who go there to celebrate the Day of Youth.

Celebration of the Day of Youth in Kumrovec, 2004.
Photo: M. Belaj.

An Ordinary Man with an Extraordinary Life

The period of Tito's statehood (1953 – 1980) is often labeled Yugoslavian so-cialism, communism or Titoism; moreover, Tito is identified with Yugoslavia, communist ideology, the Communist Party, Socialist Revolution, the People's Liberation Struggle, etc. He stands at the center of the Yugoslavian symbolic opus, as its savior and liberator, and a fighter for its welfare and progress. Many identity markers of former Yugoslavia have found their personification in Tito.

I belong to a generation that was at primary school during the final years of Tito's life. Tito's presence in our everyday lives was intensive and diverse. And I am not referring only to the schools, streets, squares, bridges and towns that were named after him, nor to his statues which adorned each and every town in the former state, or the numerous instances of Tito's name in relief, sited on hills so that they could be seen from the air. I am also referring to school lessons overflowing with stories about his childhood in the countryside, his arduous struggles as a worker, his heroic and uncompromising achievements during and after World War Two. During class we were constantly watched over by his picture on the classroom wall, a mandatory part of school and of-fice inventories. At home we were watched from television screens, where he would mainly appear in a white suit or a marshal's uniform.

In the first class at primary school, on the *Day of the Republic* (29 Novem-ber), we joined *Tito's Pioneers* (an organization of children aged 7 to 14). In our hundreds, dressed in pioneer uniforms with red neckerchiefs and blue caps with a red star (the *Titovka* – Tito's Star), we recited in unison the initiation oath which bound us to pursue moral values like 'diligence' and 'good comrade-ship,' as well as to respect everyone who 'strives for liberty and peace.' But the same oath also bound us (though we were unable to fully comprehend it) 'to love the self-managing homeland and to develop brotherhood and unity and ideas Tito [had] fought for.' Admission to the pioneers was a symbolic separa-tion from political innocence and neutrality, marking the first step in the state care of children's education as part of the process of developing their political socialization, a sense of belonging to an ideological collective: 'It was the first of a series of initiations which had to produce a fully acculturated member of a socialist community.'[3]

In the seventh grade of primary school, we were admitted into the Socialist Youth Alliance. By receiving the red booklets, a little larger than the Pioneer ones, on the Day of Youth (25 May), we became *Tito's omladinci* (Tito's youth). Every year this state holiday would culminate in the stadium of the Yugoslavian People's Army in Belgrade (Serbia). Besides the spectacular *slet*, a massive gymnastic display performed in the stadium, Tito would be given a baton containing a congratulatory message, which had been relayed for months across Yugoslavia.[4]

At my school, a ritual event would take place each year on the Day of Youth, the content of which remained unchanged for years. There were also sport events. The school and its courtyard were decorated with stars, state flags and the Party's flags, and framed banners that shouted at us, reminding us that Tito 'is all of us,' that he was 'a white violet,' and that we should 'swear' to him not to 'deviate from his path.'[5] The same messages were repeated in songs played over the sound system, which were more combative. However, because such iconography was inherent to all important events, it is difficult today to determine whether, in terms of décor and music, this was characteristic of the Day of Youth or some other state holiday.

When I was admitted into the *omladinci*, Tito had already been dead for three years. However, up until the late 1980s, schoolchildren would still write letters to Tito on the Day of Youth, plant schoolyards with 88 rosebushes or trees for Tito[6], and on special occasions greet each other with the learned phrase: 'For the homeland with Tito.' The last Baton of Youth was relayed in 1987, and the last admission into the Pioneers took place in 1989. In 1985, five years after Tito died, the largest banknote (5,000 dinars), featuring Tito, was put into circulation.[7] Although he was no longer amongst the living, the law sanctioning acts of impiety against his character and work was still effective. This is illustrated by what happened in 1984, when members of the rock band *Zabranjeno pušenje* were subjected, like enemies of the state, to police oppression (interviews, home searches, telephone tapping) because of an 'incident' involving their lead singer at a concert in Rijeka. When their amplifier, made by the Marshall Amplification company, broke down, the band's frontman sadly announced to the audience: 'Hey folks, the marshal's dropped dead'

(*Raja, crko maršal*), referring to Tito by his rank of marshal. This, and many other examples, illustrates the use of Tito as a source of legitimacy in ideological efforts after his death. Tito was used as a fulcrum to maintain unity and stability. American historian Nina Tumarkin writes: 'A regime that derives its legitimacy from a single ruler risks instability upon his death. But if after death that ruler becomes the object of a cult predicated on his continuing living power, then the cult can serve as a stabilizing force' (Tumarkin 1997: 165).

Although there can be no doubt that Tito was turned into a kind of instrument of communist rule after he died, he has also retained an important place – as an ideal, a friend, a guardian – in the private spheres of life for many individuals. Commenting on communist versions of Tito's biographies, Croatian historian Maja Brkljačić perceives two different aspects: on the one hand, biographers emphasize Tito's poor background and his craft of locksmith (also presented in Tito's birth house in Kumrovec), which tie in perfectly with the 'glorious' history of the proletarian movement in Yugoslavia; on the other hand, they present a struggle for humanity in different periods of Tito's life embedded in events in Yugoslavian history. 'If combined, these two empha-

Groups of Croatian and Slovenian visitors in front of Tito's statue, September 2006. Photo: P.J. Margry.

ses tell a story of an ordinary man with an extraordinary life (...). In a sense, what was pictured was a perversion of the "American dream": he was quite a normal guy with a very suspicious background, and he did become president and the most celebrated figure of the country during all its existence, but you cannot even dream to come close to his fame, because he was after all very extraordinary in all his "ordinariness"' (Brkljačić 2001). Brkljačić also observes that Tito is never portrayed as cold or aloof, but is often called a 'teacher,' 'guardian' and 'friend.' In addition, his biographers insisted on elements of intimacy and friendship. In letters written to Tito by Yugoslavian Socialist Youth, just before he died, we find a similar discourse to that used when religious people describe their feelings about their patron saints. Brkljačić concludes that it is this kind of portrayal of Tito as a friend and protector that made him so close to the masses, without disturbing his position of power: 'One was supposed to believe him not on the grounds of fear but love' (Brkljačić 2001).

The fact that people have continued to speak of the role of Tito's life within their lives after 1980 has led Brkljačić to name the final chapter of her work on symbolization connected to Tito's funeral *Dead Man Walking:* 'In a sense, Tito remained roaming around like a good spirit, a vampire of a sort – not alive, but not completely dead either' (Brkljačić 2001).

A lively and non-institutional veneration of Tito after his death can be seen in occasional actions of citizens of former Yugoslavia, such as the banner saying 'This is Marshal Tito Street' (*Ovo je ulica Maršala Tita*) in the main street of Sarajevo. This banner was erected by citizens of Sarajevo in response to an attempt by the authorities to change the name to Alija Izetbegovic Street, in honor of the first president of the independent state. Tito's name, based on the symbolization contained within it, is often recognized and offered as a 'saving solution' in problematical situations. For example, a 33-meter-high cross illuminated by six spotlights was erected on Hum, a hill in Mostar, to mark the occasion of the 2,000[8] anniversary of Christ's birth. One sector of multi-denominational Mostar saw it as provocation against Muslims.[8] A citizen proposed the following as a possible solution to the problem: 'They should pull down the cross and write TITO [...] or all those symbols, but that the star is adopted as a valid atheist symbol and that it becomes constitutive as if it were a religion, that is, a personal conviction (...) therefore, knock down everything and in big bold letters write TITO.'[9]

Expressions of direct and personal attachment to Tito give an especially vivid account of his life after death, usually referring to communication with him and the need to bring him closer and make him more familiar. There are many such expressions, for example on 'Tito's official page' http://www.tito-ville.com/ (*Tito's Tribune*).[10] Incidentally, it is worth noting that the homepage of this Internet site says: 'Josip Broz – TITO (Kumrovec, 7. 5. 1892 – Ljubljana, 4. 5. 1980 – Internet, 22. 7. 1994).' As the postings on these pages show, the practice of writing letters to Tito – albeit now in digital form – has never been abandoned. The authors of these messages congratulate him on his birthday,[11] they are ashamed of their forgetfulness, and they send requests,[12] they evoke a friendship,[13] they express intimacy and comment on ideology,[14] and they curse him.[15] Furthermore, even fifteen years after his death, Tito's portrait, already removed from public spaces, still occupies a special place in many private houses (Bringa 2003: 153). Some people now regret removing them from their walls and throwing them away. For example, during my research on beliefs in patron saints in the North Velebit region, an informant showed me pictures of patron saints hanging on the walls of her home, and said: 'I have St. Anne and St. Anthony. I also had Tito, and I'm always sorry I threw it away.'[16] Tito was placed in a similar context by another informant I talked to in Gračišće in Istria: 'When it's tough, when you're ill, when facing difficulties, you'll believe everyone – Tito and a monk and the Pope.'[17] This quotation makes it clear that Tito is invoked in the same way as Catholic saints in order to bring relief or help.

Having examined this kind of personal communication with Tito, I will now attempt to present contemporary events in Kumrovec which take place once a year – at the celebration of the Day of Youth. As these events seem to show, not only has the Day of Youth continued in spite of its official abolition, it also survives as a focal point in the calendars of many of Tito's admirers. The central element in this celebration is the statue of Josip Broz, situated beside his birth house.

The Day of Youth and the Statue of Josip Broz in Kumrovec

Statues are dead people cast in bronze or carved stone. They symbolize a specific famous person while in sense also being the body of that person. By arresting the process of that person's bodily decay, a statue alters the temporality associated with the person, bringing him into the realm of the timeless or the sacred, like an icon. For this reason, desecrating a statue partakes of the larger history of iconoclasm (Verdery 1999: 5).

The statue of Josip Broz at his birth house in Kumrovec was made by the Croatian sculptor Antun Augustinčić and was erected in the courtyard of Tito's birth house in 1948. Today this statue can be viewed as a stage on which dialogue or, to be more precise, conflicts between different collective memories take place.

Several times in the last few years the statue has been the 'victim' in a conflict between the two dominant political factions in Croatia – those who respect the Yugoslav past and those who condemn it – about their differing interpretations of history. At the very end of 2004, the latter group placed explosives beneath the statue, which was seriously damaged and had to undergo restoration. This event was a major story on the national news service. Since it was about Josip Broz Tito, a person whose portrayal ranges from 'the greatest son and teacher of our peoples' to 'a butcher, criminal, and a dictator,' it is obvious that these attributes, characteristic of a real person, are often – and certainly in the above-mentioned conflicts – attributed to the statue representing him. For some of the opponents, the statue represents something untouchable, 'sacred' and, at the same time, intrusions are seen as 'sacrilege.' To others, the very existence of the monument is 'sacrilege.'

Such phenomena are not a distinctive feature of Croatian society, and nothing would seem out of the ordinary[18] were it not for the fact that Tito and his admirers and followers, in line with Marxist ideology, publicly renounced religion. Moreover, religion was not even mentioned, apart from the sense of *das Opium des Volks*. This therefore raises an important question: how can an admirer of Tito perceive his statue as the real person, without this experience

Touching the statue of Josip Broz Tito in Kumrovec, 2004.
Photo: M. Belaj.

being in a certain way religious? Does Tito's statue arouse anything religious in the experience of a visiting admirer? It is the celebration of the Day of Youth in Kumrovec that has proven to serve as the perfect training ground for this kind of political imagery. 'Identities are not at first hand a question of ideas but of ordinary practice – the tactile, sensual and practical relationship to the natural and humanly created environment' (Frykman and Gilje 2003: 11). In this context, instead of discussing what the statue of Tito in Kumrovec represents, it seems more interesting to deal with what happens around it, and with its impact on those *using* it. What kind of a dialogue takes place between the statue and participants in the Day of Youth celebration, or in other words, how does the statue affect the participant, and how in turn does the participant bring the statue to life?

Celebrations of the Day of Youth in Kumrovec are organized by the Josip Broz Tito Society in Zagreb.[19] As their president Tomislav Badovinac points out, the Society's intention is not to create a personality cult[20] because 'he is dead, he's gone,' but to draw attention to the *life and work* of Josip Broz. Explaining the essence of the notion of Tito's work, the Society's president lists five historic moves by Josip Broz: (1) the uprising against the Germans and the Quisling government in Croatia, (2) independence, freedom and justice, especially in contrast to the Stalin regime, (3) self-government, (4) communal property, and (5) the Non-Alignment Movement. Delegations of other societies that admire Tito's life and work attend the celebrations as well.

In honoring Tito, society members seem to follow a strict protocol. For example, a delegation from one of the societies formed a line with almost military precision and advanced towards the statue in a few, apparently choreographed movements. It was prearranged who was to bring the flowers and who to lay them down. In their procession towards the statue, they looked at each other to avoid making a mistake in the protocol. They laid the flowers and stood in silence in front of the statue. After about a minute, the leader of the delegation said: 'Glory be to comrade Tito!' Everyone replied firmly: 'Glory!' – it sounded as if they had been rehearsing it on the way to Kumrovec. In fact, they have probably had many rehearsals at all the commemorations and memorial gatherings over the years. What added to the distinctiveness of this protocol was the vocabulary and gestures used by the delegation members to pay their respects – greetings like 'Death to Fascism!' or 'With Tito into the future!,' sometimes accompanied by the Communist military salute (pressing the fist to the temple).[21] This, one could almost say ritual, vocabulary was particularly instrumental in creating an impression of authenticity.

This strict adherence to the protocol characterized every delegation. On completion of the protocol, the groups would disband, so it seems that for most delegations laying down the flowers and paying their respects before the

Saluting the statue of Josip Broz Tito, 2004.
Photo: M. Belaj.

statue was the climax of their formal involvement in the visit to Kumrovec.

The paying of respect was nothing but an acknowledgement of the *life and work* of Josip Broz Tito, as the phrase went. In fact, when Tito died, a number of his sympathizers and followers actually *vowed* to continue his work. For example, the end of the proclamation issued jointly by the Presidency of the Central Committee of the Yugoslav Communist League and the Presidency of the Socialist Federal Republic of Yugoslavia on the day of Tito's death, 4 May 1980, reads: 'The generations of today and those to come owe profound gratitude to comrade Tito and will continue his immortal work.'[22] A similar note echoes in newspaper articles of the day: 'And in all the written vows, words and thousands of signatures, there is found one common message: that the magnificent work of President Tito should be the guiding star of our future, that we should follow in his steps and thoughts'; 'We have before us today a great moral obligation to continue this great work.'[23]

The recognition of Tito's *life and work* had a more powerful effect on all members of the delegations than any personal experience of the statue – it was, judging from Badovinac's words, programmatic. However, only about a dozen delegations performed such protocols in front of the statue that day. The overwhelming majority of those who came to see the statue were individuals who experienced and expressed their encounter with the statue in a very personal way. They talked to it, saluted it, cried while looking at it, and touched it. Were they thinking of *Tito's work*, or was their experience of the statue of a totally different kind?

I was standing very close to one lady who picked a small branch of lilac in order to have her picture taken beside the statue. Then she laid the branch beneath the statue, and kissed and stroked it. She then looked at me and said very gently: 'You were his Pioneer.' I do not know whether she was trying to advise or encourage me, but that is not all that important. What matters is her open and intimate contact with me. It was not hard to approach her or the others. They addressed each other very openly, sometimes even euphorically, as if they knew each other very well. They addressed me as well, not for one moment imagining I had some other reason for coming – for them, the fact I was standing there was enough to consider me 'one of them.' Moreover, my comparatively young age seemed to make me particularly welcome and to bring great joy to these, mostly elderly, people. It reminded them of their own past as a youth pioneer.

A lady from Križ (born in 1928) looked at the statue in tears, but she said she was happy and explained how in 'those days' people had different values. She told me about her personal experience of the time, of her own emancipation and starting a family, of a morality marked by family values and solidarity instead of materialism. As she emphasized, Josip Broz deserves credit for this, and therefore 'his feet should be kissed for it. (...) Not just the feet, we should kiss the pedestal itself. Because what he did... for man...' There were no great historical facts in her story, nothing about the *life and work* of Josip Broz. She shared her memories in a warm and direct manner, often entering into moral instructions with an almost religious tinge. It is difficult to believe that a statue can evoke these memories and, occasionally, even instructive narrations. I was sure that she saw a real person – Josip Broz himself.

She carries this experience to her home as a memory, and it encourages her to come again, as the following dialogue points out:

Q: 'You'll go back home, the statue will stay here. Do you know how you'll feel?'
A: 'Relaxed. Relaxed. I'm glad. I come here every year. (...) Because this is who we are and we can't be any different. We can't. Even if I wanted to, I couldn't. Because it's in me. This is how I raise my children (...).'
Q: 'Do you make special preparations for coming here? Do you think about it in advance?'
A: 'Yes – yes, yes. To us it is an extension of life. An extension of a duty we'd performed. You understand me? (...) To us it, I mean it extends our life. I'm an old woman, born in 1928. I guess this is my fourth country, you know (...) But there is something within you which carries you, which no one will ever destroy. And can't. This is how I raise my children. And we are all like this. And I have grandchildren, and they also... I'm saying that for as long as I can, I'm, you know, my soul is at peace.'

Many participants in the Day of Youth, mostly women, approached the statue, kissed it, stroked it, touched the hand at the back, some in awe, some completely calm. 'Hey there, Stari,[24] if you only knew what happened to us,' a man said to the statue, after bowing and crossing himself.

One lady ran excitedly into the courtyard, making her way to the statue. She stroked it several times, saying at every stroke, 'This is for Radenković, this is for Majda...,' and she kept listing names of her friends and relatives. After that, she kissed Tito's coat, and then withdrew several steps, content, and stayed close to the statue.

There were groups of women who circled around the statue touching it, while some would simply touch it and cross themselves. Others spoke to the statue or simply saluted it. Many lit a candle beneath the pedestal.

On that day hundreds of people expressed their experience of the statue in similar ways.

Lighting candles in front of the statue of Josip Broz Tito, 2004.
Photo: M. Belaj.

The religious domain is often revealed in small talk, for example, while queuing to be photographed with the statue. While we were standing in line, one man from Varaždin (northwestern Croatia), watching the people taking pictures, said: 'He was too gracious.' When I drew his attention to the people touching the statue, he explained: 'Well you see, he was a god. He is a god. And we will touch him.' When our turn came, we placed our palms on Tito's coat, and he added: 'Now we're close.' If he had touched a random statue, wouldn't he have felt only the coldness of the material instead of this experience of being close to Tito?

During the four to five hours of the event, thousands of photographs were taken of visitors touching Tito's coat, his feet, the statue's pedestal, or leaning on it, or posing alongside it, saluting. Almost everyone had a camera, and those who did not exchanged addresses to have the photos sent to them. To have a photograph of themselves with the statue of Josip Broz was so important that they were also willing to pay for it. The encounter with the statue of Josip Broz represents one of those events worth recording and preserving, and sharing with those to whom they will show the photograph.

However, conversations overheard in the streets of Kumrovec during the celebration also suggest a certain religious experience of the whole event, not just the statue:

'I'll tell you why I'm here – Tito is a god! I'm not religious, but Tito is a god' (an Istrian man in his early 20s).

['Is there any other day in the year that is so important to you?'] 'Yes, Easter is important, and Christmas too' (a woman in her early 20s from Kumrovec).

['Which part of the celebration was the most important to you?'] 'Look, everything is important. First we went to Tito's monument. I talked to him and kissed him. I do that every time' (a woman in her mid-40s, from Varaždin, northwestern Croatia).

'When I tried to organize a visit to Kumrovec, someone said "I've already been". And I replied: "My friend, my dear mother has never said to me, I've already been to church. She goes again and again. That's how I do this – again and again"' (a 65-year-old man from Zagreb).

We read similar comments in the guest book ('In my heart you remain immortal; Blessed is the one who lives forever'), on banners ('Tito lived, Tito is alive, Tito will live'[25]), and even in a speech that opened with a personal address to Tito, who is seemingly *present*: 'Tito, our comrade! I am speaking to you on behalf of...'

New Perspectives on Tito and Kumrovec

The experiences of the visitors to Kumrovec when encountering Tito's statue point on the one hand to the presence of the past in that time and place – the past relating to the period of personal development, starting a family, bringing up children, etc. The evoking of memories reflects nostalgia, but not – as is generally believed – for a political creation, but for one's own youth. The visitors connect the creative and prosperous period of their lives with their then leader, 'the greatest son of these lands,' Josip Broz, who in their eyes achieved what is elsewhere called the *American Dream*. He is perceived by the participants in the celebration as the embodiment of exemplariness and of ideals.

The statue of Tito also invites special gestures, actions and emotions which, in turn, transform the statue into the person it represents. Many of these actions and gestures are not simply suggestive of the religious, but are in fact taken from religious practice – expressions of experience of Tito's statue are similar to forms of religiosity found in the worshipping of saints. Above all, I am thinking here of people touching and kissing the statue, walking around it, talking to it, lighting candles and laying flowers at its feet, and especially the gesture of crossing themselves in front of the statue.

For most of these participants, the very meeting with the statue represented the culmination of their visit to Kumrovec – a visit motivated primarily by their need to pay respect to Josip Broz, who was in their eyes exemplary and ideal and, indirectly, to thank him for the creative and successful period of their lives. The visit triggers powerful emotions, great affection, and sometimes even euphoria, which is manifested in laughter accompanied by tears and in unrestrained behavior in general. The atmosphere is one of feeling connected with the other participants, so that communication is direct and often intimate. But being in Kumrovec on the Day of Youth does not end when the participants arrive home. They still have a photo of their encounter with the statue, or a memory of the experience, which demands a revisit; it is even a *duty*, as the lady from Križ said.

All this indicates a special kind of journey, the ultimate aim of which is to meet Tito's statue – a pilgrimage, as explained by the Croatian ethnologist Vitomir Belaj (1991). He discusses crucial features of a pilgrimage which distinguish it from other visits to sacred places. Among other things, he mentions the following elements of a pilgrimage:

- the motivation that starts the pilgrimage, which is a specially close contact with the sacred in order, for instance, to show reverence or express gratitude;
- an anticipated beneficial effect of the pilgrimage, such as a material effect or spiritual grace given by the divinity;
- the goal, which could be a picture or a statue and which presents an embodiment of exemplariness and ideals;
- forms of piety, such as touching, kissing, talking to the statue or picture, walking around it, etc.;
- remembrance of the pilgrimage, supported by a photograph or a memorized experience, and also the preservation of the need for further pilgrimages, in which word of mouth plays an important role.

In Kumrovec, it would seem, a process has happened involving the 'spatialization of charisma.' Anthropologists John Eade and Michael Sallnow, discussing a particular kind of Christian places of pilgrimage, paraphrase Weber in their use of this term: '"spatialization of charisma": the power of the living person is sedimented and preserved after his death in the power of place.' In other

Slovenian women from the city of Koečevje, which is near the Croatian border, singing Tito's favorite folk song (Plenička je prala pri mrzlem studenc), September 2006.
Photo: P.J. Margry.

words, as the authors state, we are dealing with loci of supernatural power or rather of 'place-centred sacredness' (Eade and Sallnow 1991b: 8). In this context, Kumrovec can be viewed as a place of pilgrimage, but primarily for participants who come there in order to make close contact with Josip Broz. However, the other participants, who pay respect to Tito's *life and work* with actions predetermined by protocol, do not *a priori* show characteristics of religiosity in their attitude towards the statue and their motivation.

Nevertheless, the encounter with the statue represents the culmination of the visit to Kumrovec for them too, and the strictness of the protocol suggests that its performance leaves no room for error, thus pointing to some common characteristics of a ritual act (cf. Belaj 1998: 30). In this regard, Eade and Sallnow state the following: 'A pilgrimage shrine is also – sometimes predominantly – an arena for the interplay of a variety of imported perceptions and understandings, in some cases finely differentiated from one another, in others radically polarized' (Eade and Sallnow 1991b: 10). Sacred places are given the characteristic of a universality which is not constituted by discourse unification, but rather by the potential of the cult to support and maintain plurality (Eade and Sallnow 1991b: 15-16).

Even more intriguing is the translation of a form of behavior from one domain into another, or rather the presence of popular piety in the context of the celebration of a secular – indeed, communist – holiday such as the Day of Youth. It is important to note that twenty years ago allegiance to Josip Broz was not publicly displayed in forms of popular religiosity. Furthermore, the Day of Youth, which was introduced as a political holiday, ceased to be a state holiday about fifteen years ago when political changes occurred. Among those still firmly upholding communist values, this historical distance resulted in the disintegration of the anti-religious barrier and was thus able to produce a previously unimaginable commingling of world views, without anyone being held responsible. In addition, the event itself, as a temporary break with everyday life, leads to emotional and mental excitement that in turn encourages analogous changes in physical behavior. The break with everyday life and the common environment 'lays people open to possibilities of behavior which they embody but ordinarily are not inclined to express' (Jackson 1983: 334–335). I do not wish to judge the extent to which popular religiosity was present in the daily lives of those participating in the festivities. What I have in mind is the celebration of the Day of Youth and the living cult of Josip Broz, which today are not only far removed from everyday experience, but are often relegated to the margins and sometimes even perceived as 'ridiculous.'

Kumrovec continues to be a place of pilgrimage, at least on this one day of the year. Of course, it is not so in and of itself. It is made 'sacred' by the participants in the Day of Youth festivities. McKewitt notes: 'The sacred is not a given or something fixed, but must be constantly created and recreated. A conscious effort is required on the part of the pilgrim to use the appropriate symbols, myths, and rituals in order to vivify the experience of pilgrimage and to make real the sacredness of place' (McKewitt 1991: 79). Nowadays, the initial idea that placed Kumrovec on the political map of the time is dead, and therefore meaningless. Participants in the celebration of the Day of Youth, as far as activities involving the statue are concerned, have replaced it with another, completely different idea. They come to pay their respects to the person embodied in the statue, which is why they touch it, greet it, talk to it, and light candles at its feet. There is no doubt that the marginalization of communist ideology, present in contemporary society, as well as the freedom of thinking (and speaking) about Tito as the bearer of this ideology have strengthened individuality and the variety of behavior at the celebration in Kumrovec, thereby creating the basis for the development of a new form of devotion. Surely it does not come from the initial ideological framework in which Kumrovec was created, nor does it have anything to do with the official creed of the church. It is a newly created cultus which, due to its expressions, represents a form of popular religiosity.

In order to complete the picture of the visitors to Kumrovec, I wish to present at the end of this article a particular group of visitors to the Kumrovec statue. I am referring here to those who do not visit Kumrovec on the Day of Youth and who cannot be considered tourists, but who from time to time remember the statue or pay a visit. They address it with insults and threats, behave aggressively towards it, and leave explosive devices instead of candles and flowers. We could therefore conclude that for them, too, this statue represents a person, the only difference being the way in which the statue is experienced and the kind of needs they seek to satisfy in encountering it.

Finally, I would like to justify the research I conducted in Kumrovec in relation to an observation by Mary I. O'Connor. Dealing with the subject of pilgrimages, she has noted that anthropologists tend to research only certain aspects of a pilgrimage (religious, social, political, and economic), rather than viewing it as a whole (O'Connor 1999: 369). In spite of her criticism, I have focused in this study almost exclusively on a single aspect of a pilgrimage, the religious one, in order to draw attention to it in the context of a single event – not just non-religious but also anti-religious. Apart from that, the research was conducted in one sitting, thus leaving many particulars unrecorded, especially those which would point in detail to other aspects of a pilgrimage. However, familiarity with one aspect opens up opportunities to research others during a subsequent visit, and it would take all of them to make the picture complete.

Notes

1 From material held in the Croatian State Archives, quoted in Kristić 2006: 111: Program uređenja Starog sela Kumrovec, Institute of Ethnology at the Yugoslavian Academy of Sciences and Arts, May 1973. Croatian State Archives, box 4: 9-10

2 From material held in the Croatian State Archives, quoted in Kristić 2006: 103-104: Selo Kumrovec povijesni spomenik, Croatian State Archives, box 4:1

3 *'Bila je to prva u nizu inicijacija koje su kao ishod trebale da imaju potpuno akulturalizovanog člana socijalističke zajednice,'* see Erdei 2006: 209.

4 Every May 25 between 1945 and 1987, mass youth relay races were organized throughout Yugoslavia. The runners would carry batons containing a congratulatory birthday message for Tito. The first Youth Relay Race set off from Kumrovec in 1945. Each subsequent year, it would start in a different Yugoslav republic, with the batons carried along stipulated routes throughout the country. Every day the media would inform the Yugoslav public about the relay's progress and its top participants.

5 'Comrade Tito, we swear to you that we shall not deviate from your path' *(Druže Tito mi ti se kunemo da sa tvoga puta ne skrećemo)* is a verse which generations of Yugoslavian citizens used to sing at every major event. The song is an important part of the collective memory concerning the soccer tournament between Hajduk and Crvena zvezda at the stadium in Split. The match was stopped at the moment of the official announcement of Tito's death. Many players fell to their knees in tears, and the whole stadium spontaneously started singing this song.

6 The number 88 refers to Tito's age at the time of his death.

7 It is worth mentioning that this banknote bore an obvious printing error when it entered circulation: 1930 instead of 1980 (the year that Tito died). Four percent of the total of 14 million banknotes contained this error. The banknote was not withdrawn from circulation although international laws on banknote production oblige a state to withdraw such notes if more than 1% are faulty (http://hrvatskanumizmatika.blog.hr/arhiva-2006-02.html, last accessed on March 1, 2007).

8 Cf. Ko je prekrstio Mostar? at http://drzava.blogger.ba/arhiva/2006/01/31.

9 From: tataratira; written: 25/08/2005 11:45; http://www.sarajevo-x.com/forum/viewtopic.php?t=17786&sid=a576930a58da0cc92670b1a5e9536a04; last accessed on February 3, 2007).

10 The page is maintained by two young Slovenians, Matija Marolt (Assistant Professor at the Faculty of Computer and Information Science in Ljubljana) and Martin Srebotnjak (a director from Ljubljana).

11 From: TMN; date: Mon, May 24, 2004 16:36:11 -0400; subject: Happy Birthday 'Dear Mr. Broz, I wish you a happy birthday. Hope you will have a good party as you used to have. Regards, TMN' (http://www.titoville.com/tribune2004.html, last accessed on February 12, 2007).

12 From: 'Diana Petronio'; date: Sat, May 15, 2004 16:36:58 +0200; subject: danes, ko postajam pionir... 'dear Tito! I've forgotten the pioneer oath (shameful, I know), but I'd like to refresh my memory. I look forward to receiving your reply and thank you in advance for your hep. [What could this abbreviation refer to?] death to fascism! Diana PS. I'm happy you've returned among us! *(dragi Tito! zal sem pozabila pionirsko prisego (sramotno, vem) sedaj pa bi rada osvezila znanje. vnaprej se ti zahvaljujem za kakrsnokoli pomoc. smrt fasizmu! Diana p.s. me veseli, da si se vrnil med nas!;* ibid).

13 From: Bogdan Milanovic; date: Sat, Feb 12, 2005 17:47:05 +0100; subject: none 'Dear comrade Tito, I'm turning 15 this year. [...] I won't call you by name, don't think that I'm uneducated ☺. I only want it to seem as if comrade Tito was closer to me [...] Well, that would be all from me... I'll keep in touch. Bogdan' (Ibid).

14 From: 'Danko Drasko'; date: Fri, Aug 6, 2004 22:04:11 -0400; subject: Hvala 'Comrade Tito,

thank you for everything, when I need peace and nice memories I just come to your site and pay you a visit so that my mind's at peace [...] PS. If Religion-ideology is the opium of the masses, you have certainly fattened us with cocaine' (Ibid).

15 From: Tatjana Novakovic Ostojic; date: Thu, Jan 15, 2004 14:29:07 -0800; subject: anatema 'You're never going to drop dead, are you? ' (Ibid).

16 Quoted from transcripts of my unpublished research Belief in patron saints, Krasno, 2005.

17 Quoted from transcripts of my unpublished research Belief in patron saints, Istra, 2002.

18 By destroying statues of former rulers and dictators, supporters of the new order not only avenge certain injuries and washing away the sins, but also unequivocally mark the boundary between the past and the present. 'To pass judgement on the practices of the old regime is the constitutive act of the new order' (Connerton 1989: 7).

19 The society, a member of the Association of Josip Broz Tito Societies, was founded in 1996.

20 The term personality cult was popularized by Nikita Khrushchev in a 1955 address. Implicitly referring to Stalin, he used the term to describe excessive adoration and uncritical praise of any individual as well as blind submission to his will (Klaić 1990: 765). According to Christian beliefs, personality cults in contemporary totalitarian societies constitute a form of modern idolatry (Rebi 2002: 493).

21 I collected this data, as well as the data later in the text, during the 2004 celebration.

22 *Samoborske novine*, May 15, 1980, no. 10; ed. XXX, *Samobor Samoborske novine* 1980, no. 10: 2–3; *Vikend*, a family magazine, May 9, 1980, no. 624; *Zagreb. Vikend* 1980, no. 624: 5–8.

23 *Samoborske novine* 1980, no. 10: 8 and 14.

24 Stari was Tito's nickname; it means 'old man,' with age symbolizing authority.

25 Once again, this construction seems to link Tito with Lenin. The same sentence, but with Lenin's name, appears in Komsomolskaya (1924), written by Vladimir Vladimirovich Majkovsky.

Chapter 4

Patriotism and Religion:
Pilgrimages to Soekarno's Grave

Huub de Jonge

Introduction[1]

Pilgrimages to graves are a widespread phenomenon in Indonesia. They can be observed in almost all regions and in most of the country's cultures and religions. In Java alone, there are thousands of graves which are visited by varying numbers of pilgrims. This does not mean, however, that such pilgrimages are non-controversial. Orthodox Muslims, for example, condemn the practice, although it is very popular among less strict fellow believers with a more syncretic approach.[2] Among the graves that attract disproportionate numbers of visitors are those of ancestors, village founders, religious apostles, religious leaders, shamans, heroes, monarchs and secular leaders. Although not all these deceased figures are seen as saints or holy men, their graves are considered sacred places (De Jonge 1991; Chambert-Loir and Read 2002).

One of the most-visited graves of a secular leader is that of Soekarno who, together with Mohammad Hatta, proclaimed Indonesian independence in 1945 and was president of the Indonesian republic during the first 27 years of its existence. Today, Soekarno's grave attracts several hundred thousand pilgrims a year from all over Indonesia. His is not the only grave of a secular leader or freedom fighter to have become a place of pilgrimage. Some final resting places of monarchs of former realms in the Indonesian archipelago draw large numbers of pilgrims, although fewer now than in earlier times. The graves of other national figures are also visited regularly, but not on the same scale or in the same way as Soekarno's burial place.

In this article, I will attempt to describe the nature, form and meaning of pilgrimages to the grave of Indonesia's first president. I will discuss the physical and spatial changes that the grave has undergone during the years of successive political regimes, the sort of people who visit it, and the reasons why.

In this way, I shall attempt to draw out the religious dimension of this homage or veneration or, more accurately, show how the secular and the spiritual relate to each other. Further, I implicitly compare the pilgrimage to Soekarno's burial place with visits to the graves of monarchs, apostles and other revered people. To set the scene, I begin with a brief summary of Soekarno's significance for Indonesia and Indonesians.

Soekarno

Soekarno (1901-1970) played a leading role in the nationalist movement in the Dutch East Indies, in the independence struggle and in political developments after independence. He was very active in politics from a young age. In 1927, he founded the Partai Nasional Indonesia (PNI) and a federation of political organizations[3] striving for independence. This rapidly made him a nationalist leader of importance. Ideologically, he advocated a coming together of nationalism, Marxism and Islam. His Marxist or socialist doctrine, labeled Marhaenism, comprised a number of Marxist ideas relating to the specific situation of Indonesian peasants.[4] Because of his fierce opposition to the colonial regime, he was imprisoned in Bandung for a year, and spent eight years in exile in Ende on Flores and in Bencoolen on Sumatra. Together with Hatta (1902-1980), with whom he formed a kind of political duumvirate for many years, he opted in 1942 to cooperate with the Japanese occupying forces, in the expectation that this would bring about independence much sooner. A few months before independence was proclaimed, he presented the Pancasila, the five (*panca*) principles (*sila*) on which the Indonesian state should be based: nationalism, international brotherhood, democracy, social justice and belief in one God (monotheism). Standing next to Hatta in the capital Jakarta on 17 August 1945, two days after Japan capitulated, he read out the text proclaiming the Indonesian Republic. The next day the Committee for the Preparation for Independence chose Soekarno as president and Hatta as vice-president.

Between 1945 and 1949, Soekarno led the violent struggle against the Dutch, who refused to recognize the new republic and who tried to reinstate their authority through two *politionele acties* or police actions (July-August

1947; December 1948-January 1949). At the start of the second police action, or the second military aggression as the Indonesians called it, Soekarno was again arrested by the Dutch and exiled to Bangka for six months. He was released in July 1949 once it was clear that Indonesian independence was inevitable. With the recognition of Indonesian independence in December of that year, Indonesia (first a federal state, and from 1950 a unitary state) became a constitutional democracy with Soekarno as ceremonial head of state. However, as a result of increasing discord between political parties, proponents and adversaries of an Islamic state, Java and the outer islands, rebellions in Sulawesi and Sumatra, coupled with a succession of impotent cabinets, Soekarno took more and more power into his own hands. At the end of the 1950s, to save the country from chaos, he resorted to what he called 'Guided Democracy.' In 1959, the parliamentary system was replaced by a presidential system, and in 1960, he instituted a people's congress that included representatives of regions and interest groups in addition to members of parliament. As in the 1920s, he promoted close cooperation between nationalists, Marxists and Muslims, which he called NASAKOM,[5] the chief difference being that it was now imposed from above.

Soekarno also asserted himself internationally. In 1955, he organized the Asian-African Conference in Bandung, a meeting of primarily newly independent nations who refused to accept the partition of the world into American and Soviet spheres of influence. State visits to the USA, the Soviet Union and the People's Republic of China in 1956 increased his international prestige still further. With foreign support, he was able to expand Indonesian territory in 1963 by annexing Papua (the former Dutch New Guinea), an area that the Dutch had refused to hand over at the time of transfer of sovereignty. In the same year, he was appointed 'President for Life.'

Soekarno was clearly at the peak of his power. Thanks to his contribution to the independence struggle, his charisma and his passionate speeches at mass meetings which carried away the man in the street, he was placed on a pedestal by millions of his compatriots. He was without doubt the most popular person in the country. Yet, despite the credit he had built up and the room for maneuver he had created for himself, he was unable to solve the

Soekarno reads out the Proclamation of Independence, while Hatta (on the right) listens, 17 August 1945.

Soekarno in front of the Proclamation of Independence.
From the H. de Jonge collection.

huge problems facing the vast country. On the contrary, his political arrogance caused great damage to the economy. To overcome this impasse, he increasingly lent his ear to the Partai Komunis Indonesia (PKI), against the will of the army and other political parties. His international reputation was damaged when he turned against the formation of the federal state of Malaysia in 1963, distanced himself increasingly from the 'Old Established Forces,' as he disparagingly called the West, and showed increasing enthusiasm for the People's Republic of China, which he saw as the leader of the 'New Emerging Forces.' Instead of a leader who could better the lot of his subjects, Soekarno increasingly became an obstacle to development.

His downfall was ushered in by an attempted coup d'état on 30 September 1965, in which pro-Soekarno soldiers killed six pro-Western generals thought to be preparing a putsch against the president. General Soeharto, who quelled the *kudeta*, saw the communists as instigators of the murder of his colleagues.[6] It led to a round-up of political opponents that resulted in half a million to one million victims, with Java and Bali being the most affected areas. Soekarno refused to identify the PKI as the culprit, which strengthened his opponents' view that he knew of or had even helped stage the attempted coup. Now that his NASAKOM policy was seen as bankrupt and the PKI effectively crushed, he became increasingly sidelined. After protest campaigns by students and Muslims, with tacit support from the army, he was forced to hand over his powers relating to the country's security and stability to Soeharto. His honorary title of 'President for Life' was removed in 1966, and all his remaining powers were transferred to Soeharto in 1967. In March 1968, Soeharto was officially appointed president, and Soekarno was placed under house arrest. He lived the last two years of his life completely stripped of all privileges, suffering regular interrogations, and largely in isolation. The Old Order, as the Soekarno regime was now called, had ended. For a long time, despite the continuing multitude of adherents and admirers, Soeharto's New Order, which would last until 1998, offered no place for public memories of Soekarno in speech, print or elsewhere.[7]

A Simple Grave

In an interview with Cindy Adams (1966: 312), who was compiling a biography, Soekarno said that he did not want to be buried in a grave 'with all kinds of decorations,' as Nehru had done with Gandhi. He said, 'I yearn to rest under a leafy tree, surrounded by beautiful landscape, beside a river with fresh air and a lovely view. I want to lie among rolling hills and serenity. Just the beauty of my beloved country and the simplicity from which I come. And I wish my final home to be the cool, mountainous, fertile Priangan area of Bandung where I first met Farmer Marhaen.'[8] Later he added that he hoped for a grave near his villa in Batu Tulis, close to Bogor, which he had designed himself at the end of his presidency and which met all these criteria. When Soekarno died at the age of 69 on 21 June 1970 in the Gatot Subroto military hospital in Jakarta, his successor, President Soeharto, took a different decision. Against the wishes of Soekarno's wives and children, who themselves were divided in their views as to his final resting place, he decided to bury Soekarno near his mother's grave in Blitar in East Java, far from the center of the country (Soeharto 1989: 246). This choice was seen as an affront by Soekarno's followers – as a banishment after death. He had been politically sidelined; now his remains were to be marginalized.

Blitar is a small, quiet provincial town (having grown from 75,000 inhabitants at that time to 127,000 today), by road about 160 km southwest of Surabaya. Many Indonesians believe that Soekarno grew up there, but that is not entirely correct. He was in fact born on 6 June 1901 in Surabaya, the capital of East Java, where his father, Raden Sukemi Sosrodihardjo, was employed as a teacher. Before moving there, his father had worked in Buleleng on Bali, where he met his wife, Njoman Rai Serimben, and where his daughter, Soekarmini, was born. After leaving Surabaya, Soekarno's father taught in several East Javanese towns including Ploso, Sidoardjo and Modjokerto. Not until 1917, a year after Soekarno entered secondary school (HBS) in Surabaya, did the family move to Blitar, where his father was appointed head of the normal school, set up to train Indonesian assistant teachers. His parents decided to remain there when they retired (Giebels 1999: 25-44, 186). Thus, Soekarno only knew Blitar from the summer holidays he spent there with his family in

The initial, simple grave (under the black parasol).
From the H. de Jonge collection.

his youth and the few visits he made to his parents during his political career. However, he did know the region around Blitar well, as his paternal grandparents lived in neighboring Tulungagung, where he had once stayed for a year as a child. In Soeharto's eyes, these were sufficient reasons to defend the choice of Blitar.

Despite the recent exile of his predecessor, Soeharto did not deny him a state funeral. Following his death, the body of the former president lay in state at Wisma Yaso in Jakarta, in the house of his Japanese wife Ratna Dewi. Of his nine wives and former wives, only Dewi, his fifth, and Hartini, his fourth, kept watch by the body as thousands of Jakarta's inhabitants filed past. The next morning, Soekarno's body was flown to Malang, from where it was transported by car to Blitar. There was much more interest in his native East Java than in the capital. Millions of people lined the route, causing considerable delays. In an Islamic ceremony in the late afternoon, Soekarno was interred in a simple grave beside his mother in the Karang Mulyo general cemetery in the Bendogerit ward on the outskirts of the town. His body was draped in the

Indonesian flag, and his burial was accompanied by gunfire. The only people to speak at the grave were Panggabean, the army commander, representing the government, and Soekarno's brother-in-law on behalf of the family (Syariffudin 2001: 5-7). Many dignitaries attended, but almost no-one from the government. Soeharto pointedly remained in Jakarta.

Soekarno's final resting place in the *Taman Makam Pahlawan* or 'Heroes' Cemetery,' a separate section of the graveyard housing freedom fighters from the 1945-1949 period and victims of the violent aftermath of the 1965 coup attempt, was initially barely distinguishable from the other graves.[9] The only sign that a distinguished person was buried there was the parasol shading the grave, an unintentional symbol of the government's approach to Soekarno. In the years following his death, his name could not be mentioned in public, and at least in governmental offices and public spaces, there were no portraits or statues of him to be seen. While a visit to his grave would not be openly thwarted, it would certainly not be encouraged. Those aspiring to a political or bureaucratic career wisely avoided showing up in Blitar. In those days, it was mainly poor peasants and landless laborers from the surrounding area with nothing to lose who made a pilgrimage to the grave. It was not until the second half of the 1970s, when Soeharto was firmly in control of the country, that it was once again acceptable to write about Soekarno, albeit in a reserved way. However, censorship would be imposed if any criticism was leveled at Soeharto's New Order.

A Mausoleum and Gradual Rehabilitation

In 1978, Soeharto felt that the time had come to upgrade the grave by giving it the appearance of a modest mausoleum. The population would see this as a posthumous gesture towards his predecessor, which would hopefully increase his own popularity.[10] The foundation stone was laid on 21 June 1978, eight years after his death (this length of time, a *windu,* is significant in the Javanese calendar). Exactly one year later, the mausoleum was officially opened by Soeharto. It was the first and last time he visited the location.

To make room for the mausoleum, all the people buried in the *Taman Ma-*

kam Pahlawan area of the cemetery, with the exception of Soekarno's mother, were moved to a new graveyard elsewhere in the city. The new, walled funeral complex, now officially called Makam Bung Karno[11] (Grave of Brother Karno) consists of three levels, from south to north: the courtyard, the terrace around the mausoleum and the mausoleum itself. These levels symbolize the three stages of life distinguished by the Javanese: *alam purwo*, the time spent in the womb, *alam madya*, the transient time on earth, and *alam wasono*, the hereafter. Pilgrims enter the courtyard through an imposing southern gate in the style of Madjapahit, a glorious Hindu-Buddhist empire (1300-1500) whose center was located in East Java.[12] There are two sacred *waringin* (banyan) trees and two buildings, a small mosque and a rest room where visitors can prepare themselves for the final steps of the pilgrimage. Barefooted, they move on to the bare empty terrace that gives access on all sides to the *pendopo*, an open-sided, covered building, where Soekarno is buried with his parents. The remains of his father, who died in Jakarta in May 1945, were brought here shortly before the opening. The parents are each entombed, while Soekarno

The Soekarno Mausoleum, seen from the library, 2007.
Photo: H. de Jonge.

lies in a plain, flat grave behind which stands a rough stone of black marble bearing the words:

Here lies

Bung Karno

Proclaimer of Independence

and

First President of the Indonesian Republic

Born June 6 1901

Passed away June 21 1970

Spokesman of the people

The addition of external horizontal beams gives the brass roof of the *pendopo* a three-tiered structure, a modern variant of the traditional Hindu-Javanese architectural style, which had become popular during the New Order period. The ceiling of teakwood is carved with flames and clouds representing the struggle and energy that Soekarno gave to his people and fatherland. Behind the mausoleum is a small garden dominated by a leafy tree, an acknowledgement of how Soekarno wished to be buried.[13]

The upgrading of the grave in 1978 was the first step in a carefully orchestrated rehabilitation of Indonesia's first president by the New Order regime. A statue of Soekarno and Hatta was unveiled in 1980 at the location where independence was first proclaimed. In 1985, the new airport near Jakarta was named Soekarno-Hatta and a year later both founding fathers of the republic were declared Heroes of the Proclamation. In the same year, 1986, on Independence Day, members of the government went on a pilgrimage to Blitar, something which became a yearly tradition. That was enough as far as the New Order administration was concerned. Soeharto emphatically refused to publicly acknowledge any other merits that Soekarno might have had, such as his role in the nationalist movement and the independence struggle, and as the devisor of the Pancasila, the official state ideology, which was in fact strengthened during Soeharto's rule. Apart from the proclamation of independence, the deeds of his predecessor were concealed or ignored as much as possible, or attributed to both Hatta and Soekarno (Schreiner 2002: 200-201).

Soeharto was forced to step down in 1998, paving the way for an open and more balanced discussion of Soekarno's place in Indonesia's history. This resulted in further changes at the funeral site. Previously, for more than 20 years, the three graves were initially surrounded by a high glass partition, and later by a low wooden fence, which kept the pilgrims literally, but also spiritually, at a distance. This was increasingly seen as an obstacle to fulfilling appropriate rituals, such as praying beside the grave, and strewing flowers and burning incense on the grave. Consequently, Abdurrahman Wahid (President 1999-2001) ordered the fence to be pulled down, emphasizing that Bung Karno was owned by the whole population. The marble floor of the *pendopo* could now accommodate about a hundred pilgrims at the same time.

In 2004, President Megawati Sukarnoputri, herself a daughter of Soekarno, opened the impressive Soekarno Library and Museum that was built on the south side of the entrance gate. As far back as the 1980s, East Javanese members of the Partai Demokrasi Indonesia and the Partai Persatuan Pembangunan (United Development Party), parties established by the New Order government in 1974 to merge oppositional secular and Islamic-oriented parties, respectively, had been calling for a museum in Blitar in memory of Soekarno. During the *reformasi*, the process of political change that followed the fall of the New Order and led to a flourishing of new political parties, this demand resurfaced, winning widespread approval in government and political circles. The plan gained momentum and was rapidly realized during the regime of Megawati (2001-2004), who incidentally owed her position almost exclusively to the fact that she was the daughter of the *pater patriae*.

A design based on an American concept was eventually chosen for a presidential library with an exhibition hall and film theater. The ultramodern building, consisting of two parts connected by a walkway, was designed by an architect from the Institut Teknologi Bandung, where Soekarno had received his civil engineering degree in 1926. The shape of the building is inspired by the 14th century Panataran temple that lies not far from Blitar at the foot of the Kelud volcano. Fifteen houses[14] were demolished to make way for the library and since, for reasons of respect, it could not stand above the mausoleum, the hill on which they stood had to be leveled.

The library is generally seen as an important addition to the mausoleum, while almost all pilgrims visit the museum. The museum holds photographs of the president's political and family life as well as a selection of his personal possessions, such as the Indonesian flag used at the proclamation, made from a blouse of his second wife Fatmawati and the red skirt of a fellow freedom-fighter's wife, and the suitcase he took with him to his places of exile. They all point towards the role Soekarno played in the creation of the Indonesian state. Photographs with nationalists from the early days, with comrades during the independence struggle and with people from all ranks during the early years of his regime emphasize his position as an energetic and binding force in those formative years. Photographs with the great statesmen of the twentieth century – Eisenhower, Khrushchev, Mao, Nasser, Tito, Nehru and Kennedy – show the heights to which he had risen. The library itself, a branch of the national library in Jakarta, has an enormous collection of publications and clippings about Soekarno, books once owned by the former president, and writings and draft speeches in his own hand. In the open space between the library and the museum stands a statue of a seated Soekarno with a book in his hand, a reference to his repeated calls to his people to become acquainted with their history and to develop themselves. Many visitors, in particular women, touch the statue and place their hand on their heart.

Between the library and the stairway giving access to the courtyard is a long pond, flanked on one side by 21 pillars, a reference to the date of Soekarno's death. The tops of the pillars are decorated with ornaments from all over Indonesia, some of the many symbols that refer to important dates in the president's career and in the history of the Indonesian nation. Along one of the walls near the pond, a long bronze relief depicts 17 memorable events in Soekarno's life, such as his birth, the lawsuit in Bandung where he defended himself with a plea known as 'Indonesia accuses,' the proclamation of independence, the conference of non-allied countries in Bandung and 'Nawaksara' (the nine intentions), his last speech in parliament. The library complex unmistakably rectifies the limited place in history that Soeharto had planned for his predecessor. The pilgrims who make their way, as is now the custom, from the library, past the pond to the grave are more than ever conscious of the greatness of the man they have come to revere. From an unpretentious grave, Soekarno's burial place has finally become a national site that befits a man of his stature.

The sharp rise in the number of pilgrims in recent years has also led to an increase in commercial activities around the funeral complex. Numerous shops have sprung up along the road to the grave, renamed after Soekarno in 2006, selling posters, T-shirts, stickers and other souvenirs with pictures or slogans from Bung Karno. A popular one, which underlines Soekarno's devotion to and sacrifices for Indonesia, reads: 'I love my family, but I love my country more. As I have to choose, I choose for the sake of the country.' Near the entrance, women sell flowers for the grave and photographs of the funeral and of relatives of the former president. Having kept a low profile for years, these days the town of Blitar promotes itself explicitly as the town where Soekarno is buried. It now calls itself Patria City and the 'Kitchen of Nationalism,' referring here also to a local uprising by Indonesian auxiliary troops (Peta) against the Japanese occupation in February 1945.[15] Since its renovation in 1998, the house of Soekarno's parents has been an important attraction. The walls are decorated with family portraits showing the president as a loving son and an affectionate husband and father.

The Pilgrims

On a typical working day, Bung Karno's grave is visited by 500 to 800 pilgrims, with numbers swelling to several thousand a day on weekends and holidays. On special days, such as the anniversary of his birth and Independence Day, the site attracts tens of thousands of visitors. The busiest day of the year is the anniversary of his death, when Blitar is almost overwhelmed.

Most of the pilgrims are from Java, Bali, and Madura, although visitors come from other parts of Indonesia almost every day. During my stay in Blitar, I spoke with people from Sulawesi, Kalimantan, Sumatra, Flores, and even Papua. Most of those from the outer islands had come to Java for business, a family visit, on holiday, or to study, and had taken the opportunity to visit the grave. Some, however, came especially to honor Soekarno. Most visitors are

Megawati Sukarnoputri (on the right) at her father's grave in the 1990s.
From the H. de Jonge collection.

Pilgrims praying at Soekarno's grave, 2007.
Photo: H. de Jonge.

accompanied by relatives or friends; only a few people each day come alone. A number of pilgrims from Java and the neighboring islands – members of a women's society, a prayer group, laborers from a factory, or pupils from a school – make the pilgrimage as a group. It has become fashionable in recent years to visit the grave as part of a tour of pilgrimage sites and historical locations. One of the most popular is the *wali sanga*, or nine Muslim saints' tour, visiting the graves of the apostles of Islam in Java. In traditional Muslim circles, Soekarno is sometimes seen as the tenth *wali*.

The pilgrims span all ages, men and women, members of different ethnic groups such as Javanese, Acehnese, Batak, Minangkabau and Chinese, and of different religious groups including Muslims, Christians, Hindus and Buddhists, as well as adherents of various political persuasions. They come from all levels of society, although poor and lower-middle class citizens tend to dominate. Since the end of the New Order, Makam Bung Karno has been attracting more politicians, bureaucrats and officials than before. It is increasingly visited by heads of villages, districts and regencies, plus ministers and other political leaders. The national figures who have come to the mausoleum include Abdurrahman Wahid, who visited several times, Susilo Bambang Yudhoyono, before he replaced Megawati, and Amien Rais, the former chairman of parliament and current leader of a modernist Muslim party. Even the senior officials in the Golkar party, founded by Soeharto, no longer avoid the place. Local and national religious leaders are also regularly spotted at the grave.

Since the opening of the mausoleum, pilgrimages have become increasingly regulated. Pilgrims have to register at the entrance, where they are also asked for a cash donation. While in the past it was possible to visit the grave day or night, it is now only open from 8.30 am to 5 pm. However, the municipal authority that administers the site can grant an extension of the opening hours. Soekarno's relatives and VIPs with their entourages who wish to avoid the crowds are granted such permission without difficulty. Rich businessmen can usually pay on the spot for similar favorable treatment.

On normal days, it is forbidden to talk aloud, make speeches, sing or make music in the mausoleum, or to give a *selamatan* or communal meal, or to place anything other than flowers on the grave. Officially, you cannot spend longer

Pilgrims praying at Soekarno's grave, 2007.
Photo: H. de Jonge.

than 15 minutes at the grave. In practice, the grave's guardian, who welcomes the pilgrims, is flexible in applying such rules. He takes the religious backgrounds of the visitors into account and will, for example, allow Balinese and Chinese pilgrims to burn incense. He also does not object if pilgrims pray or meditate longer than the official time, or wish to take flowers from the grave home for their healing properties. The rules are only strictly enforced for visitors devoted to superstitious practices and fanaticism, or who disturb the peace and order.

Tranquility and serenity usually reign supreme in the mausoleum. Pilgrims are impressed by the location, fulfil their ritual obligations, pray in silence or in whispers and show respect for one another. On popular days, however, it is difficult to maintain this decorum. Pilgrims crowd around the grave, and the normally subdued atmosphere gives way to cheerfulness and excitement.

One of the busiest pilgrimage months is June. The first is remembered as the date on which Soekarno introduced his *Pancasila* state philosophy in 1945. Celebrations start in the town center with the reading aloud of the original

address, after which five mounds of different kinds of vegetables, symbolizing the five principles, accompanied by groups of one, six and forty-five
(1-6-1945) inhabitants dressed in the traditional palace uniform, are carried
through the streets of Blitar to Soekarno's burial place. On arrival, the mountains of vegetables are 'plundered' by the onlookers, who hope this will bring
them blessings. The day closes with a ritual meal at the grave itself. Although
Pancasila celebrations are held in several places across the country, only in
Blitar is it considered to bring good luck.

Soekarno's birthday and death are commemorated on June 6 and 21, with
the 21st in particular attracting more pilgrims every year. In the early 1990s,
Soekarno's *haul* (the term for the anniversary of the death of an important
person) was attended by thousands of visitors, but nowadays we see crowds
numbering several tens of thousands. On both June 20 and 21, the mausoleum is open around the clock to allow as many people as possible to pray near
the grave. The celebration, which is organized by relatives and family sympathizers, officially begins at dusk on the 20th (since according to the Javanese
calendar a new day starts at sunset) in the former house of Soekarno's parents, where a grandchild of his sister now lives. After prayers and a communal
meal for next of kin and invitees, the crowd (members of which have come
from far and wide) is addressed by a descendant of Soekarno, plus political
and religious celebrities. Recently, this has often been Rachmawati, a younger
sister of Megawati, who has spoken on behalf of the family. Then, until deep
in the night, dance and musical groups from several regions entertain the audience from a stage built for the occasion. While this is going on, or the next
day, the relatives visit the grave. To the disappointment of many visitors, not all
of Soekarno's descendants attend the annual *haul*, some preferring to make
a private visit at a quiet moment to pay respects to their father and grandfa-
ther.

During the New Order period, the authorities would intervene in the program held at the parental home to ensure that the government was not denounced. The *haul* was often used by opponents of the then current regime
to praise Soekarno's thoughts or to express discontent with the social situation. In 1986, when the celebration was combined with *Hari Pahlawan* on

10 November, the day when all the national heroes are commemorated, a public discussion between politicians from different parties was broken up by the police.[16] The experiment, intended to downplay Soekarno's merits, was not repeated. In 1995, by which time Megawati had political aspirations and Rachmawati was thwarting her career, the authorities played them both off against each other and took over organizing the 25th haul. They forbade both Megawati and Adurrahman Wahid, who were seen as successful opponents of the regime (the former from the Partai Demokrasi Indonesia and the latter from Nahlatul Ulama, the conservative Islamic organization) to speak in public. Two days later, and together, they paid a furtive visit to the grave, an event which afterwards received wide publicity. Roeslan Abdoelgani, a well-known politician from the former PNI and a good friend of Soekarno, was also encouraged to stay away. In this period, only local officials attended the jubilee meetings on behalf of the administration.

Since the reformation, cooperation between the authorities and the family has improved markedly. In 2001, President Adurrahman Wahid himself spoke at the haul; this was followed by the performance of a lyrical drama about Soekarno's struggle against the Dutch and the development of Marhaenism, or Indonesian socialism. That year, the haul attracted 50,000 visitors. When Megawati became president, the rehabilitation of her father was further enhanced. National and provincial dignitaries now not only attend the haul, Independence Day and heroes' day events, but are also seen on days of only minor importance.

Secular, Magical and Religious Goals

The meaning of the pilgrimage and the way in which it is performed depends heavily on the religious convictions and cultural background of the pilgrims, the power they ascribe to Soekarno and the objectives of their visit. Most pilgrims are traditional Muslims who adhere to a syncretic variant of Islam which includes, alongside Islamic beliefs, varying degrees of animistic and Hindu-Buddhist elements, concepts and practices. In contrast to orthodox Muslims, who consider pilgrimages to graves as heterodoxy, they see it as a normal if not essential part of their faith. This does not mean that orthodox Muslims do not visit the grave (they form a small minority). However, in general, they make the pilgrimage for purely secular motives, while for others it has a strong religious dimension. Many versions can be distinguished within the syncretic variant (De Jonge 1993). One of the most extreme forms is widely known as *Kejawen*, in which Islam is no more than a thin veneer (Koentjaraningrat 1985: 324-379).

After arriving at the grave, most traditional Muslims read or recall from memory a chapter of the Koran, Yassin, repeat the confession of faith ('There is no God but Allah and Mohammad is his Messenger') and recite words of praise to Allah, as is common in all Muslim countries where grave pilgrimages are practised. The adherents of *Kejawen*, on the other hand, usually confine themselves to a short meditation. They prefer to fast and pray for a much longer time – a day, a night, or even several days and nights. During the first decade following Soekarno's death, this was a common ritual, performed individually or in groups, particularly on auspicious days such as Sunday *Kliwon* and Friday *Legi*, when a certain day of the five-day Javanese week coincides with a specific day of the seven-day week. Since the renovation of the grave in 1978, the authorities have tried to discourage these mystical practices, which they see as superstitious and irrational. Nowadays, mystical groups need to ask permission in advance. They must also end their gatherings before midnight and are no longer allowed in the mausoleum, but have to carry out their rituals in the courtyard or near the pond.

Adherents of other religions are less conspicuous than Muslims. Aware that they are visiting an Islamic grave, they confine themselves to silent prayers, although Catholics can be identified when they make the sign of the cross. The Balinese are somehow more emphatically present, perhaps because Soekarno's mother was Balinese. They usually burn incense, bring Balinese offerings and often wear ritual garments, especially when they come in a group. As with the Muslims, most of the other believers, and even non-believers, scatter flowers over the three graves (starting with Soekarno's parents) and touch the grave or the stone bearing the president's inscription. As a rule, a photo is taken of the visit. Pilgrims from afar wash themselves ritually and pray beforehand in the mosque in the courtyard, so as to enter the mausoleum physically and spiritually purified.

Pilgrims visit the grave for various, often overlapping reasons. Primarily, they make the pilgrimage to honor Soekarno as the founder of the Indonesian state, as first president, as the father of their country. As almost every visitor acknowledges, no-one else has devoted as much effort to the birth, integration and development of the nation. His whole life – the pre-war years, the Japanese occupation, the independence struggle and his period of government – is seen as being devoted to such ideals. When asked, pilgrims spontaneously offer a host of examples of his exceptional virtues. Several quote well-known Soekarno sayings such as 'We want to found a country, not for one person, not for one group, but everything for everybody' or 'Hello, colonialists…! You want to imprison me, but you cannot imprison my soul.' Frequently, they relate Soekarno to their place, region or island of origin. A Catholic pilgrim from Flores told me that Soekarno found the inspiration for his Pancasila ideology during his exile on the island ('under a tree with five branches'). A family from Bandung told me all kinds of details about his politically formative years while studying in that city. A Chinese from Surabaya invited me to visit the house of the president's first political mentor, Tjokroaminoto, the chairman of the Sarekat Islam – the first mass political association founded in 1912. Soekarno had stayed there during his secondary school years. A visit to Soekarno's grave cannot be dissociated from the history of the country; by visiting the grave, pilgrims also show their love for the country, their solidarity and their concern for the nation. They see themselves as patriots, with Soekarno as their idol and as a personification of the struggle endured by the fatherland. During the pilgrimage, people of different ethnic origins, social standing and religious persuasion mix easily with one another, sit together at the grave, and exchange thoughts and ideas outside the mausoleum. They speak about Soekarno's significance or about national or daily affairs. They see themselves as fellowcountrymen, and rarely feel closer to each other than at this time. Pilgrims are also attracted to Soekarno because he stood close to the poor, understood and shared their worries and sorrows, and called himself 'the voice of the people.' They see him as somebody who effaced himself for others, and they emphasize the sacrifices he made for the country: imprisonment, exile, bomb attacks, the negative effects of his political career on his private life, his removal from office, and his passing away in isolation. Despite his exalted position, people are able to identify with him. His 'suffering' forms a frame of reference in which to accept the setbacks they themselves experience in life. At the same time, pilgrims remain impressed by Soekarno's charisma, his personal allure and personality. Even today, he continues to have a greater aura than other nationalists and independence fighters, including Hatta. With his rhetorical skills, he knew how to hold on to people and to make them feel that they could solve their problems.

Soon after Soekarno's burial, his grave became a place where people wanted to show their approval or disapproval of the political and social situation. During the New Order era, many inhabitants felt nostalgia for Soekarno's years in power, when people were poor, but corruption, collusion and nepotism were not very widespread. They came to express their longing for democratic relationships and better times. A visit to the grave was therefore a protest against the policies of the new government. Even today, now that Soeharto is gone, there are still visitors who come to recall Soekarno's just rule and to hold it up as an example. I have often heard how everyone had equal chances to enter university, to obtain land, a job, or a fair legal hearing during the Old Order regime. One old lady said that he was the only president who had not enriched himself or his relatives (a clear reference to Soeharto's children, who had all acquired fortunes). Her granddaughter added pointedly that he 'never liquidated opponents, but always looked for peaceful solutions.' However, it is not only the government's opponents who appear at the grave. Followers of Presidents Adurrahman Wahid and Megawati made the pilgrimage to show their satisfaction with government policy and to show their gratitude for the continuity between Soekarno and these successors. The grave's political importance is apparent from the visits paid by campaigning politicians and officials. They claim to draw inspiration from it, make statements (of varying degrees of honesty), and thus hope to gain votes.

As well as revering Soekarno as a revolutionary and statesman, believers come to Blitar to pray to God for the repose of the former president, and for the spiritual welfare of the country, their relatives or themselves. Some see Soekarno as an intermediary between God and themselves, and his grave as an appropriate holy place (*kramat*) to ask for help. There are also many pilgrims who do not pray to God, but direct their prayers to Bung Karno himself, frequently to ask or thank him for something tangible, such as offspring, examination success, a job, recovery from ill health, or wealth. For example, at the grave I met a couple who thanked him for their son becoming a policeman after years of unemployment, and a man who expressed his gratitude for his business success.

Adherents of *Kejawen* in particular, but also the more syncretic believers from outside Java, attribute the first president with *sakti* (supernatural powers). They refer in this respect to the eruption of the Kelud volcano and the appearance of a comet in the firmament around his birthday, his birth at daybreak, his gift of prophecy and his healing powers. It is said that he could be present in two places at once, that he could bring rain, that he communicated with deceased rulers and that his bathwater had curative qualities. In this way, people place him in the tradition of the Hindu-Buddhist monarchs and *wali sanga*, who dispensed magical-spiritual power (Lindsey 1993: 171). According to Wessing (2003: 204), rulers in insular Southeast Asia were seen 'at least' as the 'shadow on earth' of a Hindu deity, Buddha or Allah. Some were even considered to be deputies or reincarnations of gods. Like them, Soekarno is seen as regularly receiving divine revelations and having a godlike radiance (*wahyu*). Lubis (1969: 181) reproaches Soekarno and his followers for cultivating this 'aura of semigodliness.' Soekarno himself seems to have said that he was a descendant of the rulers of Kediri, the first East-Javanese kingdom (1045-1221). Others believe that his father was actually Susuhunan Paku Buwono X (1866-1939) from the former Central Javanese principality of Solo, or descended from the 15th or 16th century Sunan Kalijogo, one of the most famous *wali* (Labrousse 1994: 179). As a result, many believe that 'what he spoke could never be other than the truth; whatever he did was always right and true. He was all wisdom and justice, all magnanimity. He was father; he was god. Anybody who dared to disagree with him, let alone oppose him was evil. He was Krishna, he was Vishnu' (Lubis 1969: 182).

Among his admirers, we find people who see him as a *ratu adil*, a just king who was born in difficult times to bring social justice and peace to his people. Joyoboyo, a former king of Kediri, predicted in the 12th century that in the future Java would be occupied for a long period by white people from the west, who would soon be driven out by yellow people from the north, to be followed by a local ruler who would bring order, harmony and prosperity. Although Soekarno was not the first to be seen as a *ratu adil*, his historic 'timing,' following the Dutch colonial period and the Japanese occupation, meant that he satisfied the preconditions, as no other had before him, of those awaiting a messianic figure. Many Indonesians see this task as unfinished, and are hoping that he will return. More than once I heard from pilgrims that Soekarno is not dead, but has ascended into heaven and will return at an appropriate moment. One of them cited as evidence a photograph in Soekarno's parental home, taken at the moment that Soekarno was being interred and showing, between the clouds, a clear shaft of light, along which he allegedly departed. Some visitors said that a Japanese investigation in the 1970s had established that the grave contained no remains. These collective fantasies are particularly popular among *Kejawen* adherents. Even people who do not believe in the just king, or its Islamic equivalent the Imam Mahdi, accept that Soekarno has started a new cosmic cycle and, as in the Buddhist world, has taken up, as Tambiah (1976: 38) puts it, the role of 'virtuous wheel-rolling world ruler' and 'ordinator in the evolving and restless commotion-ridden world.'

Soekarno's virility, reflected in his many wives, mistresses and affairs, is also justified by pointing to the comparable position of former Southeast Asian rulers. Their masculine vigor and energy were indications of their power, and its loss a sign of their decline. As Benedict Anderson (1972: 18) wrote about traditional Javanese power-holders: 'The fertility of the ruler was seen as simultaneously invoking and guaranteeing the fertility of the land, the prosperity of the society, and the expansionist vitality of the empire. The Soekarno period once again provides a striking model to this old idea.' Pilgrims not only accept his exceptional sexual energy, they would like to possess a fraction of it, and do not hesitate to ask his blessing in that regard. A childless couple told me confidentially that they visited the grave to stimulate the man's potency and the wife's fertility.

Leaders of mystical groups or sects claim to be able, after falling into a trance, to make contact with Soekarno. They receive messages or instructions and claim to hear his voice or see his shadow. Members of such groups usually come together to hear what the former president thinks of the country's situation or future, or to pose specific questions. One of the groups I came across was wondering if Susilo Bambang Yudhoyono, the current president, was the appropriate person to lead the country as the first years of his tenure had been hit by a series of catastrophes: a tsunami, earthquakes, landslides, a mudflow, plane crashes and naval disasters. Soekarno apparently let it be known that the president would not make it to the end of his term or, if he did, would not be re-elected. A member of the group told me that their leader had 'heard' that a male descendant of Soekarno would take over the presidency. Although most people see these predictions as nonsense, there are a significant number of pilgrims who attach importance to them. Such predictions find their way into the general populace, and certain figures, such as politicians, are prepared to use them to their advantage.

Although the number of pilgrims to Blitar increases year by year, there are tens of millions of Indonesians for whom Soekarno remains a controversial figure. Although they respect him as the founder of the nation, they also see him as the person responsible for wrecking the country during his presidency. To his followers, his 'sacredness' sometimes appears limitless. In certain conservative Islamic circles, Soekarno has in recent years been ascribed a more active role in the process of Islamization of the country than he played in reality. Although he saw Islam as one of the pillars of the state, he was never an overly pious Muslim concerned with fulfilling prescribed rituals. This 'canonization' does, however, follow a somewhat traditional path, one previously trodden by earlier Javanese rulers. As time goes on, it will become increasingly difficult for those who believe in him to distinguish between myth and reality.

Concluding remarks

In pilgrimages to Soekarno's grave, the secular and the religious go hand-in-hand. The secular is influenced by the religious to a large extent, while the religious tends to have a firm grasp on the secular. Their interrelationship becomes apparent in various ways. Firstly, the physical and spatial changes at the burial site have given Soekarno's grave the character of a holy site, comparable to those of the *wali* or Javanese apostles of Islam and canonized former monarchs. Secondly, an overwhelming majority of the visitors use religious rituals in honoring the former president. Further, many pilgrims visit the grave for both secular and religious reasons; it is a place for commemoration and a place of worship. It is also a place where blessings have both religious and secular overtones. Increasingly, Soekarno is seen as a sacred person and a man with supernatural powers. In addition, feelings of communitas (Turner 1969: 96) and harmony, which are often experienced at pilgrim sites, have here a secular as well as a religious dimension. The pilgrimage consolidates and re-inforces to some extent feelings of being Indonesian, emphasizes the unity in diversity to which the country aspires (reflecting Indonesia's heraldic device) and, at least temporarily, makes people forget regional and ethnic tensions. At the same time, it brings together believers from different denominations. Religious differences, although clearly visible at the site, are tolerated, and religious boundaries temporally fade into the background. A visit to Soekarno's grave confirms Eade and Sallnow's observation (1991: 15-16) that pilgrimages are 'capable of accommodating diverse meanings and practices.'

Soekarno's burial site is, however, not only a place of solidarity and reconciliation; it is also a place where secular and religious differences are fought out in a figurative sense. Pilgrimages lend themselves to contestation as Coleman (2002) has made clear. By visiting the grave, pilgrims are making statements, intentionally or unintentionally, about their perception of Soekarno's role in the history of Indonesia, the policies of successive governments, the general political and economic situation, and their political ideas and preferences. In performing their rituals, through the objectives striven for, and the meaning they attach to the pilgrimage, they are making a statement about their religious identity and, as such, are calling the beliefs of other denominations or interpretations into question.

The main difference from other pilgrimages in Indonesia is without doubt the fact that, alongside personal goals in prayer and thought, a major place

is given to national affairs and questions. The hope for a change for the better in their own situation is linked to a wish for improvement at the national
level. The personal effects are, however, the same: pilgrims find inspiration,
energy and mental resilience to start anew, to go on with their life, or to realize a specific plan. As a poor peasant once told me about his regular visits to
Soekarno's grave: 'He is able to revive the lives of those who are still alive.'

Notes

1 Most of the information for this article was collected during a stay in Blitar in February 2007.
I am very grateful to Robert Wessing with whom I had several discussions on the supernatural
powers attributed to Soekarno and who generously showed me his field notes on this project.
2 Orthodox Muslims only recognize one pilgrimage: the hajj, the pilgrim's journey to the Holy
Kabbah (a shrine, not a grave) in Mecca.
3 The Permoefakatan Perhimpoenan-Perhimpoenan Politiek Kebangsaan Indonesai (PPPKI) or
Consensus of Indonesian Political Organizations.
4 During his secondary school years in Surabaya, Soekarno stayed at the house of the Indonesian nationalist Tjokroaminoto where he met several left-leaning Indonesians and Dutchmen. In
Bandung, he became acquainted with the librarian Marcel Koch, a member of the Indisch Sociaal
Democatische Partij, who introduced him to the works of Kautsky and Bakunin (Giebels 1999:
61-65, 79-81).
5 NAS for nationalism, A for Agama or religion, and KOM for communism.
6 This is the most popular interpretation of the military confrontation in the capital, but there are
many others.
7 For details on Soekarno's life and career, see Lambert Giebels (1999, 2001), Bob Hering (2001,
2002), J.D. Legge (1972) and C.L.M Penders (1974).
8 He adopted the name of this small peasant farmer he met in the 1920s near Bandung for his
Indonesian version of Marxism or socialism (Marhaenism)
9 There are many of these types of cemeteries in Indonesia, mainly in the cities.
10 A request by relatives and some of his followers to move Soekarno's remains to Batu Tulis or
Jakarta was ignored.
11 Bung is an affectionate form of address which was very popular during the independence
struggle.
12 Soekarno was an admirer of Gadjah Mada, one of Majapahit's most successful prime ministers.
Like Soekarno, he was forced to step down and spend his last years in confinement.
13 See page 4 (of this chapter).
14 One owner, on whose plot an open-air theatre is planned, continues to refuse to sell his property.
15 On this rebellion, see Adrianatakesuma 1973. The Peta, an abbreviation of Pembela Tanah Air,
or Defenders of the Fatherland, was founded by the Japanese in October 1943.
16 According to Schreiner (2002: 186), Indonesia has more than one hundred *Pahlawan Nasional*
(national heroes), not to be confused with the thousands of heroic freedom fighters also referred
to as *pahlawan*.

II The Musical Realm

Chapter 5

Rock and Roll Pilgrims: Reflections on Ritual, Religiosity, and Race at Graceland

Erika Doss

Although Elvis Presley died on August 16, 1977, he is hardly forgotten. On the twentieth anniversary of his death, more than 70,000 fans paid their respects at Graceland, Presley's home and gravesite in Memphis, Tennessee. Eight years later, in 2005, some 10,000 fans attended Elvis Week, an annual festival organized by Elvis's estate that culminates in a reverent all-night Candlelight Vigil at his grave. Elvis is buried in Graceland's Meditation Gardens, along with his parents, his paternal grandparents, and his stillborn twin (Jesse Garon Presley). During the Elvis Week vigil, fans wait in line for hours (some for more than 24 hours) to pass through Graceland's gates and slowly circle his burial site. All year round, Elvis's grave is piled high with gifts from his devotees, including flowers, teddy bears, candles, photographs, records, letters, and poems. During Elvis Week these gifts dramatically escalate, so much so that Graceland's grassy grounds and white picket fences also become thickly adorned with floral bouquets, handmade signs, and numerous other offerings.

For more than half a century, ever since he bought Graceland in 1957, Elvis's estate has been a site of pilgrimage. Each year, over 600,000 people visit Graceland, making it the most popular house tour in the United States. For multitudes of fans, Graceland particularly holds a special meaning; as one 35-year-old fan from Bayonne, New Jersey, explained in 1996: 'Graceland is like the worshipping ground for all Elvis fans.'[1] This essay reflects on Graceland's status as a modern site of pilgrimage, and on the motivations and desires of its pilgrims.

Pilgrimage has been interpreted in terms of its unifying, integrative, and communal capacities; as Victor Turner and Edith Turner asserted, 'pilgrimage is very much involved in perennial, universal drama, cutting across cultures, societies, polities, language groups, and ethnicities' (Turner and Turner 1978: 16). Yet pilgrimage to Graceland is marked by competing and often conflicting meanings and practices. Graceland's great appeal, of course, directly corresponds to Elvis's persistent deification as the quintessential American icon. Indeed, Elvis Presley was a multifaceted and even complex figure who played an important role in shaping and directing post-World War II understandings of American popular culture by consciously challenging restrictive barriers of race, class, and gender. However, much of his posthumous appeal – and popular culture canonization – rests on the religious and racialized assumptions of certain American fans who imagine Elvis as an icon of whiteness: as a powerful and unique 'all-white' figure who symbolizes their beliefs in white cultural dominance and superiority. Their Elvis Week rituals and pilgrimages to Graceland reaffirm these beliefs and also work to redefine Elvis's meaning within the larger American imaginary. Their capacity to do so stems from both the ubiquity and multivalence of Elvis's image and the resurgence of a divided and oppositional race consciousness in contemporary America.

Elvis's Image

Thirty years after his death, and fifty years after he became fixed in national, and global, popular culture consciousness – ever since millions of television viewers watched him gyrate on *The Ed Sullivan Show* in 1956 – Elvis Presley remains omnipresent. When he died, there were 65 Elvis fan clubs; today there are more than 500. In 2002, Elvis had a best-selling album – *Elv1s 30#1 Hits* – and a hit single – 'A Little Less Conversation' – that topped the charts in the UK and half a dozen European countries. In 2003, Elvis toured Europe – or rather, former band members and a sixteen-piece orchestra performed in front of giant video screens featuring Elvis concert footage from earlier decades, to wildly enthusiastic crowds in England, Scotland, Ireland, Belgium, France, Switzerland, and Holland. In 2004, for the fourth year in a row, *Forbes* listed Elvis as the world's 'top earning dead celebrity,' netting some $40 million for his estate, Elvis Presley Enterprises (EPE). In 2005, billionaire media mogul Robert Sillerman (owner of the hit TV show *American Idol*) purchased

Graceland and EPE, and announced plans to extend the Elvis empire with a Graceland-themed Las Vegas casino and a series of 'interactive, multi-media' extravaganzas to be produced by Cirque du Soleil (Serwer 2005). And in 2006, Graceland was designated a National Historic Landmark, joining Mount Vernon, the Alamo, Pearl Harbor, and some 2,500 other historically significant US properties.

Marketing plays a big role in Elvis's posthumous popularity. Sillerman, for example, sees Graceland as an underdeveloped asset with the potential to become another Disneyland and aims to expand Graceland's visitor center and exhibition spaces to highlight thousands of items of Elvis memorabilia that have long been locked away and never before seen. But the mass appeal of those items, and the resonance of Elvis's contemporary popularity, lie with Elvis's multifaceted image and the manner in which his fans respond to, and reimagine, his image.

There are many different images of Elvis, beginning with the rockabilly rebel of the mid-1950s who soared to teen culture adoration and critical rebuke with an explosive and explicitly sexual performance style. Elvis's first appearance on *The Ed Sullivan Show* (September 1956) drew an estimated 82% of the American viewing public (54 million people), who watched him gyrate to 'Don't Be Cruel' and 'Love Me Tender.' By the time of his second appearance on Sullivan's show (October 1956), Elvis's records were selling at the rate of $75,000 a day and accounting for more than 50% of the profits for his record label, RCA (Pierce 1994: 104-33). Although some critics complained that popular music had 'reached its lowest depths in the "grunt and groin" antics of one Elvis Presley,' and others dismissed him as a 'whirling dervish of sex,' Elvis's sensual and erotic image accelerated his popular culture hold in post-World War II America (Guralnick 1994: 285).

Elvis was also postwar America's most obvious 'white Negro,' a teen version of the white hipsters that Norman Mailer portrayed as being infatuated with the sights, sounds, and styles of urban black culture (Mailer 1957: 311). Indeed, much of Elvis's earliest popularity, and the media attention he received, can be ascribed to his cross-race stylistics: to the ways that he mixed black and white music and black and white performance styles into the emergent hybrid of rock-and-roll, thereby negotiating the nascent terrain of 1950s civil rights to participate in the creation of a more democratic American popular culture.

Yet Elvis's postwar image as a rebellious race-mixer is complicated by his image among many fans as a working-class success story: as a 'blue-collar guy in blue-suede shoes,' a poor white kid who worked hard, followed his dream, and became 'The King' of rock-and-roll. Born in the middle of the Great Depression, in 1935 in Tupelo, Mississippi, Elvis was the son of an itinerant laborer who served time in Parchman Farms Penitentiary for forgery; his mother worked as a seamstress in a textile factory. Graduating from high school in 1953, Elvis himself worked as a machinist and a truck driver before making it big in rock-and-roll.

Labor historian David Roediger argues that the terms 'work' and 'working class' are deeply imbricated with whiteness, as the formation of American working-class identity in the nineteenth century was anchored to assertions of white racial superiority (Roediger 1991). Fearing their growing dependency within a capitalist system of wage labor, white workers sharply distinguished themselves from the slaves and former slaves with whom they shared economic oppression. Artificial, alienating, and yet powerfully convincing categories were established whereby white laborers self-consciously defined themselves as hard working, independent, skilled, honest, and industrious, in direct counterpoint to nonwhite (black, Asian) workers whom they viewed as lazy, needy, unskilled, undisciplined, and untrustworthy. The racist underpinnings of an American working class emergent in the Industrial Age remain prevalent today; in everyday language, as Roediger observes, 'the very term *worker* often presumes whiteness (and maleness)' (Roediger 1991: 19). This is not to imply, of course, that racism is only or even particularly a working-class disease, but to assert the complicated intersections between race and class identity. Thus, when many white working-class fans highlight Elvis's image as a rock-and-roll pioneer, and when they romanticize his (and their own) working-class leanings, they speak to their shaping of his essentially white racial identity.

Elvis's image as 'The King' of rock-and-roll is also problematic. A moniker that he apparently disliked and many contemporary black musicians and critics, not surprisingly, despise, crowning Elvis 'king' relegates everyone else in the pantheon of rock-and-roll as lesser figures, including the many black musicians who influenced Elvis and whom *he* repeatedly credited with inventing rock-and-roll: including Fats Waller, B.B. King, and Muddy Waters (Spencer 1997: 112-113; Rijff 1987: 75, 178; Guralnick 1994: 369). As Gil Rodman argues, 'Elvis's coronation implicitly helps to reinforce the resegregation of the musical world into neat and (supposedly) mutually exclusive racial categories' where whites dominate (Rodman 1996: 46). Or as funk bassist Me'Shell Ndegé Ocello protested in 1994: 'If Elvis is King, then who the fuck is James Brown – God?' (Plasketes 1997: 59).

Many contemporary Elvis fans, however, persist in his deification as rock-and-roll's 'king' and also tout his image as a Las Vegas superstar. Elvis played 1,126 shows in eight years in Las Vegas during 1969-1977, and played hundreds of others in arenas across America. He was, his fans assert, 'the hardest working man in show business': a tireless entertainer who performed in front of thousands of people wearing a lily-white jumpsuit. Among his many guises, this image best embodies the values of work and whiteness held dear by many fans. The white jumpsuit has a lot to do with it, resembling the uniform worn by World War II parachutists and then by America's postwar blue-collar workers, albeit gussied up into royal grandeur. And it is white: the color of purity and power, 'of positive myths that celebrate imagined virtues and conceal real failings' in the popular American imagination (Lopez 1996: 167). Elvis's image in a bejeweled white jumpsuit especially conveys the man that many fans imagine: a white guy who made it big the 'right' way through talent, ambition, and sheer hard work.

These conflicted images of Elvis are accompanied by many others, including: Elvis the Southern gentleman, squire of Graceland; Elvis the soldier (Elvis was drafted in 1958 and spent two years as a tank driver in Friedberg, West Germany); Elvis the B-movie idol (Elvis made over thirty movies from the late 1950s through the 1960s); Elvis the family man (Elvis married Priscilla Beaulieu in 1967 and their daughter, Lisa Marie Presley, was born nine months later); Elvis the philanthropist (Elvis rather impulsively liked to give diamond rings and Cadillac Eldorados to total strangers, and money to Memphis hospitals and police departments); Elvis the Nixon admirer (Elvis visited the White House in December 1970 and offered President Richard Nixon his services as an honorary 'Federal Agent at Large' in order to rid the USA of 'drug abuse and Communist brainwashing'); and Elvis the drug addict (Elvis consumed hundreds of pills a week, and autopsy evidence showed a body stuffed with Dialaudid, Placidyl, Valium, Quaaludes, Percodan, Demerol, Seconal, Nembutal, Phenobarbital, morphine, codeine, cortisone, and lots of other uppers, downers, and painkillers).

Many fans also embrace an image of Elvis in pain and talk about how Elvis suffered: how despite his success and fame, he died alone, addicted to drugs and grossly overweight. One fan writes: 'I read that Elvis once said, "The three keys to happiness are: someone to love, something to do, and something to look forward to." I don't think he had any of those things toward the end of his life.' Another remarks: 'I feel very sad at times for Elvis. Such talent, wealth, and everything going for him and to end up like he did.' Some fans blame themselves for Elvis's suffering, feeling guilty that their demands were more than he could bear. 'The fans who supposedly "loved" him made his a very difficult life,' writes one Michigan fan. 'He was mobbed everywhere he went. He could not shop, take a walk, ride a motorcycle, or even go to an amusement park without elaborate security, secrecy and much planning. These restrictions, I feel, were probably the reason he resorted to alcohol and drugs.'

Intertwined and oppositional, Elvis's image was, and remains, ambiguous and contradictory, solid but unstable. This is not surprising: American popular culture has always been an unstable 'site of conflicting interests, appropriations, impersonations' (Lott 1993: 92). Elvis's hybridic and unsettled imaging in American popular culture corresponds to how he is seen, and by whom (Lipsitz 1990: xiv). By extension, Elvis's 'longevity' as a cultural icon 'is largely due to his flexibility – his willingness to take the shape of what we most wanted to see. Whether our fantasies were psychic, sexual, cosmic, financial, or religious Elvis accommodated all of us' (Quain 1992: 255). Interestingly, Elvis's musical reputation, with the exception of his mid-1950s rock-and-roll creolization, is almost inconsequential in terms of his contemporary iconicity. Elvis's albums are never included on VH-1's 'Top 100' lists, for example, and few contemporary performers cite Elvis as a primary influence on their own work. 'There was so little of it that was actually good,' remarks David Bowie. 'Those first two or three years, and then he lost me completely' (Patterson 2002: M-13).

Rather, Elvis's abiding presence as a popular culture icon centers on his multifaceted image. More particularly, it centers on what these diverse and conflicted images mean to the people who look at them, make them, and collect them: his fans. Their cultural production of Elvis's meaning, which is hardly monolithic and is layered in contradiction, is key to his posthumous celebrity. By extension, the narrative instability of Elvis's image corresponds to certain tensions evident in the larger public sphere of postwar America, especially racial tensions. The complexity of his image is further apparent in a consideration of Elvis's iconic meaning in religious terms, and how Elvis fans regard him as a figure of popular culture canonization.

Saint Elvis

One fan, a former teacher who emigrated from Greece to Memphis in order to be 'closer' to Elvis, spends every spare moment at Elvis's grave, tending it and honoring him with small shrines and hand-made offerings, engrossed in vigils of prayer and remembrance. A devout Catholic (raised Greek Orthodox), this fan does not worship Elvis but sees him as a mediator or an intercessor between herself and God. As she says: 'There is a distance between human beings and God. That is why we are close to Elvis. He is like a bridge between us and God' (Harrison 1992: 68, 53). If she imagines Elvis as a saint, she also sees him as a redemptive figure. 'I believe in Jesus Christ and I believe in God,' she remarks, 'but Elvis was special. Elvis was in our times, he was given to us to remind us to be good.' Understood as a servant of God and Christ-like savior, Elvis brings this fan joy, intensity, pleasure, and purpose. 'I don't go to church much now. I don't ask for anything else from God, my prayers have been answered,' she says, acknowledging that her personal relationship with Elvis and the rituals she performs that express that relationship are the most meaningful cultural and social practices in her life.

'The worship, adoration and the perpetuation of the memory of Elvis today, closely resembles a religious cult,' states former BBC Religious Affairs Correspondent Ted Harrison (Harrison 1992: 9). Elvis's posthumous popularity has 'transcended the familiar contours of a dead celebrity cult and has begun to assume the dimensions of a redemptive faith,' asserts writer Ron Rosenbaum (Rosenbaum 1995: 50). Scholars have probed the Celtic, Gnostic, Hindu, and Vodun derivations of Elvis's cult-like status and contemplated Graceland's manifestation as 'sacred space' (Alderman 2002; Ebersole 1994; King 1992; Lardas 1995; Vikan 1994). Some attribute the entire phenomenon to the highly successful marketing schemes of Elvis Presley Enterprises and to the susceptibility of an apparently passive public bent on escapism through, especially, the 'transformative' ideology of consumerism (Fiske 1993; Stromberg 1990). 'Explicit manifestations of "Elvis Christ" did not exactly evolve,' carps British journalist John Windsor. 'They were cunningly contrived for a mass market' (Windsor 1992: 33).

Still others cynically cite the quasi-religious conditions that seem to confirm Elvis's contemporary deification: how in the years since his death a veritable Elvis religion has emerged, replete with prophets (Elvis impersonators), sacred texts (Elvis records), disciples (Elvis fans), relics (Elvis memorabilia), pilgrimages (to Graceland and Tupelo), shrines (such as his gravesite), temples (such as the 24 Hour Church of Elvis in Portland, Oregon), and all the appearances of a resurrection (with reported Elvis sightings at, among other places, a Burger King in Kalamazoo, Michigan).[2] Ritual activities that occur in Memphis each August during Elvis Week (nicknamed 'Death Week' by more sarcastic observers) are cited as further evidence of Elvis's cult status.

Explanations that Elvis's iconic omnipresence and the devotion of his fans embodies a cult or a religion prompt many questions, including the issue of religious essentialism. That is: what is it about the revered images, ritual practices, and devotional behaviors among Elvis fans that is religious? Do these images and practices constitute the making of a religion? Why is it that *images* of Elvis have taken on the dimensions of faith and devotion, viewed by many fans as links between themselves and God, as ex-votos for expressing and giving thanks, or as empowered objects which can fulfill wishes and desires?

Many fans dismiss the idea that Elvis is a religious figure or that Elvis images and Elvis-centered practices constitute any sort of Elvis religion. 'It's only the media who seem to be obsessed with turning Elvis into a religion, you don't hear normal fans discuss it,' says one fan. Fans worry, and with good reason, about being ridiculed as religious fanatics. Others object to how they are often represented as lower class, uneducated, and irrational worshippers of a 'fat, pill-filled Vegas singer,' as Elvis was described in one *New York Times* article (Rosenbaum 1995: 57). Given this media marginalization, it is hardly surprising that many Elvis fans deny fidelity to any sort of Elvis cult or religion.

Without discounting their objections, however, it is important to recognize the following: from John Winthrop's 'city on the hill' creation myth to the present-day proliferation of New Age spirituality and the growth of fundamentalism, religious expression – mainstream and fringe – remains central to American self and national identity. As a profoundly religious people, Americans tend to treat things in religious terms, apply religious categories, and generally make a religion out of much of what is touched and understood. According to one public opinion poll from 1980, Americans 'value religion' and maintain 'strong religious beliefs' to a far greater degree than the citizens of any other Western industrial nation (Hatch 1989: 210). According to another poll conducted in 1994, 96% of Americans believe in God (Bishop 1999: 38).

Yet, Americans tend to be predominantly private and diverse in their religious beliefs and practices (Berger 1967; Luckman 1967). Indeed, historian Nathan Hatch observes that much of America's 'ongoing religious vitality' can be attributed to the longstanding democratic or populist orientation of American Christianity (Hatch 1989: 212, 218). As 'custodians of their own beliefs,' Americans have traditionally shaped their religious practices to mesh with individual rather than strictly institutional desires (Bellah 1985: 220-221; Roof 1993). It may be that when Elvis fans protest that their devotion to Elvis is not 'religious,' they are really objecting to an institutional definition of the term. In fact, their privatizing veneration of Elvis and its diverse manifestations follow from historical patterns of American religiosity.

Religion constitutes those practices and attitudes that imbue a person's life with meaning by linking him or her to a transcendent reality: that which is beyond purely immanent or secular experience and understanding. Creating Elvis shrines and going to Graceland are not religious acts and practices in and of themselves. But they can become religious if they affect a transcendent and all-powerful order that can influence human affairs and is not inherently ap- prehensible. Elvis's religious import hinges on his multifaceted image, which for many fans is imbued with a certain mystical greatness and looked upon for access to a transcendent reality. It is longstanding, too: as early as 1957, some fans tried to start an 'Elvis Presley Church' (Pierce 1994: 136). And in 1995, a Saint Louis group (The Congregation for Causes of Saints) sought his canoni- zation. It is most obviously revealed in terms of pilgrimages to Graceland.

Graceland as Pilgrimage Site

Pilgrimage, and particularly American pilgrimage, is summarized as 'a set of ritual actions involving specific human communities, institutions, and organi- zed travel to and from sacred places' (Campo 1998: 41). Pilgrims make their way to shrines, the sites of saints, sacred relics, or miracles. Generally enclosed and set apart from the secular world, shrines are located wherever the special qualities of a holy person, thing, or event are 'believed to be more concen- trated' than anywhere else. Pilgrims visit shrines 'in order to commune more intimately' with whoever (or whatever) is thought to be sanctified there; as Mary Lee Nolan and Sidney Nolan argue, a place becomes a shrine 'if people think of it in that way and behave accordingly.' Furthermore, pilgrimage sites are commonly marked by two features: they are centrally located, to attract the largest number of devotees, and they are often located in uncomfortable and hard to get to places (Nolan and Nolan 1989: 13, 36, 291-292). A shrine's special or sacred character is enhanced, in other words, by the difficulties of pilgrimage.

Set back on a hill, a hundred or so yards from a four-lane highway, and enclosed by fieldstone walls and white picket fences, Graceland is conceptua- lized by many Elvis fans as an especially sacred site. Fans have visited Grace- land since Elvis first moved there in 1957. But since his death twenty years later, in a second floor bathroom, visitations have escalated and have become increasingly institutionalized by his estate, and ritualized by his fans. Particularly during Elvis Week, Graceland becomes a site of veneration for tens of thousands of fans. Going there is a deeply significant and often formidable act for many of them. Graceland itself is easily accessible, located just a few miles from Memphis International Airport and near the crossroads of several major interstate highways. But going to Graceland in August, amidst the torrid heat and humidity of the southern summer, makes this a demanding pilgrimage. By extension, pilgrimage to Graceland is expensive: the average fan spends hundreds of dollars on travel, car rental, motel costs, meals, tickets to Graceland (which range from $22 to $55 per adult), and souvenirs. Rarely impulsive, pilgrimages to Graceland are deliberate journeys which entail careful planning and saving.

Despite these pilgrimage hardships, going to Graceland is the deepest desire of most Elvis fans. 'My dream was to see him in concert and see Graceland,' writes a fan from Chisholm, Minnesota. 'Well,' she adds, 'one dream came true when my husband took me to Graceland on our honeymoon.' Many fans try to go as many times as they can: 'My husband surprised me with a trip to Graceland and it was so special,' writes a fan from San Leandro, California. 'We have been back a second time and are planning to be there for the 20th anniversary of Elvis's death.' As the focus of their pilgrimage, Graceland is special because fans make it special: their beliefs and behaviors transform it from historic home to shrine. To be sure, Elvis Presley Enterprises facilitates their faith, eager to profit from Graceland's significance. But fans themselves manufacture its sacrality.

For most fans, the desire to see and experience Graceland is akin to the desire to see and feel Elvis. 'Seeing his home, Meditation Gardens, the planes and many of his personal belongings, I realized that he was a real person with a real life,' writes one fan. 'I was on cloud nine walking around there, seeing in person how Elvis lived and played,' exclaims another. 'It's so hard to describe the feelings when you're there,' still another says. 'To know you're in his home, walking where he has walked.' Fans go to Graceland to walk in Elvis's house, gaze at his things, mourn at his gravesite, and be that much closer to the man they adore. Some leave things for Elvis: a tour guide who worked at Graceland in the mid-1980s recalled finding slips of paper tucked under vases or hidden behind curtains with messages like 'Elvis, we miss you. Love, Bob and Marge.' Other visitors take a little of piece of Graceland home with them, pocketing leaves, pebbles, sticks, and pinches of dirt as tokens of their pilgrimage, and their brush with Elvis. The stuff of material culture – Graceland itself and its relics – is pivotal to the devotional practices and beliefs of Elvis's fans (Doss 2002: 63-86).

Graceland itself isn't that remarkable: a pseudo-Georgian Colonial structure of about 4,500 square feet and a small guitar-shaped pool. If it is ironic that this mundane mansion has now become the most popular house shrine in America, the fact that Elvis Presley died and is buried there has a lot to do with it. Elvis was originally interred at Memphis's Forest Hill Cemetery, but after reports of vandalism, Vernon Presley had his son re-buried at Graceland. It was a smart move. As seen in the growing public presence of ephemeral shrines, contemporary Americans are increasingly drawn to the sites of tragic death: to the Oklahoma City Federal Building (where 168 people were murdered in 1995); to Columbine High School (where 15 people were killed in 1999; Grider 2007); to the World Trade Center (where 2,752 people were murdered on September 11, 2001).

The desire for visceral experience, for intensified modes of sensation that may permit empathetic response, encourage ideological attachment and, especially, confirm our own reality, draws people to these sites of tragic death. Some deem this disrespectful and distasteful, as a kind of 'tragic tourism' tainted by 'insidious elements of voyeurism and sensationalism' (Lippard 1999: 119). Yet it is also, increasingly, the subjective, personal, and hence 'authentic' kind of ritualistic performance out of which Americans (among others) make meaning of tragic death and traumatic loss. These experiences are constitutive: visiting sites of tragedy is not simply something Americans do but part of who Americans are (Scott 1991). These feelings are ritualized, becoming shared and socially permissible through grieving, gift-giving, and intimate participation at these sites. However morbid it might seem to make the pilgrimage to Elvis's grave, even on a honeymoon, fans go to Graceland to emotionally indulge themselves, to become overwhelmed by their feelings of love, loss, and loneliness for Elvis. Elated inside his house, many fans openly weep beside his grave.

Of course, not everyone who goes to Graceland is an Elvis fan. As with any shrine, Graceland's audience is a blend of pilgrims and casual tourists: as Juan Eduardo Campo notes, pilgrimage and tourism 'are seldom easily distinguishable' today, especially as patterns of travel, information, and economics are significantly reshaped (Campo 1998: 53). Other scholars have more closely analyzed Graceland's visitation demographics: in a study based on data collected in 1984, Jim Davidson defined visitors to Graceland as 'tourists' and 'pilgrims' and divided the latter group into 'transient pilgrims,' or fans who are frequent visitors, and 'immigrant pilgrims,' or fans who had actually moved to Memphis in order to be 'closer' to Elvis (Davidson 1990). However diverse the average crowd at Graceland, it is safe to say that most are drawn there to try to come to terms with Elvis's abiding popularity. Their presence feeds the phenomenon: even the most ambivalent tourist, who goes to Graceland to see why everyone else goes, adds to Elvis's popular culture canonization.

That isn't to say that all of Graceland's pilgrims share the same insights about Elvis. Especially during Elvis Week, Graceland draws a mixed crowd of tourists, fans, journalists, and documentary filmmakers. Some fans humor the press, even making up stories about 'when I met Elvis' or 'when I dated Elvis.' Most, however, resent the intrusion of 'the media' and other outsiders into Elvis Culture (Doss 1999: 25-27). Some are even suspicious of recently declared fans making their first trip to Graceland, eyeing them as 'fake fans' and inauthentic wannabes. In a seemingly classic and debated model of pilgrimage as *communitas*, going to Graceland brings many different people together (Turner and Turner 1978: 20). But Graceland is also a site of conflict as pilgrims argue over who Elvis was and what his image represents. This is most obviously realized in a consideration of racial tensions evident during Elvis Week, and in Elvis Culture in general.

Elvis Week

Graceland's shrine-like sensibility is especially apparent during Elvis Week, when pilgrims engage in specific rituals including musical revues, impersonations, benefit concerts, art contests, memorabilia auctions, talks, memorial services, and movie screenings. Fans tour Graceland, buy souvenirs at nearby gift shops, eat in special 'Elvis Rooms' in local restaurants, and participate in window-decorating competitions in area motels. Ordinary spaces such as motels and restaurants become sacred spaces during Elvis Week, because Elvis fans occupy them and fill them with images and objects that they deem to have special significance. Simultaneously a shrine and a shopping mall, Graceland's thirteen-acre complex resembles other pilgrimage sites where devotional practices, material culture, and commercialism are commonly mixed, from Lourdes to the Basilica of the Virgin of Guadalupe in Mexico City.

Elvis Week culminates in the Candlelight Vigil. Beginning on the afternoon and evening of August 15, fans gather at Graceland's gates. Around 9 pm a ceremony with prayers, poems, and Elvis songs starts, and shortly thereafter, fans walk up the mansion's driveway to the Meditation Gardens for a brief personal tribute to Elvis. The procession goes on all night, until every pilgrim has had a chance to visit Elvis's grave. Each solemnly holds a glowing candle, lit from a torch at the start of the procession (which is itself lit from the eternal flame at Elvis's grave); once back down the driveway and outside Graceland's gates, they snuff it out. The tone of this ritual is clearly borrowed from traditional religious practices such as midnight mass services at Christmas and vigils at the Shrine of Saint Jude in Chicago, where candle-lighting marks the beginning and the end of each pilgrim's journey (Orsi 1991: 222). It also resembles secular rituals such as flicking lighters at rock concerts to lighting the Olympic Torch. For those who cannot physically attend the Candlelight Vigil, EPE offers an online 'VigilCast' that can be viewed anytime. Indeed, Elvis's burgeoning presence in cyberspace is seen in the dramatic growth of Elvis websites and chatrooms in recent years.

For most pilgrims to Graceland, the Candlelight Vigil is a hushed and somber ceremony, the cathartic moment of a highly emotional week. Rituals have special meaning because of their sensuality, and this one is especially sensual.

The sounds of cicadas, low murmurs, hushed cries, and Elvis's music, broad-cast over strategically-placed loudspeakers all over Graceland's grounds; the visual spectacle of Graceland lit up at night, of flickering candles, and crowds of fans; the smells of wax, perfume, magnolias, roses, and sweat; and, of course, the damp and steamy heat, made even more oppressive by standing in line pressed against thousands of other fans for hours on end, all combine to make the Candlelight Vigil an especially physically powerful ritual.

Its special character is enhanced by the offerings that fans leave at Elvis's tomb. Traditional pilgrimages usually involve confessional components, and the gifts left by Elvis's fans are comparable. Many specifically request Elvis's intervention: a gift left at his grave during Elvis Week 1996, for example, fea-tured a photo and a hand-printed letter that read: 'Dear Elvis: Miss Yoko was here at Graceland last summer but can't make it this time because she died in a car accident in September last year. You don't know how much she loved you but we hope she is with you in the heaven. Her friends from Japan.' Other of-ferings, especially those which feature images of Elvis, are like ex-votos, or *mi-lagros*: small metal objects shaped like body parts (hearts, hands, feet) that are commonly left at the shrines of holy figures and serve as petitions or thanks (Wilson 1983: 21). Offerings of Elvis dolls and Elvis pictures placed where he is buried seem to have a similarly powerful meaning for the fans who leave them. They are also expressions of gratitude: physically and visually expressive focal points of fan tributes to Elvis's significance in their lives.

As much as fans find pleasure in Elvis's image, pain and sorrow are also evident during Elvis Week. Aside from assassinated political figures such as Abraham Lincoln, John F. Kennedy, and the Reverend Martin Luther King, Jr., Americans have historically embraced few secular realm martyrs. Elvis's suffering, his drug-addict death in a Graceland bathroom, his failure to find happiness *despite* achieving the American Dream may be what attracts so many of his fans, who are likewise caught up in pursuing the myth of the American Dream. Many fans imagine Elvis as a fellow sufferer, which may explain that the image of Elvis most loved by contemporary American fans, and most frequently evoked by his impersonators, is that of the Las Vegas Elvis, the 'Fat, Pain-Racked, Self-Destructive Elvis' (Gottdiener 1997: 189-200,

Rosenbaum 1995: 62, 64). This image of the suffering Elvis, dressed in an all-white jumpsuit and working extra hard to entertain his fans, also reaffirms fan assumptions of Elvis's 'all-white' cultural superiority.

All-White Elvis

During the 1950s, many fans embraced Elvis's cross-race stylistics: his borrowings from and dependence on black culture. Many contemporary fans, however, are unaware of or more blatantly refute Elvis's undeniable appropriation of African-American rhythms and sounds, his own acknowledgement of lessons learned from black musicians, and his personal commitment to racial and cultural integration. Instead, they image an all-white Elvis that corresponds to their nostalgia for an American culture that never really existed, but which they fear is fading from national consciousness. Like the supporters of virulent anti-immigration measures such as Proposition 187, the 1994 'Save Our State' initiative aimed at cleansing California of undesirable – meaning 'nonwhite' – immigrants, most Elvis fans deny they are racist (Lopez 1996: 144). They say they are simply 'taking care' of Elvis and preserving his memory, but their limiting image of Elvis betrays their racial animus. Pilgrimage practices observed during 1993 through 1996 and surveys from fans collected in 1996-1998 substantiate the following remarks (see also Doss 1999: 163-211).

Pilgrimage to Graceland is predominantly white. Although Elvis is popular in countries such as Brazil (where Sao Paulo's Gang Elvis Brasil fan club regularly draws 600 fans to monthly meetings) and Japan, and foreign fans are present during Elvis Week, most of those who go to Graceland are white. Although there are African-American Elvis fans and Graceland is situated in a predominantly black neighborhood (called Whitehaven), few blacks visit. Indeed, going to Graceland, or to Memphis in general, did not even rate on a 'color comfortable' tourism list assembled by the African-American magazine *Ebony* for its majority black readers, who were advised, instead, to visit Walt Disney World, Las Vegas, New Orleans, and the Zora Neale Hurston Festival in Eatonville, Florida (Anon. 1997: 58-60). Neither Memphis, despite being the 'birthplace of the blues,' nor Graceland project a race-friendly image. While black workers staff Graceland's shops and restaurants and supervise its tours, most view Graceland, and Elvis Culture in general, as a 'white thing.' Black absence in Elvis Culture is due to the concerted manner in which the culture itself has been organized as a distinctive and deified site of whiteness.

Admittedly, some fans recall Elvis's own acts of racial goodwill and fellowship: 'Elvis crashed through barriers, bringing the people of the world together via his gifts,' writes one fan, while another adds: 'The love Elvis shared with all of us came straight from the heart without manipulation or prejudice or guile.' But few fans closely consider why African-Americans might feel unwelcome in a racialized fan culture whose favored images include Elvis the working class hero, Elvis the Southern separatist, and Elvis the Las Vegas showman: all images which reinforce assumptions of a culturally-dominant whiteness that many fans extend to Elvis himself.

Brouhaha over Elvis's image on a 29-cent US postage stamp reveals the racial chasm in Elvis Culture. Shortly after Elvis's death, the US Postal Service was besieged by fan demands that Elvis join the flag and the eagle as lickable national icons. Vermont fan Pat Geiger headed fan lobbying efforts, writing daily letters to the US Postmaster General and organizing petitions from fan clubs. In 1992, the first nationwide vote for an American stamp was orchestrated, and the post office printed five million ballots offering a choice between an image of Elvis the rebellious rock and roller or Elvis the Las Vegas showman. Certain politicians decried the campaign: 'What are we saying to our young people?' growled Representative Marge Roukema, a New Jersey Republican. 'We're trying to teach them to say no to drugs, then look who we're lionizing on a stamp.' And certain philatelists sneered: 'Elvis is to stamps what Barbara Cartland is to serious literature' (Brown 1992: 1, 31).[3] Fans, however, focused on promoting their preferred image of Elvis in a high-collared white jumpsuit. While thrilled by Elvis's impending honorific status, they worried about democracy in action. As the president of the Elvis Love Forever Fan Club sniffed: 'A lot of non-fans and people who don't know very much about Elvis will vote [and] I'm not sure you will get the nicest picture.'

Indeed, fans were dismayed when the American public picked the 1950s

Elvis over the Las Vegas image by a three to one margin (over a million votes were cast). Fans were even more upset by Elvis's inclusion in the US Post Office's 'Legends of American Music' series, along with Ritchie Valens, Dinah Washington, Buddy Holly, Hank Williams, Patsy Cline, Otis Redding, and Clyde McPhatter. 'I don't like the idea of Elvis being part of a group because he is too unique,' complained Geiger. Other fans were similarly peeved that the US Post Office sought to contextualize Elvis within the country and western, rhythm and blues, gospel, and pop musical cultures from which he actually emerged, thus making him one of *many* popular culture legends instead of *the* legend.

Fan beliefs in Elvis's 'unique' and culturally-dominant whiteness were most blatantly revealed in the summer of 1994, when Lisa Marie Presley announced her marriage to Michael Jackson. Many fans denounced the celebrity union as an act of race treason: 'It was a sin for her to marry a black,' wrote one fan; 'I feel Lisa Marie disgraced her heritage,' wrote another. One longtime Elvis fan from South Carolina, who had started a fan club in 1956, stated that Elvis 'would NOT have given his Blessings' to the marriage because 'Southern roots go DEEP and 99% of us Black and White folks DO NOT believe in mixed marriages.' During Elvis Week that year, the fieldstone walls in front of Graceland featured the following graffiti: 'Elvis: Lisa Marie made a big mistake marrying that jerk. Come back and straighten her out!' and 'Elvis: Too bad your son-in-law is a faggit nigger' [sic]. The newsletters of some Elvis fan clubs printed similarly racist outbursts (Doss 1999: 200-202). And proprietors of various gift shops near Graceland noticed a dramatic increase in sales of Elvis flags: banners featuring Elvis's face in the middle of the Confederate battle flag, the premiere symbol of white supremacy.

The marriage of 'The King' of rock-and-roll's only daughter to a black entertainer universally hailed as 'The King of Pop' obviously generated deep-felt anxieties among many white fans about Elvis's presence and authority, and their own, in an increasingly multicultural America. Their race-based condemnation of his daughter's second (and shortlived) marriage and their invectives against Michael Jackson speak to the racialized and racist narrative that also underlies Elvis's popularity in contemporary America. While many white fans eagerly embraced Elvis's appropriation of black sounds and styles in the 1950s and championed the colorblind 'family of man' *Zeitgeist* that Elvis promoted in his 1970s concerts, many of today's fans have re-formed his image, and hence his historical meaning and memory, into one of reified whiteness.

In 1956, while Elvis was topping the charts and gaining national attention on prime-time TV, the Reverend Martin Luther King, Jr. was leading the Montgomery, Alabama, bus boycott and drawing national attention to civil rights. Today, many fans who mourn for Elvis at Graceland forget that another highly revered King died in Memphis (in 1968), murdered at the site of what is now the National Civil Rights Museum. In the early twenty-first century, the United States of America is dominated by a loss of faith in liberal humanism and racial equality, and King is no longer an icon: his vision of an integrated American Dream no longer commands credibility. The Elvis who shared King's dream of American racial harmony is no icon, either. Today's Elvis, as personified by many of today's fans, symbolizes white privilege and cultural dominance. Locked into an oppressive ideology of racial essentialism, many of the fans who make the pilgrimage to Graceland carry an image of Elvis that represents a divided and oppositional race consciousness. In their segregated and stifling world, there is no room for the liberatory and barrier-breaking image of the original, interracial Elvis.

Notes

1 Unless otherwise noted, all quotes from fans in this essay stem from author interviews conducted in Memphis or elsewhere from 1993 through 1996, or from surveys of Elvis fans collected in 1996-1998.

2 Cf. The living on or reincarnation of Jim Morrison mentioned on page 145.

3 Barbara Cartland was a very successful British writer of sweet romance novels.

Chapter 6

The Pilgrimage to Jim Morrison's Grave at Père Lachaise Cemetery:
The Social Construction of Sacred Space

Peter Jan Margry

The paradox could hardly have been greater: Jim Morrison (1943-1971), the American rock star and poet who refused to be constrained or pushed around by anyone, has been thrust into a straightjacket more than thirty years after his death. The *espace Morrison*, the area around his grave at the Parisian cemetery of Père Lachaise, had gradually evolved into a kind of sanctuary where his fans brought him to life again, as it were, and where his musicality, his lifestyle, and his poetic and philosophical legacy were evoked and propagated. But on April 15, 2004, the authorities unconditionally put a stop to these informal, communal gatherings that annexed the grave and its immediate environs. The erection of a closed iron ring of anchored barriers marked the culmination of almost thirty years of confrontation between Morrison fans and the established order. By their actions, the authorities have somehow managed to invert the meanings and functions of his grave, confronting some visitors with a curious paradox. Dorothea, a single woman from Hamburg who was born in 1966, was painfully struck by this during her visit on July 3, 2004.[1] 'It hurt me most for Jim Morrison himself,' she said. 'For him, barriers were the worst thing there was. The things that Jim had always wanted to guard against have become reality thirty years after his death. They've finally managed to lock him up.'[2]

In this contribution I will analyze the way in which Jim Morrison fans transform his grave into a sacred place and how the cult surrounding this idol has acquired performative shape in the public space. At the same time I will seek to establish whether there are forms of religiosity involved in the fan culture and Morrison cult on and around his grave and whether it is possible to speak of a Morrison 'pilgrimage.'

Mythologizing

Notwithstanding his international fame, Morrison was buried almost anonymously five days after his death in Paris on July 3, 1971.[3] In part to prevent hysterical scenes involving fans, an austere ceremony was decided on. Morrison was interred without fanfare – no rituals, poems, or prayers – in less than ten minutes and in the cheapest available coffin. The grave was little more than a nondescript, rectangular patch of sand, known as a *pleine-terre*, demarcated by bluestone blocks and with a plaque for the purposes of identification.[4] The plaque was replaced in 1972 by a simple headstone, which was later replaced by a larger stone bearing an inscription.

It was not until the late 1970s, however, that interest in Morrison received a new impetus, a revival that occurred more or less in parallel with the rediscovery of 'his' band, the Doors. This was prompted by the posthumous release of a special LP containing nothing but recordings of Morrison reading his own poems, accompanied by music adapted by the three surviving band members. It also marked the beginning of a mythologizing process around the band and its front man, with Morrison increasingly being profiled as a writer. Added to that, 1979 saw the release of Francis Coppola's anti-war film *Apocalypse Now*, in which the mysterious, dramatic Doors' song 'The End' featured prominently. *No one here gets out alive* appeared one year later. This successful – and controversial – Morrison biography presented for the first time in print various speculations about the final year of Morrison's life in Paris and about how he met his end. Informal confirmation of this process and of the growing iconization of Morrison as a male sex symbol, dark-star musician and *poète maudit* came with the September 1981 edition of *Rolling Stone*, the pop music magazine with an international audience. A photo of Morrison was emblazoned on the cover, together with the words: 'He is Hot, He is Sexy, and He is Dead' (Fowlie 1994). While Morrison and the Doors were subject to a worldwide re-evaluation among older and successive younger generations, his friends, acquaintances and 'hangers-on' began publishing a string of insiders' books, all of which continued to create, maintain, unmask, or embellish new myths. Above all, it was the fact that Morrison's body had only been seen by his girlfriend and a Parisian doctor before being interred in a sealed coffin that triggered considerable speculation that Morrison 'lived on' (Fowlie 1994: 94-96; Seymore 1991). This idea was given further credence by the fact that his 'official' biographers believed he was perfectly capable of such an 'escape' (Hopkins and Sugerman 1980: 373). Finally, the emergence of a new literary genre of Morrison fantasy biographies and novels, like those by Strete (1982), Farren (1999), Verheul (1999)[5], Pierce (2003) and Meunié (2005), in which he continues to experience bizarre adventures on earth or in the afterlife, has only lent more weight to the idea that he is not dead, that he lives on or has been reincarnated, and that he has a supernatural status.[6]

This denial of death, the belief in the existence of a life after death, or the attribution of an eternal life has many parallels in world religions and could point to the presence of religious perceptions in relation to Morrison. Just as the day of a saint's death marks the birth of his heavenly life and the beginning of an intermediary function, so too do some Jim Morrison devotees believe that they can still communicate in some way with him and/or his spirit. Different stories – from fantasy novels and accounts from witnesses or visitors to Morrison's grave about Morrison continuing to live and experience things – have influenced and complemented one another.

Oliver Stone's successful 1991 film *The Doors* gave a whole new impetus to this mythologizing. The film was essentially a disguised biography of Morrison, based on Stone's own understanding of the central character. The film partly confirmed the existing image but added new, powerful iconographies and narratives. Stone's personal feelings and viewpoint were highly influential because he himself was a devoted fan who claimed that the Doors had completely turned his life around when he was young. For him, Jim Morrison symbolized the central preoccupations of the 1960s, particularly the search for new forms of heightened consciousness and freedom. Thanks to his physical resemblance to Morrison and his superb acting ability, actor Val Kilmer managed to more or less convey Morrison's reputed charisma in the film. The result was an international success that shaped Morrison's image, and to a lesser extent that of the Doors, for new generations of fans.

For our purposes, it is important to point out how the film uses manipulation to highlight Morrison's supposed shamanistic abilities. The film opens significantly with a mystical representation, set to music, of how Morrison took on these qualities as a small child by means of 'spiritual transmission' from a dying Native American in the New Mexico desert. With references made in passing to the secularization – the 'loss of God' – of American society, the film continues with the words 'the ceremony is now to begin' and jumps ahead in time to the adult Morrison. His interest in the occult and his shamanistic trances and performances during concerts are shown at length. There is no doubt that these filmic narratives have exerted a powerful influence on his fans' perception of Morrison as someone with supernatural or transcendental qualities.

The media's continued inflation of Morrison in relation to the Doors met with a worldwide response, leading to a broad iconization of the Morrison phenomenon. An early Morrison photo, a 1967 portrait from Joel Brodsky's *Young Lion* series showing a bare torso and a head of abundant curly hair, became the canonized image of the idol par excellence (cf. Ortíz 1998: 63-64).[7] Distributed internationally, this series has had such a powerful impact over

Postcard of a Morrison picture from Joel Brodsky's Young Lion *series of 1967, with signature. Collection Meertens Institute.*

the years that it has helped shape the way in which Morrison is perceived. In discussion forums on the Internet, it has triggered observations like: 'He looks so primal, ferrel [sic] -- like a wild cat (...) also the look in his eyes is so confrontational. (...) If man was made in the image of G(g?)od [sic], then this is the mirror' and 'Great photos, ... talk about looking like a god.'[8] Not only did fans see him as someone divine, for many fans these photos functioned as images of the human ideal: for women, the man of their dreams and for men, the ideal masculine model. This is expressed in the frequent attempts by in-group fans to imitate and copy Morrison's lifestyle and outward appearance.

Fan Scene vs Heritage

The growing iconization also had an impact on Morrison's grave. The opportunity to de-anonymize his minimalist grave came in 1981, ten years after his death. Fans wanted some link with and attribution to their idol, as well as acknowledgement and recognition that this was indeed his final resting place. A larger headstone with his name was erected. Someone made a bust of Morrison (which was later stolen) and placed it on the headstone so that fans could picture him. In 1991, twenty years after his death, Morrison's parents arranged for a larger, more formal headstone with a bronze plaque.[9]

The grave underwent not only material changes. Because of the fan culture (the 'scene'), the immaterial changes were much more far-reaching. In the 1980s and 1990s, the growing presence of the fan scene had given rise to the *espace Morrison* – the physical, central reference point for fans and devotees from all around the world. This had evolved into a socio-cultural space where the identification with and the *imitatio* of the life of Morrison took shape. It was an informal annexation of the surrounding gravestones and crypts where fans drank excessively, smoked, took drugs, removed their clothes, had public sex, slept, and put into practice the non-conformist ideas and lifestyle championed by Morrison. But they also recited his poems or lyrics, played recordings of his music or played the music themselves. The headstone usually functioned as a table, or 'shrine' as it was increasingly referred to, where they revered and paid homage to Morrison. The shrine continued to be the central

Postcard showing the grave of Jim Morrison adorned with a bust and graffiti,
approx. 1987. Collection Meertens Institute.

focus for visitors and the focal point of an ever-growing social and sacred
space, at the same time underscoring the importance of *locality* in this context
(Bennett 2000: 195-198). The literal appropriation of the space by gatherings
of Morrison fans was so informal, chaotic and 'anarchistic' in nature – fully in
keeping with the idol worshipped there – that the site became increasingly
contested. This had already led to a temporary closure in 1988-1989 that failed
to relocate or eliminate the cult; it would be effortlessly revived again later
(Söderholm 1990: 303). Thus, the site continued to exert its power, becoming once again the subject of conflict and eventually being permanently and
physically cordoned-off from the public.

Grave of Morrison with gifts from visitors, 8 December 2003.
Photo: M. Campbell.

The fans were active not only during the day; in the evenings and at night-time they would creep into the closed cemetery to gather at the grave. In 1991, to put an end to these gatherings and to the 'profaning' of the cemetery, solid, spiked railings were erected on top of the cemetery's outer walls, a measure that sparked off fierce clashes with fans on the anniversary of his death later that year. After that, there were daily checks to ensure that fans did in fact leave the cemetery before closing time and were not locked in. This failed to prevent disturbances of the peace during the day, however. New confrontations were not long in coming, especially as the entire area around the grave was severely

An analogy of the church altar: fanscene has covered the new gravestone for
Jim Morrison with drugs and alcohol, 1990. Photo: M. Campbell.

marked and damaged by graffiti and inscriptions in the thousands. This was
the permanent confrontation of the informal Morrison cult with the order and
sacrality of the cemetery. Also at that time, in response to the newly launched
heritage policy and to burgeoning tourism, the cemetery was declared a historic monument, which meant that Père Lachaise – although still a functioning cemetery – became subject to a process of museumization. This served to
heighten tensions with the Morrison scene, who were held partly responsible
for stripping the cemetery of almost all of Morrison's funerary paraphernalia.

However, the introduction of tighter security measures did not altogether
halt the alienation of objects. Visitors still tried to remove sand from the area
around the grave, to take objects from the vicinity or to leave behind etched

proof of their visit. For that matter, treating the dead with respect and the meaning of 'property' are relative concepts for the fans. Because of the sacred significance of objects that have come into contact with the grave and the site as whole, objects or letters placed there by fans often hold an irresistible attraction. Personal gifts – like poems, drawings, photos, flags and packets of marijuana (cf. Thomas 2006: 17-22) – tend to disappear very quickly. The number of gifts has fallen since barriers were erected in 2004, but anything left behind is still usually removed.[10] And when the Père Lachaise security guards are absent, there are always fans who will jump over the barriers to appropriate something.

Hence the decision by the cemetery management to cordon off the grave.[11] The primary reason was the damage to Père Lachaise – described as 'la plus spectaculaire profanation permanente de sépultures' – as a cultural monument and as part of cultural heritage (De Langlade 1982/2002: 71). In 2004, the cemetery's historian inadvertently attracted worldwide notoriety after stating in a Guardian interview about Morrison: 'We'd like to kick him out, because we don't want him; he causes too many problems. If we could get rid of him, we'd do it straight away' (Henley 2004). This view, held by certain Parisians but never before articulated so brusquely, came to the attention of the world press. It shocked not only Morrison's followers but also the Paris authorities, who hastened to explain that the American rock star's grave was part of French cultural heritage and there would be no question of relocation. This announcement was quite unrelated to the fact that, like most graves at Père Lachaise, Morrison's grave was given in perpetuity to the family and for that reason could not possibly be relocated.

Nevertheless, the grave has remained Morrison's lieu de mémoire par excellence. Despite all of the problems, his final resting place has continued to work its way up the ranks at Père Lachaise. Today, it is the cemetery's most visited grave, and together with the Eiffel Tower, Notre Dame and the Louvre, it is one of the top tourist attractions in the French capital.[12] It was not only Morrison's grave that became a focal point; owing to the growing importance of the Morrison cult, any place that recalls his stay in Paris has acquired a significant, albeit subsidiary, role within the Morrison memorial tour. Fans can take a route past all the sites that are somehow connected with Morrison's life in Paris in 1971, such as the Hotel George V, the apartment on the Rue Beau-treillis 17, the Le Beautreillis restaurant in the same street, Café de Flore, and the L'Astroquet and La Palette bars.[13]

At Père Lachaise, 'hidden away' in an unsightly corner, Morrison fans will still find a simple grave that fails to correspond to prevailing esthetic norms or to what is usually deemed worthy of tourist attention. This monument oc-cupies quite a different position from an attraction like Graceland, the grave and home of Elvis Presley, which in terms of design, management, and mer-chandising is entirely controlled and administered by Elvis Presley Enterprises and which has long since assumed Disney World proportions (Doss 1999). In comparison, Morrison's grave seems above all to emanate humility, simplic-ity and modesty, as if it were the material representation of a Catholic saint's classic virtues. How then should we classify Morrison?

Idol, Icon or Saint?

In his book *Heiligen, idolen, iconen* (1988), the Dutch historian Willem Frijhoff published a programmatic manifesto about the relationship, past and present, between conceptual terms like saint, idol and icon. Combining a cultural-his-torical perspective and an anthropologizing approach, he brought together his insights on the broad theme of personal sacrality. In so doing, he gave new direction to research evaluating the deeds, virtues and vices of the social elite, and he broadened the concept of sainthood in analytical terms. In this regard, Frijhoff stated that social groups could also ascribe sainthood to exemplary, non-church-related lives – including idols or icons – that are orientated to other than strictly material and individual values (Frijhoff 1988: 19-20; 39-51; 52-78).[14] They can then perform specific functions, including in the sphere of spirituality and religiosity. The Morrison case is an example that ties in well with this model.[15]

This broadened analysis also permits us to establish the degree to which religiosity has a place within popular and pop music culture. The German sociologist Thomas Luckmann was the first to carry out systematic research

An Italian admirer of Morrison asks for his support, also on behalf of his friends who have signed a card that bears a message, 3 July 2004. Photo: P.J. Margry.

into hidden and implicit forms of religiosity (Luckmann 1967: 115-117). In the early 1960s, he identified the rapidly growing discrepancy between the subjective autonomy of the individual and the objective autonomy of the primary (religious) institutions in the public domain. At that time, the traditional religious domain in Western societies was beginning to fragment, in connection with processes of secularization and, interacting with this, de-secularization or sacralization (Berger 2002). Increasingly, individuals withdrew into the private sphere and attached greater importance to their subjective autonomy, thereby giving rise to new forms of religiosity. Cultural globalization and fragmentization, new religious movements and individual appropriation practices involving customs, rituals and symbols began to accommodate non-institutionalized forms of religion that are manifested, individually or in groups, as social constructs.

Although as a rule there is only a small religious element in the fan cult surrounding Morrison, we do in practice see constantly recurring connections (assemblages) with Christian culture, rituality and religion, forms that have been introduced by his fans. For example, we regularly find photos placed on the grave depicting Morrison's head and a crown of thorns, an image of the dead musical messiah. When he was alive, Morrison himself encouraged a blending with existing religious traditions. First of all, there was his constant identification with the shaman. However, for a time he also wore a golden crucifix around his neck, saying, 'I like the symbol visually, and it may confuse people' (Fowlie 1993: 82). This symbol and Morrison's explanation may be what prompted visitors to place crosses and crucifixes with Morrison's name on the grave. But he also turned against the Christian church in his texts, saying, 'let's reinvent the Gods.' These ideas are expressed most clearly in his fondness for Native American spirituality and shamanism. At that time some reviewers were already describing the Doors' concerts as performances in the tradition of shamanistic evocations. In their view, Morrison created heightened powers of observation, using them – as he once said in relation to himself – to 'mediate between man and spirit world' (Morrison 1970: 71). Even band member Manzarek attested to this: 'I've never seen a performer like Jim – it was as if it wasn't Jim performing but a shaman.' In his film about the Doors, Stone left nothing to the imagination, on several occasions using filmic dissolves to transform his idol into a shaman. We see Morrison being initiated into the metaphysical world of Native Americans and shamans. Stone suggests that Morrison constantly had visions or supernatural experiences throughout his life and during his performances; in the film, Morrison's hallucinations and those of the shaman flow into one another. However much the 'divine' image of Morrison as a shaman and Dionysian incarnation may have been promoted by Morrison himself and by those close to him (Riordan and Prochnicky 1991: 183-200; cf. Seay and Neely 1986: 229-237), there can be no doubt that the film's textual and visual narratives have exerted a powerful influence in this respect. The perception of Morrison as having supernatural, transcendental and healing powers acquired ever-greater importance within the fan culture (cf. Fournier and Jiménez 2005).

The element of the intermediary also emerges in his experiments with mind-expanding drugs. Morrison was inspired by the mystical, symbolist lyrical poetry of artist William Blake (1757-1827), whom he greatly admired and who had a strong belief in the liberating power of the imagination. Blake wrote: 'There are things that are known and things that are unknown; in between are doors...' (Fowlie 1993: 11, 76). According to Hopkins, Morrison's biographer, Morrison would like to have taken on this role of door (Hopkins and Sugerman 1980: 58). The idea of putting this into practice through drugs came after reading Aldous Huxley's *The Doors of Perception*, which details the author's experiences when taking mescaline. Morrison consequently named the band after these doors of Huxley, thereby presenting himself at one and the same time as a key to another, subversive world.[16] He was suggesting that he and his band could play an intermediary role between the known and the unknown, between the perception of everyday life and the life beyond.

The Espace Morrison

Fieldwork at Père Lachaise has demonstrated how the many visitors and the active fan culture have expanded the material *pleine-terre* of a rectangle of sand as a social construct to become the performative *espace Morrison*. Today, the barriers guide and constrain both the behavior and freedom of movement of the public and the performativity of the grave in general. As a result, although opportunities for communication, contemplation and rituality, for approaching the monument, showing homage, placing objects or taking photos may have changed, they have not disappeared. The measures were designed to protect the site and to safeguard the cemetery against behavior deemed inappropriate. The result is that people tend to make shorter visits, and in-group fans who appropriate and demarcate the space by sitting or lounging around have become a thing of the past. Given that, in the past, Morrison fans had in effect erected their own barrier around the *espace Morrison* through their behavior; the disappearance of this behavior has made the grave more accessible to visitors who do not belong to the in-group fan culture.

In my fieldwork, I have been able to identify different groups of visitors.[17] Firstly, there are those who visit the grave as a tourist site or as part of cultural heritage. This includes tour groups on general Paris tours (group A), guided

A visitor draws the grave as part of a process of spiritual communication with Jim Morrison. Photo: P.J. Margry.

tours organized by the management of Père Lachaise for those interested in the cemetery and its famous dead (group B), and individuals and families who visit Père Lachaise independently as a cultural-historical monument, perhaps in connection with the celebrity route set out by the cemetery's management (group C). Visits by groups A and B are generally fairly large-scale, quantitatively dominant, and of short duration. They tend to be casual spectators who cast a brief glance at the grave, and who usually just say the singer's name aloud, out of surprise or in verification. For the rest, they include Morrison fans who have chosen this particular excursion so that they can visit the grave in an easy, organized way.

Secondly, there is a less easily definable group of Morrison and Doors 'fans.' The term is a broad, diffuse one, as Hills has revealed (Hills 2002). However, without wishing to suggest that other visitors are not fans (they often are), I use the term 'fan' to mean those who see themselves as 'true' fans, as part of the Morrison scene around his grave. The narratives about how they became fans and how they profess this closely resemble the conversion stories from fans of other music idols (cf. Cavicchi 1998: 38-59). The fan scene around the grave is the second general category, and it can be further subdivided into three subgroups.[18] One group (group D) is interested primarily in the music of the Doors/Morrison. A second, smaller group (group E) focuses on the music and lifestyle in close connection with Morrison's iconic dimensions. The music is also important for a third, smaller group (group F), but they visit the site for its intrinsic qualities arising out of Morrison's spiritual-religious significance and that of his vision and writing. Although groups E and F, which may some-times overlap, are considerably smaller than (hundreds) the first groups, these fans tend to stay longer at the grave, returning regularly in the course of a day or several days. Their visits also specially take account of Morrison's birthday and the anniversary of his death.

The grave has become increasingly contested as a result of growing num-bers of visitors with different backgrounds, motivations and behaviors. Within all visitor categories, we find a heterogeneous international origin, with the vast majority being white Europeans and North and South Americans. They include proportionately more Americans, Canadians, Germans, Italians, Eng-lish, French, Dutch and Swiss. Generally speaking, these groups – which are roughly distinguishable and certainly not mutually exclusive – can be identi-fied by the way in which they come to the grave and the behavior that they exhibit there. The tour groups are instantly recognizable, but so too are the fans in general, primarily through their appearance, their clothing and the at-tributes they bring with them. Almost all carry explicit references to Morrison, either in the form of tattoos on their body or texts, images, or objects printed on or attached to their clothing. A significant proportion of fans use boots, clothing (leather), jewelry, sunglasses, or hairstyle to try to imitate Morrison's appearance. In addition, the fans in group E make their presence felt through their high spirits and boisterous behavior. Group E consists of a core group of several dozen people, spread across different generations, most of whom come back every year, plus a changing ad hoc group who show an affinity and join in temporarily with the core group during their visit to the grave. These fans are characterized by a strong sense of group membership, with a shared collective identity based on adoration of their idol. Because of their close, intimate bond, the core group also calls itself a *family* (cf. Fournier and Jiménez 2004). However, Maffesoli's theoretical concept of *tribus* seems to be more appropriate for group E as a whole. After all, this group is global in character and is only constructed at the site of the grave and its surroundings. They see the site first and foremost as a meeting place of kindred spirits where a certain ambience subsequently arises, a state of mind which is expressed through the Jim Morrison lifestyle (cf. Maffesoli 1996: 98). Because of this collective identity, the social context and their behavior, group E fans differ markedly from those in group F. The latter usually visit the grave individually or with a traveling companion with whom they share a strong bond of trust. They approach the site much more cautiously, before opting to spend time in quiet reflection or contemplation at the graveside.[19] As Erving Goffman says, they have drawn a 'circle of the self,' as it were. An authority on Père Lachaise wrote in 1982 that the more spiritually-inclined fans would sit close to the grave and 'remain thoughtful, usually with their head in their hands, for a long time, a very long time' (De Langlade 1982/2002: 72).[20] When the site fills up with groups of tourists, these fans withdraw to the background. The tension between the groups is illustrated by F., a Dutchman (1967) who says: 'I avoid the days commemorating his birth and death, because that's when you often find the most irritating 'fans': loud and coarse in their efforts to be like Jim. I prefer to go on quiet days.' H. (1973) has this to say: '[I] always try to be alone, then I can talk to Jim in my thoughts.' Group F fans tend to spend longer at the grave and to view it from different vantage points. More than the other groups, they are the ones who bring a text from home to deposit at the grave and who are more critical and particular when capturing the site on a photo. They quite often come alone or in pairs, a small majority are women, they are often single, and for most, their year of birth is spread fairly equally between 1960 and 1990.

A visitor analysis makes it clear just how much the Morrison grave has become a polymorphous sacred site, but also how much tourism, 'tribal cult,' and pilgrimage run parallel and overlap with one another. This picture, born of a broad socio-cultural stratification with a wide variety of ritual repertoires, ties in closely with Eade and Sallnow's theoretical model of contested places of pilgrimage (Eade and Sallnow 2000).

The Religious Factor

In this section I will attempt to show whether, within the fan scene around his grave, Morrison is viewed as someone with certain divine or sacred qualities, or at least as someone who can arouse religious or spiritual feelings among his fans. Or in other words, is there for visiting fans also a certain religious perspective in the way they approach the person of Morrison and make a pilgrimage to the grave as a holy place?[21] Such a perspective, and here I am following Clifford Geertz, would move fans 'beyond the realities of everyday life to wider ones which correct and complete them, and its defining concern is to accept and have faith in those wider realities' (Geertz 1973: 112). The question is whether that indeed is the case. In more general terms, however, it has been established that young people construct personal frameworks of meaning and religiosity within the cultural fragmentization in which they live (Prins 2006). Research in the Netherlands and elsewhere has revealed that in the group of 18- to 30-year-old non-church members, almost half believe that they can derive religiosity and/or inspiration from pop musicians (Kregting and Sanders 2003: 14).[22] With regard to the musical supply, Schwarze

Visitor in reflection at Morrison's grave, 2000. Photo: M. Campbell.

established that rock and pop music articulates an individualized, non-institutionalized and estheticized ('gnostic') religiosity (Schwarze 1997: 241-248).[23] This is reflected concretely in ethnographic research into Bruce Springsteen fans (Cavicchi 1998: 184-189).

It is against this backdrop that I have linked my fieldwork data to Glock's still useful theoretical scheme, comprising five categories or dimensions (ideological, experiential, ritualistic, intellectual and consequential). Charles Glock, an American sociologist of religion, devised these dimensions in order to identify and label the various components of any religious perspective within a given phenomenon (Glock 1962; 1974). I will now discuss these dimensions one by one in relation to my fieldwork observations.

1. The ideological dimension ('doctrine') concerns religious commitment: what those involved believe or believe in. However, there is no formal discourse about a general ideology, let alone theology, surrounding the person of Jim Morrison. Nonetheless, when asked, most visitors in groups E and F articulate the ideological meanings that Morrison has for them. Nineteen-year-old Mandy, a percussionist and saxophonist from Muskegon in Michigan, 'feels

Visitor to the grave, May 2004. Photo: P.J. Margry.

the freedom.' For her, the visit to his grave is 'the reaffirmation of being confronted with a sort of big thing; something bigger than life.' Another American (29) thought that Morrison had a 'higher stature,' 'he makes people think; he is a free spirit.' For two women (25), friends from Dunkirk, he represents a mystical form of '*l'espoir*' [hope] because 'what you don't understand, he makes comprehensible.' Two young men from Darmstadt (23) felt that Morrison 'can give something, or something different, that the church can't give.'[24] According to them, Morrison had an idea, namely the 'insight that meaninglessness of life – as a fact – can open up other ways.'[25] He thus provides them with an alternative basis for the search for another meaning or purpose in life. For Martina (21) and Marigina (20), two students from Bologna, Jim prompted them to '*riflettare sulla vita e aldila*' [reflect on life and the hereafter]; he is able to '*risolvere problemi*' [solve problems]. Martina believed in his power within the '*supranaturale*.' In her view, because Morrison rejected the traditional social order and was influenced by Native American spirituality, he was able to create visionary poetry and an alternative spirituality. Therefore, the specific way in which fans interpret Morrison focuses primarily on his significance as a musician, songwriter and poet ('you'll always be a word man,' wrote one fan on July 3, 2005), as well as on his personal search for freedom and spirituality. In that respect, there is a connection with the intellectual dimension, including the ideological principles that Morrison put in writing.

2. The experiential dimension refers to religious feeling, or emotion, and points to the recognition or consciousness of the transcendental or divine. For a 20-year-old man from Naples, who traveled especially to Paris, Morrison's grave offered an immediate spiritual power that becomes knowable, or 'comes out' at that place, and is 'passed on.' Two Canadians were only willing to say that they found 'support' at the grave. Others experience an affinity with the mysterious, the mystical. For example, a 20-year-old from the Dutch town of Deurne felt the 'impact' that Jim has on him, but 'rituals and stuff' do not come into it for him. For another musician (24) from Naples, the visit was an '*evento*' with a '*motivo spirituale*,' something which he preferred not to elaborate on. The American musician Mandy had a 'spiritual feeling' and re-

Some visitors experience a strong need to touch the grave and/or bust, 1992.
Photo: M. Campbell.

ceived an inner power: 'I had to come to the grave.' Maria (22) from Hannover
described him as a genius: 'He determines my thoughts. Now I'm where he is
and I want to experience something with him.' Jim shows her the other side
of life, a side that he himself has already experienced and which now opens
for her like a 'new page.' Carissa (21) and Sophia (22) from the United States
have been listening to his music and reading his poems since they were twelve. For them, 'he's right about a lot of things; Jim opened our minds and, also,
sex is in the center of life.' Morrison also gives them a degree of 'guidance,
consolation and relief.' But as they themselves say, 'that is the grey area of
spirituality.' Silas from Switzerland, who was given the trip to the grave by his
mother as a present for his eighteenth birthday, visited the site in 2004 so that
he could come into closer contact with Morrison through a kind of *'spirituelle
Kommunikation.'* This was why he kept returning to the grave over several consecutive days. The above-mentioned Dorothea from Hamburg, who had been
committed to Jim and his music from the age of 16, felt 'as if the spirit of one
person enters the spirit of another' and in this way part of his aura entered into

hers. She had always felt Jim's aura and 'from time to time his spirit reappears to me at this spot and I can communicate with him.'[26]

On July 2, 2005, Ted S., an American, placed the following message on his grave:

> Dear Jim,
> Thank you for everything.
> Years ago I had a vision
> and in it you told me to
> keep the flame alive. I
> now promise you I will.
> You have my word. Please
> give me any help you
> can, and watch over me.
> I will make you proud.
> Thank you.

In these few sentences the writer declares that he had had a vision of Morrison, in which he was given a task which he seemingly, only now, has come to confirm at the grave. At the same time, he calls upon Morrison's support and protection. Clearly, Morrison occupies a supernatural and transcendental position here.

Finally, what matters to various people interviewed is their perception that their experiences or life situations are similar to Morrison's. Analogies – experiencing similar situations and viewing things in a similar way – can create a bond and thus provide support. Another fan said that Jim sensed his difficulties and recognized his frustrations. So the young man from Zürich is 'not alone' with his thoughts – 'Jim felt the same way I did.' Sometimes the experiences themselves are separate from the physical locality. A 20-year-old woman from Vilnius in Latvia experienced a 'metaphysical and peaceful feeling' just from looking at photos of the grave.[27] The different examples clearly show that, for his fans, there is a transcendental relationship between Morrison and his grave.

3. The presence of a ritualistic dimension can also point to religious practices. The public behaviors and rituals manifested by fans on and around Morrison's grave display first of all a certain communality with or resemblance to more universal practices surrounding the dead, idols or saints. Despite parallels with rituals from Christian culture, they do not necessarily or solely point to religious dimensions. To a degree, they are part of the secular fan scene around the grave. Whatever the case may be, they vary enormously in form and execution, often tailored to Morrison and the life he led – a life of singing, making music, writing poems, as well as taking drugs, activities to which the fans themselves have given performative shape in *imitatio* at the graveside. The same applies to the drinking bouts that took place there until recently. By leaving behind bottles of whisky and allowing the alcohol to drain down into the sandy grave, fans sought to ensure that the liquid reached Morrison's body. Some hoped in this way to make closer contact with his person or spirit.

The chaos, graffiti and litter that accompany all these activities are a characteristic feature of the creation of the *espace Morrison*, a chaos that is said to be typical of Morrison. Various people interviewed said that the mess and graffiti had not bothered them in the slightest: 'It just goes with Jim Morrison.' In an interview with Reuters in 2004, Christian Charlet, the cemetery's historian, said: 'People come here not to worship the dead, but think they can do what they want, as if it was a rave party.' Here he misunderstood the specific, distinctive forms of idolization being expressed by Morrison fans. Camilita (*1979) from Norway says that the texts or graffiti are 'letters of love, respect and sadness,' although many fans in fact view them as expressions of lack of respect.

The barriers now make it almost impossible to come into physical contact with the grave. While the fan scene may complain about this, it is the spiritually-inclined who are the most disappointed. Martina and Marigina from Bologna experienced it as *'brutto non toccare la tomba'* [It's mean that you can't touch the grave]. It also meant that they could not properly place the 'guiding feather' (*Piuma guida*) that they had brought with them as a tribute and offer to Morrison's bond with the Native American shaman. Another visitor, angry at the presence of the barrier, tried an alternative means of appropriating the grave for herself by making a drawing of it.

Before Morrison's bust was stolen from the headstone, almost all fans laid their hand on the stone head as part of their visit. This is the object that they miss most. They also felt an overwhelming need to touch the headstone or copper plaque at least once during their visit. But the desire for physical contact was sometimes expressed in very different ways, like the girl who straddled Morrison's grave and then bared her breasts so that she could offer herself to Morrison and still unite with him, as it were. Another fan lay down on the grave and experienced a 'reincarnation.' For others, this spot was the ultimate location for making love.

The most common ritual, which has declined significantly since the erection of the barriers, is to give or place objects or messages. We encounter the following gifts: cigarettes, drugs (joints, packets of hashish),[28] alcohol, Morrison portraits and busts, flags (some with drawings), cloths, T-shirts, shawls, caps, stones, plants and flowers. People also place burning candles and incense. Important in terms of content are the ritually deposited letters and poems, photos and drawings. A musician from Naples tossed a sheet of lyrics that he had written onto the grave, in homage to his great role model. When asked, he said that he was also hoping to bring down success upon himself. His preference would have been to burn the paper at the site in order to make a greater impact, but in the end he did not dare because of the security around the grave. This would also have been a way to keep your communication private – as indeed sometimes happens – as others conceal their intimate words or requests to Morrison by folding their message several times before throwing it publicly on the grave.

Fans not only leave objects behind; until a few years ago, they frequently took flowers, stones, or sand from the grave away with them, which meant that the sandy, open grave had to be replenished regularly. Now that the barriers are in place, items can no longer be removed, but this does not prevent fans from taking sand or pebbles, albeit from the ground as close as possible to the grave. As a young Dutchwoman explains, this is for the 'feeling that I have something of "him" at home'. For many fans, photos taken at the graveside suffice as an important souvenir of their visit.

Both today and in the past, visitors have taken objects given to Morrison, sometimes even shortly after a fan has left them behind. And if this does not happen, then it is often the guards who clear away the material after closing time.[29]

For about two decades, one of the most characteristic forms of rituality surrounding Morrison was the large-scale writing of graffiti in the area around the grave. Although the graffiti writers usually recorded their own names, or Morrison's name ('Jim'), many also quoted from his repertoire of lyrics and poems. In addition, some texts made more explicit reference to the expectations of the visitors. The occasional researcher has interpreted this as a parallel to the Catholic church's books of wishes, placed in shrines for visitors to record their reflections, prayers, words of thanks, and expressions of love and sorrow. The walls of the burial chapel seem to play a similar role here, expressing through texts the emotions that 'weigh down' fans (De Langlade 1982/2002: 72). Almost all graffiti was removed in a major clean-up operation in 2004.

Visitors with a religious or spiritual motivation (group F) tend to distance themselves from the group nature of the fan scene, desiring above all peace and quiet at the graveside, or as one young man put it: 'Peace and quiet to reflect.' For them, it is a place of contemplation and meditation. However, this group also includes people who want to touch the grave and to take something tangible away with them. The letters placed on the grave, often expressing more considered personal thoughts and reflections (see 2 above), could offer valuable insights into people's motivations, but almost all are taken by other fans or cleared away and destroyed by cemetery staff.

4. According to Glock, the intellectual dimension is a reaction to the content and meaning of the related (holy) texts. In rock music, the conscious use of lyrics for defined countercultural purposes gave the music a new social function and added more weight to them (Dunbar 2002: 4-5). Jim Morrison has made a powerful, essential contribution to that development in general. In part because he was so widely read, he built up a repertoire of lyrics in which the existential – death is never far away – is continually addressed. As Morrison grew older, his poetry became more important to him. In an interview about the art

of poetry in general, he said: 'It's so eternal (...) Nothing else can survive a holocaust, but poetry and songs' (Hopkins 1981: 55). For many fans in group F, the significance of Morrison's collected writings and lyrics transcends that of the music itself. In many respects these texts function as sources of inspiration and as a guide to the meaning of life and its supernatural aspects. There is a certain overlap here with the above-mentioned ideological dimension, in which his texts also function as a canon. For some, the visionary element that characterizes his poems is essential to his perceived supernatural qualities. In any case, we see a clear division between the readers and the non-readers of his poems. While almost all in-group fans own editions of his poems, most in group E do not read them (cf. Janssen 1994: 164). They usually find it difficult to come to grips with the content, or as Heerko (*1973) from the Netherlands put it: 'No, [I] can't follow Jim on that plane, nobody can.' Those in group F, on the other hand, are more receptive to his poetic work, turning to it and deriving support from it in times of trouble. Roby (*1984) from Bergamo says: '*Mi danno molto sostegno a volte*' [He sometimes gives me a lot of support]; a Dutchman says: 'Yes, support, but I can't really put it into words'; and Marieke (*1969) says: 'in difficult times I find support in Jim's texts.' These comments reveal that Morrison's text corpus can offer his fans support or consolation for their existential problems.

5. Finally, the consequential dimension reflects the religious effects or consequences of the form of religiosity in question: what people can expect or what is expected of them as a consequence of their religiosity. We can think here of spiritual harmony, peace of mind, freedom from care, health, well-being, release, etc.

Until the big clean-up at Père Lachaise in 2004, a large piece of graffiti – 'Thanks for helping me Jim, 14/11/92' – still adorned a crypt next to Morrison's grave. This is a clear reference to the fact that, after his death, Morrison in some way helped the person who wrote it. When her father was ill, T. (*1968) went especially to Paris to enlist Jim's help. Letter writer Ted, quoted above in 2, is a further powerful example of someone asking Morrison for help and protection. We can deduce from these and comparable texts that some fans at-

tribute to the deceased Morrison a special, effectual power. We observe something similar with a 33-year-old musician from Quito who asked Morrison for
strength, inspiration and assistance in establishing his own music career. To
this end, he spent a long time at the graveside, taking photos from every possible angle. For some, Morrison is also an anti-role model in certain respects.
With his help they hope, like an 18-year-old Swiss boy, to find the strength
to either resist or overcome drug addiction. Jan K., a Danish ex-hippie, paid
homage to Jim's grave after winning the battle with alcohol at the time of the
twentieth anniversary of Morrison's death. An Englishman (*1980), knowing
that 'deep inside' Jim was against heroin, asked for his help with his own addiction.[30] During her second trip to the grave, Dorothea from Hamburg said
that he gives comfort and support for the immense 'helplessness' that she experiences in everyday life.

Relating Glock's five theoretical dimensions to the fieldwork findings has generated a better understanding of the forms of religiosity displayed around Jim
Morrison's grave at Père Lachaise. The study shows that, for a specific portion
of the fan scene, Morrison has a religious significance and function. It is not
easy to categorize this form of religiosity within what is broadly labeled 'the
holistic milieu' or part of the associated 'spiritual revolution.' Although, like
the New Age, the Morrison cult has arisen in relation to processes of secularization and individualization, I do not perceive a direct connection and regard it as an independent form of religious expression linked to a clear cult
object, originating from that same massive subjective turn of modern culture
(cf. Heelas and Woodhead 2005: 129-130). For one specific, reflective group
of fans, singer/writer Morrison is therefore a person of transcendental significance who gives them meaning. For the E group, the in-crowd of Morrison
followers, his importance is determined largely by an 'all-significant philosophy of life,' as Söderholm has shown.[31]

Conclusion

This study examined the different fan cultures exhibited on and around Père Lachaise by visitors to Morrison's grave. It became apparent that although the different narratives constructed in past decades around the person of Jim Morrison and his grave may in general be shared, their meanings differ markedly.

There is no doubt that the fan cultures have constructed the grave into a special, sacred and performatively powerful place. Morrison is 'represented' there by a broad fan scene as an idol and role model. My next step was to examine the fans from a religious, transcendental perspective. I wanted to identify the extent to which the many references to pilgrimage, saint, and cult owed their existence to a religious or spiritual inspiration or motivation among certain visitors or whether these were purely metaphorical attributions of pilgrimage.

The processing of the fieldwork data clearly demonstrated that for part of the fan scene – the more individually and reflectively-inclined fans (group F) – a religious inspiration or dimension played a vital role in their visit and in their lives. As a result of his charisma, his performances and verbal and writing abilities, Morrison presented and created alternatives that differed in a socio-religious sense from those of mainstream society and Christianity. For these fans, he emerges as a source of spiritual inspiration in their personal lives, and acts as an intermediary between different spheres or domains, namely that of everyday life and the metaphysical. In visiting this place, these visitors are seeking salvation.

Therefore, notwithstanding the cultural interferences that cloud the picture somewhat through mediatization, Christian and other religious-ecclesiastical connotations and symbolism, this study highlights the fact that for a specific group of fans, Morrison functions as an independent cult object and as a more-or-less independent cult that is not part of a broader system of meaning. These fans regard his grave as a holy place. They clearly do in fact make a pilgrimage there, in part because of the site's supposed supportive and healing qualities.

The study shows that this last point does not apply to other groups of fans like the close-knit Morrison tribe (group E), let alone the touristically-inclined visitors. As a rule, they have little or no affinity with Morrison as a poet or thinker, or with any metaphysical qualities he might have, or his religious im-manence. For them, Morrison is first and foremost a rock idol, a performer and, in lifestyle terms, a role model. One thing is certain, all these different group perspectives have made Morrison's grave a contested space where po-pular culture, global tourism, neo-tribalism, individualism and religion en-counter one another.

Notes

1 All visitor quotes come from fieldwork carried out by the author at and around Morrison's grave on May 20-23, July 2-4 and December 8, 2004, and July 2-3, 2005, and from a separate question-naire sent out in 2005.

2 'Vor allem tat es mir weh für Jim Morrison selber. Für ihn waren Barrieren ja das Schlimmste was es gab. Die Dinge, die Jim immer hat verhüten wollen, sind dreißig Jahre nach seinem Tode doch Wirklichkeit geworden. Er ist schließlich dennoch eingesperrt.'

3 The most important books about his life and death are Hopkins and Sugerman 1980; Riordan and Prochnicky 1991; Densmore 1990; on his death, see also Van Alphen 1980: 70-73.

4 The grave is located in the sixth division of the cemetery; various publications pay attention to the grave, also visually. Jones 1990: 184-191; Campbell 2001 and 2004; Reed and Miller 2005: 34-37.

5 For example, in *The tenth life of Jim Morrison*, the Dutch writer Ineke Verheul describes Morrison as still living on. She attempts to place herself in the singer's thoughts and spirit and describes his adventures after his death.

6 An American journalist, Brett Meisner, claims to have proof of Morrison's death from a 'miraculous' photograph taken in 1997 on which the 'ghost' of Morrison appears next to the grave in Paris; cf. the video footage on www.brettmeisner.com/, last visited on December 3, 2007.

7 See http://archives.waiting-forthe-sun.net/Pages/Players/Professional/brodsky.html.

8 http://messageboard.thedoors.com/lofiversion/index.php/t27378-50.html (November 5 and 29, 2005, page last visited on October 24, 2006).

9 This plaque reads: 'James Douglas Morrison 1943 – 1971 Kata ton daimona eaytoy.' The Greek text means 'in accordance with his own spirit,' which can be interpreted as a reference to the ob-stinate way in which he led his own life. Even this text has spawned a host of weird and wonderful translations and interpretations about what happened to Morrison.

10 At least once a week, cemetery workers remove all materials thrown onto the grave; it is then taken away as litter.

11 This was not the first time. The grave was temporarily closed to the public during the second half of 1988; see Söderholm 1990: 303.

12 In 2001 more than one million visitors (the city published an official figure of 1.5 million); no formal counts are conducted, however.

13 Rainer Moddemann, Jim Morrison. Paris – Führer (www: Kreutzfeldt Electronic Publishing, 2003); an abridged version in English can be consulted on the Internet: The complete Paris Guide for Jim Morrison fans: http://www.geocities.com/SunsetStrip/Palladium/1409/jimparis.htm; see also: Rainer Moddeman, Jim Morrison's Quiet Days in Paris (1999).

14 Frijhoff has repeatedly made critical evaluations of his own model; he now recognizes the

importance of including the concept of 'heroes' in the analysis, either placing it alongside or substituting it for 'saints'; see Van Eijnatten 2007: 419-438.

15 See my contribution to the publication to mark Prof. Frijhoff's departure. Contributors were asked to submit articles based on Frijhoff's research model (Van Eijnatten 2007: 377-392).

16 For example, the word 'snake' that recurs in his lyrics is supposedly a metaphor for a consciousness-expanding journey, as an expression of 'subversive fantasy.' See Rodenberg 1983: 166-181.

17 This stratification is often not properly recognized. For example, in an interview in 1993, the well-informed Gilles Yepremian reduced visitors to mere tourists: 'Now the grave is like a tourist monument, not because of Jim but for curiosity. This image was refined by Fournier and Jiménez in 2004.

18 Fournier and Jiménez (2004) distinguish three other categories: *'admiradores,' 'seguidores'* and *'fanaticos.'*

19 In addition to conversations with visitors in general, I also observed the visitors and held interviews with fans (groups E and F), whom I identified on the basis of their behaviour and external appearance.

20 *'Demeurent pensifs, le plus souvent la tête dans les mains, un long, très long moment.'*

21 I do not agree with Thomas (2006: 21-22) who classifies Morrison's grave as a 'spontaneous shrine'; being a long existing formal grave and tomb, this is definitely not the case.

22 Both academics and artists frequently compare and describe pop music and religion in general. Of the latter group, Graham made a documentary in 1984 entitled Rock my Religion, in which he uses Jim Morrison, among others, to establish a broad connection between rock, religion, sex and capitalism. According to Graham, Morrison's shamanism is comparable to Pentacostal experiences and performances. For this documentary, see Elke Town (ed.) (1986), Video by Artists 2. Toronto: Art Metropole, pp. 81-111.

23 Schwarze applied Peter Sloterdijk's religious-philosophical principle of gnosis as an open interpretation model in order to identify the features of connecting forms of religious expression, (Schwarze 1997: 103-111).

24 *'Etwas oder etwas anderes geben kann, das die Kirche nicht geben kann.'*

25 *'Erkenntnis, dass der Sinnlosigkeit – als Fakt – des Lebens andere Wegen eröffnen kann.'*

26 *'Dann und wann erscheint mir an dieser Stelle sein Geist wieder und kann ich mit ihm kommunizieren.'*

27 Email of January 5, 2001, to the official Doors website (thedoors.com), showing photos by Michelle Campbell of the scene around the grave.

28 Rainer Moddemann (April 1993): Gilles Yepremian on the initial years after 1971, 'In the beginning you could always find joints and drugs on the grave.'

29 There are several larger private collections belonging to guides and frequent local visitors who for years have taken and kept letters and other objects.

30 From an email of May 5, 2004, to the official Doors website (thedoors.com).

31 Söderholm's study, in Finnish, is rarely cited because it is difficult to access, both physically and in terms of language.

Chapter 7

The Apostle of Love: The Cult of Jimmy Zámbó in Post-Socialist Hungary

István Povedák

It must be added at once that such a profane existence
is never found in the pure state.
To whatever degree he may have desacralized the world,
the man who has made his choice
in favor of a profane life never succeeds
in completely doing away with religious behavior.
(Mircea Eliade)

The present study deals with Jimmy Zámbó, a Hungarian pop singer who has sharply divided public opinion, triggering unreserved adoration or absolute rejection. Jimmy Zámbó died in the early morning of 2 January, 2001. After his tragic death, fans spontaneously flocked to his house. Thanks to the Hungarian commercial media, his death became the first mass mourning event in 21st-century Hungary. Fans continue to visit his grave. In order to understand Jimmy Zámbó's impact on people, it is necessary to outline socio-cultural developments since the 1989 regime change. After the collapse of the communist regime, the spread of Western mass culture had a far-reaching effect on Hungarian society. The cultural policy of the communist era – based on the strong selection and censorship of Western culture and all branches of culture (including pop music) – collapsed.[1] Post-communist Hungary was subsequently annexed by globalization. However, mass culture emerged there in forms that differ from Western ones. Although most Western cultural trends can indeed be found, remnants of the communist era are also present, leading to a great differentiation in public taste. The influx of new ideologies created an extensive ambivalence among the bearers of Hungarian popular culture. While younger generations accepted ideologies from the West, many of the new elements were rejected by older generations. One reason for this is not only the freeing-up of politics and culture but the transformation of the economy into a market economy, resulting in an ongoing downturn in the standard of living. That is why older generations show a certain nostalgia for the Kadarist 'soft dictatorship'[2] and for financial security. This phenomenon was further reinforced by typical social changes of modern mass culture: the atomization of society, changes in social networks, individualization, desacralization, moral crisis, etc.

This nostalgia created the figure of Jimmy Zámbó, who became the greatest 'sacralized' icon in modern Hungarian society. Hungarian popular culture can therefore be seen as a typical 'accumulated popular culture' similar to other post-communist countries, where the almost rootless Western trends exist side-by-side with vestiges of communist mass culture.

The Tale of Jimmy Zámbó

Jimmy Zámbó, originally Imre Zámbó (1958-2001), is one of the most successful and ambiguous figures in Hungarian pop history. His musical talent was recognized at an early age. He sang in the Hungarian Radio Children's Choir and later graduated from the Music Conservatory, specializing in jazz. He began his professional career in 1982 as a bar musician and left the country in 1986 for the United States. Like other emigrating musicians, his main motivation was the freedom, professional opportunities and better financial conditions in the West. He sang and played the piano in Los Angeles bars, performing jazz and blues songs. American audiences started calling him 'Jimmy' because they couldn't pronounce 'Imi,' Zámbó's nickname. He decided to return to Hungary in 1988, and that year he won the Interpop music festival. In 1990, he gained immediate fame when he sang on the album *Movie Hits in Hungarian.'* After that, he released new records each year (a total of 13 during his lifetime), all of which went multiple platinum. Sales figures show him to be the most successful Hungarian performer of the 1990s. The key to his success is complicated. On the one hand, Jimmy Zámbó built on international pop icons such as Elvis Presley and Demis Roussos. He used elements of their image: appearance, costume – such as Elvis's white scarf – and romantic songs. On the other hand, he returned to the romantic style of Hungarian pop singers of the 1980s like Pál Szécsi (who died in 1974 at the age of 30) and Péter Máté (who died in 1984 aged 37).

In addition to the social changes mentioned, Zámbó's success can be attributed in musical terms to his four-and-a-half-octave range and to his deeply romantic repertoire, regarded as 'kitsch' by many Hungarians. His success was achieved despite the fact that commercial radio stations and music TV networks barely broadcast his songs. He was called 'King,' a reference to international popular music icons Elvis Presley ('The King') and Michael Jackson ('King of Pop'). It therefore came as a shock when Zámbó died unexpectedly in the early morning of 2 January, 2001, at the peak of his career. According to police reports, he died at a New Year's after-party when, pointing a gun to his head, he accidentally shot himself. His fans, however, talk in terms of 'murder' and 'mysteries.' Already bestsellers, his albums sold at an even greater rate after his death. Several biographies were published, and hotels, pubs and even musical awards were named after the dead artist.[3] Despite all this acknowledgement, perceptions of Jimmy vary considerably. In addition to the great number of Jimmy fans, there is still a small sector of Hungarian society that rejects his persona and the style of music he represents.[4] It is therefore worth investigating Jimmy Zámbó's life from an ethnological perspective and seeing how he was brought into Hungarian popular culture. Somewhat simplified versions of significant elements in the singer's life appeared in the Hungarian tabloids, with certain parts emphasized and other insignificant or embarrassing elements left out, resulting in a life that resembled that of folktale heroes. The themes became part of Hungarian culture, and fans started making and circulating their own versions. An analysis of the media reveals the following main stages in Zámbó's life:[5]

1. *The youngest son*: he was the youngest son of a big family.

2. *Exceptional talent, the element of destination*: his musical talent was recognized at an early age. He both sang and played different musical instruments, such as the piano, drums, guitar, and flute.

3. *Poverty*: his father died early, so he grew up in poor, but loving, circumstances.

4. *Wandering, the element of loneliness:* he began singing, but unable to find a helping hand, he emigrated to the United States.

5. *Returning home*: some years later he returned home, won a pop festival and achieved nationwide fame.

6. *Rejection and success*: his achievements came in spite of rejection by a significant proportion of the musical elite. Even commercial radio stations did not play his songs. However, he released one album after another, which became bestsellers; his popularity broke all records.

7. *Example of an honest father:* despite his pop-music career, he was a decent, caring father to his three children.

8. *Sudden, mysterious death*: he died unexpectedly and under suspicious circumstances, at the peak of his career. His death ended his family idyll, and conflicts emerged, but it also triggered a new idyll among his fans, who 'sanctified' him.

These stereotypical plot elements of his life story draw attention to Eric Hobsbawm's argument about the similarities in outlaw myths and their artistic representation at different times and in different nations (Hobsbawm 1985: 2). He claims that there are two basic reasons for these similarities: (a) the similarities of ethnic-regional relations and historic situations, and (b) the uniformity of traditional community expectations about the 'hero' role, hence the similar behavior of heroes. Hobsbawm's statements can be applied not just to outlaw heroes but to all hero types. Heroes have lived, live and will live forever; heroes can be rulers, political leaders, outlaws, or in this case, performers like Jimmy Zámbó.[6] However, the problems of a given historical period can only be solved by a person from that period who is gifted with special talents. All historical ages therefore have their own heroes who were brought to life by a characteristic void (Barna 2003: 109).[7]

It is important to point out that the really popular celebrities in modern societies tend to be those who have some kind of connection with the lives and social situations of their fans. That is how they can become role models who embody the ideal life in the eyes of their fans. This is especially true of Zámbó. Hankiss states: 'Whatever people lack in everyday life is condensed into them: richness, power, beauty, talent and a life of great importance filled with heavenly harmony, ecstasy and flutter. The fullness of life. Finally the triumph of life over death' (Hankiss 2002: 105). This desired life cannot break away entirely from the roots and social sphere from which it originates; they must remain the sons and daughters of ordinary people, as articulated by informants visiting Zámbó's grave. A 43-year-old Hungarian woman said: 'He was very informal... others didn't come to see the people after concerts but Jimmy was not stuck up because he was a singer. Those who struck it rich only say it, but in fact, they don't give a damn about us. But Jimmy, he didn't change. He was humble and never misused his fame... He helped in whatever he could. He helped the poor.' A 70-year-old woman added: 'I never go to funerals, but Jimmy is different. He was one of us and he sang his music for us. And I really regret that I didn't come out last night to the church, but you know because of my age...'[8]

Jimmy Zámbó did not break away from his social group in a mental and emotional sense. He remained 'one of them.' His songs communicate this message to his fans, filling a space in their everyday life and comforting them when they have problems. The lyrics are about love that has passed, about infidelity, about the dissolute man regretting his mistakes. For example, he wrote the song 'Love me the way I am' for the album *Jimmy II* (1992):

The words still hurt, I wasn't good
And I'm still imperfect, there are crazy days and moments.
But love me even if I'm bad,
It will all return to you,
Love me the way you love a child.
'cause I'm a child.
Love me even when I'm bad,
There are crazy moments,
Love me the way I'm
Here with you!

In 1995 the album *Love me so that I love you* came out. It contained the song 'A good woman forgives me,' with the lyrics:

The night was long, the company was great.
I went home late and I didn't take care of you.
Oh, shame on me, oh...
A good woman forgives me,
Forgives me all the time, forgives me again.
A good woman forgives me
And darling, you are good with me.
It has always been this way,
I won't ever change.
Every night is so long,
I repeat my promises.
Oh, shame on me, oh...

Three years later, in 1998, the song 'We could live happily' on the album *Adopt me!* expressed the following feelings:

I lost all the words,
But I hear it again.
Believe me, we will find it again.
All the lost words, we will find again.
We could live happily,
We could, I feel.
We could live for our dreams,
Because there is always hope.

Those listening to Zambó's songs often relate these words and feelings to their own lives, with some perceiving it as though their partner is speaking to them. Two Hungarian women, interviewed at his grave in early 2001, said: 'You could learn love from him, in his songs he always expressed love' (aged 43); and 'He was singing of our feelings, of our thoughts and dreams, but he could express them in a beautiful way' (aged 48). A young woman (aged 27) stated: 'The fact that he won't write more songs hurts the most. No more concerts, no more lyrics which we can't express with our own words.' Zámbó reached out to all ages, as we see from the words of an elderly lady of seventy: 'He didn't just preach about love, it came from his heart...' 'When he had something to say it came from his soul and heart' (aged 40) and 'I feel that with his songs someone is standing by me and he is helping me with his thoughts...' (aged 52).

On the basis of his lyrics and what his fans say, it appears that Jimmy Zámbó could be called an 'Apostle of Love.' His fans feel that he mediates the message of love to the listeners in our alienated world and that he is able to comfort and help people with his songs.

Jimmy Zámbó became the hero of those Hungarians who were not the 'winners' in the regime change. It was mainly manual workers and the less well-educated – that is, the working class in the former communist regime – who had

The grave of Jimmy Zámbó, 2006.
Photo: I. Povedák.

placed him in a sacred sphere even when he was still alive. Barely able to make a living working eight hours a day, this social group is forced to take on additional part-time jobs. As they spend more hours working, they have less time for their families, and in many cases, their leisure activities and entertainment are confined to watching TV. One of the main reasons why Jimmy became an idol for them is that his songs embody their feelings and spiritual needs and therefore compensate for deficiencies in their lives. He fills the emptiness created by their inability to satisfy a certain part of their own personality or desire. The fans project themselves at the performer within the framework of a compensatory rite.[9]

Life and Death in the Tabloids

The death of Jimmy Zámbó was followed by media hysteria in Hungary. The singer's death was the lead story in the tabloids and the focus of attention on the commercial television networks. The media competed with one another, broadcasting constant updates and speculations regarding his death. The media had two key functions here. Firstly, as the main source of information, it helped in the creation of legends about the life and death of a star.[10] Secondly, with its continuous reports on the mass of mourners, it also contributed to the events themselves.[11] Thus, the media played an active role in generating the cult. Of course, I am not claiming that the mass mourning would not have happened without the contribution of the press, but the media had a generating and reinforcing role in constructing a cult around Jimmy. The media in this case can be regarded as a mediator through which the processes among the fans are given publicity and therefore strengthen the similar feelings of others. In fact, the media events after the death of Jimmy Zámbó serve as an illustration of how the events broadcast by the mass media became 'folklorized.' This means that these events are not only integrated into the memory of popular culture (that has become part of public discourse for a short period of time), but they survive for a longer period, not in a single form but in variants, and they continue to exist in accordance with the processes of folklore, as outlined by Linda Dégh:

To be sure, television might force the tale into obsolescence, without being a satisfactory substitute for it, unless the television borrows from the tale, relies on it, or places its new propositions under the protection of ancient tale conventions. Approximations, however, amount not to substitution but rather to expansion, which is a mere technicality, not affecting the deep substances of Märchen [...] it might sound strange to those early theorists of folklore, but television is the main dispenser of certain forms of folklore, including the tale. (Dégh 1994: 35–36)

And:

Thus the 'interference' of mass media vehicles not only accelerates the folklore process but also contributes to a numerical growth, indeed a never-before-experienced inflation of folklore [...] our generation is witnessing the return of folklore on the wings of the media, with more vigorous circulation, gaining more significance than ever, emerging as a crucial response to the vicissitudes of life in the modern age. (Dégh 1994: 24)

Thus, the investigation of the Hungarian mass media has revealed another interesting phenomenon that sheds light on the present materialistic culture: although Jimmy became popular independent of the mainstream mass media, mass media became the key maintainer and beneficiary of Jimmy's memory after his death.[12]

'Secular' Pilgrimage

After the death of Jimmy Zámbó, unprecedented spontaneous public events and rituals took place in post-socialist Hungary. I use the term 'secular' pilgrimage to distinguish these events from the pilgrimages of traditional religions. Although the two terms are closely related, I believe it is important to distinguish them.

I wish to demonstrate in this section that Zámbó's grave became sacred for the fans because it differs from everyday time and space. Religious motivation is also present since the cult of the dead celebrity functions as a religion for the fans. An important difference is the fact that the revered person was part of the profane world. This means that during his lifetime Zámbó did not hold any religious positions; we don't even know whether or not he was religious at all. In any event, he became sacred in the eyes of his fans. This was made possible through secularization processes, by the fact that traditional religions and traditional religiosity became less important in people's day-to-day lives. However, I feel that new phenomena appear alongside traditional religions, functioning as religions but not considered formal religions. The fact that Jimmy Zámbó became a sacred person also indicates that secularization is accompanied by a desecularization of the profane world.

Zámbó's death sparked three weeks of spontaneous visits to the singer's home in the Budapest district of Csepel. Already on the night of the tragedy, hundreds brought flowers, candles and soft toys. In this case we can see a communal manifestation of the expression of grief. Fans and admirers of Zámbó said

Jimmy Zámbó. Collection I. Povedák.

prayers for his salvation in accordance with their own faith, silently paying tribute to the singer's memory. In the past decades we have been witness to similar rituals when celebrities die and a form of pilgrimage evolves in direct connection with the celebrity or the tragedy (e.g. the celebrity's home, the scene of the tragedy, the hospital). An 'internet pilgrimage' began in parallel with these rituals. A huge number of topics dealing with the singer appeared on popular internet chat rooms. We can distinguish the following thematic groups: 1) expressing condolences and regret, 2) appreciating the singer's achievements and qualities, 3) writing about the mysteries and puzzling circumstances, 4) requesting the purity of public grief, and 5) rejecting the materialistic approach of the commercial channels.

The day of the funeral was a clear indication of Jimmy Zámbó's enormous importance for the Hungarian people. A huge crowd gathered that day.[13] The Csepel cemetery, where the singer's grave is situated, became the focal point of what we shall term a pilgrimage. It is four kilometers from Zámbó's house and is surrounded by blocks of flats. Right from the start, details of the funeral and the design of the grave were made public. Jimmy Zámbó was laid out in the Greek Catholic church in Csepel. On the day and night before the funeral, crowds of fans queued for many hours waiting to be admitted. Two hours before the funeral, a huge crowd gathered in front of the church. Fans were able to watch the funeral on a giant screen. The funeral procession of about 40,000 began to pour into the cemetery. Throughout, fans sang Jimmy's most popular songs.

Another potential place of pilgrimage was opened the same day: the Jimmy Zámbó memorial exhibition which had previously been housed in Csepel's largest shopping mall. It contains personal objects which belonged to him, such as his microphone, outfits, school reports, etc. At the same time, a modern cult of memorial objects was created with the aid of the mass media. Anything relating to the dead celebrity suddenly increased in value, and the quest for relics and memorial objects began. This is best illustrated by the sales figures for books and records. Zámbó broke the Guinness World Record when his albums held the top 13 places in the Top 15 chart of the Association of Hungarian Record Publishers (MAHASZ). News captions show how the most dedicated fans were willing to pay vast sums for an object: 'A fan offering his two-room flat for a book signed by the king,'[14] 'Jimmy's guitar with his signature is for sale,' 'Offering to Buy the Singer's Jimmy-1 Mercedes' and 'The last signature of the king is deposited in a safe ... my wife considers the signature as well as the pen a relic.'[15] Further evidence of the relic cult is the theft of the singer's gravestone from the cemetery in Csepel a few days after it had been erected. The function of relics here is similar to that in traditional religions. With the help of such objects, fans hope to bring about the eternal presence of the celebrity, to make him an integral part of their lives and to reduce the distance between themselves and their beloved idols.

The Zámbó Jimmy Pub on Köztársaság Square 4, which opened three months after Zámbó's death, attracted huge numbers of visitors; it has since become a favorite haunt of the singer's fans. The owner – one of Zámbó's brothers – began adapting the pub shortly after Zámbó died. The place can be understood as a partial realization of the above-mentioned compensatory rite, in which fans project their desires and their shortcomings onto the celebrity; we see the opposite in this case, however. The pub is furnished in accordance with Jimmy's taste. We find his photos on the wall and some personal belongings. The pub serves only his favorite meals and drinks, and plays only his music. It is a place of remembrance in which to cherish Jimmy's memory and as such plays an identification role. For a short time, the fans are able to identify with the celebrity whom they regard as the ideal. What we observe is an analogy of those who follow Christ's life and example, e.g. Christians re living Christ's sufferings during Easter rituals at Golgotha in Jerusalem or in the bloody crucifixions in the Philippines. This phenomenon highlights the fact that it is appropriate to talk about 'secular' religion in this case. Here we see an analogy for identification in a profane, secular and highly simplified form. One of the reasons for this simplification is that although secular rituals in today's secular world employ traditional religious practices, they have to satisfy the requirements of our times. The phenomenon has its roots, however, in what Eliade had to say about sacred time and religious festivals (Eliade 1959: 68-73). A significant element of such festivals is in fact primordial mythical time, which is made present. The symbolic identification with Jimmy enables the fans to experience a sphere where the dead celebrity is once again omni-present; the fans themselves therefore become part of 'eternity' in a sense.

Pilgrimage Motives

First we have to differentiate between the thousands who flocked to Jimmy Zámbó's funeral and the visits and pilgrimages that have been made since the funeral. We can point not only to differences in the number of participants, but to variations in underlying motivation and behavior at the grave. However, the two types of visits are similar in that both can be understood as classical rites of passage, and we observe in both a break away from everyday life. Desperate people experience a different time and spiritual sphere in which space, time, and physical tiredness disappear. Like the traditional pilgrimage, the continui-ty of these dimensions ends when the fans reach the sacred place because this territory is detached from the surrounding cosmic milieu – implying hiero-phany – and is therefore qualitatively different (Eliade 1959: 26).

The determined, fanatical fans did not mind the bitter cold and discomfort during Zámbó's funeral. They came from all over Hungary and from neighbo-ring countries and were forced to spend the night in shopping malls, under the stars or, like fans from Transylvania, at the railway station.[16] A 30-year-old informant from Serbia had this to say:

We don't mind spending the whole day on this. We respect his lyrics, his mu-sic and his four-and-a-half-octave range. We respect and honor him, so we arrived yesterday, I don't know exactly when, and sometime tomorrow we will arrive home. Jimmy is a legend, a king and the king is dead, he isn't here. Damn it! No, boys and girls, he isn't here. I came 1,000 kilometers to light two beautiful candles, four, six, eight, I don't know how many, flowers and the church. Now we will accompany him to the funeral. Some old lady said we have to walk four-and-a-half kilometers or even five. I would go fifteen or a hundred and fifty to see him off. Now we're going to the church. That's what they said. We came now today for the last time, we will go to the church and see him off for the last time and then return to our home country.[17]

A middle-aged woman recounted similar experiences of not feeling tired. She made three visits to the King's coffin on the bier even though she had to wait for hours in the cold each time. After reaching the goal of the pilgrimage, the fans arrive at such a 'clear region' which is above the profane world, beyond profane feelings such as tiredness or pain.

As mentioned above, the huge attendance on the day of the funeral is a reflection of grief and reverence. People came to the funeral grieving for their beloved hero. It is important here to highlight the fact that fans treated Zámbó like a close relative although they did not know him personally, thus supporting my opinion on how the media transforms our social networks. It is well known from mass communication research that people enter into a fictive communication with television programs (and to a lesser degree with radio programs). With the help of fantasy, a television program appears like a real, interactive situation and real communication. Fans often confess experiences like the following from a 48-year-old woman: 'Every time I listen to his music I feel that he is speaking to me, he is singing to me and he wants to tell me something.'[18]

There seems to be little or no distance between the celebrity and his fans. They are emotionally involved, even though the relationship is one-sided since there is no feedback from the adored celebrity. To sum up, there is a parasocial relationship for fans, meaning that all relationships between the fans and their object of interest are through the media instead of through face-to-face interaction. Consequently, television can trigger real feelings such as affection, love, or fear. This is why fans grieve over the celebrity's death, even though most had no direct connection with him or her (Chris 2001; Samantha 2001).

Informants had often decorated a corner of their room with the singer's pictures and posters, thereby turning the place in a sacred space, like private, traditional Christian shrines or house sanctuaries. The Zámbó version functions as a place in which to cherish the celebrity's memory and at the same time as a place of prayer. Here I should point out that in several cases the participants in 'secular' pilgrimages, Zámbó's fans, were already religious in terms of traditional religion. The religious dimensions of the cult of Zámbó do not therefore exclude the practising of traditional religion; the two exist side-by-side. The use of traditional religious rituals in celebrity cults is most striking in the case of fans with a religious affiliation. A 30-year-old man from Serbia says: 'I am not a man of words. I come from Yugoslavia and by now it is easier for me to express myself in Serbian... I prayed the Our Father and the Hail Mary because the Our Father is the Our Father, and the Hail Mary is The Hail Mary in Yugoslavia, in Hungary or Romania. I prayed I don't know how many prayers to myself...'[19] A 52-year-old woman clearly described in an interview the interference between the different religious domains:

> Jimmy remains unique, special and perfect till the end of time! Ever since I heard about his death I can't get over it. I can't believe he left us ... I always pray to him, in the morning, at noon and in the evening ... At home I sit down in front of his poster, I light a candle and I pray. I pray to him, for him and I know he hears me, I know ... I can't be wrong. I know that he is in Heaven waiting for me.[20]

This bricolage of traditional religion and new religious forms and the relationship between them are evident in the words of fans who give the singer unambiguous religious attributes.[21] The huge number of poems written by fans also contain elements taken from Christianity, such as heaven, angels, a singer becoming a saint, a choir of angels, Jesus, Lord, Satan, etc. A woman named Betty wrote:

> You arrive in Heaven on your birthday
> And the choir of Angels sings only to You.
> You enter the gate into the glorious light,
> I hope You'll be happy in Heaven.
> The Lord protects You,
> I keep You in my heart and my soul
> As long as I live.

Another woman, named Zsuzsanna, composed the following lines:

Six years have passed since a dream is over,

On the wing of Angels the light and happiness disappeared.

God came for our dearest treasure

And took him away,

Our light and his life.

No one can replace his wonderful being

While he is teaching the Angels to sing.

He makes Heaven even more wonderful with this.

To understand the religious dimension of these poems, we have to take a closer look at the current processes of secularization and desecularization. As part of this, traditional forms of religion – in this case Christianity – are pushed into the background. However, this secularization process does not lead to a society without religion and to the decay of religion because new forms continuously appear to take their place – not necessarily of a supernatural nature or relating to any traditional denominations. Therefore, secularization weakens traditional denominations, resulting in a society with a low church-attendance rate but not without religion. Religious compensation or desecularization is found in society through new cultic forms, as in the case of Jimmy Zámbó.

In this regard, we should emphasize another phenomenon that is related in a broader sense to characteristics of the cult of celebrities. We observe that informants frequently draw comparisons between the death of Jimmy Zámbó and that of other canonized celebrities in Western mass culture. This is also manifested in the fact that even during his lifetime, from 1992 onwards, a crown appeared next to his name, symbolizing his place as the 'King of [Hungarian] Pop.' A young woman (23) explains: 'He was our king, the king of the Hungarians. Other people have Elvis, but he is our king, the Hungarians.' [22] The name 'king' refers not only to Elvis Presley or Michael Jackson but in its female form also to Lady Diana, the Queen of Hearts. Zámbó is perceived as the successor to these celebrities and has therefore gained some of their fans as well. Since the second half of the 1990s, fans have also referred to Zámbó as the 'King of Hearts.'

Since Jimmy Zámbó's death, fans have continuously visited his grave. There are always fresh flowers, drawings or stuffed plush animals on the grave. The number of visitors is larger on special occasions such as his name-day, his birthday, the anniversary of his death, Easter, Christmas or All Saints' Day. The grave then becomes a meeting point of collective and individual memories, where fans who do not know each other can enter into spontaneous communication. The community that suffers from the absence of their lost idol assembles on the holidays of the dead celebrity as a response to that absence. Collective mourning stirs up social feelings, which inspire individuals to search for closeness with one another. As a consequence, spontaneous communication develops. As this phenomenon is constantly taking place, it is not possible to collect the entire content of such communication. For this reason, I will provide only an outline of the patterns. The following thematic elements were heard:

A. Entering into communication, collective remembrance
This usually involves communication about the painful absence of the singer and the appreciation of his human greatness. A 64-year-old Hungarian woman said in 2006: 'We have lost an irreplaceable voice. Hungarian people cannot conceive how talented he was. Since his death I have watched singers and I think to myself: Is this a voice? What's this voice compared to Jimmy's? And then I turn my CD player on and it is completely different. Jimmy had such a voice that he could have even become a ... Pavarotti as well. I mean if he had started doing opera instead of pop. He had such an amazing voice, like nobody else! Not even Louis Armstrong!'[23]

Fans who do not know one another at the beginning of the communication process can only be sure that they love Jimmy's music and that they miss him.

B. Communication about the mysteries surrounding his death
In 2002 a woman of 59 said angrily: 'This was murder! I'm sure Jimmy did not commit suicide! The underworld is involved in this case because there was big money involved!'[24] A somewhat younger woman agreed, adding: 'His

eldest son had something to do with the murder, that's certain! He's still in prison.'[25]

Although police reports rule out the possibility of murder, fans have tried to maintain a sense of mystery since a hero cannot die so 'simply.' Treason or intrigue of some kind always lies behind a hero's death. This is true in the case of both legendary heroes and heroes of our own age. It is especially true in Jimmy's case. He died in almost grotesque circumstances: 'A great man like him can't die in such a silly way!'

Besides murder, the most common media version of the cause of Jimmy's death was that he was drunk and had been shooting at the neighbors' rooster because its crowing annoyed him. When Zámbó's wife tried to silence Jimmy, he put the gun to his head to show that he wouldn't shoot any more, and the gun went off.

C. Feelings about the dead celebrity

Asked about her feelings, a 22-year-old woman responded: 'Once I asked him for an autograph after his concert, he gave me one and we shook hands. My gosh! That was like God's touch on my hand! I look on him almost as a god!'[26] Another female visitor (28) gave the following answer: 'I listen to his music if we have some kind of problem. Then I definitely put his cassette into my car radio or I listen to him at home and I sit down and calm down and then I'm totally relieved. So his music is absolutely calming.'[27]

Personal meetings or connections with the celebrity give fans a special status. As we could see in the relic cult, everything directly related to the dead celebrity acquires special value and prestige. Indirect connections such as feeling an affinity of soul through listening to his music are less significant.

D. Transcendent connection with the celebrity

A woman of 44 said: 'If you knew how many times I dreamed about him! Oh my God! How many times he appeared in my dreams (…) And they were always peaceful, calm and beautiful dreams. On those occasions I woke up very calm.'[28] A woman of 38 had this to say: 'Jimmy Zámbó appeared to me as well. There was one time when he simply appeared and this time I felt as if he was telling me "Don't worry, be calm" or "Do this or do that now". It has happened several times.'[29] The dead celebrity appears to the chosen fans, sends a message to them, and they remain in touch after death as well.[30]

In this context it is important to mention the people who emphasize the hierophany of the place itself. A woman of 39 reported: 'I believe in the immortality of the soul and I was in connection with Jimmy from the first moment after his death. Jimmy stays with us forever, he is always here with us... whenever I can come here, although I don't live nearby, I live in Budaörs but I come to visit him. Sometimes I come every week because it fills my heart and my soul and gives me strength to fight my everyday problems. In a way, I feel relieved here and I can feel the peace and love which is upon me. Jimmy is here with me, I feel it.'[31] A woman of about the same age (41) claims: 'This place is wonderful. The grave is beautiful. Unbelievable, six years without Jimmy! For me he is forever new and I can never get bored with him. I listen to his music every day, his songs give me strength (...) He was my everything, he was almost like a god for me! I really miss him, but here we can reunite. I feel his love, which always shone from him. I always get something from him. Some love, some strength and encouragement. We have a spiritual encounter. When I go home I'm always refreshed.'[32]

For these fans the cemetery functions as a place of pilgrimage in a religious way. The motivation for their pilgrimage is not only remembrance, paying tribute to the singer's memory, or public confession of faith; it is also religious – they are seeking transcendent help.

E. Suicides at the grave

After the death of Jimmy Zámbó, some of his fans followed him to their own death.[33] One was a middle-aged man who went to the singer's grave to commit suicide. According to the police, he had said before he died that he wanted to die at Jimmy's grave because he had been a great fan of the singer.[34]

Pilgrims at the Sacred Place

Besides the pilgrim's personal motivation, it is worth examining the instruments of mourning, especially those that fans brought to the funeral or later on pilgrimages to the grave. I can perhaps venture to state that in this case the usual instruments like night-lights, candles and flowers[35] are not the most important ones for our purposes because they belong to the traditional accessories of cemetery visits. Similarly, this is not the first occasion that we observe a large number of stuffed toy animals (cf. Bowman 2001). It is particularly important to examine three points. Firstly, several Hungarian national flags were flying in the crowd, which is not at all typical of a pop singer's funeral. This phenomenon can be explained by the presence of diasporic Hungarians from neighbouring countries of the former Hungarian empire. For them, Jimmy Zámbó was not simply a pop singer; he was also a singer for Hungarians and therefore a special instrument for creating and maintaining Hungarian identity. A 30-year-old man stated in this regard:

Visitors to Jimmy Zámbó's grave monument, 2006.
Photo: I. Povedák.

We, Hungarians, are oppressed people in Romania and Serbia as well. And there was this guy who... who sang for us, for us, Hungarians. Jimmy is the same everywhere. Somehow Jimmy slipped into everybody's heart and even 170 kilometers beyond his heart. Jimmy sang to us sincerely from his soul with all his heart, to us, to all Hungarians around the world, from Austria to Canada, from Australia to Zimbabwe... Let everybody, every son be damned who says anything against him. Let them be damned! Because he was ours, I don't know well I don't know how to say, our Hungarian, yes, Hungarian king, or boy or I don't know, our singer.[36]

Another man (57) expressed similar feelings:

He was our king, the king of Hungarians. Every other nation has similar ones like Elvis, but he was the king for Hungarians. The king is the king... He connects the Hungarian people with his music and with his love. And his songs are still topical: we have to love each other. It is as if he saw what would happen here in Hungary![37]

These identity issues are especially important for Hungarians because since the signing of the Treaty of Trianon (June 4, 1920) that marked the end of the Austro-Hungarian empire, more than three million Hungarians are living as a minority group in Romania, Slovakia and Serbia. Poets, actors and scientists are leading the fight to protect and retain Hungarian national identity, but today, in the age of mass culture, their influence cannot compare with that of a media personality. Through his music, Jimmy Zámbó could reach all Hungarian households abroad, and as a Hungarian he acquired an important status in people's minds. He was more than just a celebrity; he was a Hungarian from a poor family whose life served as an example to fans, demonstrating that there is always hope for a 'better life' even if this 'better life' is manifested in emotional rather than financial terms.

Secondly, it is worth mentioning that there were several fans at the funeral who brought a poster or photo of the singer with them. The clothes worn by the fans, which resembled teenage fashion in the mid-eighties, seem anachronistic[38]. Also, the vast number of posters at the funeral may seem meaningless because the fans could not ask for them to be signed. The use of such cultural signals indicates the outer representation of identity and belonging to a reference group even though belonging to the singer's fan group is clearly evident in their taking part in his funeral ceremony.

We gain a fuller understanding of this phenomenon if we look at the religious aspects. From this perspective, the posters represent the community's idol and show their religious adoration of him. At the same time, they symbolize the community and hence their identity.

Lastly, we should emphasize the devotional objects referring to the singer as 'king.' Gilded mini-crowns were sold in the shops and florists nearby. In addition, there were stories in the media about a family that made a huge crown gilded with 24-carat gold and decorated with 16 turquoise stones and bohemian rubies, the stones of Jimmy Zámbó's horoscope.

Another phenomenon is worth mentioning at this point. Florists who tried to profit from the event along the route of the funeral procession were violently attacked by pall-bearers and removed. This indicates that as early as the funeral, fans perceived the ritual and the place as sacred. In a way, they were also rejecting consumer culture.[39] We can see that this phenomenon is a taboo akin to those found in traditional religions: the sacred time and place are associated with prohibitions and taboos.

Conclusion

Finally, we can address the question of the nature of the whole phenomenon. 'Secular' pilgrimage can be seen as a variant of traditional pilgrimage, evolving in a similar fashion, albeit in changed circumstances, and with similar content and objectives. However, it is not clear to what extent this phenomenon emerged as a result of the secularization process, as a sign of weakening traditional religions – especially Christianity – or its opposite, a process of desecularization. As I have mentioned above in connection with secularization, the eradication and weakening of traditional religions cannot be questioned from a social point of view. However, I do not suppose that this process would lead to a decline in religions and to a desacralized society. As Eliade says: 'In other words, profane man cannot help preserving some vestiges of the behavior of religious man, though they are emptied of religious meaning. Do what he will, he is an inheritor. He cannot utterly abolish his past, since he is himself the product of his past' (Eliade 1959: 204-209).

Humans carry the need for transcendency since it is part of human exis-tence (Eliade 1959: 204-209). However, transcendency has different forms in different historical ages and cultures. In consumer society, people, phenome-na or objects are sometimes understood as transcendent. Celebrities (not only musicians of course) can acquire sacred characteristics, people create cults around their physical and mental health, or as post-modern nationalists, they create a religion based on a national history (civil religion theory), etc. Secu-larization and desecularization are therefore closely related. In a secularized society, we find the resacralization of the world, as a result of which sacred values appear with the same function but different content.

The situation is similar for basic human feelings which we cannot elimi-nate. When we lose somebody – not necessarily a personal acquaintance – we grieve and try to extinguish this grief by visiting his or her memorial in order to 'meet' the lost person once again. In Jimmy Zámbó's case, we can also trace the desecularization process. Jimmy was 'sanctified' even though he was not very close to any traditional religions during his lifetime, which meant he be-longed to the profane world. His fans endowed Jimmy with sacred attributes, partly when he was alive and even more so after his death. Zámbó's fans believe that he went to heaven after his death. However, he is still 'present' in a transcendent form among his fans, who continue to visit his grave. The fans say that Jimmy knows when they are praying to him, and he listens to the poems addressed to him, which they often bring to his grave.

I wish to emphasize that Jimmy Zámbó has a stronger manifestation for the profane world in particular places. But his grave is the most significant place that his fans continue to visit and make pilgrimages to. The fans experi-ence hierophany, whereby the celebrity is present and the fans once again relive the idyll that ended with Jimmy's death. The fans search for relief when visiting the grave and experience an outpouring of love. They feel that the dead celebrity helps them and gives them the strength to solve their problems. The motivation, the sacred place, the manifestation of the 'saint,' all these elements underline the fact that the cult of a celebrity can function as a religion.

Notes

1 György Aczél, the communist Kádár regime's expert on cultural policy, coined the '3Ts' after the three Hungarian words *támogatás* (support), *tűrés* (toleration) and *tiltás* (prohibition). Artists were also classified into these categories. The prohibited ones were spied on, continuously harassed and in some cases imprisoned. At the end of the 1970s, violation of freedom of speech resulted in the appearance of 'anticultural celebrities' – those singers and bands who criticized the communist regime.

2 János Kádár's communist regime took over power after the 1956 revolution with the help of the Soviet Red Army. Between 1957 and 1989 Kádár established the 'soft' dictatorship by giving more 'freedom' to citizens than in other communist countries.

3 See for example the following biographies: László Bodonyi (2000), *Zámbó Jimmy nem csak dalban mondja el. Fejezetek a Király életből* [Meet the Real Jimmy Zámbó. Chapters from the King's life] Budapest: EPS Trade Kft; László B. Molnár and Jószef László (2001), *A Király szívünkben él* [The King still lives in our heart] Budapest: Hungalibri; Mari Háfra, (2001), *Szerelem a királyság előtt. Zámbó Jimmy menyasszonya voltam* [Love before the Kingdom. I was Jimmy's Fiancée] Budapest: Totem Plusz; Krisztián Tari (2001), *Zámbó Jimmy testőre voltam* [I was Jimmy's Bodyguard] Budapest: Százszorszép; László B. Molnár (2001), *Zámbó testvérek. Az összetört szívek* [Zámbó brothers. The broken hearts] Budapest: Hungalibri; Imréné Vágó (2001), *A negyedik lövés. A király halálának igaz története* [The 4th shot. The real story of the King's death] Gyöngyös: W. Stoker cop.; Krisztián Zámbó (2001), *Vallomás édesapámról* [Confession about my father] Budapest: Budapest Print; László Dalia (2002), *A dal ugyanaz marad* [The song remains the same] Budapest: Media Nox.

4 I compiled the outline of his life story on the basis of the following web sites: www.warnermusic.hu and http://zambojimmyfan.gportal.hu.

5 For the media analysis, I used the following Hungarian printed media: *Blikk, Mai Nap, Színes Mai Nap, Story, Kiskegyed, Nők Lapja.*

6 In Hungarian history such heroes include: King Matthias Hunyadi the Just (ruled 1458-1490), who disguised himself and reprimanded those nobles who shamelessly exploited the peasantry; Louis Kossuth, a leading figure in the 1848-9 War of Independence, who lived in exile and died there in 1894, but who is said to have been sighted in several places at the beginning of the 20th century; Sándor Rózsa, an outlaw from the second half of the 19th century. These are the most outstanding heroes in each category.

7 Barna: 'People need stability; they search for it, and culture can provide stability for them in a certain way. Humans created more institutions of life and culture in order to compensate for their losses. Compensation is not a reaction to the process of modernization but it gives way to it and therefore makes its destructive aspects bearable.'

8 Both women were interviewed on January 20, 2001, at the cemetery in Csepel.

9 Jimmy Zámbó differs from popular Western celebrities such as Elvis Presley or Jim Morrison. They were also sex symbols whose attractive appearance played a key role in the process of cult formation. Nevertheless, most of Jimmy's fans consider him handsome or at least of average attractiveness. This is known as the 'halo effect,' whereby someone's positive characteristic (Jim-

my's voice) is projected onto other characteristics (appearance); see Forgas 1985.

10 Adopting the fans' view, the media did not accept the official report of the police investigation into the star's death. The headlines covered the mysteries and shortcomings in the work of the police. 'The Sceptical Fans. Mysteries about Jimmy's Death,' *Blikk* January 17, 2001. 'No-one investigates the real causes,' *Blikk* January 15, 2001. For months, the newspaper ran the headline 'You know something? Call the Blikk!'

11 'The general public can also visit the pub, which is very likely to become a place of pilgrimage,' *Mai Nap* February 18, 2001; 'A Special Coach Service for Jimmy's Funeral,' *Mai Nap* 16 January 2001; 'RTL KLUB Even Borrowed a Helicopter,' *Blikk* January 17, 2001.

12 The Hungarian tabloids released several albums, special editions, and the two biggest commercial channels engaged in a ferocious battle to broadcast the funeral live on television. A further indication of the media's role is the fact that the tabloids published the latest developments on the front page for 30 weeks.

13 Thousands of people came to Jimmy Zámbó's funeral. The organizers had expected several hundred thousand, but 'only' about forty thousand attended, presumably because of the unusual cold that day.

14 www.rtlklubonline.hu, last accessed: January 15, 2001.

15 *Blikk* January 17, 2001.

16 *Blikk* January 21, 2001

17 Interviewed on January 20, 2001, at the Csepel cemetery.

18 Interviewed on March 16, 2007, at the Csepel cemetery.

19 Interviewed on January 20, 2001, at the Csepel cemetery.

20 Interviewed on October 31, 2001, at the Csepel cemetery.

21 See illustration.

22 Interviewed on October 31, 2001, at the Csepel cemetery.

23 Interviewed on January 2, 2006, at the Csepel cemetery.

24 Interviewed on January 2, 2002, at the Csepel cemetery.

25 Interviewed on January 2, 2002, at the Csepel cemetery.

26 Interviewed on January 20, 2001, at the Csepel cemetery.

27 Interviewed on October 31, 2001, at the Csepel cemetery.

28 Interviewed on October 31, 2006, at the Csepel cemetery.

29 Interviewed on October 31, ?? at the Csepel cemetery.

30 Naturally, the mass media endeavours to satisfy society's need for miracles and transcendence. Magazines publish many esoteric and spiritualist articles about the singer's death. Astrologers analyze his horoscope, his life, his character and the highlights of his life. Other spiritualists conjure up the spirit of the dead singer and question him about the part with the aid of a three-legged chair. [See illustration].

31 Interviewed on January 2, 2007, at the Csepel cemetery.

32 Interviewed on January 2, 2007, at the Csepel cemetery.

33 'Died for Jimmy,' Mai Nap January 24, 2001.

34 *Blikk* May 4, 2006. Unfortunately, we know nothing more about his reasons.

35 Most fans brought yellow roses to the funeral because they 'heard' that this was the singer's favourite flower.

36 Interviewed on January 20, 2001, at the Csepel cemetery.

37 Interviewed in January 2, 2007, at the Csepel cemetery.

38 The funeral actually took place before the revival of 1980s fashion in Hungary.

39 This rejection is underscored by the following conversation between two fans. When a middle-aged fan asked others whether they knew that the funeral cost 20 million forints, they scolded her, saying, 'You should be ashamed. How dare you talk about money when the King is dead!'

III The Sports Realm

Chapter 8

Pre's Rock: Pilgrimage, Ritual, and Runners' Traditions at the Roadside Shrine for Steve Prefontaine[1]

Daniel Wojcik

Located on a dangerous curved road in the east hills of Eugene, Oregon, is the roadside memorial for the long distance runner Steve Prefontaine. This site, named Pre's Rock, has attracted athletes, fans, and pilgrims for more than thirty years. Prefontaine was tragically killed at this spot in an automobile accident on May 30, 1975, at the age of twenty-four. At the time of his death, he was the most famous runner in the United States and held every American track record from the 2,000 meters to 10,000 meters. Track fans continue to debate whether or not Prefontaine was the greatest American distance runner ever, but he is undoubtedly the most popular distance runner in American history. Prefontaine has inspired generations of distance runners, and his cult of personality endures to the present.

Pre's Rock has been visited by runners and fans from all over the world, where they often place personal objects and things symbolically connected to Prefontaine and the broader subcultures of distance running and track and field. Running shoes are carefully arranged around the rock, or occasionally balanced on top of it, and jerseys and race numbers are placed at its base, or tucked into its crevices, or pinned to the ivy and other plants that grow nearby. Race medals, ribbons, trophies, track spikes, and wrist-bands are scattered about, while running caps and T-shirts drape the memorial marker on some days, and food (such as energy bars) and bottles of sports drinks or beer are occasionally left here as well. People also leave photos of Prefontaine and photos of themselves, as well as hand-written notes, poems, prayers, letters, flowers, candles, coins, identification cards, and other personal objects, similar to the offerings placed at roadside memorials throughout the United States.

In this essay, I examine the traditions and rituals of commemoration as-

Fans at Pre's Rock and the assortment of objects placed there, May 2004.
Photo: D. Wojcik.

sociated with Pre's Rock, and the personal meanings of these practices for the people who travel to the site. For some individuals, Pre's Rock is considered hallowed ground, and it functions as a shrine, a place where they make offerings, seek inspiration and intercession, and communicate with the memory or spirit of Steve Prefontaine. I explore the ways that the site is sacralized by fans, how their ritual actions are expressions of vernacular spirituality, and the degree to which journeys to Pre's Rock may be considered pilgrimages.

As a folklorist and long distance runner, I have been interested in the traditions associated with Steve Prefontaine for many years. As a runner in high school and college, I was familiar with Prefontaine's accomplishments, and like nearly every American distance runner at the time, I admired his gutsy running style and enthusiastic approach to running and to life. I vividly remember the one time I ran with Prefontaine, with some other high school runners-September 8, 1973. We ran five miles alongside and behind Prefontaine, in almost complete silence, in awe and veneration of the supreme being of American distance running. I also remember the morning that I learned of Prefontaine's death; I was stunned and devastated by the news, like so many other people.

I have visited Pre's Rock during training runs over the past fifteen years, as a place to stop and reflect, or sometimes out of curiosity to observe the objects that have been left there. Since 2003, I have been present at the site after major track meets, cross-country meets, road races, and on specific ritual days relating to Prefontaine's life and death, such his birthday, death day, and Memorial Day.[2] After interviewing many of the visitors at the site, it became apparent that Pre's Rock is not only characterized by traditions of memorialization, but that for some individuals it is a place of pilgrimage, reverence, and spirituality. A number of people regard the site as a 'sacred place' for runners, or as one person stated it, 'The Church of Pre,' and they had made special journeys to the spot and brought special objects to be left here. Some of them say that they can feel Prefontaine's 'presence' or his 'spirit' here, and they seek to interact with his life and legacy. The practices and personalized spirituality expressed at Pre's Rock blur the boundaries between the sacred and the secular, pilgrimage and tourism, shrine and memorial, inspiration and supernatural intercession.

Steve Roland Prefontaine was born on January 25, 1951, in Coos Bay, Oregon. He initially had minimal success in sports as a youth, and was a small and skinny child, born with one leg shorter than the other. According to local lore and oral history, he was an outsider as a child, in part because he did not speak English until learning it in school (his mother Elfriede was a war bride from Germany, and Prefontaine spoke German at home). During his freshman year in high school, he had some success in cross-country running, and he began a rigorous plan of training, and by his junior and senior years in high school, he won every race and set an American national high school record of 8:41.5 in the two-mile race. In his lifetime, Prefontaine set fourteen American records, and on the American running scene he appeared to be almost unbeatable and super-human in the eyes of his fans. His current admirers continue to idolize him as a fearless front-runner, who punished his opponents with a brutal pace, and who often ran alone, against the clock and himself, to the point of complete exhaustion. As he put it: 'Most people run a race to see who is fastest. I run a race to see who has the most guts.' In the 1972 Olympics in the 5000 meters, at the age of twenty-one, Prefontaine ran a characteristically gutsy race, having taken over the lead and pushing the pace during the last mile, only to be out-kicked in the last 200 meters by three other runners, and finishing out of medal contention.

Although Prefontaine quickly became legendary for his aggressive running style, he also was embraced for his view that he had less natural talent than other runners, but that hard work and devotion to a goal led to his success, and that anyone could become successful through effort and dedication (Moore 2006: 323). He was known for never missing a workout or track meet despite injury and illness, as well as for his toughness and ability to endure pain, like the time he tore open his foot in a grisly accident, and then two days later, he ran on the severely injured and bleeding foot, and won a national championship in the three-mile race (Dellinger quoted in McChesney 1981: 38-39). Prefontaine had a charismatic style, and he developed a strong rapport with his fans, who called themselves 'Pre's People'; he said that he considered running to be an art form and a performance, and his zealous fans entered into the performance with him, chanting his name, stomping their feet, and screaming for him with a deafening roar when he raced.[3] Having witnessed the relationship between Prefontaine and his devoted fans, Oregon writer and counterculture icon Ken Kesey stated that 'Pre was more than a name – it was a condition' (Hollister and Lyttle 1996). Journalists have described the enthusiasm of Pre's fans as bordering on fanaticism (Newnham 1975: B1), with one writer stating, 'there is probably nothing in sports to compare with the love affair between Pre and his people' (Davis 1975: C1). His teammate Steve Bence recalled Prefontaine's charisma and crowd appeal: 'Perhaps the most poignant memory is the energy that Pre brought to the track. I compared it to bullfights that I went to while a high school student in Spain. Pre entering the track was like the bull entering the ring. He would burst on to the track, it seemed that all heads would turn and the excitement and anticipation in the place would take off. He helped create a very special environment.'[4] One of Prefontaine's roommates, Pat Tyson, had a similar recollection: 'When he stepped out on the track, he was like a rock star (...) He made running cool' (Anderson 2005: B5). Prefontaine was also known to be generous to the mobs of children who wanted his autograph after each race, and he was equally friendly to his fans, often hanging out at local taverns, drinking beer and happily socializing with 'his people' (McChesney 1981: 3-4, 22). Many of his female admirers found him physically and sexually attractive, adding further to his cult of charisma and personal magnetism. Some of Prefontaine's fans actually attributed uncanny and supernatural powers to his presence, and in the local folklore of Eugene, Oregon, it is often recounted that the sun would shine through the cloudy and rainy weather whenever he stepped onto the track to run (McChesney 1981: 13,16; Jordan 1997: 3-4).

In addition to his charisma, Prefontaine cultivated a rebel persona and was frequently referred to by his fans as the 'James Dean of track and field.'[5] Prefontaine's appeal is also related to his small-town roots, working-class masculinity, and his rise from hometown hero to national fame, and his involvement and contributions to the local community.[6] Some of his fans view him as a vocal opponent of perceived injustices, a 'champion of the underdog' who fought 'the establishment,' such as the bureaucracy of the American Amateur Union, the governing body of track and field in the United States, which exploited amateur athletes at the time.[7] Finally, Prefontaine is venerated for not being driven by greed and staying true to his personal goals and ideals. For example, when he was struggling to pay his bills, subsisting on food stamps, and living in a trailer, he was offered more than $100,000 to run professionally, but he refused the money, because taking it would have cost him his amateur status and prevented him from competing in the 1976 Olympics.

Prefontaine's story has the elements that appeal to American audiences, as he seemed to embrace and epitomize attitudes of independence, dedication, courage, and success-a runner's version of the 'work hard and you shall be rewarded' narrative and the related rags-to-riches story, although he died before he became rich. As a folk hero and icon of American sports, Prefontaine has been celebrated in two feature films, *Prefontaine* (1997) and *Without Limits* (1998) as well as in the documentary film, *Fire on the Track: The Life Story of Steve Prefontaine* (1996). These films have brought his life story to a much wider audience beyond the local community and track and field enthusiasts and contributed further to the cult of personality surrounding Prefontaine and have definitely inspired an increase in the number of people visiting Pre's Rock in recent years. In interviews with fans at the site, I discovered that many of them had learned about Prefontaine through these films and that the films were the motivating factor for their journeys to the site, or their 'Pre pilgrimage,' as some of them called it.[8] Not all of these 'pilgrims' were runners, but athletes in other sports (swimming, wrestling, cycling, football, basketball), and many of them were in high school or college. A number of them told me they watched the films about Prefontaine before athletic competitions, sometimes as a ritual, alone or in groups, to get inspired. Others said that they watched the films for inspiration in general or to get 'psyched up' for whatever reason. Some of the young people who visit Pre's Rock are not athletes at all. In June 2005, several hours after the annual Prefontaine Classic track meet, a young man at the site said he liked Prefontaine because he was gutsy, and that 'Pre was like punk rock before punk rock, [but] he was not just about running, but doing whatever you loved with passion, going all out, balls to the wall, trying your hardest at what you did.' He then quoted verbatim various lines from the films on Prefontaine, as if he were quoting scripture, while others at the site nodded knowingly and in approval at his words.

Prefontaine's legacy also endures because of his connection to the Nike company. Prefontaine's legendary coach at Oregon, Bill Bowerman, was the co-founder of Nike along with Phil Knight, and the company was established in Eugene, Oregon. In the early 1970s, when the company was just beginning, Prefontaine wore the various shoes that Bowerman designed, such as the Nike waffle-soled shoe that Bowerman created using an old waffle iron. Since Prefontaine's death, the Nike company has embraced Prefontaine as someone who helped define the ethos of the corporation and during the past decade has increasingly promoted his image and legend, through various products, advertisements, and media productions.[9] Nike's reverence for and promotion of Prefontaine have had a significant influence in the renewed interest in Prefontaine among young people, and the resulting increase of visitors at Pre's Rock.

During the course of my research, I documented dozens of stories told by people about how Prefontaine had inspired them or had influenced their lives in a positive way. Mark Lansing (aged 47), whom I met at Pre's Rock in the summer of 2004, provided a representative narrative. Formerly a competitive runner and now a lawyer in Portland, Lansing was visiting the site with his niece and his nine-year-old daughter, a runner. He told me that he had been to the rock dozens of times, first beginning in the late 1970s when he attended the University of Oregon and was a runner, and he said that Prefontaine had been a major inspiration throughout his life:

> You could probably make the argument that Pre has influenced my life more than anyone (with the exception of my parents). In 1970 I was 13 years old and I wanted to be a runner. Pre was certainly the role model for that particular aspiration. I always enjoyed the way running made me feel, and Pre was the guy who made running cool. It was sort of a James Dean thing. Pre wasn't just good, he was the best, and the *way* he did it was equally impressive: lots of style and grit (...) I think that Pre's fingerprints are all over the things I did and do. More than anyone else, he lit that path for me, and the things that are good in my life have come from following it. Thank you, Mr. Prefontaine.[10]

Paul McMullen (aged 32), an American national champion 1,500-meter runner who ran in the 1996 Olympic Games, also visited Pre's Rock in 2004 because of the influence Prefontaine had on his approach to running and recalled his experience there: 'I vividly remember walking up to the rock and the hair stood up on the back of my neck. It was as though I was visiting the gravesite of a close friend that understood what drove me to attempt what others thought to be impossible. Fate is a peculiar thing and so is fame. The main reason Prefontaine has risen to folk hero status is because his death kept maturity's shades of gray from blurring his uncompromising nature.'[11] Prefontaine's death at the age of twenty-four was devastating to people locally and nationally: 'It was as if God had died ... he was the best person we had, a local hero. He was thought of as God-like,' recalled Shannon Rettig (aged 51), who was an Oregon college student in the 1970s when she learned of Prefontaine's death (Andujar 2007: 1).

Immortalized through legend and memory, Prefontaine's life has many of the common elements associated with other American folk heroes: he rose from the ranks of the common man; he was endowed with seemingly super-human powers of physical strength and endurance; he had personal magne-tism, exceptional vitality, and lived life with gusto; he was a rugged individua-list and confronted the elite establishment; he boasted and performed feats of audacity and daring, yet was good-natured and kind-hearted (Dorson 1977: 199-243). For his fans, Prefontaine was the embodiment of courage, rebellion, and the pursuit of one's dreams with complete abandon; and in his races he exhibited an almost martyr-like willingness to suffer for his goals and for 'his people,' running through the pain barriers to the point of near oblivion as thousands cheered him on. As an athlete dying young, the tragic ending of Prefontaine's life also has two important features of the classic 'hero of tra-dition' pattern identified by Lord Ragland: the hero meets with a mysterious death, and he has one or more holy sepulchers (Ragland 1956).

As I discovered during the time spent at Pre's Rock, the circumstances surrounding Prefontaine's death were a common topic of conversation, as his admirers speculated about how he died and the 'mysterious' events associa-ted with his death. According to the official report, Prefontaine was returning home after a party and was drunk when his MGB sports car veered across the dividing line in the center of the road and then crashed into the wall of rock alongside the roadway. His car flipped over on top of him, trapping him underneath, and he apparently suffocated from the weight of the car on his chest, with no broken bones and only a few scratches on his body, although his cause of death is still debated (2006: 326).[12] He was not wearing a seat belt, and his blood alcohol level was at 0.16, significantly above the legal limit of 0.10 (Jordan 1997: 154). However, for many, including Prefontaine's family and close friends, controversy still surrounds the events of that night, and this was reflected in the various narratives expressed by Prefontaine's fans at the memorial, many of whom believe he crashed his car attempting to avoid an oncoming vehicle in his lane.[13] Some of the narratives also assert that Prefon-taine was not intoxicated, citing evidence that the procedure for testing his blood alcohol level was done improperly (Jordan 1997: 154).[14] I even heard conspiracy theories that Prefontaine may have been killed by his 'enemies,' whether members of the AAU track and field federation that Prefontaine had challenged and embarrassed (such rumors also exist on a few websites and blogs) or foreign espionage agents from the countries of his competitors, perhaps the KGB.

Regardless of the narrative told at the site, the majority of stories assert that the accident was not Prefontaine's fault and dispute the official account of his death-an unacceptable and senseless death for his fans, and an unfitting ending for a young athlete and local hero so full of life and at the pinnacle of his career. The narratives that people tell not only challenge the official version of Prefontaine's death, but construct new meanings from the death event, just as the activities at Pre's Rock create a meaningful narrative from his death and reaffirm his life. Individuals at informal memorials and sites of tragedy do more than commemorate or grieve, they attempt to understand what happened, to make sense of the disaster, or to seek action against those responsible (Margry and Sánchez-Carretero 2007: 2).

Pre's Rock

Like other spontaneous memorials, the place of Steve Prefontaine's death immediately became a commemorative site. Friends, neighbors, fans, and others in the local community spontaneously visited the place of the automobile accident and left flowers or objects that were somehow connected to Prefontaine, his accomplishments, and their memories of him. Soon after the accident, the following inscription was painted in white on the slab of rock where the car crashed by Arne Alvarado, a teenager who lived in the neighborhood:

PRE
5-30-75
R.I.P

Later, a small bronze casting of Prefontaine running was fastened to the rock. Initially, the wall of rock was the place of commemoration, with people placing objects at its base and in its crevices. Kenny Moore, who lived near Pre's Rock, observed over time the ways that people sought to remember Prefontaine: 'After Pre died, I did live here for years and years and I watched the shrine grow up almost immediately. People wanted to connect with him in a way that was powerful, and so, consistently for thirty years there hasn't been a time when there hasn't been some little memorial left here, because Pre affected people so profoundly.'[15] Similar to other roadside memorials, Pre's Rock offers a tangible place in the landscape to commune with the deceased and commemorate individually and as a community. Because informal memorials are regularly visited and attended to, they may become places of endearment, forming the basis for continued interaction with the dead as well as interactions with others.

After two decades as an informal roadside memorial, Pre's Rock was somewhat formalized in 1997 with the placement of a black granite marker at the base of the rock where Prefontaine died. The idea for this tribute to Prefontaine came from prison inmates at the penitentiary in Salem, Oregon, where Prefontaine had volunteered and had helped establish a running program that is still in existence today. In consultation with members of the Oregon Track Club and with help from a local rock and quarry company, the granite marker containing the following inscription about Prefontaine written by a prison inmate was installed:

'PRE'
For your dedication and loyalty
To your principles and beliefs...
For your love, warmth, and friendship
For your family and friends...
You are missed by so many.
And you will never be forgotten...

The memorial stone also contains a photograph of Prefontaine's face, apparently one of the last photos taken of him before he died, and individuals who visit the site often are especially moved by the photograph, with some of them commenting that it is soulful, haunting, and 'intense.' Most people have responded favorably to the installation of this official marker, although a few people, especially longtime visitors to the site, are ambivalent about the granite marker, stating that it alters the ambiance at Pre's Rock that has existed for decades and that it appears imposed, or that it looks like a gravestone.[16] But the vast majority of Prefontaine's fans seem appreciative of the ongoing development of the site, and most of the new visitors assume the marker has always been there, and many people kneel next to the marker and have photographs taken of themselves beside the image of Prefontaine. As one high school runner remarked: 'This is my picture of me with Pre. This is as close I can get to him.'

Prefontaine is buried in Sunset Memorial Cemetery just south of his hometown of Coos Bay, Oregon. Although a few individuals I spoke with had made the journey to Prefontaine's gravesite, most had not, stating emphatically that Pre's Rock is the place to visit, the spot where 'Pre lives,' where his memory and 'spirit' survive. This crash site where Prefontaine died has replaced his grave as the primary place of remembrance, and it has become the cultic and iconic focus for most of his fans. Leah Worthen (aged 20), a student and runner at the University of Oregon, grew up in Coos Bay and visits Prefontaine's grave every Memorial Day with her family, and they leave flowers there. But she says there are relatively few offerings at his grave, and not nearly as many visitors there throughout the year compared with Pre's Rock; the rock, she says, 'is a testament to the "idea" of Steve, that he's somehow part of the "spirit" of Eugene and runners worldwide. His grave site, however, simply marks the place of his dead body.'[17]

Although Prefontaine's fans journey to Pre's Rock to commemorate and celebrate his legacy, the site also continues to be a place of sadness and loss. Prefontaine's sisters Linda and Neta have stated that they appreciate objects left at the site, but they rarely visit it because it is too emotionally painful. When I spoke with Prefontaine's parents Elfriede and Ray as they visited Pre's Rock after the Prefontaine Classic track meet on June 19, 2004, they also said they had not been to the roadside shrine for their son for many years because it brought back such painful memories. The Prefontaines were visibly moved by the objects left at the site, and after they placed flowers at the base of the marker, Mrs. Prefontaine kissed her hand and touched the image of her son's face, as the crowd of forty to fifty people at Pre's Rock gathered around her in hushed silence.

After Prefontaine's parents left, the activity at the site returned to normal, with dozens of people crowding around the rock and standing in the street in front of it. People walked about, touched the rock, stood or knelt beside it, took photos, kissed their hands and touched the rock, and left things. Some were silent or spoke quietly among themselves, others were animated, talking excitedly about Prefontaine or the performances at the recent track meet at Hayward Field, or the 'mystery car' and various theories about what really caused his death. Many people examined the assemblage of objects that had been left at the site-medals, ribbons, shoes, Mardi Gras beads, race numbers, bracelets, photos, notes, flowers in a Powerade sports drink container. One young woman gently placed a pair of worn-out shoes at its base, and a few minutes later another teenager pressed his crumpled race bib number into one of the crevices in the rock. Cars regularly pulled up to the site, with passengers paying respects as they drove by, or the cars sometimes stopping in the middle of street, creating a dangerous and somewhat carnivalesque scene. A man in a convertible drove up to the site, stopped in the middle of the road, jumped out of his car, put flowers in a plastic container, and then drove away. Moments later, a large middle-aged man suddenly appeared out of nowhere, and quickly approached the rock. Striding up to it, and smoking a big cigar, he kissed his hand and then gently touched the rock, all in one motion, and then continued walking down the road.

The sorts of things that people do at the site vary considerably, and there are no set rituals, although one common practice involves running to the site, either alone or as a group, and touching or kissing the rock, and leaving an object. One tradition that occurs after the Oregon state track and field championship races involves runners placing their recently-won and highly-prized award medals at the site. As runner and graduate student Cody Loy (aged 24) observed:

A runner bends down to kiss the image of Prefontaine at his memorial marker, 2006. Photo: D. Wojcik.

As I marveled at these few medals that the greatest runners of the year had left for Pre, I found one such medallion that had a note taped to its backside. On the note read: 'A piece of greatness can never compare to the greatness you have given to us. Rest in peace, Pre.' I remember the writing to this day because the idea stood out to me while also giving me a new insight: so many of the great athletes and runners produced in the state of Oregon today attain their level of ability and athleticism only because they strive to be what Pre has been to so many like myself: an indicator of what can be achieved by the human will when one sacrifices everything for the sport and its legacy. And as Pre once said: 'To give anything less than your best is to sacrifice the gift' (Heinz 2007: 1).

Roadside Memorials and Spontaneous Shrines

As a vernacular place of commemoration and veneration since 1975, Pre's Rock has been actively maintained longer than most American roadside memorials, spontaneous shrines, and gravesite shrines, including Graceland. Although the current practices associated with Pre's Rock are similar to those at more recent informal memorials, they also have antecedents in previous and longstanding folk traditions. The practice of marking the place of death has existed for hundreds of years in the United States, with the origins of such traditions often located in indigenous practices, folk Catholicism, and Spanish and Mexican cultures, such as the practice of creating roadside crosses or *descansos* (places of rest) to indicate the place of death. Similar memorial practices, including the tradition of creating wayside shrines, have a long legacy in many cultures throughout the world. In more recent decades in the United States, large spontaneous shrines occasionally have emerged as expressions of collective sorrow, such as the memorial created in Dealey Plaza in Dallas after the assassination of John F. Kennedy in 1963, or that for John Lennon in New York City after his death in 1980. During the past twenty years in the USA, traditions of spontaneous memorialization have proliferated (Santino 2006a), attributed in part to the influence of the media coverage of the mourning rituals associated with the Vietnam Veterans Memorial (dedicated in 1982). After the outpouring of offerings left at its base, it became much more acceptable to express personal grief in public spaces (Hass 1998).

The increasing presence of spontaneous shrines and roadside memorials is also related to public awareness of the informal memorials that were created after the bombing of the Murrah Federal Building in Oklahoma City (1995), the death of Princess Diana (1997), the shooting at Columbine High School in Colorado (1999), and the terrorist attacks on the World Trade Center in New York City (2001) and the trains in Madrid (2004), and other tragic events. Vernacular memorialization now has become a pervasive, accepted, and almost obligatory way to express grief and remembrance in the event of tragic and violent death in American culture and throughout the world.[18]

As various writers have asserted, in the modern era the mourning rituals provided by dominant institutions in society, whether by religious organizations or the funerary industry, often seem inadequate and may not fulfill the emotional needs of those concerned (Aries 1974; Haney, Leimer, and Lowery 1997: 167-170; Huntington and Metcalf 1979: 187-211; Santino 2006b). The rituals that occur at spontaneous memorial sites provide alternative and personally meaningful ways of expressing sorrow and remembrance, in response to the depersonalization of death and the inadequacy of institutional and traditional mourning rituals. Unlike the memorialization of death that occurs in cemeteries or religious institutions, which tend to be private and restricted to family and friends, spontaneous memorials also provide places to mourn for people normally not included in traditional rites. Like other roadside memorials, Pre's Rock is interwoven into the landscape of everyday life and continues to be a vibrant site of folk expression, and it differs from most cemeteries which are generally hidden from public view and which usually restrict tangible outpourings of emotion, the leaving of objects, and the gathering of crowds.

These popular sites of commemoration have been called both shrines and memorials, and there is no universal agreement about the exact meanings of the terms. Both of these concepts reflect the notion of symbolic and ritual space invested with significance. Memorials are usually regarded as places of commemoration of an individual or a group of people, while shrines are frequently defined as sites of ritual, prayer, contemplation, and sometimes pilgrim -age. However, in the realm of popular expression, these categories may blur and overlap, as people's behavior at such sites is variable. For example, while the Vietnam Veterans Memorial is an official memorial and place of commemoration, for some people it is also a place of pilgrimage and functions as a shrine, and it is considered a sacred site, where people leave symbolic objects, engage in ritual behavior, and communicate with the dead (Hass 1998: 87-102; Dubisch infra, drapters).

In 1992, folklorist Jack Santino proposed the term 'spontaneous shrine' to refer to sites that are created by people in response to instances of sudden and tragic death. As Santino notes, 'spontaneous' indicates the unofficial and 'folk' nature of these sites, that they are 'of the people'; and term 'shrine' indicates those sites that are more than memorials and that have become places of pilgrimage and communion between the living and the dead (Santino 2006b: 12). Folklorist Sylvia Grider shares Santino's view that these places are more than secular memorials because they become sites of ritual offering, pilgrimage, and sacred meaning (Grider 2001: 2-4). In a discussion of the various types of official and informal shrines, folklorist Jeannie Thomas describes the folk religiosity associated with such sites: 'Shrines mark hallowed spots; they are composed of culturally or personally significant relics. We travel to shrines to express our devotion and pain, to ask for help, to reach toward other worlds, to remember, and to heal' (Thomas 1996: 17). Although the media has sometimes referred to sites such as Pre's Rock as 'make-shift memorials,' these places are not haphazard displays, but are heartfelt, popular constructions usually characterized by certain underlying principles and common themes shared with other informal environments that have been created through the processes of assemblage and bricolage (Grider 2001; Santino 2001, 2006b; Margry and Sánchez-Carretero 2007; Wojcik 2008). As Grider notes: 'These spontaneous shrines are among the deepest expressions of our shared humanity, combining ritual, pilgrimage, performance art, popular culture, and traditional material culture' (Grider 2001: 2). Such sites also have been referred to as 'performative commemoratives' (Santino 2006b) or 'performative memorials' (Margry 2007) because they are publicly created and enacted for others, inviting participation, presenting significant personal and cultural issues, and frequently communicating political concerns (Santino 2006b: 10-14; Margry and Sánchez-Carretero 2007).[19]

Like other spontaneous memorials, the place where Steve Prefontaine died immediately became a bounded ritual space where people attempted to emotionally grasp and manage the trauma of sudden death. The accident site, a place of tragedy, was symbolically 'cleansed' by the actions of people and transformed into a consecrated place of remembrance, love, and communion. Pre's Rock is participatory and 'open' to all, friends and strangers alike, and it emerged from the public need to mourn and remember. Like other folkloric forms of expression, the varied traditions and personal practices at the site exist without official guidelines and are not controlled by official institutions and authorities.

Shrine, Pilgrimage Site, Spirituality, and Inspiration

Although Pre's Rock emerged as a spontaneous roadside memorial in 1975 as a site for people to mourn, it soon became a place for admirers to pay tribute to the accomplishments and life of Steve Prefontaine. Today, for many who come here, especially young athletes in high school and college, Pre's Rock is a source of inspiration, a place for devotees to experience the cult of personality and legendary status that Prefontaine has attained, comparable to fans visiting the graves of Jim Morrison or Elvis Presley, or the crash sites of Princess Diana's or James Dean's death'[20]

The terms 'shrine' and 'pilgrimage,' when used to describe Pre's Rock, evoke ideas about religious devotion, sacred space, and communication with intercessory beings that may seem inappropriate and that probably would disturb Steve Prefontaine himself. Certainly, some of the people who visit the site are tourists, and many others come to remember and commemorate Prefontaine's life. Yet for a number of individuals that I spoke with, Pre's Rock fulfilled the functions of a shrine, as a ritualized space, where they gave thanks, made offerings, asked for help and intercession, and attempted to interact with the 'spirit' of Prefontaine, as a venerated person and object of devotion. Furthermore, some of these individuals referred to their journey to Pre's Rock as a 'pilgrimage.' But can this place of remembrance on the side of the road actually be considered a pilgrimage site? The attributes and parameters of pilgrimage continue to debated and contested by scholars (Badone and Roseman 2004, Cohen 1992, Eade and Sallnow 1991/2000, Morinis 1992, Reader and Walter 1993), but for the purposes of this essay, I utilize the definitions of pilgrimage proposed by Emily Socolov (1997), Alan Morinis (1992), and Peter Jan Margry (see chapter 1). Pilgrimage is defined by Socolov as 'the journey of individuals in homage to highly esteemed places, individuals, or artifacts with the aim of deriving some benefit therefrom' (Socolov 1997: 647). According to Morinis, 'the pilgrimage is a journey undertaken by a person in quest of a place or a state that he or she believes to embody a valued ideal' (Morinis 1992: 4). Margry gives us a thorough characterization of pilgrimage, as follows: 'A journey that individuals or groups undertake based on a religious or spiritual inspiration, to a place that is regarded as more sacred or salutary than the environment of everyday life, to seek a transcendental encounter with a specific cult object, for the purpose of acquiring spiritual, emotional, or physical healing or benefit' (see: chapter 1).

These definitions suggest that Pre's Rock is both a shrine and a pilgrimage site for some individuals, a ritually demarcated cultic space, believed to be sacred, where one honors a being or force that may function as an intercessor, and where one offers petitions, prayers, and votive objects. People travel to the site not only for reasons of commemoration or curiosity but to receive personal benefits in the form of inspiration, aid, or blessings, and they speak of feeling renewed or transformed as the result of their visit. Some of the people who journey to Pre's Rock say that the place provides an encounter with the 'true spirit' of Prefontaine and the 'essence' of the culture of running. In this regard, Pre's Rock, like other folk shrines, represents an embodiment and enshrinement of the valued ideals and the ethos of running that are central to people's lifestyle and belief system: 'All runners know this is the sacred spot for runners. Eugene is the Mecca for running and Pre's Rock is the shrine to guts and courage,' said Ben Ackerly, a high-school track coach, who said he had 'made a pilgrimage to the rock' from Virginia.[21]

Journeys to Pre's Rock are often referred to as pilgrimages in various online postings, with the following comment by a high school runner being fairly representative: 'I really want to go to Oregon this summer (...). Visit the memorial to the Pre, and maybe run a workout on the infamous Hayward Field. It would be somewhat like a pilgrimage, a deeply religious experience.'[22] This idea of Pre's Rock as a source of inspiration that embodies valued ideals and existential meaning was expressed by Prefontaine's sister, Linda, who considers the rock to be 'a symbol for all runners. It's a place they can go for a purpose for running, for goals in life, to have inner peace.'[23] Similar ideas were stated by many runners at the site, who frequently told me that they visit Pre's Rock to get inspiration or give thanks for the inspiration they received. Matt Gray, who had driven from northern California to attend the Prefontaine Classic track meet in June 2007, said that he visits the site every time he is in Eugene. After the track meet he was at the site with friends and discussed their visit to Pre's Rock: 'It's the pilgrimage. If you're a runner, it's what you do. If you're in Eugene, and you don't go to Pre's Rock, you're not a runner' (Christie 2007: A1, A9). Gray left one track shoe next to the rock, as an offering of thanks to Prefontaine for helping him set some high-school records, and he kept the other shoe for himself.

Many athletes have a tradition of journeying to Pre's Rock on significant dates or in relation to important events, whether one's birthday or before or after championship competitions. For example, after the conclusion of the Oregon state track and field championship meet, the coaches at Crescent Valley High School in Corvallis, Oregon, Ted Pawlak and Pat Wilson, ritually run with their athletes from Hayward Field to Pre's Rock, a distance of several miles, with the last part up a steep hill. As Pawlak stated, 'This is the special place if you are a runner, and we always run here, we have done it for years now. It gives these kids a sense of Pre's legend, as one of the greatest runners of all time. When they visit, they feel connected to him, and he becomes a part of them.'[24] At the beginning of the cross-country season, the team also drives to Eugene from the town of Corvallis and gathers together at Pre's Rock, where they make a vow to do the best they possibly can during the season.

Such traditions and the other forms of ritual behavior expressed by people who come to Pre's Rock resemble the actions traditionally associated with pilgrimages to shrines for superhuman beings or culture heroes: the journey to the cultic site requires a physical hardship or sacrifice; the experience at the site removes the individual from the ordinary world and everyday life, and involves an encounter at a unique and revered place that is believed to embody the history and heritage of the culture of running; individuals engage in rituals and sometimes spiritually-inspired actions, whether participating in a communal vow, leaving personal gifts of gratitude, or asking for help or intercession (see Margry: chapter I; Morinis 1992; Reader and Walter 1993). Although journeys to Pre's Rock initially may not appear to be as explicitly spiritual as the religiously-motivated pilgrimages to established holy places, in some cases people's experiences at the site reflect personal forms of spirituality, and the journeys exhibit the structure of the rites of passage model proposed by Arnold van Gennep (1960) and developed by Victor Turner and Edith Turner in their characterization of pilgrimages: a separation from society and one's previous self as one journeys to the site; the liminoid and reflexive experience at the shrine itself, as a place of power and the embodiment of highly-valued ideals; then the return home and a reincorporation into the ordinary world (Turner and Turner 1978).[25] Like most contemporary pilgrimage experiences, special journeys to Pre's Rock are generally not as dramatically transformative as traditional rites of passage that provide an entirely new social identity or status.[26] Yet people may be changed by the journey and their experiences at the site, may feel more connected to significant values and beliefs, and rene-wed in some way.[27]

Pilgrimage sites, as 'energized' and extraordinary places, are points of con-vergence for communication between humans and deities or supernormal forces, sites where the supernatural is manifested and where divine favors may be attained. The actions and statements of some of those at Pre's Rock reveal the belief that Prefontaine's life-force, essence, or power is present at this place and that it can be experienced here: 'Pre had a tremendous strength and will-power in his life, and great determination, and this is the last place

An individual poses for a photo next to the memorial marker at Pre's Rock, as others wait to do the same, 2005. Photo: D. Wojcik.

where he was in this world. I think there is some kind a power here, I don't know what exactly, it is like the last part of him, his life, the last place he was alive, and he still lives on here, somehow ... some kind of energy.'[28] Such ideas and related folk beliefs are widely accepted in vernacular culture, with the site of death considered to be a liminal space, a threshold where the sacred and secular intersect. In popular belief and vernacular imagination, the exact spot of death, as the place where the soul leaves the body, is often believed to be infused with the spirit of the deceased and remains a permanent place of contact between this world and the afterlife.

For some individuals, Pre's Rock is experienced as a sacred place of contemplation and spirituality. Kate McInerny, who attended the University of Oregon from 1971-1975 and knew Prefontaine, said she returned to Eugene for the first time in twenty years to attend the Prefontaine Classic in 2004, and at the track meet she learned about people visiting Pre's Rock: 'I was interested to hear about the "pilgrimage" to Pre's memorial site the day of the meet (...). My visit the next morning to Pre's Rock was very quiet. The image of Pre set in the rock is timeless – I felt haunted because I sensed "life" in his eyes – he had very intense eyes! I felt that it was as important and vital to visit the site as it was to attend the meet. Visiting the site is a very powerful spiritual experience.'[29]

Like other sites of popular spirituality, the beliefs and spiritual meanings associated with Pre's Rock are largely personal, private, and experiential, and exist at an informal level among people apart from formal religious institutions and authorities (Luckmann 1967, Yoder 1974, Primiano 1995, Wojcik 1996, 1997). One example of the individualized spirituality connected to Pre's Rock was expressed by Michael Regan, a senior Deputy District Attorney in Oregon City, who drove up to the site with his sons after the Oregon high-school championship track meet because they wanted to see the site. Regan said when he went to school at the University of Oregon between 1975-1982, he would stop for reflection at the rock during his training runs, and he continues to visit the site for the same reasons today:

That spot to me represents a simple tangible place to pause and reflect ... not only on Steve Prefontaine but about the spiritual side of running. All of us who run persistently through life, whether as seriously as Pre or just for fitness, come to recognize the role running plays in clearing our mind and soul. Throughout life, when you come up against stress, pain, heartache, depression, challenges, decision-making moments, or even joyful occasions, that time simply putting one foot in front of the other, alone, hearing nothing but your breathing and your mind's random meandering, is a spiritual and therapeutic activity, which over the years has saved me a lot of money on therapists. Coming to the Rock, and recognizing how amazing a runner Pre was, and how his life ended in such tragedy, makes you feel connected to him at some amorphous spiritual level which I can't really explain.[30]

Although sometimes difficult to describe in words, runners and non-runners alike stated that they considered Pre's Rock to be a place of spirituality, contemplation, or 'presence.' Kenny Moore and Steve Bence, former friends of Prefontaine who have visited Pre's Rock many times, said that the site is a place where people attempt to make a 'connection' to the spirit of Prefontaine, whether regarded as inspirational or spiritual.[31] Graduate student Thomas Pellinger, from the University of Oregon, stated that he regularly runs up to Pre's Rock on training runs, where he stops to see what people have left, to reflect on Prefontaine as a runner, and 'ask for Pre's energy.'[32] Susan Stater (aged 59), a retired high school teacher who visited the site, said she 'felt a sense of being surrounded by an almost mystical energy, a quiet sense of reverence' (Stater 2007: 2). Stater's friend (aged 50) who often visits the site stated: 'I go there when I am so fed up with the junk in my life that I feel like giving up. Somehow, there is a presence at his memorial that touches me deeply, and I get courage to go on (...) when I go there I feel a sense of connection with Steve as well as a connection with other people who have stood there to honor the memory of a great person' (Stater 2007: 2).

The Spirit of Steve Prefontaine: Intercession, Prayers, and Blessings

While many people referred to Pre's Rock as a place to connect with Prefontaine's presence, whether in terms of spirituality, inspiration, or commemoration, there were a few individuals who believe that Prefontaine's soul or ghost,
as a disembodied spirit, is present at the site on some occasions, and that his
spirit continues to interact with the living. Such ideas are common at other
roadside memorials, reflecting widespread and traditional beliefs about the
spiritual state of people who died 'unnatural deaths,' whether unexpectedly
or in a manner that is considered unusual or 'bad' within a particular culture (murder, suicide, tragic accident, etc.). A recurring belief cross-culturally
and within Christian folk tradition is that the souls of individuals who die
in an unusual or violent manner continue to haunt the place of death and
are 'trapped' between worlds. Such souls, it is widely believed, are unprepared
for death or, in some cases, are unwilling to make the transition to the afterlife
and remain attached to this world (Bennett 1987: 36-49). In vernacular traditions, these 'troubled souls' require the prayers and actions of the living to help
them successfully enter the other world.

Concerning Pre's Rock, people have occasionally expressed beliefs about
Prefontaine's ghost appearing at the site, and one of Prefontaine's girlfriends,
Mary Marckx, claims that his ghost has been haunting her for years, and she
has written a manuscript about the experiences in the hope of liberating his
spirit (Hauser 1997: A21). In 2004 when I was at the site, a neighbor who was
at the crash scene the night Prefontaine died invited me into his home and
showed me a photograph that he took of Pre's Rock, exactly ten years after
Pre's death. On the photo, there was a blurry, smoke-like image that he said
might be Pre's spirit. Like other spirit and miracle photographs, photos of 'Pre's
ghost' reflect broader ideas about the ability of photography to 'capture' and
reveal souls and spiritual beings on film, an enduring aspect of American vernacular belief (Wojcik 1996).

Yet unlike beliefs about spirit hauntings at the place of tragic death, ideas
about Prefontaine's soul or presence were almost universally positive, with
some people referring to him as an angel or existing in heaven (sometimes

in 'Runners' Heaven' or 'running in Heaven, with God,' or running with other deceased Olympians and legendary athletes in the afterlife). Such ideas are similar to beliefs expressed at other informal roadside shrines, in which the death site is considered sacred and heaven is the new home for the deceased (Jorgensen-Earp and Lanzilotti 1998). Neta Prefontaine, in an interview about her brother, stated that she considers him one of her 'guardian angels' (Miller 2006), and the letters and notes left by people at Pre's Rock occasionally express similar sentiments:

> Dear Pre,
> You have helped me
> You have guided me
> You are an angel to me,
> Thank you
> Sara B.

In popular belief and tradition, those who are admired and loved in life are often regarded as angelic beings who intercede and help the living, despite the fact that such ideas are doctrinally unacceptable in institutionalized forms of Christianity (Godwin 1990). But folk eschatology, fueled by the affection, devotion, and yearning for loved ones, creates its own alternative afterlife, a personally meaningful realm where the deceased are transformed into angels who now run interval workouts and tempo runs in heaven.

Whether people literally consider Prefontaine to be an angel or not, he often seems to have a similar symbolic function and is believed to be an intercessor and mediating force in some people's lives. Like other intermediary deities, spirits, and folk saints, Prefontaine is often regarded as an inspiring and benevolent presence that helps people in various ways. Some runners I spoke with referred to being influenced or 'possessed' by Pre's spirit or ghost, especially after they ran a particularly good race, asserting that they ran faster, farther, harder, and with more 'heart' and 'soul' because of Prefontaine's influence. One runner from Seattle (aged 20) stated: 'Pre's helps me in races, oh yeah. I focus on how ballsy he was, and I get a surge, some kind of strength. Some people run with Jesus, I run with Pre.'[33]

In some cases individuals may have been speaking metaphorically about Prefontaine's assistance in races, although often it was difficult to tell. However, a few individuals clearly spoke of Prefontaine as an intercessor who had a spiritual or supernatural influence on their lives. For instance, Jay Kimiecik, a professor at Miami University in Oxford, Ohio, says he had several encounters with Prefontaine's spirit, who offered words of inspiration, with the first experience occurring in a hospital emergency room (Kimiecik 2006). As a result, he was inspired to make a trip to Pre's Rock and to Hayward Field, where Prefontaine raced, to run in a national championship competition for runners over the age of forty, and he says that Prefontaine's spirit actually intervened in the last part of his painful 1,500 meter race: 'This hurts so much, I want to quit (...) My lungs are going to burst (...) Help me, Pre. Help me, God (...) A heaviness came over me on the backstretch unlike any I have ever known. I felt as if death was near. And then I was on the home stretch-the final 100 meters-and

Images of Prefontaine running with his friend and 1972 Olympic teammate, Jeff Galloway, being placed at Pre's Rock by Joe Henderson at Galloway's request, July 2007. Photo: D. Wojcik.

I felt lighter as if someone was carrying me along' (Kimiecik 2006). After the race, Kimiecik realizes Pre's spirit supported him physically and spiritually, and as a final expression of gratitude, he completes his spiritual journey by going to Pre's Rock, where he thanks Prefontaine for helping him transform his life: 'Pre's ghost had been calling me out to Eugene-to help me kill off the part of me that I didn't need anymore (...) bringing me back to life (...) I am forever changed, forever transformed' (Kimiecik 2006).

Kimiecik's narrative resembles other memorates involving numinous, first-hand encounters with benevolent otherworldly beings, such as angels, saints, or the 'good dead,' who intervene in human affairs and may spiritually transform the lives of people (Bennett 1987: 50-81; Brown 1981; Godwin 1990). Such intermediary beings are seen as accessible, and they respond to the prayers and petitions of individuals, helping people with their problems. Although Kimiecik's narrative is more elaborate than most of the stories associated with Prefontaine and Pre's Rock, there were other runners who expressed gratitude about being transformed or helped in a positive way because of Prefontaine's influence or inspiration. John, in his mid-40s, was at Pre's Rock after the Prefontaine Classic track meet on June 4, 2005. He lives in Portland, and he told me that he tries to visit the rock whenever he is in Eugene: 'I'm a track nut, and the Pre meet is the best meet in the US. I used to be a pretty serious runner, and I was a big Pre fan. He was my idol. So now I come here to pay my respects (...). I also get strength from this spot. Pre was strong. He was determined, he never gave up. I need that kind of strength in my life. I have a drinking problem, but I'm dealing with it. And coming here helps me deal with it. Pre liked to drink too, you know.'[34]

Younger runners attempt to communicate with Prefontaine for other reasons, seeking his support, guidance, and supernatural influence on their lives. For example, various websites, blogs, and Myspace pages include accounts of Prefontaine sending signs and blessings, and runners requesting help from him before races: 'hey Pre can you through [sic] down a blessing for tommorrows meet (...) Thanx, Javi'; 'I have a race tomorrow, so can you throw down a blessing or somethin? Thanks, Pre'; 'hey man can u help my friend do good in his DMR 2morrow? its his first big race.'[35] The following personal petition to Prefontaine, written on stationery, was tucked into a crevice in the wall of Pre's rock:

> Dearest Pre,
>
> I've come from Bakersfield, CA to see Eugene, Oregon (...) I've come here to your place of passing for your blessing for myself and for the one I love dearly (...) He wants to be great, Pre (...) Give him your strength: to overpower his competition. Give him your speed: to keep all other runners to his back & give him your infamous ability to endure stress and pain; so he can fight himself to the dying end & become forever immortal in the sport he loves so much (...) I ask you to grace him when it is necessary to do so (...)
>
> An eternal fan, Erica
>
> B.C. C X C & Track.

While some individuals leave notes and request blessings and help, others who visit Pre's Rock take things from the site, such as stones or dirt, or even the objects left by others. They often take photos, which similarly function as tangible mementos of their experiences and presence at the site, and documentation of the hierophanous power of the place. As mentioned, some runners kiss the rock or memorial marker, while others touch the rock or marker, sometimes with shoes or an article of clothing. For example, one local high school runner disclosed the following ritual: 'Oh yeah, I don't tell too many people about this, though, they think it's dumb, but I got my little good luck thing I do. Before a big race, I come here, touch the rock, touch my race shoes to rock to get the 'Pre power'-you know what I mean? [he laughs] Yeah, I ask Pre to help me run fast, to give me his strength. And I run with Pre in my mind. It helps, it can't hurt. And I didn't just make this up, I know other runners who have done this too.'[36] Touching racing shoes and other items to Pre's Rock to absorb Prefontaine's power or energy resembles magico-religious ideas about the spiritual force or sacred power associated with saints' relics and other objects of supernatural power, which are believed to help, heal, and protect people in various ways (Brown 1981, Wilson 1983). The practices of Prefontaine's devotees who touch things to the rock or memorial marker for good luck or to obtain 'Pre's power' also suggest the underlying concept of contagious magic. This seemingly universal belief holds that objects once in contact with each other continue to influence each other at a distance through a secret sympathy (Frazer 1979). At Pre's Rock, this concept is reflected in the practices and beliefs centered around the idea that Prefontaine's life power and aura infuses his place of death, and that his beneficial energy, spirit, or magic emanates from the rock and is available to those who seek it.

Gifts and Votive Offerings

Yet another practice, by far the most common at the site, involves leaving a personal object, often related to one's recent racing history, such as a jersey, a shoe, spikes, a race number, a hat, or some other piece of clothing. Visiting Pre's Rock with his team for the first time as a freshman runner, Cody Loy says he was 'compelled to leave something of myself (...). I laid my lucky pair of socks across a small piece of granite near the base of the Pre's rock. These socks had been worn for every race I had completed that year, and had senti-mental value to me. Maybe leaving something as simple as socks seems trivial, but from one runner to another, the idea of parting with something that you feel gives you strength equates to what Oregon lost on May 31st, 1975' (Heinz 2007: 1). George Forte, from Massachusetts, made a special journey to the rock with his daughter in July 2004, the day before her race in the National Junior Olympics. At the site, she placed a gold medal she had previously won on the memorial, just above the image of Prefontaine's face. The next day she ran a personal best to finish eighth in the country and was named an 'All American.' Her success was attributed in part to the 'good karma' she received from Pre's Rock, and as she received her medal on the podium, she thought of Prefontaine and his influence.[37]

While the objects left at Pre's Rock express a personal connection to Pre-fontaine, many of the offerings have been worn in races or in training, as things that have been in direct contact with the exertion, the sweat, the blood, the pain, and the accomplishment of the athlete. These gifts are not just objects that one has touched, but personal and symbolic pieces of oneself, imbued with one's effort, energy, or being, whether the shoes worn in training runs day in and day out for months, or a jersey saturated with sweat, or the racing spikes from a major competition. One representative offering, with the following note, was openly displayed at the site:

Dear Steve,

I have travelled across the country to see the place where you breathed your last breath. Your impact on my life has been of gigantic proportions. My life is dedicated to run with the same ardor that you did. I am leaving you my first singlet which I won my first USA Track and Field title with. You will always be with me in my runs and journeys. Best wishes, Stephen D.

In addition to articles of clothing, shoes, and race-related offerings, other common items left at the site include gifts of food and drink, particularly sports drinks such as Gatorade or Powerade, and energy bars and energy gels, as well as candy, including on one occasion an unopened box of chocolate-covered Macadamia nuts from Hawaii. People also occasionally leave bottles of beer (unopened as well as empty containers), and one afternoon at the site there was a small handwritten note next to a sealed can of Pabst Blue Ribbon beer that read: 'Pre, Thank you for the inspiration. I wish I could have known you and run with you. This one is on me. Cheers, W.D.'

During the cold and rainy months in Eugene, people have draped sweat tops, windbreakers, jackets, and even a leather coat over the memorial marker, as if to keep Prefontaine protected and warm, while the offerings of food, sports drinks, and beer appear regularly, seemingly to satisfy his appetite and quench his thirst all year round. The gifts left at the site express affection and mediate between the living and the holy dead, and resemble the widespread practice in varying cultures of leaving the favorite foods, beverages, and objects for the recently deceased and for ancestors, such as the *ofrendas* placed at Mexican Day of the Dead altars.

Many individuals also leave things at Pre's Rock that identify and represent themselves in some way, such as business cards, identification cards, personal

The memorial marker at Pre's Rock and various objects placed at the site, 2005. Photo: D. Wojcik.

portraits, race photos, or team pictures. At Pre's Rock on June 19, 2004, I spoke with Paul McMullen, who had just run a sub-4:00 minute mile at the Prefontaine Classic track meet. After the race he visited Pre's Rock and left a photo of himself running at the 1996 Olympic Games, with the note, 'Today I gave all I had, what I've kept is lost forever. Thank you Pre. #18, 19 June 2004.' He said he placed the photo on the rock 'as a token of my reverence to what Pre inspired me to do. Of course he is dead, but those that visit his shrine might say that those who run today run with Pre's spirit in their hearts (...) Thank you Pre for setting an example of how to piss off those people who have no passion, and inspire those who have it.'[38]

The letters and objects left at Pre's Rock express thanks for benefits received, help, and inspiration. In the instances in which medals, trophies, ribbons, or other awards are left at the site, the objects may represent proof of the 'success' of Prefontaine's influence and are presented as a public gesture of gratitude, much in the same manner as the votive offerings left at shrines for folk saints. Whether such objects and hand-written notes express appreciation for inspiration or for actual supernatural 'power' believed to be provided by Prefontaine, the continual presence and magnitude of the offerings reflect

Pre's Rock and the photo of Sam Haughian that was left by his friend James Thie, June 2004. Photo: D. Wojcik.

the ongoing relationship with him either as memory or as an intermediary force, with his spiritual magnetism located at the site. The presence of visitors and the images of themselves or personal objects that they place at Pre's Rock express a desire to be near and to interact with the deceased, a juxtaposition of the living and dead that symbolically connects them.[39]

The idea of Pre's Rock as a liminal site that allows communication between realms is expressed repeatedly by the individuals who leave notes, objects, and images there. Few objects were as poignant as the framed photo of Sam Haughian at the site, which contained the following hand-written message:

RIP Sam Haughian 24, UK, 5KM 13:19 (aged 22)

Dear Steve, Please look up Sam for us he would love to get some 5KM [5 kilometer] sessions in with you. He was a big fan of yours, he loves to run hard, and enjoys a nice beer or two. Look after him for us. Best wishes, James Thie and Friends.

Like Prefontaine, Haughian was a world-class runner killed in his prime, dying tragically in an automobile accident at the age of twenty-four, the same age that Prefontaine died. Haughian's friend, James Thie (aged 25) from Wales, who was running in the Prefontaine Classic track meet in 2004, made a special trip to Pre's Rock to place the photo at the base of the memorial for the following reasons:

> The similarities between Prefontaine and Sam are scary, they were both amazing 5km runners that loved to run hard and enjoy life (...) Their times were almost the same and I found out at Sam's funeral that he had cried when he finally ran a few seconds faster than Pre's best 5000m, he was Sam's hero as well. I took over with me a picture of Sam, and decided to place it with a message at Pre's rock. I thought that Sam would have liked this and asked Pre whether they could hook up for some training and some beers in the magic training centre in the Sky! This experience of losing Sam as a friend, but also the not knowing how good he could have been left me understanding more about the void left by Pre.[40]

Various photos and letters commemorating the life of someone who has died have been left at Pre's Rock on other occasions, as well as commemorative objects, such a piece of driftwood, one meter long, that contained the following inscription: 'I Love U 4 the memories dad. I hope you are in heaven running with your heroes Steve Prefontaine, Jim Fixx, Roger Bannister, and all the rest (...) that made running their life.' Such personalized and creative forms of memorialization often would not be permitted at cemeteries or more formalized memorials, yet for some people, such expressions are the meaningful equivalent of lighting a votive candle or saying a prayer in a formal religious setting.

Secular objects placed at the site, like running shoes and lucky socks and bottles of beer and Gatorade, are personal offerings of remembrance, as well as a way for some people who are not particularly religious to express feelings of communion and appreciation for the deceased. Steve Prefontaine, because of his accomplishments and the aura of his personality conveyed through oral traditions and the mass media, seems to have inspired forms of veneration that resemble the devotion to extraordinary individuals who have been deified at the vernacular level in other cultures and contexts (cf. Griffith 2003, Wilson 1983). His fans feel that they can communicate and talk to him, because he was a man of the people and a folk hero, and they reach out to him in death to keep his spirit alive.

Conclusion

In February 1999, the formalizing of Pre's Rock proceeded further after it was rumored that the site and surrounding acreage might be sold for private development. Friends of Prefontaine, including Phil Knight who knew Prefontaine in college, contributed money to preserve the site, so that it could be donated to the city of Eugene, with plans to eventually create a one-and-a-half acre memorial park in the hilly area surrounding the site. The city of Eugene widened the road and added parking places for four cars near the site in 2003, and also placed street signs at various locations pointing the way to Pre's Rock (although the signs are regularly stolen as souvenirs). Efforts by the Oregon Track Club, Lane County Tourism members, and other groups dedicated to promoting Eugene, Oregon, as 'Track Town, USA' and a 'runner's paradise' have resulted in a runner's map for the area that gives directions to the site, which is no longer referred to as Pre's Rock but as the 'Steve Prefontaine Memorial.' There are rumors that the future memorial park at the site will include benches and trails to honor Prefontaine and possibly a life-sized statue of him. How will the site be transformed as it becomes increasingly formalized, and to what extent will the practices and desires of Prefontaine's fans be acknowledged, ignored, or restricted in the years ahead?

With the United States Olympic Trials scheduled to be held in Eugene, Oregon, in the summer of 2008, the popularity of Steve Prefontaine will no doubt increase, and his image and legacy will be highlighted and promoted through film, media, and commercial products. An entire clothing line of Prefontaine-branded apparel is already for sale, as are posters, coffee mugs, and other paraphernalia. Some individuals have been critical of the commercialization of Prefontaine and the corporate use of his image (see Walton 2004).

Nonetheless, most of those who visit Pre's Rock seem to embrace and enjoy the various Prefontaine products now available, and some of them wear their Pre T-shirts to the site, and occasionally leave a Prefontaine-themed object at place where he died.[41]

Regardless of the commodification of Prefontaine, for many of his devotees, the power of the legendary runner's aura resides at Pre's Rock. Inspired by the legends, lore, and media portrayals of Prefontaine, his fans come here seeking a tangible connection, an 'authentic' encounter with their hero that is not commercialized or mass-mediated. At this peaceful place on the side of the road, nestled in the verdant overgrowth and beneath a canopy of trees, the memory of Prefontaine is revived and nurtured through the desires of those who admire him. His fans have transformed his place of death into a vibrant ritual space that is constantly in the process of creation. Here, Prefontaine's life-force infuses the landscape, and his spirit is present and accessible to those who kneel beside his image for a photo, kiss the rock or the memorial marker, and offer hand-written notes and objects to him. For more than thirty years, Pre's Rock has been sustained by the folk traditions and vernacular spirituality of Prefontaine's admirers, and this pilgrimage site and roadside shrine for a fallen runner will continue to attract Pre's people in the future, as a grassroots expression of their love, yearning, and reverence for Steve Prefontaine.

Notes

1 I would like to thank Arne Alvarado, Tom Atkins, Steve Bence, Beatrice Caponecchia, Larry Norris, Jack Santino Kelley Totten, Konrad Wojcik, and the students in my classes for their interest and help with this project; special thanks also to the individuals who have allowed me to quote them in this essay. I am especially grateful to Peter Jan Margry for his patience and encouragement.
2 When I began my research at Pre's Rock, I was initially somewhat uncomfortable asking people about their reasons for visiting the site, but I soon discovered that most individuals willingly and often enthusiastically talked about their presence at the site and Prefontaine's importance to them. Unless otherwise noted, all the quotes included in this essay come from author interviews at the site or correspondences by telephone and email.
3 Fans frequently cite the following quote by Prefontaine when referring to his 'artistic' style of running: 'Some people create with words, or with music or with a brush and paints. I like to make something beautiful when I run. I like to make people stop and say "I've never seen anyone run like that before." It's more than just a race, it's a style. It's doing something better than anyone else. It's being creative' (Jordan 1997: 161). Oregon runner and author Kenny Moore compa-

red Prefontaine's charisma to that of a seasoned performer, always aware and responding to his audience: 'He did it the way a great actor does in a theater, who draws the crowd into a performance, who senses what the crowd wants that night, who changes things and conspires to do things by the throng' (Anderson 2005: B5).

4 Steve Bence (Beaverton, Oregon), 12 July 2007, personal communication.

5 Alberto Salazar, former American record holder in the 5,000 meters, 10,000 meters, and marathon, said that Prefontaine was the primary reason he came to the University of Oregon, and characterizes his lasting impact: 'Pre inspired a whole generation of American distance runners to excel. He made distance running cool. He created the whole idea of training really hard and going for it. Runners setting goals for themselves, wanting to go all out and be really tough. That was his example' (Jordan 1997: back page).

6 Prefontaine is remembered for counseling at-risk youth and volunteering at the Oregon State Prison, where he organized a running club. He also testified before the Oregon State Senate against the practice of field burning in the region (which produces toxic smoke and extreme air pollution), and he lobbied locally for bark running trials after learning about them when competing in Europe.

7 As an outspoken critic of the Amateur Athletic Union and the injustices of the American sports system at the time, some of Prefontaine's statements were considered not only rebellious but unpatriotic: 'People say I should be running for a gold medal for the old red, white, and blue and all that bull, but it's not gonna be that way. I'm the one who had made the sacrifices. Those are my American records, not the country's. I compete for myself. To hell with love of country...' (Amdur 1975: B1).

8 Individuals from varied racial and ethnic backgrounds visit the site, although the majority of visitors are white, and range in age from children and young runners to older fans, with a significant number of visitors, both male and female, in high school and college.

9 Nike provided the financial backing for the documentary about Prefontaine, *Fire on the Track*, and former friends of Prefontaine now affiliated with Nike have been involved in the production of the feature films about Prefontaine. Nike co-founder Phil Knight has stated that Prefontaine 'not only set a tone for his sport, for me at least, he set a tone for this whole company' (Anderson 2005: B5). At the Nike headquarters in Beaverton, Oregon, the Prefontaine Hall is where the company showcases its achievements and products, and where new employees go through orientation; and when employees are given a tour of Eugene, to see where Nike originated, they end the tour with a stop at Pre's Rock (Christie 2007: A1; Steve Bence [Beaverton, Oregon], 12 and 13 July 2007, personal communication).

10 Mark Lansing (Portland, Oregon), 6 August, 22 August 2004, personal communication.

11 Paul McMullen (Grand Haven, Michigan), 6 July 2007, personal communication.

12 Arne Alvarado (Eugene, Oregon), 18 May, 29 May 2004, personal communication; Kenny Moore (Eugene, Oregon), 13 July 2007, personal communication.

13 While a few people believed that Prefontaine may have swerved on the curved and narrow road to avoid hitting an animal, or that he lost control of the car as he changed a John Denver cassette tape, the most frequent narratives dealt with speculations about a 'mystery car' associated with the accident. According to the police report, there was a second car that arrived at the scene immediately after the accident, the driver of which then sped off to notify his father, a doctor. Neither the father nor the driver returned to the scene of the accident to aid the victim, although they did call the police. As a result, the police initially suspected a potential hit-and-run case, but there were no scratches on the second car and the driver was later given a lie-detector test, which he passed, and the case was closed (Jordan 1997: 152-154; Moore 2006: 331-334).

14 Unlike other roadside memorials that have been used to convey a message about the dangers of driving while intoxicated, such as the roadside crosses at the sites of fatal accidents construc-

ted by Mothers Against Drunk Driving (MADD), Pre's Rock has never been a roadside warning against the dangers of drunk driving, in part because of the controversies associated with the accident, and the power of Prefontaine's legend. A few of the narratives told at the site did emphasize drunk driving, but the driver of the mystery car was the one said to be intoxicated. In some versions the driver was a prominent citizen who lived in the neighborhood and who allegedly drove home drunk on numerous occasions, and his connections in the community helped cover-up his involvement in the accident.

15 Kenny Moore (Eugene, Oregon), 13 July 2007, personal communication.

16 The formalization of spontaneous memorials – whether at Columbine, the Oklahoma City site, the World Trade Center, or certain roadside memorials – is often characterized by controversy and debate. These sites of death and disaster evoke a range of emotions and meanings, and people differ greatly in their ideas about how to memorialize death and tragedy. In some cases, the institutionalized creation of memorial spaces is regarded as an imposition and not expressive of the range of personal emotions and community concerns. Those involved in the memorialization of Steve Prefontaine to date seem sensitive to the feelings of the people who visit the site. Yet the very existence of such roadside memorials is offensive to some people, and in the case of Pre's Rock, a few individuals expressed displeasure with the cluttered nature of site, stating it was messy, 'an eyesore,' or that it was 'disrespectful' to Prefontaine. A few people in the neighborhood feel that the constant flow of traffic and continual visitors who flock to the site is a nuisance, if not outright dangerous, while a couple of individuals said that there was something maudlin or even macabre about the creation of the site and the non-stop visits there, as if it were some sort of morbid tourism.

17 Leah Worthen (Eugene, Oregon), 28 June 2007, personal communication.

18 The increase in the prevalence of roadside memorials in the United States also may be a response to the realization that roadways are extremely dangerous places. Approximately 42,000 people are killed on the roads each year in the United States, with more than one million people having died on the roads in the USA from 1975-2000; the vernacular practices of spontaneous memorialization have changed the landscape of American roadways, now marking them as 'deathscapes,' places of mementos and mourning (Clark and Cheshire 2003-2004: 205).

19 For instance, spontaneous shrines in Northern Ireland critique paramilitary violence (Santino 2001), and roadside crosses in Texas offer commentary on issues of public safety and drunk driving (Everett 2004: 114-116). In some cases, these improvised memorials are publicly performed events that may trigger social and political action, such as the memorials established after the Madrid train attacks which criticized the government distortion of the truth about the disaster (Sánchez-Carretero 2006), and the memorials and ensuing events related to the murdered Dutch politician Pim Fortuyn, which ultimately presented a challenge to the entire Dutch political system (Margry 2007).

20 Tom Jordan, who has written a biography of Prefontaine's life and is the director of the Prefontaine Classic track meet, says that he receives hundreds of letters and emails every year from people who say they are inspired by Prefontaine (Anderson 2005: B5). Similarly, Cliff Shirley, who collects the things left at Pre's Rock, states that people who visit the site commonly express the idea of inspiration (personal communication, 4 June 2005).

21 Ben Ackerly (Richmond, Virginia), 31 July 2004, personal communication.

22 http://j-therman-bro.livejournal.com/4712.html; posted October 15, 2005, 18:17.

23 Prefontaine's Friends Preserve His Shrine (no author), Portland Oregonian, 1 March 1999.

24 Ted Pawlak (Corvallis, Oregon), 29 May 2004, personal communication.

25 The experience of communitas proposed by the Turners (1978) as a key feature of pilgrimages, as an anti-structural and completely egalitarian state, does not seem to apply to Pre's Rock,

although a sense of bonding and community may be experienced by individuals at the site. As other researchers have noted, communitas as described or imagined by the Turners does not necessarily occur at some pilgrimage sites and is an idealized concept (Eade and Sallnow 1991/2000).

26 According to Margry, to be labelled as a pilgrimage, the journey should be transitional and religiously inspired (Margry: infra).

27 The 'sacra' at Pre's Rock, defined as those sacred objects, narratives, and performances at the site, perhaps would be the shared ideals and legendary stories associated with Prefontaine's life, the ritual actions and meaningful objects left at the site, and the rock itself as a life-source, a place of contemplation and meaning.

28 Kyle L. (Eugene, Oregon), 4 June 2005, personal communication.

29 Kate McInerny (Marin County, California), 21 June, 25 June 2004, personal communication.

30 Michael Regan (Oregon City, Oregon), 26 August, 30 August 2004, personal communication. Mr. Regan is not alone in his thoughts about the spiritual and therapeutic aspects of running. As various writers have observed, distance running may evoke religious feelings for some people, who say that the solitude, concentration, and physical challenges of running provide experiences of inner peace, meditation, deep meaning, euphoric states, and spiritual renewal (see Sheehan 1978; Higdon 1992).

31 Steve Bence (Beaverton, Oregon), 12 July 2007, personal communication.

32 Thomas Pellinger (Eugene, Oregon), 24 June 2004, personal communication.

33 Thomas A. (Seattle, Washington), 28 May 2006, personal communication.

34 John W. (Portland, Oregon), 4 June 2005, personal communication. Prefontaine's legendary drinking exploits are well known in local runner's lore and have been recounted by those who knew him (cf. McChesney 1981) but have been largely de-emphasized in the media accounts and films about him.

35 http://profile.myspace.com/indexcfm?fusaction=user.viewprofile&friendid=9098819.

36 Ryan C. (Eugene, Oregon), 20 May 2005, personal communication.

37 George Forte (Rehoboth, Massachusetts), 12 August 2004, personal communication.

38 Paul McMullen (Grand Haven, Michigan), 6 July 2007, personal communication.

39 In particular, the photographic images left at Pre's Rock, as extensions of oneself, invite the spirit of the deceased to be part of this world and to join a community of other images--family, friends, admirers-carefully arranged with the array of colorful objects and flowers left at the site, bringing life to the place of death.

40 James Thie (Cardiff, Wales), 7 July 2007, personal communication. Thie, a self-proclaimed 'Pre nut' who named his springer spaniel puppy 'Prefontaine,' says he had made a previous pilgrimage to Pre's Rock in 2002 after running his first sub-4:00 minute mile in San Francisco: 'Even being a British kid a few thousand miles away we grew up hearing the Pre stories and knew what happened to this amazing young runner. For that reason visiting Eugene and Pre's rock became something that I always wanted to do' (Thie, 7 July 2007, personal communication).

41 There are even runners who exhibit a Prefontaine-inspired style, what several people at the site knowingly referred to as 'the Pre look'-shaggy '70s hair groomed like Prefontaine's; some version of the 'Pre mustache' or the 'Pre sideburns'; and an overall physical presence bearing a resemblance to Prefontaine. But these 'Pre impersonators,' unlike Elvis impersonators, are relatively rare.

IV The Realm of Life, Spirituality and Death

Chapter 9

Going with the Flow: Contemporary Pilgrimage in Glastonbury

Marion Bowman

Introduction

Glastonbury is undoubtedly the most multivalent pilgrimage site in Britain. It has a long history of drawing people to it (Bowman 1993), inspiring myth, speculation and (many would claim) transformation. However, while that might be said of any number of traditional pilgrimage destinations, perhaps the most striking feature of this small Somerset town is the extent to which it acts as a magnet for an ever-increasing variety of pilgrims, with varied forms of pilgrimage and multiple understandings of what pilgrimage might mean or be. Because a variety of people come to Glastonbury with assorted interests, aims and expectations, a spectrum of pilgrimage activity can be seen here, from more traditional Western Christian models, through interfaith pilgrimage, Goddess pilgrimage, Celtic calendar-related activity, conference/symposium attendance, earth energy-inspired journeying, one-off instances of spiritually significant co-presence (which may or may not be considered pilgrimage), and virtual pilgrimage.

Much of the contemporary spiritual interest and pilgrimage activity in Glastonbury relates to the projection of Glastonbury as a sacred center far back into the pre-Christian past, as well as assertions of its importance as a sacred site of particular relevance and potency now (Bowman 2005). Myth and speculation abound concerning Glastonbury's prehistory; great claims are made for its status as an ancient cultic center of Goddess worship, as a Druidic seat of learning, and as the Avalon of Arthurian legend. Glastonbury's Christian status as the earliest site of Christianity in England, allegedly visited by Joseph of Arimathea and perhaps even Jesus himself, and as the possible repository of the Grail, is likewise wreathed in legend and conjecture. Claims concerning its magical properties, its closeness to the Otherworld, its special energies, and its national, international, and planetary significance further add to its magnetism.

Knott (2005: 33) claims that 'the particularity of a place arises from the complexity of its social relations and the sum of the stories told about it,' an observation that in many ways encapsulates Glastonbury's attractions for a wide variety of residents, visitors, spiritual tourists and pilgrims. Glastonbury's contemporary drawing power could be said to have at its heart a flexible corpus of myths[1], distinctive natural and landscape features (wells, hills and trees) and since the early twentieth century, a remarkable spiritual sub-culture (see Benham 1993).

To get to grips with this multiplicity of personnel, praxis and interpretation, I shall briefly introduce Glastonbury, establish its many and varied credentials as a pilgrimage site, and then discuss some forms of traditional and non-traditional pilgrimage that occur and have occurred there. First, though, I shall deal with the context of this study, touching on ideas of spirituality, the sacred, mobility and proximity.

The Context

The material relating to pilgrimage in Glastonbury in this chapter has come from a variety of sources, including academic literature, 'insider' literature relating to Glastonbury of the type popular with visitors and pilgrims (e.g. Jones 2000; Maltwood 1964; Howard-Gordon 1997) and publicity material for events there; websites connected in various ways with Glastonbury; and fieldwork, participant observation and interview.[2]

This analysis of pilgrimage in Glastonbury is located within the academic context of what Leonard Primiano has termed 'vernacular religion,' which involves 'an interdisciplinary approach to the study of the religious lives of individuals with special attention to the process of religious belief, the verbal, behavioral, and material expressions of religious belief, and the ultimate object of religious belief' (Primiano 1995: 44). Of particular interest to us here will be 'the verbal, behavioral, and material expressions of religious belief' to be found in various forms of pilgrimage activity, as well as the 'bidirectional influences of environments upon individuals and of individuals upon environments in the process of believing' (Primiano 1995: 44). However, as this study ranges from traditional to non-traditional forms and understandings of pilgrimage, in some cases those involved might be uncomfortable with the idea of 'religious belief,' preferring the term 'spirituality.'

In the latter part of the 20th century, many people started to use 'spirituality' to denote a particular understanding of religious and spiritual matters. Religion for some in the West became a term with negative connotations – institutionalized, hierarchical, patriarchal, oppressive, 'out of touch,' worldly – that is to say, whatever they disliked about or disapproved of in their experience or perception of 'conventional' religion. Spirituality, by comparison, became a positive term, perceived as a personal, intuitive, experiential involvement with the divine, the supernatural, or the Universe. While there are, of course, a great many people for whom religion continues to have very positive connotations and who would regard the idea of spirituality divorced from religion as puzzling (if not absurd), spirituality for those who, in Grace Davie's (1994) words, are 'believing without belonging' is regarded as 'purer' and more all-embracing than religion. As one young woman told me, 'religion is about boundaries; spirituality is about lack of boundaries.' Challenging, 'fuzzying' and dissolving boundaries is very much part of the contemporary discourse in places like Glastonbury, as boundaries and distinctions are often regarded as part of 'old order' forms of religiosity which need to be displaced in favor of a more 'evolved,' universalized outlook. As one Glastonbury shop owner told me, 'I am Christian, I am Buddhist, I am Hindu – of course I am not *really* all those things, but I can take the best, the essence from all those traditions.'

Spirituality has thus become a word with a number of emic and etic meanings, covering those who are within or on the peripheries of an identifiable religion, and those who, although non-aligned (i.e. not committed to any particular religious group or 'spiritual path'), perceive themselves to be 'spiritual' or involved in spiritual activity by virtue of their worldview and lifestyle. The 'autonomization' of spiritualities from religions, as Hanegraaff (1999) puts it, and the 'turn to subjective life' (Heelas and Woodhead 2005) are particularly obvious in Glastonbury in the 'integrative spirituality' of those who exercise consumer choice in relation to ideas and practices from a wide variety of religious, historic, indigenous and esoteric traditions in order to produce highly personalized forms of religiosity. However, while such an approach might be characterized as DIY (do it yourself) religiosity, the fact that you have to 'do it yourself' is not the same as doing it *by* yourself. Glastonbury is considered a good place to pursue spirituality – in whatever direction and with whatever degree of intensity the individual wishes – because there are so many people engaged in similar pursuits, and because the place itself is thought to be supportive.

It is worth noting two aspects of contemporary spirituality that have particular resonance in relation to pilgrimage: interconnectedness and 'synchronicity' (or meaningful coincidence). Interconnectedness refers to a 'holistic' way of regarding relationships between different people, between different places, between human and non-human beings, between people and planet, between the seen and the unseen, between the past and the present. In highly personalized spiritual contexts or, perhaps more correctly, in contexts where authentication comes though personal experience, synchronicity is considered highly meaningful. Frequently, when people talk about feeling 'drawn' or 'called' to Glastonbury, they tell of a number of circumstances or 'coincidences' that either gave them the idea of coming to Glastonbury or enabled them to get there to immense spiritual benefit; it is not uncommon for people to refer to themselves, in retrospect, as 'unconscious pilgrims.' As I was told recently: 'People often come without fixed purpose, but find themselves finding something.'

The notion of Glastonbury as a site of the sacred is key to understanding its ubiquitous appeal. As one Glastonbury-related website claims:

> The growing interest in sacred places has led to a modern awakening in the value of Pilgrimage. In every age there have been Pilgrims travelling to the sacred sites and places of the world as an act of spiritual devotion to their particular creed (...) The difference now is that the modern Pilgrims visiting the sacred places are of many different beliefs and often of no belief. They do not necessarily come to be in touch with any specific divinity but they come to be in the energies of the sacred places and by being in

these places to understand themselves more clearly and to see their role in the world.[3]

'The sacred' is accorded the highest degree of respect, awe and seriousness by many in Glastonbury. However, just as spirituality is now widely regarded as a somewhat 'free form' and/or 'form free' quality, precisely what the sacred is, and what makes a place sacred, is open to a wide spectrum of explanations. Glastonbury is considered to be a place endowed with a *number* of sacred sites, and experiencing sacred sites is thought to bring myriad benefits including healing, self-knowledge, resolution of problems, and simply 'feeling good.' One regular attendee of the annual Anglican Pilgrimage declared: 'It's quite a sacred place, it has a nice friendly feel, and even if you weren't terribly religious you'd still get a lot out of it. There's definitely something about Glastonbury.'

I met a woman who had once been given a gift from Chalice Well that she had particularly liked; some years later, in a state of bereavement and exhaustion after the death of her elderly parents, she remembered the gift and decided to come to Glastonbury for a break and stay at Chalice Well. During her stay, she had 'deeply meaningful experiences' each day in the Chalice Well gardens, culminating in a sense of 'profound peace'; all this she attributed to the sacredness of Glastonbury in general and Chalice Well in particular. In the Glastonbury context the presence of 'the sacred' (whether undefined and unarticulated, or differently defined and articulated) is broadly accepted as an explanation of the town's drawing power.

Coleman and Eade in *Reframing Pilgrimage: Cultures in Motion* (2004: 18) identify in contemporary pilgrimage 'diverse processes of sacralization of movement, persons and/or places.' Such concepts have resonance for the varied manifestations of pilgrimage in Glastonbury for, as we shall see, people not only travel purposefully to Glastonbury to experience and participate in the sacred, but also self-consciously to help activate the sacred and to sacralize the landscape. Whether reclaiming, reactivating, or creating the sacred, people come to Glastonbury to 'participate in sacred-making activities (...) according to paradigms given by the belief systems to which they are committed' (Anttonen 2000: 281).

Though not specifically directed towards pilgrimage *per se*, the work of sociologist John Urry on mobility and proximity is useful in relation to understanding the different forms of pilgrimage in Glastonbury. Urry starts with the basic question 'why do people physically travel?' and concludes that to answer this it is necessary to understand the importance of proximity and co-presence. Urry identifies three 'bases of co-presence, face-to-face, face-the-place, and face-the-moment' (2002: 262).

Firstly, a variety of people 'intermittently come together to "be-with" others in the present, in moments of intense co-present fellow feeling' (2002: 261). Although festivals, conferences and seminars are cited as examples, pilgrimage could very easily figure in the list of occasions he identifies as co-presence. Such moments of co-presence are necessary to sustain normal patterns of social life often organized on the basis of extensive time-space distanciation with lengthy periods of distance and solitude (Urry 2002: 261). One regular attendee of the annual Anglican Glastonbury Pilgrimage commented: 'When you're here, you're amongst your own. Perhaps in this day and age that's one of the most important things, we all come together, we're all here as Christians.' Similar sentiments have been expressed by women who regularly attend the annual Goddess Conference, regarding it as their 'annual fix' of being 'part of an international Goddess community,' while an individual pilgrim said that whereas in normal life it was easy to feel a bit 'odd and isolated,' in Glastonbury, where there are many spiritual seekers and people are open to the pursuit of different paths, one felt like 'part of a bigger picture.'

The importance of 'facing-the-place' is also self-evident in pilgrimage: 'Not only do people feel that they "know" someone from having communicated with them face-to-face, but they desire to know a place through encountering it directly. To be there for oneself is critical. (...) Thus there is a further sense of co-presence, physically walking or seeing or touching or hearing or smelling a place' (Urry 2002:261).

In conversation with a couple who regularly come to Glastonbury on their own 'mini pilgrimage,' the woman said, 'It's just so spiritual here, it makes your knees knock!' Finally, Urry describes 'facing the moment': 'There is a further kind of travel to place, where timing is everything. This occurs when what is experienced is a "live" event programmed to happen at a very specific moment. Co-presence involves "facing-the-moment"' (Urry 2002: 262).

While artistic, celebratory and sporting occasions are given as examples of the latter, events coinciding with saints' days or Holy Week or with full moons, solstices, and significant points on the so-called 'Celtic' or eight-fold calendar observed by many modern pagans could all be seen as temporary and temporally constituted instances of co-presence. The Harmonic Convergence of 16 August 1987, when hundreds gathered on Glastonbury Tor as part of a global attempt to 'activate' sacred sites around the world (Ivakhiv 2001: 85; 2007: 265-266), could also fall into this category. Urry talks of 'the globalization of intermittent co-presence,' concluding that 'whatever virtual and imaginative connections occur between people, moments of co-presence are also necessary' (Urry 2002: 264).

All three 'bases of co-presence' – alone or in combination – can be recognized in both traditional and non-traditional pilgrimages. 'Face-the-place' has obvious resonance for 'place-centred sacredness' (Eade and Sallnow 2000: 8). In pilgrimage, 'face-to-face' might be extended not only to one's fellow travelers, but to the significant figures who are the focus of 'person-centred sacredness' (Eade and Sallnow 2000: 8), such as Jesus, Joseph of Arimathea and the Goddess in Glastonbury. Most interesting from our point of view are the importance and persistence of co-presence even in an age of 'virtual pilgrimage' and increasing individuality in the sphere of religiosity.

Simultaneous Pilgrimage in Glastonbury

Superficially, Glastonbury is a small market town (population ca. 9,000) in the southwest of England, in the Somerset 'Levels' (low-lying drained marshland). If it is misty, it is possible to get some inkling of what it was like before the Levels were drained, when Glastonbury was essentially an island; this is one reason why it has been equated with the Isle of Avalon, where according to legend King Arthur was taken for healing after his last battle.[4]

The center of the town is dominated by a large green space, containing the ruins of a great medieval abbey, now a heritage site. On a summer weekend, the Abbey grounds might be full of Anglicans (if it is a Saturday) or Roman Catholics (if it is a Sunday), for both groups celebrate Mass there as the highlight of their annual pilgrimages to the place where St Joseph of Arimathea reputedly established the first church in England and where, some firmly believe, Jesus himself visited.[5] People wishing to celebrate Glastonbury's past status as a great center of Marian devotion on other occasions might seek the Shrine of Our Lady of Glastonbury housed in the 1940s Catholic church across the road from the ruins. However, at other times of year one might see individuals with dowsing rods pacing the Abbey grounds, lost in concentration as they follow leylines; members of the Sufi Naqshbandi-Haqqaniyya visiting the place Shaikh Nazim al-Haqqani al-Qubrusi has identified as 'the spiritual heart of England'; a lone woman clutching a copy of Kathy Jones's *In the Nature of Avalon* (2001) in a place she believes was sacred to the Goddess before Christianity was 'imposed' upon it; or some of the many people (frequently American) who come to see the site of King Arthur's tomb.[6]

For such a small place, the High Street can be surprisingly busy. Each summer there is the Goddess Conference and its Goddess Procession, with participants following an effigy of the Goddess, singing Goddess chants and bearing banners with images of female deities. Occasionally, the sound of a 'Hare Krishna' chant alerts one to an ISKCON procession. People with an interest in cereology (crop circles) visit for their annual symposium, while some hope to experience the 'buzz' of Glastonbury which is allegedly caused by the earth energies there, testing the local rumor that the pedestrian crossing on the High St is built on a leyline. Just off the High Street is an area collectively known as the Glastonbury Experience, a major focus for many pilgrims and visitors to the town. Set around an outer and inner courtyard, the complex houses the Glastonbury Goddess Temple, the Library of Avalon (set up as successor to the once great library of Glastonbury Abbey), the Isle of Avalon Foundation (a center for spiritual learning in the tradition of the alleged Druidic university), the Bridget Healing Centre, a restaurant, and shops selling stone and crystals ('Stone Age'), incense ('Starchild Apothecary') and books ('Courtyard Books'). Beyond the High Street, some converge on the converted church that houses the Maitreya Monastery for Dharshan with His Holiness

Spirituality and Shopping: Multifaith shrine area in Stone Age, *a crystal shop within the Glastonbury Experience courtyard. In addition to assorted crystals and items from Buddhist and Hindu material culture, there are notebooks in which customers can write requests for healing for themselves or others, 2007. Photo: M. Bowman.*

Gyalwa Jampa, an American who claims to be an incarnation of both Jesus and Buddha (see Bowman 2003-2004), while others come for an Anglican retreat at Abbey House or a 'Holistic Retreat' at Shekinashram (in the building that formerly housed the Satya Sai Baba Centre). Wandering round town at any time of year there might be a Baha'i, mindful of the Glastonbury connections of Abdu'l Baha (son of Baha'u'llah) or someone drawn as a result of reading Marion Bradley's highly influential novel *Mists of Avalon* (1986), set in Glastonbury. Fans of the popular singer Van Morrison might even be taking the advice that 'Anyone planning a tour of important Van places should put Glastonbury high on their list.'[7]

Glastonbury Tor, topped by St Michael's Tower, showing some of the contours that are endlessly speculated upon. It is said that whatever time of day or night you look at the Tor, there is sure to be someone up there, 2006. Photo: M. Bowman.

On one edge of town a strikingly shaped hill, the Tor, rises up steeply, and it is easy to understand why people speculate endlessly whether it is an impressive man-made labyrinth, the 'spiral castle' of Celtic mythology, or part of a landscape figure of a Goddess (see Howard-Gordon 1997:9-20) or, more mundanely, whether its contours are the result of erosion or strip lynch agriculture. On the Tor one might find a gathering of Druids and pagans celebrating a significant point on their eight-fold calendar, considering themselves part of a Celtic tradition stretching back to the time when Glastonbury was reputedly 'a great Druidic center of learning.' Some people might be walking with great concentration along the lower contours of the Tor, tracing a three-dimensional ceremonial maze, or there might be a group of women creating sacred sound for their own and the planet's healing.

At the foot of the Tor is Chalice Well, the chalybeate, red staining water of which is associated by some with the Chalice used at the Last Supper and Christ's blood, by others with the menstrual blood of the Goddess. The wellhead might be decorated with holly, mistletoe and other seasonal greenery at Winter Solstice, an individual might bathe a crystal in the water, or a group of

The wellhead at Chalice Well, decorated for Lammas, 2003.
Photo: M. Bowman.

people could be engaged in Buddhist meditation. At a tap in the outer wall of Chalice Well, people collect the water in bottles, possibly tying a piece of ribbon on the overhanging branches. Opposite Chalice Well is the White Spring, which for a period in the 1990s was 'reclaimed' as an 'ancient' rag well, and which some believe marks the entrance to the Underworld ruled by Gwyn ap Nudd, King of Faery (Howard-Gordon 1997: 70).

On Wearyall Hill is a small, bent thorn tree, according to local legend on the spot where St Joseph of Arimathea's staff took root to become the Glastonbury Thorn, that flowers both in spring and around Christmas. On the feast of St Joseph, one might find a short service and tree blessing taking place under the auspices of the Celtic Orthodox Church. Some visitors tie material onto the tree as a symbol of the prayers or 'intentions' voiced there or simply to honor the tree; others leave offerings of flowers or candles at its base. Alternatively, as Wearyall Hill is regarded as the fish of the sign Pisces on the Glastonbury Zodiac (some discern a huge zodiac in the landscape in and around Glastonbury), Pisceans might visit with the expectation of feeling particularly in tune with the energies there, or people might be taking part in the

Glastonbury Milky Way Pilgrimage, 'a 21 mile pilgrimage across the Glaston-bury Zodiac.'[8] In an area beyond the remains of Glastonbury's defunct leather industry is Bride's Mound, associated by some with the Celtic St Bridget, by others with the Goddess Bridie, focus of an annual pilgrimage on 1 February (St Bridget's Day in the Christian calendar, and Imbolc on the 'Celtic' calen-dar). Meanwhile, far beyond the town, people from all over the world can experience Glastonbury 'virtually' through one of its many websites, such as Sig Lonegren's 'The Glastonbury Pilgrim's Trail.' Such is the immensely varied nature of pilgrimage in Glastonbury.

This snapshot of Glastonbury has neither taken in all its sacred sites nor exhausted all the forms of pilgrimage to be found there. It should, however, give a flavor of the diversity of places, persons and practices to be found there. Furthermore, this multiplicity of pilgrimage and visitor activity has given rise to a vibrant and varied spiritual service industry of specialist shops, cafes, as-sorted spiritual tour guides, a range of spiritual souvenirs, and accommoda-tion which provides the healing, therapy or meditation of choice (see Bowman

The ruins of Glastonbury Abbey in the centre of town; many non-Christians also regard it as a sacred site for a variety of reasons, 2006.
Photo: M. Bowman.

1993: 49-54; Drown 2001). Shekinashram, for example, is 'an ashram and ho-listic retreat center' that describes itself as a western evolution of an ancient tradition where sacred space is created away from the world where individuals come to both cultivate and draw upon spiritual sustenance.[9] It offers B&B accommodation, daily morning kirtan and meditation, organic vegan raw food lunches, sauna, complementary therapies, and hosts courses on such varied topics as Working with Crystals, Foot Reading, Reiki, Bhakti Yoga, Shamanic Training, Thai Massage, Sound Healing and Fire Walking. It is the sheer variety and simultaneity of activity and belief that makes Glastonbury such a multivalent pilgrimage destination.

Vernacular Christianity

As I have pointed out elsewhere (Bowman 2000, 2003-2004), although Christianity has frequently been regarded as the marker of 'conventional' religiosity, against which 'alternative' spiritual activity has been measured and contrasted, Glastonbury's Christian history and status are based heavily on vernacular myth and tradition that can hardly be regarded as mainstream. The central legend is that Joseph of Arimathea brought Christianity to Glastonbury shortly after the crucifixion, erecting a church on what was later the site of Glastonbury Abbey, and bringing with him the staff that was to root and become the Glastonbury Thorn (celebrated annually in the Holy Thorn Ceremony; see Bowman 2006), the chalice used at the Last Supper (the Holy Grail) and possibly also some of Christ's blood. Furthermore, the reason for Glastonbury's continuing attraction for many Christians is the myth that Jesus himself came to Glastonbury as a boy. Elements of Christian vernacular myth and practice in Glastonbury have been and remain beyond the approval and control of conventional Christianity. In addition, the alleged 'discovery' of the body of King Arthur by monks in the grounds of Glastonbury Abbey in 1191 seemed to confirm popular associations between Joseph of Arimathea and the Grail, the Holy Grail and Arthur, and Glastonbury and Avalon, so contemporary variations on Arthurian themes also owe a lot to vernacular Christian traditions.

The Blessing of the Holy Thorn on Wearyall Hill by the Celtic Orthodox priest on the Feast of St. Joseph of Arimathea, 31 July 2006. In the distance, also making their way to the Holy Thorn, a procession of Spanish women in Glastonbury as part of a series of pilgrimages throughout Europe 'rediscovering' Mary Magdalen. Photo: M. Bowman.

Although Glastonbury ceased to be a major Roman Catholic pilgrimage site after the brutal dissolution of the Abbey in 1539, the town continued to attract attention intermittently, and in the late nineteenth/early twentieth centuries there was considerable esoteric Christian activity (influenced by both Theosophy and the Celtic revival), with concomitant renewal of some informal pilgrimage activity. In 1907/1908 the Abbey grounds and ruins came into the possession of a Church of England-based trust, and from 1924 regular Anglican pilgrimage activity was established. On one weekend each summer, there is now an Anglican pilgrimage on a Saturday, followed by a Roman Catholic pilgrimage on the Sunday. Additionally, the ultra-conservative Society of Saint Pius X holds a Glastonbury Pilgrimage on alternate years. In 1978 there was a 15-day Ecumenical Walking Pilgrimage from Arundel to Glastonbury, and various other Christian organizations have visited or held events in the town (including specifically youth-oriented phenomena such as the evangelical Hearts on Fire celebrations and the Roman Catholic Youth 2000 weekends)[10]. Christian pilgrimage in Glastonbury is undoubtedly subject to some contestation between denominations and factions (see Bowman 2004), but there is also an awareness of celebrating Glastonbury's Christian heritage in the face of the many claims being made on and for Glastonbury by a great variety of spiritual seekers. One woman spoke of the 'importance of witnessing through pilgrimage,' while the Anglican Pilgrimage was described by a participant as 'the Church cheerfully militant.'

In Christian pilgrimage to Glastonbury, there is a celebration of Glastonbury's person-centered sacredness (Jesus, Joseph of Arimathea, Celtic and other saints associated with the site) as well as the commemoration of Glastonbury's status as a great Marian pilgrimage center in the Middle Ages when the Abbey was at its height. In form, the annual pilgrimage weekend with its processions, banners, crosses, statues, singing and ritual activity looks very much the model of 'traditional' Christian pilgrimage. People have traveled purposefully to be in a special place, at a specific time, to 'be with' likeminded others, celebrating (and some would claim experiencing) person-centered and place-centered sacredness. Although attendance at the formal Anglican and Roman Catholic pilgrimages is dropping, they remain powerful and enjoyable experiences for those who do participate. Glastonbury is considered by the pilgrims I spoke to at the Pilgrimage weekend in 2007 to be 'peaceful,' 'sacred ,' and above all to have 'a special atmosphere.' Even the Abbey's ruined state is turned to advantage, as a number commented on the particular 'feel' of holding the service outdoors: 'Somehow having the service in the open air always seems a bit more spiritual, you're under God's heaven,' and 'You're out in the open, so you feel your prayers and hymns are going straight up to God.' Many felt that traveling in the coach with other people from their diocese strengthened the sense of a church community at home, as well as reminding them that they are part of a larger Christian community: 'Every year it's a pleasure, lovely being with a crowd of people all doing the same thing.' One Welsh woman attending the Anglican Pilgrimage found the procession down the High Street 'very impressive and uplifting; but when you get into the ruins [of the

Abbey] it's like, as if you're out in the countryside, it's so quiet and peaceful, with everyone there, it's like a little community, just the feeling that you have when you're all together.'

Avalon, King Arthur and the Goddess

It has long been said that there are two types of people living in Glastonbury, the Glastonians, who think they are living in a small Somerset town, and the Avalonians, who *know* they are living in Avalon.

Glastonbury's Arthurian and Avalonian connections have given rise to a variety of pilgrimage activity, as Arthur has proved a particularly versatile character in contemporary spirituality (see Bowman 2007). A high percentage of visitors to the Abbey – particularly Americans – give Arthur as the reason for their visit to the site. Still a Christian hero for some, he is immensely significant for Celtic-oriented Pagans and Druids, as well as becoming an icon of the New Age spiritual seeker. As one Glastonbury resident and self-styled 'New Ager' told me: 'The whole idea that he lies here sleeping and will rise again, some people interpret that as meaning he'll rise again to lead us into a New Age, a new cycle, a new beginning, a new phase in world evolution.'

In the 1920s Theosophist and artist Katherine Maltwood claimed to discern in the landscape in and around Glastonbury a huge planisphere, the Glastonbury Zodiac (Maltwood 1964; Carley 1996). She argued that the events described in the grail stories had in fact taken place in the Glastonbury area, the different characters and creatures encountered simply reflecting the movement through the year. Some thus consider the Zodiac to be the true 'Round Table' of Arthurian legend. Chris Trwoga's *Grail Quest in the Vales of Avalon* (2001) lays out seven journeys in the Glastonbury area, allowing the individual to 'literally follow in the footsteps of the knights of Britain's Heroic Age as they searched for the greatest treasure of all – the Sangreal – the fulfillment of all we have ever yearned for' (publicity leaflet). The Glastonbury Zodiac Companions have held regular walks to different sites at appropriate points in the astrological year for many years, while some individuals seek particular areas on the Zodiac according to their star sign. On the Glastonbury Zodiac, Aquarius is represented by a Phoenix whose beak dips into Chalice Well, for example, so there is an expectation that Aquarians might feel particularly drawn there, as well as the association between Glastonbury and the Age of Aquarius. The construction of the Glastonbury Zodiac has been attributed to Sumerians or Atlanteans, while some regard it as 'a spontaneous creation of the Earth itself' (Ivakhiv 2001: 111); it is also significant to those interested in UFOs and crop circles, for many contend that the Zodiac must have been planned from above, thereby 'confirming' their belief in Glastonbury's long association with extraterrestrials.

However, there are different visions of the nature and significance of Avalon. Many have been influenced in their 're-visioning' of Avalon by Marion Zimmer Bradley's novel *The Mists of Avalon* (1982), a female-oriented retelling of the Arthurian saga. Kathy Jones, long-term Glastonbury resident and an influential figure in the Goddess movement there, claims:

> Today Avalon is the Otherworldly counterpart of the small country town of Glastonbury in Somerset, England. It is a magical land where the Goddess has lived from time immemorial and still lives today. It is a place of birth, transformation, death and rebirth, a place where we can let go of the old and assist in birthing the new.[11]

Many involved in Goddess spirituality claim to discern various figures and symbols of the Goddess in the very landscape of Glastonbury; the Tor forms the left breast of one alleged reclining Goddess figure, the red waters of Chalice Well are regarded as her menstrual flow, while some envisage Glastonbury encompassed by the figure of a huge swan, symbol of Bridget.

The Goddess movement contributes to some of the most high-profile pilgrimage activity in contemporary Glastonbury, in connection with the Glastonbury Goddess Conference held since 1996, for many years co-organised by Kathy Jones and Tyna Redpath of *The Goddess and the Green Man* shop. The Conference always coincides with Lammas (1 August), and each year in rotation a model of the maiden, the mother, or the crone goddess is made for the Goddess in the Cart Procession, the most public aspect of the event.

As I have commented elsewhere (Bowman 2004), the Goddess community is fighting patriarchy with pageantry, self-consciously using the procession as a means of re-possessing Glastonbury for the Goddess, re-asserting 'Her' presence in the town. In producing practically a mirror image of the Christian pilgrimage processions, with images of the Goddess, goddess banners, processions, chanting and ritual, the Goddess community is physically encompassing Christian Glastonbury and spiritually reclaiming aspects of the Christian tradition there, such as devotion to the Virgin and St. Bridget. [Jones claims, for example, that 'where we find St. Bridget we know that the goddess Bridie was once honored' (2000: 16).] The processional element of the conference is highly creative and fluid, and it has increased significantly since 2000, in terms of sites visited and ground covered. It is undoubtedly the form of pilgrimage in which contestation for and of Glastonbury is most marked.

The seriousness with which goddess pilgrimage is regarded and undertaken, both within and outside the conference context, should not be underestimated. Pilgrimage is at the heart of the Glastonbury Goddess Conference, as the 2003 conference publicity makes clear:

> (...) we will once again be making collective and individual pilgrimages to the Goddess throughout the course of the Conference. We will be journeying physically, emotionally, psychically and spiritually into the Heart of Her Mysteries as they present themselves here in Avalon.

Delegates to the conference are always organized into 'Pilgrimage Circles' (groups of thirteen) for as the 2004 conference program explains, they 'play an essential supportive role in the Conference so that everyone has companions on their pilgrimage journey.' There is the expectation that pilgrimage will be an individually significant experience and that, within the context of the Goddess Conference, people might benefit from a sort of community. While some come with partners or friends, people attending the Goddess Conference are less likely to arrive (as in the case of Christians attending the Pilgrimage weekend) as part of a group. Over the years various women have stressed that attending the Conference and taking part in the Procession gives them their one opportunity in the year to be part of a group; to dress flamboyantly (both in honor of the Goddess and as a celebration of their own divine femininity); to learn new songs and chants for the Goddess; to participate in beautifully crafted ritual; to experience healing; to 'share experiences with people who understand' and 'to feel really close to the Goddess.'

Writing in *In the Nature of Avalon: Goddess Pilgrimages in Glastonbury's sacred landscape,* Jones stresses the importance of preparation (Jones 2000: 33):

It is traditional to prepare oneself for a pilgrimage, spiritually, mentally and emotionally as well as physically. It is important to spend some time beforehand thinking and praying about your purpose in making such a journey. You may be making a pilgrimage to Avalon out of curiosity, to see if you can feel something, to see if you can penetrate the Veil. Or your pilgrimage may be an act of devotion to the goddess – walking with consciousness in her sacred landscape, offering her your love, offering yourself to her. You may be asking the goddess to help you to become more conscious of her presence or asking her to open you to deeper insight or to shower you with her blessings. You may be making a pilgrimage to ask for healing of your physical, emotional, mental or spiritual wounds. You can make a pilgrimage on behalf of others – family, friends or the wider society. It can be a good idea to write down your intentions before you begin and then record your experiences as you walk and when you are complete.

Jones also elaborates on the nature of goddess pilgrimage (Jones 2000: 28):

To make a goddess pilgrimage is to journey to her holy places as an act of spiritual devotion, an act of love for the goddess. Traditionally there are four phases to any pilgrimage. The first is the pilgrimage to the sacred place itself, your journey to Glastonbury made with spiritual intent. The second phase is entry into a defined sacred enclosure or *temenos*, in this case the sacred landscape of the Isle of Avalon. The third phase encompasses your personal prayers to the goddess at the various energy centres, power spots and natural and human made altars, within the sacred landscape.

The fourth and final phase is your return to everyday reality bringing the fruits of your communion with the goddess back into the world (...).

In thus describing preparation and motivation for pilgrimage and the stages (including what in Turnerian terms would be separation and reintegration), Jones is articulating an understanding of pilgrimage that would be familiar and acceptable to pilgrims from a wide range of religious and spiritual backgrounds, as well as underlining the special nature of Glastonbury as a Goddess-imbued location.

Goddess pilgrimage activity thus occurs in Glastonbury in a variety of forms and contexts. Urry's 'intense co-present fellow feeling,' 'face-to-face' and 'face-the-place' are particularly marked in the Goddess Conference. Within Pilgrimage Circles and conference workshops and as part of large-scale, exuberant, high-profile processions, people who often follow their spiritual path in isolation can experience community, and as with the Christian pilgrimage weekend, there is also an awareness of public witness and 'reclamation'

Exterior of the Goddess Temple in the Glastonbury Experience which demonstrates the broad and syncretistic way in which the Goddess is envisaged and celebrated, 2003. Photo: M. Bowman.

especially in the procession. However, small groups and individuals also come as pilgrims, seeking the Goddess in the Glastonbury landscape or visiting England's first officially registered Goddess Temple throughout the year, at significant points on the Celtic calendar, or simply when they feel 'called by the Goddess' to be there.

Multifaith Pilgrimage

Such is Glastonbury's high status within the UK spiritual scene that a variety of religious groups has had and continues to have some sort of presence in Glastonbury, whether through having a shop front, a 'center' of some kind, or simply through regular meetings or occasional events. In addition to a range of Christian denominations, Druids, pagans and non-aligned spiritual practitioners, assorted Buddhist groups, exponents of different schools of Yoga, members of the Baha'i faith, ISKCON adherents, followers of Sai Baba, Osho and Mother Meera, practitioners and teachers from a variety of indigenous traditions, and different Sufi groups might be found in the town.

In the years before the Millennium, there was growing interest in multifaith discussion and activity, and there was an ambitious plan to build a 'Sanctuary' in Glastonbury, 'to recreate a spiritual powerhouse at the center of Glastonbury,' ideally in the Abbey grounds:

> We hold a vision to build and maintain a great Sanctuary in Glastonbury, ancient Isle of Avalon, dedicated to the divine essence within all spiritual paths. Our aim is to create a sacred space of prayer, peace, meditation and healing in the centre of Glastonbury where pilgrims of all faiths and spiritual beliefs can meet and celebrate together. We believe this is a wholly unique venture on the planet now, which will progress religious and spiritual ideas and structures in ways which we cannot yet imagine. (...) Drawing on the traditions of the past and present, it will be a seed of spiritual regeneration for the third millennium.[12]

The Sanctuary Group promoted 'Sanctuary Soundings' – a 'spiritual discussion group between people of all faiths in Glastonbury' – and it hosted
a 'Multifaith Pilgrimage.' Kathy Jones wrote an account of this 'Multifaith
Pilgrimage around the sacred sites of Avalon' which took place on 25 May
1998 for *Avalon: A Journal of Transformation from Glastonbury* (1998:4-5). With
around 30 participants, the event started with a tour of the Abbey ruins led by
John Sumner (of the ecumenical Christian group Quest) and a short Christian
service, after which the group walked to the Satya Sai Baba Centre[13] where Sai
Baba devotees played and sang 'a special selection of bhajans or devotional
songs dedicated to the gods, goddesses and gurus of all faiths' (Jones 1998:4).
The group then walked up Pilgrim's Way onto Chalice Hill, and at Bushey

*Procession up Wearyall Hill in honour of Bride/Bridget during the Glastonbury
Goddess Conference 2004; Glastonbury Tor in the background.
Photo: M. Bowman.*

Combe a Buddhist teacher led them through a walking meditation, 'helping us to become truly present in our pilgrimage' (Jones 1998: 4). Following a walk up the Tor, the group 'prayed, sang and danced in praise of the Goddess' (Jones 1998: 4). In the afternoon, a 'Celebration of Peace and Unity service' was held in a room 'full of local and visiting pilgrims' in the Glastonbury Experience, led by Maria Jory from the Temple of All Faiths in Reading, including prayers for peace by 'Rev John Sumner, Swami Sivarupananda from the Vedanta Centre at Bourne End, Mohan Dogra – a Sikh priest, Ervad Bhedwar who is a Mobed of the Zoroastrian community, Philip Koomen of the Bahai [sic] faith and Kathy Jones who loves the Goddess' (Jones 1998: 5). On this occasion (reversing the Christian pilgrimage route) people set out *from* the Abbey and visited a number of traditional pilgrimage sites within Glastonbury, ending up at the Tor, but encountering an unusual variety (even for Glastonbury) of verbal and behavioral expressions of religious belief and spirituality en route, including different forms of movement.

To some extent the Multifaith Pilgrimage, and more importantly the ambition to build the Sanctuary, typify the assumption in Glastonbury that humanity needs to move beyond the more traditional and historical boundaries and demarcations of religions. (Although the plan for the Sanctuary has not come to fruition, there are those who believe it will do so when the time is right.) In the Multifaith Pilgrimage, adherents of a variety of paths felt able to journey together in Glastonbury, with pilgrimage as a vehicle for communication, participation and aspiration.

Virtual co-presence in Glastonbury

People may be in Glastonbury for a wide range of reasons, drawn by myths, beliefs and assertions from a variety of sources. Websites have become increasingly important in the past decade, not simply in terms of providing information as to what is on, but in shaping expectations through personal accounts of experiences in and of Glastonbury, and giving currency and a sort of authority through repetition to Glastonbury's many myths and 'spiritual histories.' For example, the information site for the 2004 Glastonbury Symposium on crop circles, the Druidic university and its perpetual choir, and Glastonbury's status as a stone age pilgrimage site are all given equal, 'factual' status with its documented medieval Christian importance.[14]

Moreover, while many people come to know about Glastonbury, its varied myths and claims to significance through the Internet, that is also the means whereby people can in some ways connect with and 'visit' it. It is possible to 'virtually' visit the Roman Catholic Shrine of Our Lady of Glastonbury through a website for example;[15] petitions made on the site will be printed out and placed before the statue in St Mary's Church within 24 hours. At the Glastonbury Goddess conference of 2005, the following 'invitation' was to be found on fliers:

Yearning for Avalon?

An Invitation

Do you feel you have a soul connection with the Ancient Isle of Avalon, with the Glastonbury Red and White Springs, the Tor, the Chalice Well, and that only circumstance or maybe karma prevent you from being here in this life, perhaps as Priestess or Priest of the Goddess?

If you have travelled here for the Goddess Conference but hate the thought of leaving Avalon behind – join our email group and be welcome in our virtual community.

The group was recently started as a service by Priestesses of Avalon who had an intuition of the need and desire that many people have to be connected to Avalon.

Among the considerable number of websites relating to Glastonbury, some offer a virtual pilgrimage experience of Glastonbury, including *The Glastonbury Pilgrim's Trail: The sites and sights of Glastonbury*, by Sig Lonegren,[16] before leading the virtual pilgrim round various sites (the Abbey, Chalice Well, Wearyall

Hill, Bride's Mound, the Tor). Through such websites people become familiar with various versions of events in Glastonbury's past and with the layout of the town and different sites within it. However, ultimately, these simply inform and whet the appetite. As the Glastonbury Pilgrim's Trail concludes: 'This is the end of our pilgrimage trail. There are many other magical places in this special pilgrimage town – it's a matter of coming here and moseying round – taste it for yourself!' While there are modern mechanisms for helping people feel part of or in touch with Glastonbury (just as more traditional shrines have had newsletters and confraternities), there is nothing quite like facing-the-place.

Facing the Moment: the Solar Eclipse and Millennium Eve

The Solar Eclipse of August 1999 received considerable media coverage and captured the popular imagination in Britain. For hundreds of people of varying spiritual and ritual orientations, it seemed appropriate to be experiencing it, celebrating it, and participating in it at Glastonbury. In particular, as the highest point in Glastonbury, and as the town's most mythologized feature, the Tor appeared the natural place from which to witness this spectacle. Some people were there in groups, overtly taking part in spiritual or ritual activity in small circles, but there were also many individuals, couples and family groups. Some were exotically costumed, but most were casually attired. Some were sitting in meditation positions, others had crystals laid before them on the ground to absorb whatever energy might be released by the event. The image of the Crone Goddess from that year's Glastonbury Goddess Conference was taken up the Tor a second time – on this occasion, I was told, to witness the beginning of the eclipse of patriarchy! Local television news cameras were there to record the scene. It was a cloudy day and tension as well as expectation mounted, as there was a common worry that it would not be possible to see the eclipse. The sky darkened and it became distinctly chilly as the eclipse commenced. There was a momentary silence then a cacophony of ululations, drumming, cheers, tears, Goddess and other chants, and lots of hugging among strangers. Having, in Urry's parlance, 'faced the moment' and shared an intense experience of 'co-presence,' the crowd dispersed.

On 31 December 1999, thousands of people gathered at Glastonbury. Again, a special time demanded a special place, so a variety of people headed for Glastonbury. A large ecumenical Christian service was planned for the Abbey grounds, but it was clear that this would not be suitable for many of the town's non-Christian residents, and that numerous other people would come to Glastonbury for the Millennium experience for whom the Christian celebration would likewise be inappropriate. The National Trust gave permission for a huge bonfire at the foot of the Tor. Glastonbury resident and parapsychologist Serena Roney-Dougal had the literally spectacular idea of creating a double spiral of flares along the contours of the Tor, with 100 flares on each of the seven 'terraces' of the Tor, and a circle of 70 lanterns on top of the Tor. Each of the seven pairs of safety stewards was supposed to carry a lamp, to make a total of 777 lights. In order to raise enough money, Roney-Dougal and her team had the idea that people could sponsor a flare and write a card with their prayer or wish for the millennium, so every flare was lit with someone's message tied on to it. Roney-Dougal comments:

> Everyone in the town was included which is I think unique as normally the townspeople will have nothing to do with the alternatives – but that wasn't the case here. I felt so pleased. (…) It was a major ritual which actually worked for all participants – a fantastic night.[17]

Community artist Liz Beech also wanted to create something as 'an offering for the celebration' and for there to be something that 'the whole town could put itself behind,' residents and visitors of all persuasions. She decided to create an enormous metallic figure of a phoenix, which took seven people five days to make. On the Glastonbury Zodiac the Tor forms part of the sign of Aquarius, represented as a phoenix, and Beech subsequently discovered that the phoenix is sometimes used as a symbol for Jesus. Although Beech admits that in retrospect it seems naïve, she simply did not envisage that the phoenix and its procession up the Tor would make such an impact. The phoenix group set out from the Market Cross at seven o'clock in the evening. She said it seemed appropriate to stop at the War Memorial and contemplate war, though she did not direct anything, and simply asked for a moment's silence: 'People can be trusted to respond appropriately, they don't need to be stage managed.' As the phoenix was a heavy structure carried on a litter with poles, progress towards the Tor was slow, and the procession gathered more and more people en route; many just came out of the pubs and joined in, and there was plenty of opportunity for people to help carry it. As they would pass Chalice Well on the way to the Tor, Beech had asked if the Guardians of the Well would like to ritually exchange some Chalice Well water in return for fire (from the incense burner at the center of the structure), so there was a small ceremonial interlude at that point, then a stop at the bonfire, and eventually the phoenix reached the top of the Tor. Meanwhile, the flares were lit from nine o'clock onwards so all were alight by midnight, creating a striking pattern of lights, accentuating and celebrating the Tor's distinctive shape. An estimated 3,000 people gathered on the Tor. Liz Beech describes it all as a great 'collective': 'Not in the sense of one idea, for there were as many ideas as people, but communal.' She says of events such as Millennium Eve: 'We're required to seize the moment, spontaneously to gather when appropriate.' Glastonbury's status as a pilgrimage/sacred site for Christians and other spiritual seekers was instrumental in their decision to gather there to face the Millennial moment.

Individuals and Intermittent Co-presence

Urry talks of the importance of people 'intermittently com[ing] together to "be-with" others in the present, in moments of intense co-present fellow feeling' (Urry 2002: 261), while Coleman and Eade refer, in relation to contemporary pilgrimage, to the idea of 'meta-movement – the combination of mobility itself with a degree of reflexivity as to its meaning, form and function' (Coleman and Eade 2004: 18). The publicity for 'Pilgrimage to Avalon' with Judith Tripp ('a Transpersonal Psychotherapist, workshop leader, musician and Labyrinth facilitator') to some extent demonstrates a combination of such reflexivity and the coming together of spiritually individualistic and diverse people in pilgrimage:

I invite you to come with me on a journey of adventure, self-discovery and inspiration. Glastonbury and her environs have been a place of pilgrimage throughout the ages. From the days of the Earth-centered religions of the stone circles, through Celtic, Druidic, Arturian [sic] and Christian times, people have come here to remember their soul's purpose.

Our journey is simultaneously inner and outer. It is purposive. We will use meditation, Yoga, movement, music, and various healing arts to open to the next step in our individual spiritual paths. We will meet daily in practice and group process to affirm and integrate our experiences.[18]

It is probably fair to assume that going on and coming together in pilgrimage has always been a highly subjective experience, with different motives, preparation, expectations, degrees of difficulty and outcomes. We also know that sacred sites are frequently contested, so that the vision or significance of a place is not necessarily shared by all who encounter it. However, while some have rejected the Turners' (1978) notion of 'communitas' within pilgrimage as overly idealistic (e.g. Eade and Sallnow 2000), it seems that 'moments of intense co-present fellow feeling' (Urry 2002: 261) are very significant in contemporary society, including for those who are following a highly individual, personally 'customized' spiritual path. Drawing on French sociologist Michel Maffesoli's work on 'tribalization' and the emergence of 'neo-tribes' (1996), Finnish scholar Tuomas Martikainen comments:

The unifying element in all tribes is *puissance*, the basic vital energy of sociality, and the emotional community. (...) The New Age spiritualist is a perfect example of a neo-tribal identification. Most of the time, the person is by himself with his books, thoughts and actions, but every now and then, the tribe gathers for lectures, Internet newsgroups, and fairs, and they enjoy the *puissance* of the like-minded (Martikainen 2001: 122).

Whether we think in terms of a neo-tribal *'puissance* of the like-minded,' 'communitas,' or 'intermittent co-presence,' many of the people who come together as individual pilgrims, to participate in the Goddess Conference or

Cereology Symposium, on the eight-fold calendar, for the Millennium, or as part of the Pilgrimage to Avalon described above, are able to find in Glastonbury either broadly like-minded people or at least an environment that can embrace, accommodate, and affirm an immense spectrum of belief and praxis. There is contestation, certainly, but there is also often consensus built on the act of spiritual seeking – regardless of what is being sought, found or experienced. This returns to the point that spiritual individualism should not be equated with isolationism.

Consensus and Communitas: Earth energies

The notion of earth energies is taken immensely seriously and seen – or, more to the point, experienced – as a powerful and tangible force in Glastonbury (see Ivakhiv 2001: 108-110). Almost the first act of one businesswoman, on taking possession of her shop on Glastonbury High Street, was to identify the exact position of the leyline running through it and to bury three thousand pounds' worth of crystals on either side of it to direct the energy positively into her premises; she attributes the 'good feel' of her shop to that and considers it a very worthwhile investment. Another shop owner, who sells crystals and is a passionate advocate of crystal healing, feels that:

> There is a lot of crystal energy in this town, and crystal energy lifts things up and transforms negative energy into positive energy, that's one of the things it does, and you know we have a lot of crystals in this town. That is because Glastonbury wants crystals because that's part of its, crystals promote transformation and Glastonbury is a town of transformation, so they go really well together, that's what I find.

For some, visiting the town is quite literally about 'feeling the buzz' or 'recharging'; as one man said, it 'gives you a new energy to go back to the rat race with.' A woman long resident in Glastonbury told me that from time to time she had to go and stay somewhere else for a couple of nights when the energy got too much for her. Dowsers can frequently be found at various sites in Glastonbury, seeking or identifying different types of energies; the site for the projected Sanctuary at Glastonbury has been located by dowsing in the Abbey grounds, for example. Glastonbury is frequently described as an 'energy center' and – along with Iona and Findhorn – as part of an 'energy triangle.' As Ivakhiv points out, such 'power places' or 'power spots' are seen 'as places of personal transformation, and pilgrimages to them are considered a tool of such transformation' (Ivakhiv 2007: 267).

Though by no means the first work on the subject, John Michell's *The View Over Atlantis*, first published in 1969, was extremely influential in populari-zing ideas relating to leylines, earth energies and sacred geometry in relation to Glastonbury. Some claim that the presence in Glastonbury of the Druidic university was dictated by its status as an 'energy center,' and that Jesus was attracted here by its healing energies. Furthermore, it is claimed that the early Celtic Christians (said to have inherited esoteric knowledge from the Druids) knew of and utilized this power, particularly an energy line connecting the Tor with the High Altar in Glastonbury Abbey:

> The Abbey itself lies east west, directly on the east west energy line con-necting Glastonbury to Stonehenge and Canterbury, now the power base of the ruling Archbishop of the Church of England. When the priests said mass from the High Altar as well as invoking the energies of Christ, they also had access to the governing energies of the southern half of the British Isles (Jones 2000: 153).

Among the leylines people believe can be detected at Glastonbury are the Mi-chael and Mary Lines, reputedly lines of male and female energy, respectively, so named because it is claimed that they run through numerous sites where Christian churches dedicated to St Michael and the Virgin Mary have been built on older pagan sites. The Michael and Mary Lines are said to meet at the Tor (see Miller and Broadhurst 1990).

As conduits of earth energy, leylines are sometimes described as the ner-vous system of the planet. The assertion that Glastonbury is at the node of a number of leylines, linking to other significant sacred sites, is used as evidence of Glastonbury's global significance. As one Glastonbury resident said:

> There are more and more people now that are just accepting this, that Glastonbury is the heart center, if Gaia is the living planet and is literally the *body* of some kind of intelligence, then that intelligence must have energy centers, and often these coincide with holy places, whether they're Mecca, or Ayers Rock, or Glastonbury.

Leylines are envisaged as quasi-physical embodiments of the notion of inter-connectedness, linking apparently historically, geographically, culturally, and religiously disparate places like Glastonbury, Stonehenge, Ayers Rock (Uluru), Mecca and the Great Pyramid into a global network of earth energy, power and sacredness.

We have seen that a range of pilgrimage activity, group and individual, occurs in Glastonbury and that at certain times people feel that they have to be there, whether on a regular, annual, intermittent or one-off basis. For those for whom earth energies are potent forces, the rationale for pilgrimage and the reasons that a variety of people feel drawn to sacred sites are fairly self-evident. Glenn Broughton, Sacred Circle tour guide, makes the point that 'ancient sacred sites are not just dead relics of a bygone age':

Many are still animated by serpentine currents of Earth energies which fluc-tuate according to the seasons, the phases of the moon and even day and night. This is a living, vibrant, organic force with which we can interact today. Maybe this is what is calling us to the sites. An inexorable call by the Earth to come back into resonance with her. It is the same call that prompted millions throughout the ages to undertake arduous pilgrimages encountering many perils on the journey and even risking death on [sic] route, so strong was the call. It is a call to our mind, body and soul. Our mind alerts us to the call, our body sets off in search of the prize and it is our soul that seeks the satisfaction of harmony and balance with our source once again (Broughton 1999: 72).

Such energies are often associated with healing, so the traditional connection of pilgrimage and healing is reaffirmed:

> Our entire world is an intricate web of energies, and when we see the
> ancient sacred sites as such then they become vibrant living spaces within
> which we can effect healing on both a personal and planetary level. What
> makes the crucial difference between a tourist visit and a transformative
> experience is our intent. Intent is what activates the healing potential in
> each of us (Broughton 1999: 74).

Moreover, not only are people connecting with the land and its energies, but
with those who have journeyed before – a communitas of past and present:

> Through Sacred Circle I take people to places which have been revered
> for thousands of years. Many of them have a history of continuous use
> for spiritual purposes right up to the present day. By making a journey
> ourselves we become part of this unbroken lineage, and connect in subtle
> ways with the living heritage of this land. For some it is a quest, for others
> a pilgrimage, for others still a healing; it is what we allow it to be and it is
> always transformative on some level (Broughton 1999: 74).[19]

Indicative of the contemporary and growing interest in pilgrimage, earth
energies and spirituality is the Gatekeeper Trust, an educational charity founded in 1980, 'devoted to personal and planetary healing through pilgrimage'
which 'seeks to rediscover the ancient art of pilgrimage as a way of journeying with an awareness of the sacred nature of our environment.'[20] The Trust's
leaflets and website highlight the benefits of sacred journeying:

> Each of us knows at least one place where we feel special – somewhere
> that makes us seem more alive, more in tune with the world, more truly
> ourselves. It is here that we connect with the spirit of place and find uni-
> versal harmony.
>   As we care for places in the landscape, we find that places in ourselves
> become healed. Journeys through the outer landscape can create within us

new frontiers of inner perspective; we can discover new depths of potential in ourselves that may have lain hidden before; new gifts can be released in us.[21]

These are strong incentives for 'facing-the-place.' In 1997 a Gatekeeper Trust event in Glastonbury introduced participants to 'the special energies and celebrations around wells on each of the [Glastonbury] Zodiacal signs and their use as spiritual gateways' (Gatekeeper Trust Programme for 1997), while more recently it has publicized the 'Glastonbury Milky Way Pilgrimage,' described as 'a 21 mile pilgrimage across the Glastonbury Zodiac.'

However, the relationship between people and the Earth is not simply a one-way process in terms of benefits. Gatekeeper Trust publicity explains how walking helps the Earth:

With an understanding of how energies move through the Earth, it can be realised that just as acupuncture can restore the healthy flow of vital energy in Humans, so walking can help Mother Earth. Today this way of **caring for the Earth** is mostly a lost knowledge. Yet, historically, pilgrimage formed a central core to society. In medieval times, for instance, pilgrimage routes were established all over Europe. The Australian Aborigines still go on their "**walk abouts**," walking the "**song lines**" very much in tune with the needs of their land. Walking in this way can enhance the natural energies that flow through the Earth's crust, as can dance, song and prayer, helping to bring **healing** and balance to the environment and to the planet as a whole.[22]

Thus, 'superficially' varied pilgrimage and praxis are understood to have at their core the *same* spiritual purpose and benefits, and universal applicability.

During the 2004 Glastonbury Goddess Conference, for example, there was an extended ceremonial pilgrimage to four sites within Glastonbury specifically 'to generate healing energy and to radiate it to all parts of Brigit's Isles and beyond' (Goddess Conference Programme 2004: 7). The Earth Ceremony on Chalice Hill was typical of the day's events:

As we face outwards to all the directions we will sing our Earth Chant and send clearing and healing energy outwards from Avalon through the meridians and energy lines of the Earth, which is Her sacred body, to the whole of the land which is Brigit's Isles, and connecting to the land of Europe and to all the continents (Goddess Conference Programme 2004: 9).

The morning after these events, conference delegates were told that they had truly sent their and Brigit's healing out across the land, and that 'something has changed in the landscape because of the work we did yesterday.'

As the quotations in this section have indicated, there is a growing body of opinion concerning earth energies and leylines that has a number of implications for perceptions of and attitudes to pilgrimage. Earth energies are perceived to have connective roles between different eras, localities, cultures and worldviews. Earth energies can both account for and accommodate a broad spectrum of belief and praxis, whether 'serially' in history or simultaneously at the present time, and are used to support the idea that literally 'beneath the surface' seemingly disparate spiritual outlooks have some common elements or are in some way related. In this context, pilgrimage to Glastonbury is seen as a timeless, natural, instinctive and beneficial (for both person and planet) activity, whether conducted collectively, individually, or as a collective of individuals.

Conclusion

'Pilgrimage and Glastonbury are synonymous,' claims Sig Lonegren on his Glastonbury Pilgrim's Trail website.[23] Undoubtedly, many people who feel drawn to Glastonbury are consciously thinking of it as pilgrimage and have the clearly articulated purpose of visiting it as part of their spiritual journey because they consider it a sacred place. Urry's three 'bases of co-presence, face-to-face, face-the-place, and face-the-moment' (Urry 2002: 262) are amply demonstrated in Glastonbury, underlining the importance of pilgrimage for many Europeans, Americans and Antipodeans, *despite* the technological availability of virtual pilgrimage. Journeying with a purpose, physically covering ground for spiritual reasons, evidently remains of considerable importance. Furthermore, what we clearly see in connection with various forms of contemporary spirituality is 'the combination of mobility itself with a degree of reflexivity as to its meaning, form and function' (Coleman and Eade 2004: 18). Some pilgrims come as part of a group with ostensibly the same worldview, sharing a similar perception of Glastonbury's sacred significance, while for others pursuing a more solitary spiritual quest or practising in isolation, one of the main benefits of pilgrimage to Glastonbury is to have a fleeting, spiritually-nourishing sense of communitas among the 'fellow travelers' to be found there. Contemporary integrative spirituality, with its assumptions that there is no 'one size fits all' religion and that the individual is on a perpetual spiritual voyage of discovery, actually reinforces the desirability of visiting sacred places and exposing oneself to new experiences and insights. Alternatively, there are those who find themselves in and benefiting from Glastonbury as the result of 'coincidence.' The experiential aspect of pilgrimage to Glastonbury is thus varied and complex, for people come seeking a variety of experiences, from communitas with fellow believers to connectedness with the universe; for healing for themselves or for the planet; to discover the Goddess or to find their true selves; to benefit from or to enhance earth energies. And of course, in the context of integrative spirituality, they might do a number of these simultaneously. New Age Pilgrimage, according to Ivakhiv, 'represents a multitude of desires':

> To heal the sores and imbalances of a society perceived to be broken, to feel strange energies and open mysterious portals into the unknown, to map out the alternative universes exposed by New Age theories and gnostic impulses (Ivakhiv 2007: 283).

There are temporal as well as spatial dimensions in pilgrimage activity in Glastonbury. Pagan, Druid, Goddess, and Christian pilgrims not only come to what they all perceive to be a special location at significant times (whether points on the eight-fold calendar, important days in the Church calendar, or during the Goddess Conference or the Pilgrimage weekend) but to some extent to celebrate, connect with and temporarily reactivate a Golden Age, the period in the past when (as they see it) their path was dominant in Glastonbury.

I stated earlier that Glastonbury's contemporary drawing power has at its heart a flexible corpus of myths, distinctive natural and landscape features and a remarkable spiritual subculture. Vernacular religion in Glastonbury is suffused with the 'bidirectional influences of environments upon individuals and of individuals upon environments in the process of believing' (Primiano 1995: 44). People perceive themselves to be inspired and physically affected by Glastonbury, and they in turn color the landscape with speculation, interpretation and 'sacred-making activities' (Anttonen 2000: 281). Glastonbury's myths are constantly rewoven to incorporate ever more 'insights'; its landscape is regularly re-interpreted as different ways of 'reading' or understanding it emerge. New 'facts' increasingly become incorporated as a matter of course into accounts of Glastonbury's past and present status. Some tend to talk not about the town's history, but its 'mythtory.' This cumulative 'knowledge' about Glastonbury is incorporated into oral tradition, popular publications and, increasingly significant for its dissemination, into websites.

Although journeying to a sacred site is important, it may be observed in the Glastonbury context that the journey to Glastonbury itself in many cases seems secondary to the journey *within* Glastonbury. This is not to make light of the many personal experience narratives I have collected over the years of how events 'led' a person to Glastonbury, and for participants in the 1978 15-day Ecumenical Walking Pilgrimage from Arundel to Glastonbury or for the 'foot pilgrims' to the Glastonbury Christian Pilgrimages, it is reasonable to assume that the journey was a major feature of the pilgrimage experience. However, for the many people who regard Glastonbury as special on account of its 'place-centered' or inherent sacredness, Glastonbury's plethora of sacred sites provides the setting for 'pilgrimages within pilgrimage.' It is worth looking again at Jones's (2000: 28) positioning of goddess pilgrimage within a four-fold structure, three of which emphasize various *degrees* of being in Glastonbury:

The first [phase] is the pilgrimage to the sacred place itself, your journey to Glastonbury made with spiritual intent. The second phase is entry into a defined sacred enclosure or *temenos*, in this case the sacred landscape of the Isle of Avalon. The third phase encompasses your personal prayers to the goddess at the various energy centres, power spots and natural and human made altars, within the sacred landscape.

While other pilgrimage destinations may have more than one focus, Glastonbury is perhaps extreme in the number and nature of its 'sites within the site.'

Glastonbury's spiritual subculture has played and still plays a vital role in Glastonbury's contemporary and continuing status as a pilgrimage center. A remarkable group of people were operating in Glastonbury in the early twentieth century, making all sorts of claims for it and encouraging people to see the place and its history in new ways (see Benham 1993: Cutting 2004). Early Avalonians such as Wellesley Tudor Pole and Alice Buckton (influences on whom included Theosophy, Baha'i, the Celtic Revival, the Hermetic Order of the Golden Dawn, Freemasonry and British Israelite theories) envisaged pilgrimage as a means of bringing about the spiritual renewal of Britain, through the opening of spiritual channels in Glastonbury, Iona and an island in Ireland (it is thought that Scattery Island was the original choice, but this later changed to Devenish Island):

> These three islands were seen as 'heart centres' of the three major cultures in Britain, whose 'brain centres' were the three capitals – London, Edinburgh and Dublin. The intent was the spiritual opening and regeneration of the three cultures by means of pilgrimage – a sort of national initiation process (Cutting 2004: 99).

On a more obviously practical level, Alice Buckton bought Fair Field to donate to the National Trust, in order to preserve the 'pilgrims' path' to the summit of the Tor. Buckton also purchased Chalice Well, and although financial difficulties led to its sale after her death, eventually Wellesley Tudor Pole was able to re-establish the Chalice Well Trust in 1959, thus safeguarding Chalice Well as a place of pilgrimage. From the 1970s onwards another wave of assorted individuals brought their 'alternative' visions to Glastonbury (see Hexham 1981, 1983; Prince and Riches 2000; Ivakhiv 2001). A recent survey indicated that almost one-third of the adult population of Glastonbury are incomers who felt they had some sort of 'calling' to be there, the latest in a long line of 'Avalonians.'

An era of spiritual 'shopping around' and the necessity of trying out a variety of 'spiritual tools' as part of the individual quest, alongside Glastonbury's status and multivalence as a sacred site, afford numerous opportunities for spiritual providers and entrepreneurs. The spiritual service industry that evolved to an ever greater extent throughout the 1990s not only caters for Glastonbury's many pilgrims and visitors and encourages more to come, but also gives a variety of people a means of staying in their sacred place of choice. The latter-day Avalonians are both creators and consumers of the spiritual infrastructure, which is having an increasingly important impact on the local economy. Among those 'called' to Glastonbury are members of the Glaston Group, who consider that Glastonbury's future will be dominated by pilgrimage. They believe that the town should recognize this and make coherent provision for these special visitors.[24] Their aim is to set up a Pilgrim's Reception Centre for Glastonbury, catering for every kind of pilgrim: 'In our love of Glastonbury, we find a common purpose, the desire to serve.' Many are confident that Glastonbury will not simply persist but flourish as a focus for pilgrimage in the 21st century.

We have seen that reasons for coming to Glastonbury and what people do there can be immensely varied. To take a geological analogy, over the course of time in one place, different strata form in sedimentary rock, one on top of the other, leaving horizontal 'stripes' marking different eras. To some extent this is also how a place's religious history is normally read – one layer of belief is overlaid by another, so that there is a build-up over time of separate paradigms of religion. However, just as in a fold mountain, once horizontal strata are re-aligned so that they are vertically positioned, in contemporary Glastonbury it is as if various phases of its religious history stand together at the present time, and assorted paradigms are operating simultaneously. This certainly occasions some contestation, but it also leads to a convergence on Glastonbury of people united by one factor only – their conviction of the special nature of the place itself.

As a multivalent pilgrimage destination, Glastonbury provides a wide range of experiences and services for the pilgrims who are visiting in ever-greater numbers. However, to return to the quotation at the start of this chapter:

> (...) modern Pilgrims visiting the sacred places are of many different beliefs and often of no belief. They do not necessarily come to be in touch with any specific divinity but they come to be in the energies of the sacred places and by being in these places to understand themselves more clearly and to see their role in the world.[25]

There is a growing consensus that *whatever* the stated reason or focus of pilgrimage, underlying it all is the greater timeless, universal pull of earth energies. They are all, ultimately, 'going with the flow.'

Notes

1 I employ here the religious studies usage of myth as 'significant story.'

2 Having conducted fieldwork in Glastonbury for over a decade, I am grateful to the many people who have shared with me their time, knowledge, insights, good humour, accounts of their experiences, and company. When no specific published reference is given for a quotation, it comes from field notes or tapes.

3 http://www.glastonbury.co.uk/visitors/pilgrimage_main.html accessed 15/03/04

4 The nature of this healing, whether physical or spiritual, actual or metaphorical, is open to interpretation; one of Glastonbury's many myths is that Arthur lies sleeping at Glastonbury, and will return at some time of national emergency.

5 For many years the Anglican and Catholic Pilgrimages have taken place on the same weekend (normally in June), though the pilgrimage processions follow different routes to the Abbey. For a more detailed account of these pilgrimages, see Bowman 2004.

6 In 1191 the bodies of Arthur and Guinevere were allegedly 'discovered' by monks in the grounds of Glastonbury Abbey. In 1278 the bodies were re-buried in a magnificent tomb in the Abbey chancel in the presence of King Edward I and Queen Eleanor; the tomb and remains disappeared with the dissolution of the Abbey at the Reformation (for a summary of literature relating to this see Carley 1996:154-166).

7 According to one website, 'The lines "Did you ever hear about Jesus walkin,' Jesus walkin' down by Avalon?" from 'Summertime in England' refer to an ancient legend that Jesus once visited England. (...) Although Jesus may or may not have actually walked down by Avalon, it is far more likely that Van Morrison walked down by Glastonbury. It has been suggested that the 'Common One' album cover shows Van on Glastonbury Tor. Anyone planning a tour of important Van places

should put Glastonbury high on their list.' (http://www. harbour.sfu.ca/ ~hayward/van/ glossary/ avalon.html accessed 24/07/07).

8 http://www.gatekeeper.org.uk/gatekeeper/localevents.htm accessed 24/07/07

9 http://www.shekinashram.org/ accessed 24/07/07

10 In 2006, Youth 2000 received some unwelcome publicity when, during its procession down the High Street, some of its participants behaved in an aggressive manner towards the staff of 'The Magick Box,' as a result of which the event is unlikely to take place again in the town. It was stressed that those involved were 'outsiders'; the local Catholic priest apologized, while various Glastonbury Christians went into the shop afterwards to express their regret over the incident. In recognition of this show of solidarity, The Magick Box asked to participate in St John's Church's festival of Christmas trees, contributing a tree decorated with the symbols of a variety of religions – and miniature broom sticks! – with the caption 'COEXIST.'

11 www.kathyjones.co.uk/local/h-pages/kathyj/gdstemple-newsJuly2001.htmlaccessed10/02/03

12 www.glastonbury.co.uk/ioaf/sanctuary.html, accessed 23/02/99

13 After the Sai Baba Centre ceased to function, these premises subsequently became Sheki-nashram.

14 http://www.glastonburysymposium.co.uk/glastonbury.html accessed 24/07/07

15 http://www.glastonburyshrine.co.uk

16 http://www.isleofavalon.co.uk/gpt/index.html accessed 24/07/07

17 Email communication August 2006.

18 http://www.circleway.com/sacred.htmaccessed 24/07/07

19 Publicity for Broughton's current activities in relation to sacred sites can be found at http://the-centeroflight.net/Glenn&Cameron.html accessed 24/07/07

20 http://www.gatekeeper.org.uk/gatekeeper/about.html accessed 24/07/07

21 http://www.gatekeeper.org.uk/gatekeeper/about.html accessed 24/07/07

22 http://www.gatekeeper.org.uk/gatekeeper/about.html accessed 24/07/07

23 www.isleofavalon.co.uk/gpt/index.html accessed 24/07/07

24 In its booklet *Glastonbury: A Pilgrim's Perspective* (2005:13), the group describes itself thus: 'We are an eclectic and evolving group, with a diverse range of beliefs and interests. We too were drawn here, as pilgrims in search of truth and the sacred. Whilst some pilgrims come and go and return again, we put down our roots and stayed.'

25 http://www.glastonbury.co.uk/visitors/pilgrimage_main.html accessed 15/03/04.

Chapter 10

The Pilgrimage to the 'Cancer Forest' on the 'Trees for Life Day' in Flevoland

Paul Post

The Trees for Life Day

It is usually misty weather as the long line of cars makes its way through the polder on the last Saturday morning in November. It is also more or less guaranteed that most of the cars are making their way to the large parking area of the closed and desolate Six Flags amusement park, near Biddinghuizen, Dronten (the Netherlands). This is where the large-scale logistics operation begins. From this parking area, where long lines of mobile toilets have been set up, 44 shuttle buses transport people to the edge of the Roggebotzand nature reserve in Flevoland, a few kilometers further into the polder. From there, the people enter the Koningin Wilhelminabos (Queen Wilhelmina forest) along a fixed route and generally in small, silent groups. Wheelchairs are at the ready, and there is coffee and cake available at the halfway point.

The first destination is the memorial spot that has been cleared in this young forest; here, a podium tent with a PA installation has been set up. A bandoneon player welcomes the growing group with melancholic music as they assemble at the circle around the statue of Queen Wilhelmina, twelve trees and a series of glass plates. Folding chairs have been set out for some of the approximately 2,000 visitors. People are still arriving when the memorial service begins at 11.00 with a word of welcome and some organizational announcements. This is followed by three short speeches from the organizers, namely the Koningin Wilhelmina Fonds (Queen Wilhelmina Foundation), the Stichting Nationale Boomfeestdag (national tree festival foundation) and the Contactgroep Nabestaanden Kankerpatiënten (surviving relatives of cancer patients contact group). The speeches are followed by a song ('Heaven is a place nearby,' by the Norwegian singer-songwriter Lene Marlin) and the poem 'Een boom' (A tree) by the Dutch writer Lammy Vriesinga. This first part of the ceremony takes approximately fifteen minutes.

The unveiling of the glass plates bearing the names of this year's (2002) cancer victims is next, followed by a minute's silence. Then another poem, and the opportunity to look at the plates; people read the names, looking for family, friends, or acquaintances. After 30 minutes, the memorial service comes to an end. By this time, forest rangers in green uniforms are at the ready to lead the group to the nearby section of forest where trees will be planted. This is a walk of approximately ten minutes, but many of the visitors are infirm and have to make the journey along the forest path slowly, supported by friends and family. The visitors form a long procession. People tend to speak quietly in small groups or remain completely silent.

On arrival at the cleared space in the forest, hundreds of small saplings and many spades are lined up waiting for the visitors. After producing a receipt (proof of order and payment), each visitor is given a sapling and goes off in search of a suitable spot. Some move far away, while others remain close to the perimeter. People often hang something on their tree – a photograph, note, or letter protected by plastic, or a name, poem, doll, or drawing. Small

Monumental glass plates with the names of the deceased for whom trees have been planted in the forest.
Photo: KWF/Dutch Cancer Society

groups of people form at each of the trees, generally family members, fathers, mothers, children, grandfathers, grandmothers. People linger for varying lengths of time at the newly planted trees. Looking around, you can see the section of forest that was planted last year: The trees still bear the weathered letters and photographs. Small groups start returning to the place where the buses are waiting to shuttle back and forth to the parking area. There, the first cars for the second memorial service, which begins at 13.00, are beginning to arrive. A third round begins at 15.00. More than 6,000 people participate in this annual ritual in what is also known as the Kankerbos (cancer forest).

This Trees for Life Day, which was held for the first time in 2000, is a recently created ritual. The forest ritual represents a living memorial to loved ones who have died of cancer. The forest was named after Queen Wilhelmina, who determined that the Nationaal Geschenk (national gift) that she received in 1948 in celebration of the golden jubilee of her reign should form a contribution to the fight against cancer. This resulted in the establishment in 1949 of the Nederlandse Kankerbestrijding (KWF; Dutch Cancer Society). In 1999, Staatsbosbeheer (Dutch Forestry Commission) donated the forest to the then 50-year-old KWF at the initiative of Stichting Nationale Boomfeestdag (National Tree Festival Foundation), with which the forestry commission is associated. The first Trees for Life Day was an overwhelming success: More than 12,000 trees were planted, and the area devoted to them (20 hectares) had to be reappraised and expanded. Subsequent Days were organized more strictly and limited to 6,000 participants, in three successive sessions.

A key figure in the creation of the forest and the ritual day is the chairman of the Stichting Nationale Boomfeestdag, Peter Derksen, who combines creativity with organizational talent. The memorial forest has been created in accordance with a well-planned and, to a degree, loaded symbolic concept (Van de Bles & Hollander 2000). Life and death, the path of life, forms the guiding principle. The path to the central memorial site represents the path of life leading to the bridge that all of us must cross: the division between life and death. At the memorial site, the names of the dead who have gone before us are on display. Around the statue of Wilhelmina are twelve 'millennium trees' (spherical lime trees) in a broken circle, representing twelve provinces, twelve hours, twelve months, twelve signs of the zodiac... In the center of the circle stands a Spanish oak as a symbol of the contact that we maintain with our loved ones in memory. The return path symbolizes life that goes on, and in which memories of our loved ones have a place. A website (www.wilhel-minabos.nl) describes in detail the thinking behind the design. Since the elaboration of the initiative of the forest ritual in 1999, the next of kin of victims of cancer come together on the last Saturday in November to remember; they walk, keep silent, plant trees.

No research into this newly emerged and quickly established ritual has been done so far. I have attended the ritual on two occasions (2002 and 2003), have spoken with the organizers, and was given access to the archives containing many 'thank you' letters and letters of support, as well as reports of experiences mainly from enthusiastic and thankful participants (cf. Post 2005).

In this contribution, I formulate a number of exploratory observations on this case of an emerging ritual (Post, Nugteren and Zondag 2003; Grimes 1993; Mitchell 1995). As an analytical instrument I use the pilgrimage reference both directly and indirectly. Here, the ritual forms the primary point of departure; these are ritual observations.

Ritual Framework

First, a note on the ritual framework. I became aware of this ritual through my research into current ritual dynamics in the Netherlands, in which I focused specifically on emerging rites, holy places, and ritual landscapes (Post 1995; 1996; 2000; Foote 1997; Larson-Miller 2005). The cancer forest ritual fits a development brought to light by survey and component studies of ritual since approximately 1950 (Lukken 1999; 2004; Post 2004b). In short, it can be said that during the 1950s–1960s, a fixed Christian ecclesiastic-liturgical and profane secular repertoire was remarkably quickly dismantled, and new forms, directly and indirectly evident, were sought during the 1960s–1970s. At that time, there was considerable liturgical and ritual experimentation going on, but it was in particular a period of searching, deficiency, and vacuum. During the 1980s–1990s, new lines crystallized: Remnants of ecclesiastical repertoire were pushed back within the church confines, often appropriated as general religious life ritual; on the periphery of and outside the church, a great deal of old ritual is part of a complex process of folklorization and musealization (Post 2000: Ch. 2); and there is newly-emerging ritual, generally of the feast and festival type or the memorial type which usually marks important moments in life. The boundaries separating Christian-ecclesiastic, general religious, and secular/profane ritual appear to have become porous. Within this setting, devotional ritual such as pilgrimage is being rediscovered (Post, Pieper and Van Uden 1998; Post and Van Tongeren 2001; Post 2000).

'Sudden Unjust Deaths'

Within this schematic panorama – and here we come closer to our case – it becomes apparent how new ritual emerged in that last period of the 1980s and in particular the 1990s, around what I generally term as 'the sudden unjust death.' A series of 'mindless' acts of street violence, various disasters (ranging from outbreaks of legionnaires' disease, through explosions and plane crashes, to fatal fires in busy bars), traffic accidents, and the death of celebrities (such as Princess Diana) in different parts of the world: All in all, the sudden unjust death, as opposed to a natural death due to age or illness, is marked and surrounded by the development of new rituals that have become established as standard rituals within a remarkably short period of 10 years (Santino 2006). I reported on this in a previous publication derived from a larger project dealing with disaster ritual (Post, Nugteren and Zondag 2003; cf. Foote 1997; Stengs 2003; Larson-Miller 2005). In that context, we are dealing with the remarkable ritual of the mass silent march or procession, the public memorial service, preferably in the open air, the establishment of a memorial or shrine in a public area, and an annual commemoration. From a general ritual point of view, the entire repertoire is notable for its strong roots in the public domain and its strong relation to place and time. Religious and liturgical elements were recognized and assigned in this ritual from the beginning, both in general (ritual structure) and in specific components (ritual units). The pilgrimage and the procession in particular were mentioned here as reference (Post, Nugteren and Zondag 2003: sub 3.5).

Fellow Sufferers and Incidental Ritual Communities

It is interesting to note that these victim rituals have as a broader framework victim groups and organizations that also emerged during the same 1980s and 1990s. Besides disaster victims and their next of kin, consider here mourning groups and patient organizations. These days, every medical disorder has its own association or lobby group that in addition to acting on behalf of patients and in the interest of medical research also focuses on coping with trauma and grieving. Memorial rituals increasingly play a role here. Friends and relatives of road accident victims, for instance, gather annually for commemoration, often in a church, and the next of kin of victims of local, regional, and national accidents and disasters have their annual commemoration, with monument and annual rituals. As we can see, a broad range of shrines and rituals exists. There are the many spontaneous, local, and generally temporary roadside monuments to road accident victims (Post 1995; 1996b; Foote 1997; Larson-Miller 2005), shrines that mark disasters and those established by a variety of groups

Visitors look for the names of relatives on the glass plates.
Photo: KWF/Dutch Cancer Society

of the bereaved, designed by artists for annual memorial services. A current example of the last-mentioned type is the national monument in Utrecht for all the victims of rail-related incidents, which was unveiled in April 2004.

These groups with their shrines and rites are a good example of the formation of new communities that have a direct effect on present ritual dynamics. The classic view of community no longer suffices; it is a view that is too static, too monolithic. Community, like a great deal of ritual, is now related to events. A shared experience in connection with the event determines the group, the community. The community is incidental, momentary in character; the term 'assembly' is perhaps more appropriate here, the gathered, convened community that comes and goes, and yet is no less a community (Post 2004a). No churches as sacred places, instead shrines offering a place and a framework for these incidental communities (although churches sometimes serve as platforms).

Another relevant factor is the complex relationship between individual and community. Within the rituals, there is stratification, sometimes focused on the individual experience and expression, and sometimes on the collective. The similarity to the pilgrim community is obvious in all of the aforementioned points concerning community or assembly.

Fundamental Ritual Forms

That element of the incidental event-related community is directly connected to the ritual repertoire. Because of the already mentioned incidental nature of the gathered group, it is only possible to revert to a very general symbolic frame of reference as the shared symbolic horizon. Young and old people, ecclesiastic and non-ecclesiastic, come from all over the country, from all social classes, urban and rural, etc. It is for this reason, just as is the case in disaster ritual, that we continue to see the same fundamental or 'basic' ritual forms on our Trees for Life Day. There are no elements connected to specific religious traditions, but very general imagery encased in modern popular music or poetry dominated by archetypal symbols such as light, trees, and flowers. The repertoire of acting encompasses walking, silence, reciting names, and now also speeches. It is quite remarkable to note how these speeches – a profane/ secular form of commemoration and indication from the working and public domain – have also captured a dominant place in ecclesiastical funerary ritual (Van Tongeren 2004).

Also particularly noticeable here is the appearance of elements that typify pilgrimage ritual: walking as the primary form of expression. I will not draw normative conclusions here: is this a falling back on fundamental anthropo-logical ritual-symbolic forms of expression for want of a better alternative? Or perhaps a sign of ritual creativity and power, a ritual re-grafting to the funda-mental lines of human symbolic enactment and performance? I will, however, separately address a number of specific aspects of this ritual dimension that in my opinion are relevant in the context. As stated, I use here in particular the perspective of non-confessional pilgrimage ritual.

Inclusive Configuration

I would now like to elaborate on an aspect that has already been mentioned. The ritual in the polder is, like all disaster and memorial ritual, strongly in-clusive in character, in other words: hospitable, inviting, open. Recently, this point has been eagerly developed in ritual and liturgical studies, as well as from a practical-theological viewpoint, by differentiating between ritual con-figurations of elements of form and content in relation to the inculturation of rituals (Post 2004a; Lukken 1999; 2005). In our polder forest ritual, we have a good example of a configuration that is exceptionally inclusive in both form and content. The texts and actions are familiar, directly accessible. No drama-tic classical music, no traditional liturgy, no bible texts or complex hermetic play of language and rite. There is also more for those who require more; the already mentioned symbolism of the forest, for example, displays cosmic di-mensions, references to a supposed Celtic tree cult. However, the ritual does not depend on this. It is a bonus, as are the poems on printed color cards that are given to the participants afterwards.

The fact that the ritual takes place in the open air is determined by this in-clusiveness. The public domain is generally accessible and inclusive in nature.

From a point of view of phenomenology, open-air ritual is in nature different from indoor ritual. In components, pilgrimage contrasts with and is opposite to ecclesiastical ritual specifically through its public setting, with the baseline being inclusiveness versus exclusivity. I would like to refer to the model study on pilgrimage in the North American Protestant culture by Gwen Kennedy Neville, in which this aspect is systematically developed with the aid of the classics from anthropology (Kennedy Neville 1987).

Location-specific Shrine

The pilgrimage reference is very explicit in the strongly location-specific nature of our case, and in related victim rites. People gladly come to a specific place that they cherish, that they have designed as a ritual landscape with a center. It is holy ground. The ritual is defined considerably by this location specificity. It is based on a ritual, devotional if you will (Post and Van Tongeren 2001: 14-16), namely going to a specific place. The range of shrines is known to be considerable, as is the relation between the impact of the place and that of the journey to that place. There are classic holy places, ritual centers loaded with religious identity – Rome, Jerusalem, Mecca, Santiago, Lourdes. Then there are national places, shrines marking battlegrounds and wars, national events. We have shrines that are the graves of saints and celebrities, and places where events of great impact on nations and cities took place. There are spontaneous temporary shrines marking abductions, murders, and accidents. These days, some even go further and use shrine and place of pilgrimage more metaphorically as an indication of any place that draws interest; amusement parks, shopping malls, holiday resorts (De Dijn and Van Herck 2002). In the recent edition of the leading *Theologische Realenzyklopädie* (TRE; theological encyclopedia), we see this clearly in the voluminous entry '*Wallfahrt*' (pilgrimage), as the resurgence of pilgrimage in modern times is linked on the one hand to events substantiated by religious groups such as the Roman Catholic World Youth Days, and on the other, to events in the areas of music, media, and sport culture (TRE 2003).

Recently planted tree with letter and lantern.
Photo: KWF/Dutch Cancer Society

Created / invented and Practical

As a location-specific ritual, our case is notable through the aspect of being modeled, invented, and created. It would seem from this point of view to be a typically Dutch, and modern, place and ritual. That modeling encompasses various dimensions. This is not a ritual that has been found or handed to us via tradition or the supernatural. It was designed, invented. This is specifically evident in the location that was selected, designed, and produced. The ritual complies with the situation. The accompanying folder material repeatedly emphasizes that the participants in the ritual contribute (specifically through planting a tree) to the design and creation of the place. The modeling dimension is therefore connected to the 'do-dimension' of the ritual act. We see this all the time in modern memorial rituals: People have a desire to do something, to act. Thus the lighting of lights, walking in particular, planting trees. Commemoration becomes 'practical.'

Rites of Passage

In addition to the ritual reference of the pilgrimage, there is also that of the rites of passage (Post, Nugteren and Zondag 2003: 264-268). It is actually more than a reference. The Trees for Life Day and the already mentioned related rites surrounding sudden unjust deaths are rites of passage. I will leave aside the important question of whether we can apply to our rites of passage the classic ethnographic/ethnological genre designation 'rites of passage' with all the liminal theories surrounding it: Which transitions are actually being marked; what roles are involved in the ritual? (Grimes 2003; Hameline 2003; Brancatelli 1998). I would like to limit myself to signaling again in general terms that this involves rites of passage, more specifically a form of death ritual (Gerhards and Kranemann 2002). Just as many, perhaps even all, pilgrimage rituals are forms of death ritual, our case is a form of memorial ritual in which the central focus is on the dead. It is part of a broader whole of rites surrounding sudden death. It is the bereaved who gather. I developed this point further in the project concerning rites after disasters, and indicated how this type of newly emerging memorial ritual connects with the need for rites of passage in our culture (Grimes 2000). People are searching for an inductive, varied, and unfolding repertoire. Rituals mark events such as birth, marriage, and death, and channel human experiences and feelings at those crucial axes of life. In our culture, those ritual markings have often become events in themselves; in a concentrated rite, everything should happen at the same time, while previously, rites of passage were very complex in composition and revelation. The image of a wild river channeled through a series of locks is pertinent here. Rites are those locks. Besides funerary, burial, and cremation, people are also searching for other parallel forms, both before and after. From discussions on the bus and while walking, I came to the conclusion that many participants come from the surrounding area, from the Reformed province of Overijssel for example, and that the tree ritual in no way competes with, but is in fact supplemental to, church liturgy. Reference to the unsatisfactory cremation ritual was something I heard and read remarkably often.

Feelings and Motives

A fitting final ritual note, which will be well known from every pilgrimage research, is the classic question concerning motive: what induces people? Why are people doing this on a free Saturday? Of course, this question has already been addressed indirectly, but I would like to map out possible motives or motive clusters more explicitly. I will do this in close connection with an interesting project by Professor Lizette Larson-Miller (Berkeley), who names a number of motivations in relation to modern memorial shrines in the public domain in her research project 'Holy Ground' (Larson-Miller 2005). For my case here today, I will link her findings to those of our own project on disaster ritual.

(a) Solidarity

First, there is the important motive of solidarity. People wish to express a feeling of compassion. I refer here to what I have already said about modern communities.

(b) Commemoration

There is remembrance, commemoration; people do not want to forget the dead. People literally pause to contemplate death, an act from which they also gain hope and comfort. Notable here is the recurring element of the dead as martyrs being remembered, as warriors struggling in vain; from this perspective, the forest becomes (I quote from the official text material of the organization) 'the cemetery of honor for the people who fought against cancer in vain.' Here, remembering is the central ritual act.

(c) Fear and hope

There is also a cluster, veiled or apparent, of what people refer to as negative feelings on the one hand, and as prospect and hope on the other hand. This can involve incomprehension, despair, suffering, anger, the injustice of death, and the harm done to innocent people; it can also encompass feelings of guilt, and sometimes of revenge. Corresponding ritual notions here include invocation, penance, and reconciliation. Larson-Miller refers to the need for reassurance. Among other things, the realization that sickness, death, and calamity can happen to anyone plays a role for the participants here; participation in memorial rituals, visiting the cancer forest, functions as a kind of reality check. Yet at the same time, there is hope, prospect; by being there, by bearing witness and remembering, by rituals like walking and planting, people hope for goodness, for salvation and healing, for the dead, for the bereaved.

(d) Being absorbed into something greater

Also important is the cluster that, again in very general terms, concerns a desire to engage in something larger than oneself. This motive cluster can take many forms. It can be about the already mentioned incidental, solidarity community within which an individual can enjoy a broader frame of reference; and it can be about the healing effect of attention, which is why the presence of the media at memorial services is so important for participants, and affects numbers. It can, however, also involve religious and cosmic dimensions: the incited and cherished feeling of being part of a greater whole. The songs and poems often allude to this, the forest and nature as location evoke this, a minute's silence in which the wind rustles the leaves and the birds sing, the tree as core symbol, rooted in the earth while growing toward the heavens. I am convinced that our case is strongly religious, albeit from a general religious point of view.

(e) 'I had to do this...'

Finally, there is the strong desire to be at the specific place and to carry out specific acts. I have already referred to the location specificity and the 'practical' dimension of the ritual. People sometimes mention this very explicitly: 'I don't know why: but I had to come here today, I had to be here, I had to do this.' Here, we have a series of motives that are very connected to feelings. This encompasses known general feelings, such as grief and consolation. All of these motives are familiar, the distinction religious – non-religious is actually transcended. There is also considerable similarity to known motive clusters from pilgrimage research. This pilgrimage reference is the subject of my conclusion.

A family plants a tree in memory of a relative who died of cancer.
Photo: KWF/Dutch Cancer Society

Conclusion: Pilgrimage as a Ritual Reference

Pilgrimage has featured continuously in my exploration, albeit primarily as a passing ritual reference. This has been deliberate. I have not focused explicitly on the difference between classic religious pilgrimage and this type of newly emerging location-specific ritual. I did not proclaim the Trees for Life Day as a form of non-confessional pilgrimage in advance, as that would have focused the attention on the pilgrimage ritual, on what is characteristic of pilgrimage, on the difference between religious and non-confessional pilgrimage. Pilgrimage research shows how this has all too often been at the expense of focusing on the actual ritual performance. It is for this reason that I have applied a different accentuation: I focus on the ritual case, employing what I call the 'pilgrimage reference' as a comparative heuristic analytic instrument. Pilgrimage from the point of view of ritual phenomenology and theory evokes a certain repertoire, as do rites of passage. Assuming the primacy of the unique actual ritual act (naturally in an anthropological and cultural context) and the description, analysis, and interpretation thereof, references such as pilgrimage can be employed. The question is then not so much whether the Trees for Life Day is a form of non-confessional postmodern pilgrimage, but more how with the help of the pilgrimage reference we can describe, analyze, and interpret that ritual. I am of the opinion that the reference is very helpful in this way, as Gwen Kennedy Neville and Lizette Larson-Miller show for related ritual.

In closing, however, I would like to address the issue of pilgrimage similarity/dissimilarity. I see certain differences in accentuation, specifically at the level of the myth. By 'myth' I mean the story connected to the ritual, the holy place, the symbols and rituals there. The myth is the story that enables these things to fall into place, the exegesis in word and deed. For Christian pilgrimage, that is the story of the miraculous apparition of Maria, a story of healing, the wonder story of the saint, the death of the martyr. Stories that at the end are connected with the myth of the suffering, death, and resurrection of Christ. Such a developed and detailed myth does not ring true in the polder forest. What we hear is the story of this or that deceased, his/her life and death, and the unarticulated yearning for a broader context for that life and death and, finally, hope, prospect. That hope is mediated by the deed, by the idyll of the forest and nature, by the solidarity of the incidental community, the temporary assembly. That there is a difference between the developed Christian myth of the pilgrimage and the general myth of fear and hope with elements of ritual performance, nature, and humanity appears obvious at the level of the presented myth; however, at the level of the ritual appropriation, experience, and perception, this is less evident. Pilgrimage research makes this at least plausible, just as the suspicion has existed since the Early Church that the ritual of pilgrimage is not entirely based on the unadulterated Christian myth (*Directory on Popular Piety* 2001). Here, I will leave the normative theological question concerning the authentic Christian caliber of pilgrimage ritual for what it is; the important question concerning the religious caliber of our case, however, remains. I would be wary of brandishing judgements about vague belief in 'something-ism' ('Of course I'm religious: there must be something more...') (like Lukken 2005). Regardless of how general or unarticulated, the aforementioned clusters of motives and feelings reflect an authentic general religious desire. In the forest ritual, large groups of people find an adequate ritual expression that, it may be assumed, has a place as a supplement to Christian ecclesiastical ritual rather than competing with it. The exact relation between ecclesial liturgy and this newly-emerging general religious ritual warrants separate investigation.

With regard to the myth, yet another difference appears between the classic confessional pilgrimage and our case. Most notable to me in relation to the initial outward appearance is the aspect of the modeling, creating, inventing of our case. I have already referred to this. The foundation story, if it can be called that, is one of planning and making. The forest – every path, every tree, every bush – has been designed; the symbolism has been assembled from traditions and cultures. Nederlandse Kankerbestrijding supports a process of coping and bereavement, Staatsbosbeheer displays a socially relevant enterprise, and Stichting Boomfeestdag carries on a long tradition of planting Koningshuisbomen (royal house trees), memorial trees, birth trees, etc. in a 'cancer forest' (Post et al. 2003: 148-151). Ritual that includes place and time has been created as opposed to found. The spot was chosen because of its central location and available parking facilities. Compare here the classic story of the coming into existence of holy places and their respective rituals, where it is about finding and not inventing and creating. This is portrayed most tellingly in the latest novel by David Guterson (*Our Lady of the Forest*), which is also about a forest as a place of pilgrimage (Guterson 2003). In that story, where an American lumberjack village in decline is overcome by an apparition of Mary, the sheriff and the local priest are in despair over the sudden massive influx of pilgrims: There are no parking facilities, no forest paths, no toilets. Place and rite emerge, they are discovered, found with the assistance of a divine, supernatural clue.

On reflection, there is also less of a difference here than would appear to be the case at first sight. Guterson lets us look behind the scenes of salvation and suggests in closing that there is in fact more human planning than supernatural guidance at work. A combination of mushrooms, drugs, and cunning individuals around the sick, addicted prophetess created, construed, the voice of the Mother of God and the holy forest. Therefore, the question remains: what makes the difference?

Chapter 11

Sites of Memory, Sites of Sorrow: An American Veterans' Motorcycle Pilgrimage

Jill Dubisch

A chapel spread like a white angel's wing across a hilltop in a wind-swept valley high in the mountains of New Mexico. A memorial shaped like a giant sundial whose shadow moves across names carved on granite plaques in Frankfort, Kentucky. Red rocks framing the pathways and waving flags of a monument among the red rocks on the Navajo reservation in Window Rock, New Mexico. A campground in Colorado where a group of bikers gathers in a circle, their faces lit by the wavering glow of candles as the sun fades behind the Rocky Mountains. A school yard in Reinell, West Virginia, where a crowd assembles as schoochildren and veterans perform ceremonies in honor of all those who have served in their country's military. The black granite surface of the Vietnam Veterans Memorial in Washington, DC, where the faces of the living are reflected among the names of the dead.

These are some of the places where rituals for the living and the dead take place in the course of an annual motorcycle pilgrimage of Vietnam War veterans, spouses, supporters, and other interested motorcycle riders who travel from California to the Vietnam Veterans Memorial in Washington, DC, a journey known as the Run for the Wall (or simply 'the Run'). In the course of this ten-day pilgrimage across the United States, the participants memorialize a period in American history that has been and continues to be troubling, contentious, and painful not only for many Vietnam veterans but also for many non-veterans. Making the journey in the company of other veterans, travelling on motorcycles, and receiving the welcome given to the riders by communities along the way all contribute to the emotional effects of this pilgrimage (see Dubisch 2005; Michalowski and Dubisch 2001). But the sites that the riders visit in the course of their journey also create powerful emotions. These sites are in turn sacralized through the activities of the pilgrims, becoming places of powerful meaning, sites of memory, occasions for mourning, and opportunities for ritual offerings.

For the veterans making this pilgrimage, memories of the Vietnam War – memories that are often long buried – resurface in the course of the cross-country ride and during the rituals that accompany it. These memories are awakened in the company of others with whom they may be shared, and with support from individuals and groups who turn out along the route to honor all veterans, both those making the pilgrimage and those who never returned. 'Welcome home, brother' is the greeting given to the riders, both by fellow veterans and by those who host them in communities along the way. This welcome contrasts with the veterans' earlier return from Vietnam, a return often marked by hostile war protestors and an indifferent society. It is the support received in the course of the Run that enables many of the veterans to finally face that ultimate shrine to the Vietnam War: the Vietnam Veterans Memorial ('the Wall') in Washington, DC. Stops at other shrines and places of ceremony along the route pave the way for this confrontation and allow the participation of local communities and of those veterans who are unable to undertake this cross-country pilgrimage themselves.

History and Purpose of the Run for the Wall

The Run for the Wall began in 1989 when a group of Vietnam veterans decided to ride their motorcycles across the United States, from California to Washington, DC, to visit the recently inaugurated Vietnam Veterans Memorial. The riders also planned to join Rolling Thunder, the large motorcycle rally and parade that takes place every year in Washington on Memorial Day weekend (the last weekend in May). First established as an event for the support and recognition of veterans, Rolling Thunder takes its name from the carpet bombing of Cambodia during the Vietnam War. It has now become a large biker gathering that draws over 250,000 participants every year.

The Run for the Wall was originally planned as a one-off event, an opportunity for participants to say goodbye to comrades whose names are engraved on the Wall. However, the riders were welcomed so enthusiastically by the communities where they stopped that, as one of the original organizers told me, 'We knew we had to do it again.' Now the Run is an annual pilgrimage that draws hundreds of riders each year. Although there is a national organization that plans and oversees this event, it is not an organization to which one 'belongs.' One simply shows up during one of the Run's stops, signs in, and travels as long as desired with the group, thus becoming part of the Run for the Wall 'family' (see Michalowski and Dubisch 2001). As mentioned, Vietnam veterans are not the only participants. Veterans of other wars, family and friends of veterans, supporters of veterans and their causes, and those riders who at first just come along for the ride, but are ultimately drawn into the issues that the Run represents, also participate in this pilgrimage, either as riders or as part of the communities that welcome the riders along the way.

As emphasized by the various rituals and speeches during the course of the pilgrimage, the Run has two main goals. One is the personal healing of veterans who are still suffering from the psychological, emotional, and spiritual effects of their Vietnam War experience. These effects may be manifested in the now officially recognized post-traumatic stress disorder (PTSD)[1], or they may be the invisible wounds that still afflict many of those who participated in this conflict (see Dubisch 2005). Healing is provided not only for veterans, however: other participants in the Run may have lost a loved one in the conflict – a brother, father, son, fiancé, or some other individual who figured importantly in their lives – or they may have had relationships with those who are still suffering the effects of war. In a larger sense, the pilgrimage might be said to have as one of its goals to 'heal a nation,' a phrase that has been applied to the Run's ultimate destination: the Vietnam Veterans Memorial (Scruggs and Swerdlow 1985). More recently, the Run has attracted members of the military who have returned from or are about to be deployed to Afghanistan or Iraq (some of these are children of still-suffering Vietnam veterans on the Run).

The Run also has a political purpose: to demand a full accounting by the United States government of those who are missing in action (MIAs) or prisoners of war (POWs) from the Vietnam War (and to some extent, to call attention to this issue from other wars as well).[2] The issue of MIAs and the question of whether there might still be living prisoners of war from the Vietnam conflict are controversial,[3] but this political agenda provides a mission for the Run that offers participants a sense of riding for something beyond themselves. They are not simply 'whiny Vietnam vets' who could not manage to get their lives together after the war; rather, they are warriors on a mission, 'riding for those who can't.' But the concept of the POW/MIA is also metaphorical. Many veterans are still prisoners of the Vietnam War in their own minds because of their continued suffering, and they can be said to be still missing in action psychologically, as they have never come back to normal life since their return from Vietnam. To free both kinds of prisoners is the major goal of the Run. Veterans who ended up in therapy groups in veterans' hospitals might have had some opportunity to speak of their experiences, but many, if not most, Vietnam veterans have borne their emotional burdens alone. For this reason, the Run, with its collective rituals, its focus on places of memory and mourning, and the sense of common purpose engendered by the pilgrimage itself, has proved a powerful therapy for many of those who participate.

That the Run is a pilgrimage made on motorcycles is symbolically significant. Motorcycles are seen by many who ride them as representing American values of freedom, self-reliance, and individualism. The sense of solidarity and brotherhood that exists among bikers also comes into play during the pilgrimage, echoing the camaraderie of warriors in combat (see Wolf 1991). In addition, the physical experience of motorcycle riding – the noise, the motion, the riding in formation with several hundred other motorcycles, the hazards of the road – combine to create a psychological receptivity to the rituals carried out at the various shrines along the journey's route. And in these rituals we can see the Run as a pilgrimage of connection – connecting the country coast to coast, connecting veterans with each other and with other Americans along the way, and connecting those who returned from a foreign war to a homeland from which they may have long felt alienated.

Part of this process is also the connecting of the various shrines and, in particular, the local war memorials that honor the American dead of the Vietnam War (and other wars) to the national memorial in Washington, DC. This connection is made not only through the riders' stops at the various memorials along the route, but also through the carrying of objects to and from the local communities that welcome the Run, objects that range from flags and other symbols of patriotism bestowed upon the Run along the way to personal items given by individuals to the riders in the group. For example, on our first Run, we were given a bouquet of dried flowers in Gallup, New Mexico, by a schoolteacher who asked us to place it at the Wall in honor of one of her students who had been the first New Mexican to die in Vietnam (see Michalowski and Dubisch 2001). Another time I was given a miniature pair of moccasins by a Navajo girl, who explained that she herself would never get to the nation's capital but wanted this offering to go in her stead.

The Run is not only a pilgrimage with a sacred destination (the Wall): it also combines the individual search for healing and identity with the creation of a collective narrative, a narrative that unfolds as the Run moves across the United States. It thus serves as what Nancy Wood has termed a 'vector of memory,' a ritual performance that constructs a collective view of the past as well as contributing to the construction of a common identity (Wood 1999). It also creates spaces in which veterans (and others) can remember and mourn the losses of the war, in which they can address the memories that still haunt them and confront the often surprisingly fresh grief many still feel for the loss of comrades and for the loss of their own youth during the contentious years of the Vietnam War. The various stops, shrines, and rituals play an important role in creating such spaces, as I will discuss shortly. In these respects, the journey across America is an equally important part of the pilgrimage as the final destination, the Wall.

A Note on Methodology

Until 1995, when we participated in our first Run, motorcycle riding was simply a hobby that I enjoyed with my partner, Ray. We had been intending to spend the summer of 1995 riding across the country and attending various motorcycle rallies, but then a friend who knew of our plans handed us a flyer about the Run. As soon as we read it, we somehow felt that we had to go. As we learned later, our response was similar to that of a number of people on the Run. 'A friend told me about it, and I just knew I had to go' and 'I saw a flyer in the Harley shop and felt I had to go' were typical responses when we asked people how they came to be involved. In our case, this strong feeling was not due to either of us being veterans. We had both been opposed to the war in Vietnam and had participated in anti-war activism to varying degrees. At the same time, the war and the domestic turmoil that accompanied it were defining events of our generation and had shaped our own coming of age in the late 1960s. And so we were drawn into this cross-country journey of memory and commemoration. It was only later that we came to analyze the journey from our perspectives as social scientists and to develop the desire to write about it.[4]

Because we did not set out to study the Run and because we have been personally involved in this event and did not employ any systematic data collection in assembling the material for our writing, we have termed our method 'observant participation' (rather than 'participant observation'; see Michalowski and Dubisch 2001: 20-21). We have ridden all or part way with the Run for the Wall nearly every year since 1995 (making the journey all the way across the United States to Washington, DC, three times), taken part in annual reunions of Run participants, followed the Run website and newsletter, and become close friends with some of the Run participants. We have engaged in numerous conversations both during and after the Run, observed countless rituals along the route, shared meals, laughter, and tears, and left and received offerings along the way. We have thus become fellow pilgrims with others who take part in this journey.

The Run for the Wall as Pilgrimage

What is it that makes this journey – one that is undertaken on motorcycles, travelling interstate highways and back-country roads, to what might seem purely secular memorials and with an explicit political purpose – a pilgrimage? And it *is* a pilgrimage: 'We're not tourists – we're pilgrims,' a fellow rider declared at the beginning of one of our journeys. His sentiments were shared by most of the other riders.

But what makes the difference? One difference is that the Run participants see themselves as being on a mission: They are serious travellers, not simply sightseers (in fact there is little opportunity for sightseeing along the route, as each day of the ten-day trip is tightly scheduled). This does not mean that there is no time for fun and socializing during the Run. But participants explicitly contrast their journey with more mundane trips and particularly with purely recreational motorcycle rides. Not only are the political goals of the Run (increasing awareness of the POW/MIA issue and 'bringing them home') serious ones, but the Run is a painful, personal journey for many of the veterans. In the course of the pilgrimage, they confront memories of their combat experience and the death of comrades, as well as feelings of survivor guilt, and their own struggles and suffering since their return from the war. The physical difficulties and dangers of the journey also contribute to its distinction as pilgrimage, as these not only heighten its psychological impact, but also recreate (to some extent) the dangers and hardships of combat, as well as the sense of camaraderie (just as other kinds of pilgrimage may recreate or commemorate mythic journeys). Although they themselves do not use these terms, the participants' view of their journey as a pilgrimage clearly reflects Turnerian concepts of 'liminality' and 'communitas' (Turner and Turner 1978).

The places where the Run stops for its various ceremonies are places with a sacred character. This sacredness may come from the nature of the site (e.g. a memorial to the dead) or from the ceremonies that are performed there, which transform the site, if only temporarily, into a special and serious place. Thus, the landscape traversed by the riders on the Run is a different one from that traveled under more ordinary circumstances. It is a landscape defined not by the usual tourist sights but by places of memory and commemoration, and by both individual and collective acts of ritual and mourning, which transform both publicly-constructed memorials (particularly war memorials) and mundane spaces (campgrounds, truck stops, school yards) into shrines at which the dead are remembered and commemorated, and the living seek healing and redemption.

The Run is thus transformative for it not only transforms spaces along the journey's route into sacred places, it also transforms the meaning, history, and emotional state of those participating. This transformation takes place not only through the journey as a whole and the final accomplishment of arriving at the Wall, but also through a series of ritual steps that take place at the various stops along the way. At the same time, these stops help Run participants to lay claim to and to re-establish the meaning of a national landscape that for many has seemed alien to them since their return from Vietnam. In this respect, the experience of traversing America might be seen as being as important a part of the pilgrimage as the destination itself.

Many of the Run participants inhabit a doubly liminal status, namely as Vietnam veterans and as bikers. Motorcycle riding and biker culture have long had a particular attraction for veterans, starting with the returning veterans of World Wars I and II (Lavigne 1987; Pierson 1997) through Vietnam veterans to veterans of the Gulf War and, more recently, Afghanistan and Iraq. The sense of marginality that some veterans feel upon their return to civilian life and the difficulty they experience in adapting to that life resonate with the marginality

Motorcycles arriving for the Rolling Thunder motorcycle rally, Washington, DC, 1998. Photo: J. Dubisch.

of at least some segments of motorcycle culture, especially that of the outlaw bikers and the 'saloon' biker culture that is modeled on it.[5] The hardship and danger of motorcycle riding also provide the 'edge' and the adrenalin high that some combat veterans find themselves missing after their return from war, as well as the intense sense of camaraderie and brotherhood that they experienced in wartime conditions. The patriotic symbolism and ideology that are a part of many biker subcultures are also an attraction for some veterans. In addition, as we have heard from a number of Run veterans, motorcycle riding can have important therapeutic effects, providing a space in which veterans feel that they can 'clear their heads' (see Dubisch 2005; Michalowski and Dubisch 2001).

Motorcycle riding is also more than a symbolic or social activity. It is a visceral experience, one that transcends the power of mere words to describe. As a popular biker slogan puts it: 'If I have to explain, you wouldn't understand.' Movement itself becomes a form of therapy, taking the veteran away from the memories that haunt him and toward an open and undefined horizon. At the same time, motorcycle riding also combines the individual and the collective. As the Run speeds down the highway, each rider is enclosed in his own space of noise and movement while simultaneously being part of the larger formation that visually (and audibly) represents the collective endeavor that is the Run.[6] In this sense, the road itself – and the liminal experience of riding – becomes a sort of shrine, a space and place beyond the ordinary in which altered states of being may be experienced.

By riding motorcycles, the participants in the Run set themselves apart from those making a cross-country journey by ordinary means.[7] And while the speed with which motorcycles traverse the countryside contrasts with the often deliberately slower, more difficult pace of many pilgrimages (for example, going on foot or one's knees; see Dubisch 1995; Frey 1998), riding a motorcycle, and particularly in close formation with a hundred or more other bikers, can provide an often grueling, sometimes dangerous, and always absorbing means of travel. There is also a psychological, some would even say a spiritual, state induced by riding. The very landscape through which one rides, however familiar it might be from other journeys, suddenly becomes new and unfamiliar when one is on a motorcycle. This altered state – which on the Run is heightened by the deafening roar of a hundred or so motorcycles hurtling down the highway together at speeds of 65-75 miles an hour (105-120 kilometers an hour) – places the participants in the Run in an altered state of consciousness that contributes to their receptiveness to the experiences, impressions, and messages encountered in the course of the journey.[8]

As Turner and Turner (1978) pointed out some years ago, pilgrims create places of pilgrimage by voting with their feet (in the case of the Run, we could say they vote with their wheels). So what are the sorts of places that the participants in the Run sacralize on their ten-day journey? A description of some of these stops and of the rituals that take place there provides some idea of the sorts of places visited on the Run and the ways in which they are constructed and deployed. At the same time, it must be emphasized that the Run is ritually flexible. Although the final destination – the Wall – has always been the culminating ritual stop of the Run, other stops along the way have varied, with new ones added and old ones dropped from one year to the next. These changes are due to a number of factors, including changes in the route, requests by local communities and groups along the way, and the increasing size of the Run itself, which has made some stops more difficult (for example, the stop at the Navajo Nation Veterans Memorial described below, has been changed to a ritual at a more convenient location, due to the size of the group and the logistical problems associated with the long ride into the reservation).

While the riders set themselves apart by their mode of transportation as they ride across the country, they also seek connection, a connection that is established in the many stops that the Run makes in its cross-country journey. At small communities in the heartland of America, at veterans' hospitals, town centers and parish halls, truck stops, schools, and war memorials across the United States, the Run is greeted and hosted by a variety of local organizations and individuals: veterans' groups, motorcycle clubs, motorcycle dealers, churches, schoolchildren, community officials, and local supporters. Participants seldom pay for a meal during this ten-day cross-country journey, and in many places camping for the riders is free. In the mountainous town of Cimarron, New Mexico, for example, dinner and breakfast are provided by the local Catholic parish. At a highway rest area in Kansas, lunch was served to the group courtesy of the Kansas chapter of ABATE, which has also paid the group's highway tolls. In the impoverished mining town of Reinell, West Virginia, hundreds of riders have been fed at the local Moose Lodge Hall. It is these groups and individuals who organize many of the rituals that greet the riders in the course of the Run. Others are constructed by Run participants themselves, or in collaboration with local participants. At the same time, these rituals are experienced by the Run riders in the context of the totality of their journey, with all its physical hardships, its emotional intensity, and its collective sense of mission. Some examples of events along the route will give a sense of this experience.

Places of Ritual, Places of Power

For the last several years, the Run's first overnight stop after leaving California has been Williams, a small town in northwestern Arizona that is a tourist gateway to the Grand Canyon. Here at the campground where many of the riders stay (or more recently at the Williams Veterans of Foreign Wars Hall), a veteran from Phoenix, Arizona, brings an entire crew to cook dinner for the riders. The dinner is preceded by a ceremony in which a central role is played by a symbolic remembrance table – a table that is set for the various branches of the American military service. Each branch has an empty place with plate, silverware, and overturned glass, and each military service is honored in turn with the playing of its anthem. The empty places are reminders of the dead, who are always present on this emotional journey, and of the fact that they will not return home to drink and dine with us again. In this way, a mundane setting is turned, temporarily, into a site not only of memory but also of connection to the other world.

The next day's journey is from Williams to Gallup, New Mexico. New Mexico, with its large, mostly poor, Hispanic and Native American population,[9] gives the Run one of the warmest receptions it receives during its entire cross-country journey. In 1998, the Navajo reservation was added to the Run's landscape when the riders were invited to attend ceremonies at the then almost completed Navajo Vietnam Veterans Memorial. That particular year, the Run had endured snow on its way through the mountains of northern Arizona and temperatures hovering around 40 degrees Fahrenheit (4 degrees centigrade) as it crossed the high desert toward Gallup (with a wind chill close to zero Fahrenheit (-18 centigrade) for those riding on motorcycles). Just before we crossed the border from Arizona to New Mexico, we turned off the highway to be met by a contingent of Navajo police. After a ceremony at the Lupton schoolhouse (see Michalowski and Dubisch 2001), we sped behind our po- lice escort deep into the reservation. All along the route, groups of Navajo stood next to cars and pick-up trucks, waving and applauding as we rode by. As we pulled into the parking lot of the Navajo Nation administrative center beneath the dramatic, bridge-shaped red rock formation that gives the town of Window Rock its name, we saw crowds of Navajo gathered around the lot and on the rocks above. As we rolled to a stop, the waiting crowd burst into enthusiastic applause.

In the ceremonies that followed, the long history of the Navajo as warriors was emphasized, Navajo leaders gave the Run a Navajo Nation flag to carry to the Wall, and a Navajo folk singer performed a song he had written in memory of a brother who died in Vietnam. There was also a demonstration by the last living 'code talkers,' that is, Navajo who had used their native language to transmit military messages during World War II, a code that was never broken by the Germans.[10] Then Navajo and non-Navajo alike saluted while a bugler played taps as the light dimmed around the mystical symbol of Window Rock in a final tribute to all the warriors who had died defending their country. Here, then, a war memorial, a sacred landscape, and a powerful ceremony combined to create a space that both united and commemorated veterans.

The following day, the Run reaches another dramatic place in New Mexico that has become part of the sacred landscape of this pilgrimage: the Vietnam veterans memorial at Angel Fire, high in the mountains above Taos. Angel Fire is well known as a ski area and resort, but for many of the participants in the Run, it is a sacred place associated with their pilgrimage. The power of the site – a wind-swept valley surrounded by snow-capped peaks – is breathtaking.

And the memorial itself, with its chapel shaped like a giant white wing, stands upon a hill high above the road across the valley. We have heard from many veterans that it was here at Angel Fire, with its war museum, its chapel, its incredible natural setting, that their own memories and wounds of Vietnam were opened and their journey toward healing began.[11]

The next day in Limon, Colorado, we stopped at a campground that has regularly been the site of a ceremony by Task Force Omega, an organization of families of POWs and MIAs. Here the names of the Colorado MIAs are read in a candlelight ritual that begins at dusk. Led by both Task Force Omega members and Run participants, the ritual seeks to keep alive the memory of those still unaccounted for. One year the audience intoned 'missing but not forgotten' as each name was read. Another year, we formed into couples, and the woman read the name of one of the missing men while the man called out, 'Still on patrol, sir!' Afterwards we all joined hands in a healing circle.

The healing circle was repeated in the town park in Salina, Kansas, the next day's stop. Here, after being fed and entertained by the townspeople, one of the organizers of the event called upon us to form 'the largest friendship

The chapel at the Vietnam Veterans Memorial at Angel Fire, New Mexico, 1998. Photo: J. Dubisch.

circle we ever had.' As we sang 'Amazing Grace,' the circle moved rhythmi-
cally in and out. The line from the song 'I once was lost but now I'm found'
resonates with the feeling many veterans on the Run experience as they are
welcomed home in communities such as this.

A truck stop is the unlikely location of a roadside ceremony at Mt. Vernon,
Illinois. Here the group is fed, and ceremonies are held. The first year we participated in the Run, the names of soldiers from Illinois who died in Vietnam
were read out and an artificial rose placed in a basket for each name, the basket to be carried to the Wall. On other occasions, the remembrance table, with
its places set for each branch of the military, has been laid out here.

Some of the most important stops in the Run's itinerary are at various
Vietnam War memorials along the route, each of which honors the dead of
that particular state. Among the many such memorials dotting the landscape,
the memorial at Frankfort, Kentucky, stands out. It is in the shape of a large
sundial, with the names of the Kentucky Vietnam dead engraved seemingly at
random on granite blocks all around it. On the month and day of the year that
someone died, however, the shadow of the dial falls upon his name, transfor-
ming the seemingly random distribution of names into a celestial memory of
the war.

Until recently, the Run's last stop before Washington, DC, was always the
tiny, impoverished coalmining town of Reinell, West Virginia. Here, the riders
have received perhaps their warmest, most enthusiastic welcome. Screaming,
pom-pom-waving children lined the street as the bikers rode in and then
crowded around to collect autographs as the riders dismounted. There were
ceremonies in the school yard in which most of the town population participated; the ceremonies included the singing of patriotic songs, flag ceremonies
performed by local scout troops, and speeches honoring the veterans. Then
the entire crowd of riders, now numbering several hundred, was fed at the
local Moose Lodge.

Within the context of the rituals and other events that take place along
the pilgrimage route, being a Vietnam veteran is celebrated, not stigmatized.[12]
As the rituals of reintegration that were not available to him after the war
are enacted in the course of the Run, the veteran learns to accept his status

as a veteran. Veterans thus become reconnected – to other veterans, to the communities of 'home,' to the landscape of country and, through rituals of memory and mourning, to the dead.

Malkki speaks of 'accidental communities of memory,' individuals joined by the accidental sharing of transitory (but often powerful) experiences (Malkki 1997: 91-92). Vietnam veterans could certainly be considered such an accidental community, sharing a common experience of combat in a harrowing and controversial war. Drawing upon such a community, the Run transforms it into something more. Through the shared journey and the hardships of the road, the presumed common goals of the pilgrimage, the common bonds of biker culture and of veterans' experience, a sense of connection is created. Insofar as to participate in the Run is to show one's dedication to veterans, to their problems, and to the cause, regardless of one's own veteran status, bonds are constructed that transcend other differences that might exist outside the Run. And what we ourselves discovered in the course of our journey was that although we are not veterans, we are part of that larger accidental community of memory, composed of those who as young adults had experienced the turbulence, the pain, the fear, and the anger of the Vietnam War years. The intensity of the trip and the emotions it evokes, as well as the experience of living together in another reality for the duration of the ten-day trip, and the sense of the brotherhood of the road found among bikers (see Wolf 1991) also help to bond together those who make the journey. This bonding is particularly strong among those who go all the way together, making the entire journey from California to Washington (thus demonstrating their commitment to the cause), and is reinforced in those who repeat the trip on an annual basis.

Ritual, Narrative, and Healing: the Wall

The Run is often a painful journey. During the course of the pilgrimage, memories of the war that may have been long buried begin to surface. Indeed, some veterans who join the Run feeling that they really have nothing to get over from their wartime experiences learn otherwise once they are confronted with reminders of these experiences. And the most painful, and intimidating, part of the journey is the destination – the Vietnam Veterans Memorial. 'I'm terrified of getting to the Wall,' one veteran confided to me as we drew close to the end of the journey. For some veterans, the thought of confronting the Wall is so painful that they are unable to complete, or even to begin, the journey, despite the encouragement and support they receive from fellow veterans and others who have been on the Run.

The Wall is both the destination and the emotional climax of the pilgrimage. On the last day of its journey, the Run enters the nation's capital, Washington, DC. Parking the bikes in a field across the street from the memorial, the riders pause to collect themselves before moving singly or in groups to confront the memorial. There, face to face with the black granite surface

Veterans taking part in the Run for the Wall leave their offerings at the Vietnam Veterans Memorial in Washington DC, 1998. Photo: J. Dubisch.

in which the over 58,000 names of American dead are inscribed, the riders seek the names of departed comrades and relatives, leave offerings, offer a shoulder to those who grieve, and confront – with tears or in sober silence – the stark tragedy of war.[13] Although support is available to those who need it, the rituals performed here are individual ones. While they often involve conventional objects and forms (flags, flowers, letters, etc.), they are shaped by each participant's own experience of grief and loss. Some lay wreaths beneath significant names, others kneel in prayer, and some speak to the dead, while others make rubbings of the engraved names. For some, it is the first time they have confronted the Wall, and more experienced pilgrims are close by to offer help if needed. Others have private rituals they repeat year after year. Some veterans are so emotionally overwhelmed they must move away, seeking nearby benches on which to nurse their grief in solitude. Finally, individually or in groups, their rituals completed, the riders return to their bikes and make their way to the motel where the Run participants will spend the night. Some veterans will return to the memorial later that evening on 'night patrol,' when the crowds of tourists have dispersed, to commune with the Wall in solitude.

The next day, a Saturday, many Run participants go to Arlington to participate in the laying of a wreath at the Tomb of the Unknown Soldier, and most of the riders join the giant Rolling Thunder parade on the Sunday as it roars through Washington, DC. But it is at the Wall, on the day of the pilgrims' arrival in Washington, that the pilgrimage itself culminates. At the end of the weekend, the pilgrims will make their way home, some in the company of others, some stopping to visit friends or relatives along the way, others making a quick and solo journey back. There is no group ritual for the return. The pilgrimage itself has ended, and the participants return home on their own.

In recent years, a small group of participants has made a second pilgrimage to the Canadian Vietnam Veterans Memorial in Windsor, Ontario, once the Run is over, to honor the Canadian dead who fought in the Vietnam War. (Canadians who fought in Vietnam are not recognized as veterans by either the United States or Canada, but some participate in the Run.)

The Vietnam Veterans Memorial as a Shrine

The Vietnam Veterans Memorial has been described as America's greatest national shrine. Why this should be so is beyond the scope of this paper, but one important dimension of the Wall is the spiritual quality of this ostensibly secular monument. The concept of 'Wall magic' is one that we have heard articulated at various times in the course of our journeys. It is a quality that causes miraculous things to happen, that creates connections among people. And for many veterans, it is the Wall, not the individual gravesites scattered across the country, where their dead comrades reside. 'When you touch a name on the Wall, it brings back that person's soul,' one veteran said to me. Another veteran recounted that during the 'night patrol,' he was suddenly overwhelmed by a cacophony of voices seemingly coming from the Wall. A friend gently pulled him away, saying that he, too, had experienced the same phenomenon, as if all the men whose names were there were speaking to him at once.

The leaving of offerings at the Wall is a practice common to many pilgrimage sites. Objects left at the Wall, however, differ from the votive offerings left at religious shrines, as the latter are usually left as part of a request to a sacred figure or as thanks for prayers that have been answered. On the other hand, objects at the Vietnam Veterans Memorial are similar to those left at other sites of death or tragedy, such as the site of the World Trade Center or the Oklahoma City bombing, in that they represent a form of offering to and a memorialization of the dead.

Since its inauguration in 1982, the Vietnam Veterans Memorial has attracted such objects by the thousands (see Hass 1998). Some are generic, such as wreaths, flowers, or American flags. Others are individualized, such as photo-

A flower offering at the Wall, Washington DC.

graphs or letters to the dead left by spouses, children, parents, or friends. They may also be personal items that represent some facet of the deceased's life or personality, or of his relationship with the person making the offering. One year I watched a veteran from the Run place a newsletter from an Arizona biker club and a pack of cigarettes beneath the name of a fallen comrade. 'He loved to ride his motorcycle,' the man explained to an onlooker. On one Run (before we ourselves began participating), a brand new Harley Davidson motorcycle was taken to the memorial and left as an offering. And on the 1998 Run, the ashes of a deceased Vietnam veteran were carried in an ammunition box on the back of a motorcycle across the country, and the box was left at the Wall. Thus, offerings to the dead continue to connect them to those they left behind. (All items left at the wall are gathered and stored permanently in collections at the Smithsonian Institution.)

The carrying of objects on behalf of others, whether they are given by individuals or by groups along the way, connects communities across the country

Veterans reach out to touch a Vietnam War memorial in Colorado, 1998.
Photo: J. Dubisch.

both to the Run and to the Wall itself. Similarly, objects may be taken to the Wall and then back across the country, thus connecting the Wall to those back home. One may also take rubbings of names of individuals on the Wall; materials are provided for this purpose by volunteers at the memorial.[14] Thus, a long thread of ritual and offerings runs across the United States, connecting communities and individuals coast to coast, entwining with local Vietnam memorials in various states along the way, and finally arriving at the Wall. The fact that the Run stops at a number of local memorials, each commemorating the Vietnam War dead of that particular state, and then arrives at the Vietnam Veterans Memorial, which memorializes all the American dead, ties the local to the national, and the individual dead to the collective sacrifice.

Healing, Identity, and Memory

For some veterans, the Run has become a psychological necessity. 'I live for the Run each year,' we have heard people say. These individuals repeat all or part of the journey every year. Others participate once or twice and then do not join the Run again (though they may keep in touch with friends they have made in the course of the journey). However, the power of the Run lies not only in the support and understanding individuals receive, but also in the Run's ability to transform meaning and identity. In the context of the Run, it is not merely acceptable to be a veteran: it is a matter of pride. The Run has also introduced veterans to others in their city or state who are not only Vietnam veterans but also bikers. Such relationships can become the basis for a new social world and a new identity, once these individuals return home. Local reunions are held between Runs, and there are gatherings of Run participants for weddings or birthdays. In these ways, then, the Run for the Wall carries effects that extend beyond the duration of the pilgrimage.

The Run also offers veterans a symbolic order in which a narrative can be constructed, one that reframes the veteran's own history and identity. This is not to say that no other narratives have been available. However, such representations have generally not offered an account of the war experience with which most Vietnam veterans could identify. Indeed, I have heard more than one veteran blame pre-Vietnam movies for his own naive images of war. As one veteran put it: 'When I went to Vietnam, I was John Wayne. When I returned, I was a turd.'

Healing, then, is an important and often emphasized goal of the Run. Such healing is multifaceted, with social, psychological, and spiritual dimensions. For participants in the Run, healing has several important components. One is being honored for one's service, sacrifice, and suffering after what they perceive as years of dishonor or neglect. Another is feeling welcome in a country in which veterans did not always feel at home upon their return. Thus, the current ritual of saying 'Welcome home, brother' to a veteran becomes part of this healing process. The importance of such a ritual is illustrated by the comment one Run participant made to me after the Run's stop in the small mining town of Reinell, West Virginia. Our reception there, he told me with tears in his eyes, was 'the welcome home I never had.' Another dimension of healing is connection – not only with a society from which the veteran might have felt

'Welcome home, Brother': Two veterans embrace, 1998.
Photo: J. Dubisch.

alienated, but also with other veterans. 'Bringing veterans out of the woods' is a commonly employed metaphor, and 'lost in the woods' is sometimes a literal description of severely isolated veterans as well. Connecting with the dead is another dimension of healing, and the Run offers ample opportunity for this, both during the journey across the country and at the Wall itself. For those still suffering from prolonged grief at the loss of wartime comrades, as well as from their own feelings of guilt at having survived, this connecting is both a painful and a therapeutic process. Of course healing is a process, not an end point; there is no cure for the wounds of war.[15] As mentioned, for some of the participants in the Run, one journey is enough to start them on the healing path. For others, multiple journeys are necessary, and the Run may become a regular part of their lives.

In addition, part of the healing power of the Run lies in the construction of a new narrative that repositions the veteran in relationship to a war that constituted a controversial – and for many, shameful – chapter in American history.[16] Such a narrative involves reframing both the war itself and the veterans' role in it.

Shrines as Memory, Shrines as Forgetting

A slogan we have heard frequently on the Run is 'Forget the war, remember the warrior.'[17] As Alex King has suggested, forgetting may be an essential element in war memorials, conferring upon such monuments their sacred quality and their ability to achieve consensus (King 1999: 163). Sellers and Walter note that the Vietnam Veterans Memorial, while it refuses to shape a heroic and moralizing narrative about the war, '... allows, yet does not force, repentance for our part in the war as well as honor for those who died' (Sellers and Walter 1993: 189). Like other Vietnam memorials, the Wall separates both the living and the dead from the pain and shame that accompanied the conflict in Vietnam. This focus also separates the American dead from any larger social or global context. As Rowlands points out, the Vietnam Veterans Memorial makes 'no mention of the thousands of Vietnamese who died or the social inequalities hidden in the representation of the American dead' (Rowlands

1999: 143-142). Moreover, in its representation of sacrifice, the memorial says nothing about the United States' foreign policies, which were ultimately responsible for so much death and suffering. In this respect, the Run echoes both the Wall's remembering and its forgetting.

However, the Run is more than a political movement or a commemoration of veterans. While it is not specifically religious in its organization or its destination, and while it has overtly political purposes, the Run is nonetheless a profoundly spiritual journey.[18] Every day of the Run begins with a prayer by a Run chaplain, who asks for 'travelling mercies.' While for the most part the prayers are Christian, elements of Native American spirituality and of other spiritual traditions are also invoked by some participants. Some participants are overtly Christian (and some are even missionaries, having found in religion the peace and healing that they had sought for the wounds of war), while others are non-professing or non-religious. Nonetheless, most, if not all, are caught up in the transcendent nature of the journey and its rituals. And as a journey with and for the dead, the Run bridges the mundane and the invisible worlds. (One of the early slogans of the Run was 'We ride for those who died.') Moreover, the Run is a journey of transformation, a journey toward healing and away from pain and grief, a journey in which veterans and their supporters, in the course of their three thousand mile trip, find themselves transformed from bikers into pilgrims. The Run thus combines personal healing, rituals of mourning, political protest, and the reconstruction of history and memory. The Run creates a variety of sacred spaces along the journey's route, which in turn become places in which individuals and collectivities can remember, mourn, leave offerings, and connect to each other and to the dead. By these means, a cross-country motorcycle journey is transformed from a mundane journey into a ritual pilgrimage through a sacred landscape that it itself creates.

Notes

1 On post-traumatic stress disorder, see Dean 1997; Picquet and Best 1986; Shay 1994; Young 1995.
2 Some of those on the Run credit the current concern with the after-effects of war experience

among military personnel returning from Iraq to such efforts.

3 For a discussion of the POW/MIA issue as a social movement (one that extends beyond the Run), see Michalowski and Dubisch 2001. For two different views of the POW/MIA controversy, see Franklin 1993 and Jensen-Stevenson and Stevenson 1990.

4 I am an anthropologist; my husband Raymond Michalowski is a sociologist. Our collaborative effort has resulted in a book, *Run for the Wall: Remembering Vietnam on a Motorcycle Pilgrimage* (Rutgers 2001).

5 It should be noted that there are many different kinds of American biker styles and many different kinds of people who ride motorcycles. Neither the 'outlaw biker' image nor the image of the yuppie or rich urban biker (RUB) encompasses the range of those who ride motorcycles, and many different types of rider are represented on the Run.

6 I am indebted to 'Snake Byte' for this observation.

7 Some participants make the journey in more ordinary, four-wheeled vehicles ('cages,' in biker jargon) but they ride at the back of the 'pack.'

8 See Winkelman and Dubisch 2005. On the physiology of ritual, see Davis-Floyd 1992; D'Aquili et al. 1979.

9 Poorer states such as New Mexico, Kentucky, and West Virginia have historically provided a disproportionate number of soldiers to the United States military. In these areas, the military is an attractive career, and during the era of the Vietnam War when the military draft was active, fewer young men from these states obtained educational or other deferments than those from more affluent areas.

10 For a long time, the role of these code talkers was classified information and only became widely known when wartime documents were declassified in the mid-1990s. The code talkers' experiences have recently been chronicled in various forms, including the movie '*Wind Talkers.*'

11 For more on the power of Angel Fire, see Michalowski and Dubisch 2001.

12 This is not to say that everyone along the way is welcoming. In some cases, the riders are mistaken for a biker gang by those who are not informed of the Run's identity.

13 In all of this, nothing is said of the hundreds of thousands of Vietnamese who died. The remembrance of loss and suffering is entirely about the American dead. Some American veterans, however, have made pilgrimages to Vietnam; see Tick 2005.

14 Pilgrimage is not the only means of connection to the Wall. There are several 'travelling Walls,' replicas of the Vietnam Veterans Memorial, that tour the United States, staying for a week or so at a time in one location, allowing those nearby, who may not be able to visit the memorial itself, to experience some of the Wall's power (one of these replicas is called 'the Wall that heals').

15 On the difference between 'healing' and 'curing,' see Kleinman 1988; also Kleinman, Das, and Lock 1997.

16 For many, the war in Iraq has echoes of the Vietnam War, and returning veterans are experiencing some of the same symptoms of PTSD as Vietnam veterans. What the final 'narrative' of this conflict will be, and what the long-term consequences for veterans (and American society) will be, remain to be seen. Already, some returning Iraq war veterans have joined the Run.

17 A variation on this is 'Honor the warrior, not the war.'

18 For a discussion of spirituality vs. religion, see Heelas and Woodhead 2005; also Herrick 2003.

Conclusion

Since pilgrimage research has been broadened, and pilgrimage is sometimes referred to 'simply' as a 'realm of competing discourses,' and the metaphorical use of the concept has spread like wildfire, the meaning and the scope of the phenomenon of pilgrimage have become extremely hazy, both for people who visit secular locations and religious shrines and for researchers themselves. We therefore decided to narrow down the research perspective for the purposes of this volume: determining the religious aspect and the pilgrimage element in seemingly secular locations of memorialization and veneration. While the religious factor is defined broadly, as a sort of synonym for 'sacred,' and thus not in the sense of traditional religions and existing churches, the concepts of pilgrimage and shrine are used in a narrower sense. Here, I define pilgrimage as a journey that people undertake based on a religious inspiration, to a place that is regarded as more sacred or salutary than the environment of everyday life. The pilgrim seeks at the shrine an encounter with a specific cult object in order to acquire spiritual, emotional, or physical healing or benefit. The question is how this definition can be applied to the broad domain of what are generally called 'secular' pilgrimage sites or shrines. Until recently, very little ethnographic field work had been done to study the religious dimensions of these sites. For our study, we therefore selected a number of places around the world and categorized them into four characteristic and apparently secular realms of contemporary society. The public realms of politics, music, and sports all have powerful person-oriented veneration and idolatry. Within the realm of 'life, spirituality, and death' there is no clear cult object; instead, the pilgrims concentrate primarily on the self and/or deceased relatives, and on performing the ritual in the sacral nature of the route or location.

The ethnography made clear that people who visit the researched hybrid locations (each of which has its own rather distinct secular and religious elements and circuits) generally follow the secular or tourist circuits and are not involved with the 'essence' of pilgrimage. Usually, both the religious dimension and the number of pilgrims at hybrid places are limited, but they are nevertheless distinguished.

Against the background of the current discussions within pilgrimage research and on the basis of the perspective outlined in the Introduction and the ethnographic fieldwork executed, this book shows clearly that the contemporary pilgrimages to the persons and locations discussed here have a strongly individual character. Although the pilgrimages regularly take a collective form, their purpose and functionality are determined by the vulnerability and insecurity of daily life. The major incentive to make a pilgrimage is formed by health and social insecurities, a fundamental lack of confidence in social and political systems, and the desire for aid in the transcendental. Religion and pilgrimage are, in the final analysis, about real people, who are themselves the key to the knowledge of what really matters to them. Their longing can reveal their motivations and the values and meanings they attribute to the sacred. The study reveals that the social-cultural universality of pilgrimage lies in the *condition humaine*. The disappearance or change of traditional religious contexts can further reinforce existential insecurities and shift the focus of pilgrimage to other, apparently secular forms. The existential as motivation for pilgrimage therefore contests the idea of it as a primarily communal activity. The concentration on the self does not mean that there are no functional forms of sociability present in pilgrimage, as these for example surface in the cult around Soekarno and in the Dutch Cancer Forest, in Glastonbury, and during the motorcycle pilgrimage.

This study also shows that the crossing of a geographical or mental border is a constitutive element of pilgrimage and that, as a result, travelling to a place or a shrine is also an inextricable component of pilgrimage. Pilgrimage is in the first place transitional, a rite of passage in order to approach, enter, and experience the sacred. Since the concepts of 'journey' and 'travelling' carry a context of distance, and therefore contribute to a certain romanticization of the image of the long-distance pilgrimage, academic observation has often overlooked the mainstream pilgrimage praxis. This actually appears to be a practice in which distance is not, or is only barely, important. The journey is a much less decisive factor for the total experience and functionality of the pilgrimage. This applies to most of the pilgrimages dealt with in this work. They are mainly focused on locality and the shrine; the sacred site is the rationale of pilgrimage. Where this does not apply – as with, for example, the 'Run for the Wall' in the USA – it is the proof of the appearance of a new form of pilgrimage, at least in the Christian Western world, namely of the transit pilgrimage. Although pilgrimage has had a fairly constant pattern for centuries, in recent years this new way of pilgrimaging has emerged: pilgrimages for which the start and the finish are not or are less relevant, but that are focused on being under way. It is only in this form that pilgrimage is primarily reduced to the journey element. This may be best expressed in contemporary hiking journeys over the Camino to Compostela. They deal with the journey and not the destination. In Glastonbury in England, a combination of the two forms can be found: people go there both in groups and as individuals, and the main focus may be on the sacred sites themselves and on the journeys toward or around the town.

In a number of contributions, we find that the significance and the biographical background of the venerated person is a major factor in the development of sacrality at a secular location. This is especially the case when visitors can identify with the difficult social and psychological circumstances of the object of veneration, as in the case of Presley, Morrison, Zámbó, and Prefontaine. Life analogies of this kind, as with the suffering of the young Soekarno, provide a frame of reference for accepting the setbacks the visitors themselves have experienced in life. It is mainly in the political realm that the significance of these individuals is raised to a higher level, when a stimulating and healing effect with respect to nationalism and national identity is realized, as is the case with Falcone, Soekarno, and Tito, as well as with the Hungarian musician Zámbó. This may even lead to the venerated individuals being imbued with messianic qualities. Some pilgrims believe that these individuals are not really dead but continue to live and work somewhere, and that for example Soekarno or even the legendary King Arthur will come back one day as a redeeming messiah.

It also became clear that the role played by the media in the process of recognition and identification and thus in the creation of new modern pilgrimage shrines should not be underestimated. For example, the cultus associated with Steve Prefontaine gained impetus only after three films about him had appeared. This mediatization turned out to be the founding factor for the 'Pre-pilgrimage.' The Morrison cultus was strongly stimulated on a global scale after the movie about The Doors came out, in which a charismatic and shamanistic portrait of the singer was visualized and canonized. The modern pilgrimage sites often seem to be strongly positioned by images and representation. In this volume, representation even seems to be the determining factor, since it turns out that the sacrality of shrines is not necessarily linked to the physical remains or actual gravesites of the deceased and venerated individuals. In over half of the locations discussed here, apparently a representation suffices to generate pilgrimages: Falcone, Tito, Prefontaine, and possibly Soekarno, as well as the Cancer Forest and the Run for the Wall. And while Glastonbury remains shrouded in mythical mystery, Bowman shows convincingly that for new groups of visitors – such as New Age adepts – the idea of Glastonbury with its history and 'mythory' can become a pilgrimage in itself in addition to the existing traditional sacred dimensions. Or, to quote Bowman: 'Pilgrimage and Glastonbury are synonymous.' A new concept of religiosity is important in explaining the attraction of Glastonbury. There are 'energies' present there, and pilgrims want 'to be in the energies of the sacred places.' Glastonbury is not unique in this respect: people who visit Pre's rock and pilgrims to sites in the musical realm also experience 'energies.'

This book investigates the profane/secular and the religious dimensions and meanings of contemporary shrines and pilgrimages. One point that is made explicit is that, in addition to the secular circuits associated with the visits to or veneration of special individuals, objects, ideas, or places, there is a clearly distinguishable religious circuit in the form of veneration and pilgrimage. These pilgrimages are usually the result of the lack or disappearance of the traditional religious paradigms. A troubled human condition and a need for new religious dimensions and transcendental realms have resulted in new sacred journeys. The new pilgrims can travel these ways, usually individually, to reach significant locations where they may find assistance with and support for their existential life questions and problems. Most of the articles in fact show that powerful new sacred spaces come into being at locations where the visitors can cope with the traumatic loss of a venerated person – an icon, idol, role model, hero, or 'saint' – or where this loss is commemorated, such as at graves and roadside memorials. The value and significance of these places are then raised from the profane/secular level to a more transcendent level, so that the visit acquires a religious or sacred dimension and can then be regarded as pilgrimage. The religiosity and rituality exhibited there by people in fact mark them as pilgrims in the 'classic' sense, and therefore their visits to these places are essentially different in function and meaning from those of others who go there for non-religious reasons.

This fact also suggests that it is time for a re-evaluation of the concept of pilgrimage, to offset the dangers of using it as a broad or metaphorical container concept. This book constitutes a first attempt to do so. Against this background, it has become clear that secular pilgrimages as such do not exist but that within, or rather in addition to, the secular practice of commemoration or worship around the graves of and memorials to a wide variety of individuals, religious pilgrimages may function to a great extent independently and should be distinguished as such. It turns out that due to his primary existential insecurities, man still has the need to be able to call on higher powers. If existing churches and religious movements do not offer sufficient opportunities for this, or if those opportunities no longer correspond with modernity, then man will look for his own, new itineraries into the sacred. The perceptions of sacredness and transcendence attributed to the people and locations described in this book and the related religious praxis are the proof of this observation.

List of Illustrations

Bibliography

Abate, Ida (1997), *Il piccolo giudice. Profilo di Rosario Livatino*. Messina: Armando Siciliano.

Abdurrahman, Moeslim (2000), *On Hajj Tourism: In Search of Piety and Identity in the New Order Indonesia*. Urbana-Champaign: University of Illinois [unpublished dissertation].

Adams, Cindy (1966), *Sukarno: An Autobiography*. Hong Kong: Gunung Agung.

Adrianatakesuma, Idris (1973), *Pemberontakan Peta di Blitar*. Yogyakarta: Universitas Gadjah Mada, Fakultas Sosial dan Politik.

Agamben, Giorgio (2000), *Le temps qui reste*. Paris: Rivages.

Albers, Ineke (2007), *Heilige kracht wordt door beweging losgemaakt. Over pelgrimage, lopen en genezen*. Tilburg: Liturgisch Instituut.

Albert-Llorca, Marlène (1993), Le courrier du ciel. In Daniel Fabre (ed.), *Ecritures ordinaires*. Paris: P.O.L. / Centre Georges Pompidou, 183-221.

Alderman, D.H. (2002), Writing on the Graceland Wall: On the Importance of Authorship in Pilgrimage Landscapes. *Tourism Recreation Research* 27(2), 27-33.

Amdur, N. (1975), Prefontaine, 24, Killed in Crash. *The New York Times* (31 May), 19.

Anderson, Benedict (1972), The Idea of Power in Javanese Culture. In Claire Holt (ed.), *Culture and Politics in Indonesia*. Ithaca: Cornell University Press, 1-69.

Anderson, Curtis (2005), Pre Lives. *The Register Guard* (Eugene, Oregon, 30 May), B1, B5.

Andujar, Michelle (2007), Pre's Rock File. Randall V. Mills Archive of Northwest Folklore, University of Oregon (Summer).

Anon. (1997), Warm Winter Wonderlands. *Ebony* (January), 58-60.

Antier, Jean-Jacques (1979), *Le Pèlerinage retrouvé*. Paris: Centurion.

Anttonen, Veikko (2000), Sacred. In Willi Braun and Russell T. McCutcheon (eds), *A Guide to the Study of Religion*. London: Cassell.

Aries, Philippe (1974), *Western Attitudes towards Death from the Middle Ages to the Present*. Baltimore: Johns Hopkins University Press.

Armuri, Sandra (ed.) (1992), *L'Albero Falcone*. Palermo: Fondazione Giovanni e Francesca Falcone.

Badone, Ellen, and Sharon R. Roseman (eds) (2004), *Intersecting Journeys. The Anthropology of Pilgrimage and Tourism*. Urbana: University of Illinois Press.

Barbas, Samantha (2001), *Movie Crazy: Fans, Stars, and the Cult of Celebrity*. New York: Palgrave.

Barna, Gábor (2003), Ritualizálás és kompenzáció. In Győző Zsigmond (ed.), *Napjaink folklórja. Folclorul azi*. Bucharest: A Magyar Köztársaság Kulturális Központja, 107–129.

Basu, Paul (2004), Route Metaphors of 'Roots-Tourism' in the Scottish Highland Diaspora. In Simon Coleman and John Eade (eds), *Reframing Pilgrimage. Cultures in Motion*. London: Routledge, 150-174.

Battaglia, Letizia (1999), *Passion, Justice, Liberté. Photographies de Sicile*. Arles: Actes Sud.

Battaglia, Letizia, and Franco Zecchin (1989), *Chroniques siciliennes*, Paris: Centre National de la Photographie.

Battaglia, Letizia, and Franco Zecchin (2006), *Dovere di cronaca. The Duty to Report*. Rome: Peliti Associati.

Bax, Mart (1995), *Medjugorje: Religion, Politics, and Violence in Rural Bosnia*. Amsterdam: VU Uitgeverij.

Belaj, Vitomir (1991), Kulturološka obilježja hodoč ašćenja. *Dometi* 24, 157-161.

Belaj, Vitomir (1998), *Hod kroz godinu. Mitska pozadina hrvatskih narodnih obič aja i vjerovanja*. Zagreb: Golden marketing.

Bellah, Robert N. et al. (1985), *Habits of the Heart: Individualism and Commitment in American Life*. Berkeley: University of California Press.

Benham, Patrick (1993), *The Avalonians*. Glastonbury: Gothic Image Publications.

Bennett, Andy (2000), *Popular Music and Youth Culture: Music, Identity and Place*. Basingstoke: Palgrave.

Bennett, Gillian (1987), *Traditions of Belief.* London: Penguin.

Bensa, Albin, and Eric Fassin (2002), Les sciences sociales face à l'événement. *Terrain* 38, 5-20.

Berbée, Paul A.J.S. (1987), Zur Klärung von Sprache und Sache in der Wallfahrtsforschung. Begriffsgeschichtlicher Beitrag zur Diskussion. *Bayerische Blätter für Volkskunde* 14, 65-82.

Berger, Peter L. (1967), *The Sacred Canopy.* NewYork: Doubleday.

Berger, Peter L. (ed.) (1999), *The Desecularization of the World: Resurgent Religion and World Politics.* Grand Rapids: W.B. Eerdmans.

Berger, Peter L. (2002), Secularisation and De-Secularisation. In Linda Woodhead et al. (eds), *Religions in the Modern World. Traditions and Transformations.* London: Routledge, 291-298.

Bianchi, Robert R. (2004), *Guests of God: Pilgrimage and Politics in the Islamic World.* Oxford: Oxford University Press.

Bishop, G. (1999), What Americans Really Believe. *Free Inquiry* 19(3) (Summer), 38-42.

Bitton-Ashkelony, Brouria (2005), *Encountering the Sacred: The Debate on Christian Pilgrimage in Late Antiquity.* Berkeley: University of California Press.

Blasi, Anthony J. (2002), Visitation to Disaster Sites. In William H. Swatos Jr. and Luigi Tomasi (eds), *From Medieval Pilgrimage to Religious Tourism: The Social and Cultural Economics of Piety.* Westport CT: Praeger, 159-180.

Boltanski, Luc and LaurentThévenot (1999), *De la justification. Les économies de la grandeur.* Paris: Gallimard.

Bowman, Marion (1993), Drawn to Glastonbury. In Ian Reader and Tony Walter (eds), *Pilgrimage in Popular Culture.* Basingstoke and London: Macmillan, 29-62.

Bowman, Marion (2000), 'More of the same?: Christianity, Vernacular Religion and Alternative Spirituality in Glastonbury.' In Steven Sutcliffe and Marion Bowman (eds), *Beyond New Age: Exploring Alternative Spirituality.* Edinburgh: Edinburgh University Press, 83-104.

Bowman, Marion (2001), The People's Princess:Vernacular Religion and Politics in the Mourning for Diana. In Gábor Barna (ed.), *Politics and Folk Religion. Papers of the 3rd Symposium of SIEF Commision of Folk Religion.* Szeged: Department of Ethnology, University of Szeged, 35-50.

Bowman, Marion (2003-2004), Taking Stories Seriously: Vernacular Religion, Contemporary Spirituality and the Myth of Jesus in Glastonbury. *Temeno* 39-40, 125-142.

Bowman, Marion (2004), Procession and Possession in Glastonbury: Continuity, Change and the Manipulation of Tradition. *Folklore* 115 (3), 273-285.

Bowman, Marion (2005), Ancient Avalon, New Jerusalem, Heart Chakra of Planet Earth: Localisation and Globalisation in Glastonbury. *Numen* 52 (2), 157-190.

Bowman, Marion (2006), The Holy Thorn Ceremony: Revival, Rivalry and Civil Religion in Glastonbury. *Folklore* 117 (2), 123-140.

Bowman, Marion (2007), Arthur and Bridget in Avalon: Celtic Myth, Vernacular Religion and Contemporary Spirituality in Glastonbury. *Fabula, Journal of Folktale Studies*, 48(1/2), 1-17.

Bradley, Marion Zimmer (1986), *Mists of Avalon.* London: Sphere Books.

Brancatelli, Robert J. (1998), *Pilgrimage as Rite of Passage. A Guidebook for Youth Ministry*. Mahwah NJ: Paulist Press.

Bringa, Tone (2003), The Peaceful Death of Tito and the Violent End of Yugoslavia. In John Borneman (ed.), *Death of the Father: an Anthropology of the End in Political Authority.* London: Berghahn Books, 148-200.

Brkljačić, Maja (2001), A Case of a Very Difficult Transition: The Ritual of the Funeral of Josip Broz Tito. Available at: http://limen.mi2.hr/limen1–2001/maja_brkljacic.html. Last accessed on June 25, 2004.

Broughton, Glenn. (1999), 'Journeys of the Soul.' *South West Connection* (Aug/Nov), 71-74.

Brown, Peter (1981), *The Cult of the Saints: Its Rise and Function in Latin Christianity*. Chicago: The University of Chicago Press.

Brown, P. (1992), 2 Kings: The Postal War Over Elvis's Image. *New York Times* (15 March), 1, 31.

Brückner, Wolfgang (1970), Zur Phänomenologie und Nomenklatur des Wallfahrtswesens und seiner Erforschung. Wörter und Sachen in systematisch-semantischem Zusammenhang. In Dieter Harmening et al. (eds), *Volkskultur und Geschichte. Festgabe für Josef Dünninger zum 65. Geburtstag*. Berlin: Schmidt, 384-424.

Burggraeve, Robert et.al. (eds) (2003), *Desirable God? Our Fascination with Images, Idols and New Deities*. Leuven: Peeters.

Campbell, Michelle (1994), Jim Morrison's Resting Place in Paris. *North Atlantic Review* 6, 2-49.

Campbell, Michelle (2001), Jim Morrison Revisited. *North Atlantic Review* 13, 1-46.

Campo, J. E. (1998), American Pilgrimage Landscapes. *Annals of the American Academy of Political and Social Science* 558 (July), 40-56.

Carley, James P. (1996) *Glastonbury Abbey: The Holy House at the Head of the Moors Adventurous*. Glastonbury: Gothic Image Publications.

Caspers, Charles, and Peter Jan Margry (2003), Cults and Pilgrimage Sites in the Netherlands. In Graham Jones (ed.), *Saints of Europe. Studies towards a Survey of Cults and Culture*. Donington: Shaun Tyas Publishing, 29-42.

Cavicchi, Daniel (1998), *Tramps like us: Music and Meaning among Springsteen Fans*. Oxford: Oxford University Press.

Chambert-Loir, Henry, and Anthony Reid (eds) (2002), *The Potent Dead: Ancestors, Saints and Heroes in Contemporary Indonesia*. Honolulu: Allen & Unwin and University of Hawai'i Press.

Chidester, David (2005), *Authentic Fakes: Religion and American Popular Culture*. Berkeley: University of California Press.

Christie, Tim (2007), Feel of an Enduring Presence. *The Register Guard* (Eugene, Oregon, 11 June), A1, A9.

Clark, J., and A. Cheshire (2003–2004), RIP by the Roadside: A Comparative Study of Roadside Memorials in New South Wales, Australia and Texas, USA. *Omega* 48, 229–248.

Claverie, Elisabeth (2002), Apparition de la Vierge et 'retour' des disparus. La constitution d'une identité nationale à Medjugorje (Bosnie-Herzegovine). *Terrain*, 38, 41-54.

Clift, Jean Dalby, and Wallace B. Clift (1996), *The Archetype of Pilgrimage. Outer Action with Inner Meaning*. New York: Paulist Press.

Cohen, Erik (1992), Pilgrimage and Tourism: Convergence and Divergence. In Alan Morinis (ed.), *Sacred Journeys: The Anthropology of Pilgrimage*. Westport: Greenwood, 47-61.

Coleman, Simon (2002), Do you Believe in Pilgrimage? *Communitas*, Contestation and Beyond. *Anthropological Theory* 2-3, 355-368.

Coleman, Simon, and John Elsner (eds) (2003), *Pilgrim Voices. Narrative and Authorship in Christian Pilgrimage*. New York: Berghahn.

Coleman, Simon, and John Eade (eds) (2004), *Reframing Pilgrimage. Cultures in Motion*. London: Routledge.

Collins, C. O., and C. D. Rhine (2003), Roadside Memorials. *Omega* 47, 221–244.

Colombijn, Freek (2007), The Search for an Extinct Volcano in the Dutch Polder: Pilgrimage to Memorials Sites of Pim Fortuyn. *Anthropos* 102(1), 71-90.

Congregazione per il Culto Divino (2002), *Direttorio su pietà populare e liturgia. Principe e orientamenti*. Città del Vaticano: Libreria Editrice Vaticana.

Connerton, Paul (1989), *How Societies Remember*. Cambridge: Cambridge University Press.

Corbier, Mireille (2006), *Donner à voir, donner à lire. Mémoire et communication dans la Rome ancienne*. Paris: CNRS.

Couldry, Nick (2003), *Media Rituals. A Critical Approach*. London: Routledge.

Cutting, Tracy (2004), *Beneath the Silent Tor: The life and work of Alice Buckton*. Glastonbury Appleseed Press.

D'Acquili, E. G., C. D. Laughlin, and J. McManus (1979), *The Spectrum of Ritual: a Biogenic Structural Analysis*. New York: Colombia University Press.

Davidson, J. (1990), The Pilgrimage to Graceland. In G. Rinschede and S. M. Bhardwaj (eds), *Pilgrimage in the United States*. Berlin: Dietrich Reimer Verlag.

Davie, Grace (1994), *Religion in Britain since 1945: Believing without Belonging*. Oxford: Blackwell.

Davie, Grace (2002), *Europe: The Exceptional Case. Parameters of Faith in the Modern World*. London: Darton, Longman and Todd.

Davis, Leo (1975), Leo's Lines: Pre's People Run Out of Time. *Oregonian* (31 May), C1.

Davis-Floyd, Robbie E. (1992), *Birth as an American Rite of Passage*. Berkeley: University of California Press.

De Certeau, Michel (1982), Corps mysticus ou le corps manquant. In *La fable mystique* 1. Paris: Gallimard.

De Dijn, Herman and Walter van Herck (eds) (2002), *Heilige plaatsen. Jeruzalem, Lourdes en shopping malls*. Kapellen/Kampen: Pelckmans.

De Jonge, Huub (1991), Heiligen, middelen en doel. Ontwikkeling en betekenis van twee islamitische bedevaartsoorden op Java. In Willy Jansen and Huub de Jonge (eds), *Islamitische pelgrimstochten*. Muiderberg: Coutinho, 81-100.

De Jonge, Huub (1993), Western and Indonesian Views on the Abangan-Santri Division in Javanese Society. The Reception of Geertz's 'Religion of Java.' In Henk Driessen (ed.), *The Politics of Ethnographic Reading and Writing*. Saarbrücken: Verlag Breitenbach, 101-123.

De Langlade, Vincent (1982/2002), *Esotérisme, médiums, spirites du Pere Lachaise*. Paris: Ed. Vermet.

Dean, Eric T. (1997), *Shook Over Hell: Post-Traumatic Stress, Vietnam, and the Civil War*. Cambridge: Harvard University Press.

Dégh, Linda (1994), *American Folklore and the Mass Media*. Bloomington: Indiana University Press.

Densmore, John (1990), *Riders on the storm. My Life with Jim Morrison and the Doors*. New York: Delacorte.

Di Lorenzo, Maria (2000), *Rosario Livatino. Martire della giustizia*. Rome: Paoline.

Directory on Popular Piety and Liturgy. Principles and Guidelines. Vatican City 2001.

Donadieu-Rigaut, Dominique (2005), *Penser en images les ordres religieux (XIIe – XVe siècles)*. Paris: Arguments.

Dorson, Richard (1977), A Gallery of Folk Heroes. In *American Folklore*. Chicago: The University of Chicago Press, 199-243.

Doss, Erika (1999), *Elvis Culture: Fans, Faith, and Image in Contemporary America*. Lawrence: University Press of Kansas.

Doss, Erika (2002), Believing in Elvis: Popular Piety in Material Culture. In Stewart Hoover and Lynn Schofield Clark (eds), *Practicing Religion in the Age of the Media: Explorations in Media, Religion, and Culture*. New York: Columbia University Press.

Doss, Erika (2005a), Elvis Forever. In Joli Jensen and Steve Jones (eds), *Afterlife as Afterimage: Understanding Posthumous Fame*. New York: Peter Lang Inc.

Doss, Erika (2005b), Popular Culture Canonization: Elvis Presley as Saint and Savior. In James F. Hopgood (ed.), *The Making of Saints: Contesting Sacred Ground*. Tuscaloosa: University of Alabama Press.

Doss, Erika (2006), Spontaneous Memorials and Contemporary Modes of Mourning in America. *Material Religion* 2(3), 294-319.

Drown, Hannah (2001), *Sacred Spaces: Alternative Religion and Healing in Glastonbury, England*. Unpublished MA Thesis, Department of Anthropology, Memorial University of Newfoundland.

Dubisch, Jill (1995), *In a Different Place: Pilgrimage, Gender and Politics at a Greek Island Shrine*. Princeton, NJ: Princeton University Press.

Dubisch, Jill (2005), 'Healing the Wounds That are Not Visible': A Vietnam Veterans' Motorcycle Pilgrimage. In Jill Dubisch and Michael Winkelman (eds), *Pilgrimage and Healing*. Tucson: University of Arizona Press.

Dubisch, Jill, and Michael Winkelman (eds) (2005), *Pilgrimage and Healing*. Tucson: University of Arizona Press.

Dulong, Renaud (1998), *Le témoin oculaire. Les conditions sociales de l'attestation personnelle*. Paris: EHESS.

Dunbar, Dirk (2002), The Evolution of Rock and Roll. Its Religious and Ecological Themes. [Electronic] *Journal of Religion and Popular Culture* 2 (fall).

Dünninger, Hans (1963), Was ist Wallfahrt? Erneute Aufforderung zur Diskussion um eine Begriffsbestimmung. *Zeitschrift für Volkskunde* 59, 221-232.

Dupront, Alphonse (1967), Tourisme et pèlerinage: réflexion de psychologie collective. *Communications* 10, 97-120.

Dupront, Alphonse (1987), *Du Sacré. Croisades et pèlerinages. Images et langages*. Paris: Gallimard.

Eade, John, and Michael J. Sallnow (eds) (1991/2000), *Contesting the Sacred. The Anthropology of Christian Pilgrimage*. London: Routledge [revised edition in 2000: Urbana: University of Illinois Press].

Eade, John and Michael J. Sallnow (1991), Introduction. In John Eade and Michael J. Sallnow (eds), *Contesting the Sacred: The Anthropology of Christian Pilgrimage*. London and New York: Routledge, 1–29.

Eberhart, Helmut (2005), Pellegrinaggio e ricerca: tendenze e approcci attuali. *Lares. Quadrimestrale di studi demoetnoantropologici* 71(1) 73-98 [with a 'Commento' by Alessandro Simonicca].

Eberhart, Helmut (2006), Pilgrimage as an Example for 'the past in the present.' In Fabio Mugnaini et al., *The Past in the Present: A Multidisciplinary Approach*. Catania: EdIt Press, 157-167.

Ebersole, L. (1994), The God and Goddess of the Written Word. In Geri De-Paoli (ed.), *Elvis + Marilyn 2 x Immortal*. New York: Rizzoli.

Erdei, Ildiko (2006), Odrastanje u poznom socijalizmu: od 'pionira malenih' do 'vojske potrošača.' In Lada Čale Feldamn and Ines Prica (eds), *Devijacije i promašaji.Etnografija domaćeg socijalizma,* Zagreb: Institut za etnologiju i folkloristiku, biblioteka Etnografija, 205-240.

Eliade, Mircea (1959), *The Sacred and the Profane: The Nature of Religion.* Translated by Willard R. Trask. New York: Harcourt, Brace & World, Inc.

Everett, Holly (2002), *Roadside Crosses in Contemporary Memorial Culture*. Denton, TX: University of North Texas Press.

Fabre, Daniel (ed.) (1993), *Ecritures ordinaires*, Paris: P.O.L. / Centre Georges Pompidou.

Fabre, Thierry and Deborah Puccio (eds) (2002), *La Pensée de Midi* 8 [issue 'Retrouver Palermo']. Arles: Actes Sud.

Faeta, Francesco (1993), La mort en images. *Terrain*, 20, 69-81.

Farren, Mike (1999), *Jim Morrison's Adventures in the Afterlife. A novel*. New York: St. Martin's Press.

Fiske, John (1993), *Power Plays Power Works*. New York: Verso.

Foote, Kenneth E. (1997), *Shadowed Ground. America's Landscapes of Violence and Tragedy*. Austin: University of Texas Press.

Forgas, Joseph Paul (1985), *Interpersonal behaviour: The psychology of social interaction*. Sydney: Pergamon Press.

Fournier, Patricia, and Luis Arturo Jiménez (2004), La *familia* de Jim Morrison. El culto al Rey Lagarto entre seguidores, admiradores y fanáticos, in Elizabeth Díaz Brenis and Elio Masferrer (eds), *X Congresso Latinoamericano sobre Religión y Etnicidad. Pluralismo Religioso y Transformaciones Sociales,* ALER, Mexico 2004, electronic proceedings.

Fournier, Patricia, and Luis Arturo Jiménez (2005), Representaciones e inter-
    pretaciones del chamanismo en el rock clásico: el caso de Jim Morrison y
    The Doors. In Patricia Fournier and Walburga Wiesheu (eds), *Arqueologia y
    Antropologia de las Religiones*. Mexico City: Escuela Nacional de Antropo-
    logía, 293-314.

Fowlie, Wallace (1993), *Rimbaud and Jim Morrison. The Rebel As Poet.* Durham:
    Duke University Press.

Fraenkel, Béatrice (1992), *La signature. Genèse d'un signe.* Paris: Gallimard.

Fraenkel, Béatrice (2002), *Les écrits de septembre. New York 2001.* Paris: Textuel.

Franklin, Bruce (1993), *M.I.A, or Mythmaking in America*. New Brunswick, NJ:
    Rutgers University Press.

Frazer, James (1979 [1922]), Sympathetic Magic. In William A. Lessa and Evon
    Z. Vogt (eds), *Reader in Comparative Religion: An Anthropological Approach*.
    Fourth Edition. New York: Harper Collins Publishers, 337-352.

Frey, Nancy L. (1998), *Pilgrim Stories on and off the Road to Santiago*. Berkeley:
    University of California Press.

Frijhoff, Willem (1998), *Heiligen, idolen, iconen*. Amsterdam: SUN.

Frijhoff, Willem (2002), *Embodied Belief. Ten Essays on Religious Culture in Dutch
    History*. Hilversum: Verloren.

Frijhoff, Willem (2004), Witnesses to the Other: Incarnate Longings – Saints
    and Heroes, Idols and Models. *Studia Liturgica* 34, 1-25.

Frykman, Jonas and Nils Gilje (2003), Being There: An Introduction. In Jonas
    Frykman and Nils Gilje (eds), *Being There: New Perspectives on Phenomenol-
    ogy and the Analysis of Culture*. Lund: Nordic Academic Press, 7-51.

Geertz, Clifford (1973), *The Interpretation of Cultures*. London: Fontana.

Gerbino, Aldo (ed.) (1991), *La rosa dell'Ercta, 1196-1991. Rosalia Sinibaldi: sa-
    cralità, linguaggi e rappresentazione*. Palermo: Dorica.

Gerhards, Albert and Benedikt Kranemann (eds) (2002), *Christliche Begräb-
    nisliturgie und säkulare Gesellschaft*. Leipzig: Benno Verlag.

Giebels, Lambert (1999), *Soekarno: Nederlands onderdaan. Een biografie 1901-
    1950*. Amsterdam: Bert Bakker.

Giebels, Lambert (2001), *Soekarno: President. Een biografie 1950-1970*. Amster-
    dam: Bert Bakker.

Giunta, Francesco (1991), Santità ed eremitismo nella Sicilia normanna. In Gerbino Aldo (ed.), *La rosa dell'Ercta, 1196-1991. Rosalia Sinibaldi: sacralità, linguaggi e rappresentazione.* Palermo: Dorica, 21-27.

Glock, Charles Y. (1962), On the Study of Religious Commitment. Research Supplement to *Religious Education,* 57(4) July-August. New Haven: The Religious Education Association, 98-110.

Glock, Charles Y. (1974), Over het onderzoek van de religiositeit. In K. Dobbelaere and L. Layendecker (eds), *Godsdienst, kerk en samenleving. Godsdienstsociologische opstellen.* Rotterdam: UP of Rotterdam, 160-185.

Godwin, Malcolm (1990), *Angels: An Endangered Species.* New York: Simon & Schuster.

Gottdiener, M. (1997), Dead Elvis as Other Jesus. In Vernon Chadwick (ed.), *In Search of Elvis: Music, Race, Art, Religion.* Boulder: Westview Press.

Grider, Sylvia (2001), Spontaneous Shrines: Preliminary Observations Regarding the Spontaneous Shrines Following the Terrorist Attacks of September 11, 2001. *New Directions in Folklore* 5 (October). http://www.temple.edu/isllc/newfolk/shrines.html.

Grider, Sylvia (2007), Public Grief and the Politics of Memorial: Contesting the Memory of 'the Shooters' at Columbine High School.' *Anthropology Today* 23(3), 3-7.

Greil Arthur L., and David G. Bromley (eds) (2003), *Defining Religion: Investigating the Bounderies between the Sacred and the Secular.* Amsterdam: Elsevier/JAI.

Griffith, James S. (2003), *Folk Saints of the Borderlands: Victims, Bandits, Healers.* Tucson, AZ: Rio Nuevo Publishers.

Grimes, Ronald L. (1993), Emerging ritual. In Ronald L. Grimes, *Reading, Writing, and Ritualizing: Rituals in Fictive, Liturgical and Public Places.* Washington, DC: Pastoral Press, 23-38.

Grimes, Ronald L. (2000), *Deeply into the Bone. Re-inventing Rites of Passage.* Berkeley: University of California Press.

Guralnick, Peter (1994), *Last Train to Memphis: The Rise of Elvis Presley.* Boston: Little, Brown, and Company.

Guterson, David (2003), *Our Lady of the Forest,* New York: Knopf.

Guth, Klaus (1995), Pilgrimages in Contemporary Europe: Signs of National and Universal Culture. *History of European Ideas* 20(4-6), 831-835.

Halman, Loek, et al. (eds) (2005), *Atlas of European Values*. Leiden: Brill.

Hameline, J.-Y. (2003), Les Rites de passage of Arnold van Gennep. *Studia Liturgica* 33, 129-150.

Hanegraaff, Wouter (1999), New Age Spiritualities as Secular Religion: A Historian's Perspective *Social Compass* 46(2), 145-160.

Haney, C. Allen, Christina Leimer, and Juliann Lowery (1997), Spontaneous Memorialization: Violent Death and Emerging Mourning Ritual. *Omega* 35, 159–171.

Hankiss, Elemér (2002), Legenda Profana, avagy a világ újravarázsolása. In Ágnes Kapitány and Gábor Kapitány (eds), *Jelbeszéd az életünk 2. Szerk*. Budapest: Osiris-Századvég Kiadó, 96–123.

Harrison, Ted (1992), *Elvis People: The Cult of the King*. New York: Harper Collins.

Hass, Kirsten A. (1998), *Carried to the Wall: American Memory and the Vietnam Veterans Memorial*. Berkeley: University of California Press.

Hatch, Nathan O. (1989), *The Democratization of American Christianity*. New Haven: Yale University Press.

Hauser, Susan (1997), *Wall Street Journal* 229, no. 95 (15 May), A21.

Heelas, Paul, and Linda Woodhead (2005), *The Spiritual Revolution; Why Religion is giving Way to Spirituality*. Oxford: Blackwell.

Heinz, Nolan (2007), Pre's Rock File. Randall V. Mills Archive of Northwest Folklore, University of Oregon (Summer).

Hänel, Dagmar (2004), 'Der Kopf kann laufen': Bedeutungen und Funktionen von Wallfahrt in der Gegenwart. *Rheinisch-Westfälische Zeitschrift für Volkskunde* 49, 111-129.

Henley, John, Cemetery staff want to show rock star the door. *The Guardian*, 4 May 2004.

Hermes, Joke (1999), Diana: Death of a Media-Styled Secular Saint. In *Etnofoor* 12,2, 76-91.

Hering, Bob (2001), *Soekarno: Architect van een natie / Architect of a Nation*. Amsterdam / Leiden: KIT Publishers / KITLV Press.

Hering, Bob (2002), *Soekarno: Founding Father of Indonesia, 1901-1945.* Leiden: KITLV Press.

Hervieu-Léger, Danièle (1999), *Le pèlerin et le converti. La religion en mouvement.* Paris: Flammarion.

Hexham, Irving (1981), Some Aspects of the Contemporary Search for an Alternative Society [In Glastonbury, England, 1967-1971]. Unpublished MA Thesis, University of Bristol.

Hexham, Irving (1983), The 'Freaks' of Glastonbury: Conversion and Consolidation in an English Country Town, *Update* 7(1), 3-12.

Higdon, Hal (1992), Is Running a Religious Experience? In Shirl J. Hoffman (ed.), *Sport and Religion.* Champaign, IL: Human Kinetics Books, 77-81.

Hill, Peter C., and Raplh W. Hood (eds) (1999), *Measures of Religiosity.* Birmingham AL: Religious Education Press.

Hills, Matt (2002), *Fan Cultures.* London: Routledge.

Hobsbawm, Eric (1985), Introduction: Inventing Traditions. In Eric Hobsbawm and Terence Ranger (eds), *The Invention of Tradition.* Cambridge: Cambridge University Press, 1–14.

Hodge, Bob (2006), The Goddess Tour: Spiritual Tourism / Post-modern Pilgrimage in Search of Atlantis. In Lynne Hume and Kathleen McPhillips (eds), *Popular Spiritualities: The Politics of Contemporary Enchantment.* Aldershot: Ashgate, 27-39.

Hollister, Geoff, and Erich Lyttle (1996), *Fire on the Track* [documentary film]. Eugene, OR: Westcom Creative Group.

Hopgood, James F. (ed.) (2005a), *The Making of Saints: Contesting Sacred Ground.* Tuscaloosa: University of Alabama Press.

Hopgood, James F. (2005b), Introduction: Saint and Saints in the Making. In James F. Hopgood (ed.), *The Making of Saints: Contesting Sacred Ground.* Tuscaloosa: University of Alabama Press, xi-xxi.

Hopgood, James F. (2005c), Saints and Stars: Sainthood for the 21st Century. In James F. Hopgood (ed.), *The Making of Saints: Contesting Sacred Ground.* Tuscaloosa: University of Alabama Press,124-142.

Hopkins, Jerry (1981), [Interview with Jim Morrison, July 26, 1969]. In Peter Herbst (ed.), *The Rolling Stone Interviews. Talking with the Legends of Rock & Roll, 1967-1980.* New York: St. Martin's Press, 52-59.

Hopkins, Jerry, and Danny Sugerman (1980), *No one here gets out alive*. New York: Warner Books.

Howard-Gordon, Frances (1997), *Glastonbury: Maker of Myths*. Glastonbury: Gothic Image Publications.

Huntington, Richard, and Peter Metcalf (1979), *Celebrations of Death: The Anthropology of Mortuary Ritual*. Cambridge: Cambridge University Press.

Huxley, Aldous (1954), *The Doors of Perception*. London: Chatto & Windus.

Ivakhiv, Adrian J. (2001), *Claiming Sacred Ground: Pilgrims and Politics at Glastonbury and Sedona*. Bloomington and Indianapolis: Indiana UniversityPress.

Ivakhiv, Adrian J. (2007), 'Power Trips: Making Sacred Space through New Age Pilgrimage. In Daren Kemp and James R. Lewis (eds), *Handbook of New Age*. Leiden and Boston: Brill, 263-286

Jackson, Michael (1983), Knowledge of the Body. *Man* (N.S) 18, 327–345.

Janssen, Jacques (1994), *Jeugdcultuur. Een actuele geschiedenis*. Utrecht: De Tijdstroom.

Jensen-Stevenson, M., and W. Stevenson (1990), *Kiss the Boys Good-bye: How the United States Betrayed Its Own POWs in Vietnam*. Toronto: McClelland and Stuart.

Jones, Dylan (1990), *Jim Morrison Dark Star*. New York: Viking Studios.

Jones, Kathy (1998), Multifaith Pilgrimage around the sacred sites of Avalon. *Avalon: A Journal of Transformation from Glastonbury*, 16, 4-5

Jones, Kathy (2000), *In the Nature of Avalon: Goddess Pilgrimages in Glastonbury's Sacred Landscape*. Glastonbury: Ariadne Publications.

Jordan, Tom (1997 [1977]), *Pre: The Story of America's Greatest Running Legend*. New York: Rodale.

Jorgensen-Earp, Cheryl R., and Lanzilotti, Lori, A. (1998), Public Memory and Private Grief: The Construction of Shrines at the Sites of Public Tragedy. *The Quarterly Journal of Speech* 84(2), 150–170.

Jourdan, Michel, and Jacques Vigne (1995), *Marcher méditer*. Paris: Albin Michel.

Kaur, Jagdish (1985), *Himalayan Pilgrimages and the New Tourism*. New Delhi: Himalayan Books.

Kennedy Neville, Gwen (1987), *Kinship and Pilgrimage. Rituals of Reunion in American Protestant Culture*. Oxford: Oxford University Press.

Kimiecik, Jay (2006), The Ghost of Pre and Me (9 September), http://www. runningspot.com/ art_pre.php. (Accessed July 4, 2007).

King, Alex (1998), *Memorials of the Great War in Britain*. Oxford: Berg.

King, Christine (1993), His Truth Goes Marching On: Elvis Presley and the Pilgrimage to Graceland. In Ian Reader and Tony Walter (eds), *Pilgrimage in Popular Culture*. Basingstoke: Palgrave Macmillan, 92-104.

Klaić, Bratoljub (1999), *Rječnik stranih riječi*. Zagreb: Nakladni zavod Matice hrvatske.

Knott, Kim (2005), *The Location of Religion. A Spatial Analysis*. London: Equinox.

Koentjaraningrat (1985), *Javanese Culture*. Singapore: Institute of Southeast Asian Studies / Oxford University Press.

Korff, Gottfried (1997), Personenkult und Kultpersonen. Bemerkungen zur profanen 'Heiligenverehrung' im 20. Jahrhundert. In Walter Kerber (ed.), *Personenkult und Heiligenverehrung*. München: Kindt Verlag, 157-211.

Kregting, Joris, and José Sanders (2003), *'Waar moeten ze het zoeken?' Vindplaatsen van religie en zingeving bij jongvolwassenen*. Nijmegen: Kaski.

Kriss, Rudolf (1963), Zur Begriffsbestimmung des Ausdrucks "Wallfahrt". *Österreichisch Zeitschrift für Volkskunde* 66 (1963), 101-107.

Kristić, Karmela (2006), Tišina koja govori. Iz dokumentacije Marijane Gušić. In Kirsti Mathiesen Hjemdahl and Nevena Škrbić Alempijević (eds), *O Titu kao mitu. Proslava Dana mladosti u Kumrovcu*. Zagreb: FF press & Srednja Europa, 97-119.

Kruse II, Robert J. (2003), Imagining Strawberry Fields as a Place of Pilgrimage. *Area* 35(2), 154-162.

La Licata, Francesco (2002), *Storia di Giovanni Falcone*. Milan: Feltrinelli.

Labrousse, Pierre (1993), The Second Life of Bung Karno. Analysis of the Myth (1978-1981). *Indonesia* 57, 175-196.

Lardas, John H. (1995), Graceland: An Analysis of Sacred Space on the American Religious Landscape. Paper presented at the American Academy of Religion Annual Conference.

Larson-Miller, Lizette (2005), Holy Ground: Discerning Sacred Space in Public Places. In: Marcel Barnard, Paul Post and Els Rose (eds) (2005), *A Cloud of Witnesses*. Leuven: Peeters, 247-274.

Lavigne, Yves (1987), *The Hells Angels: Taking Care of Business*. Toronto: Ballantine.

Legge, J.D. (1972), *Sukarno: A Political Biography*. London: Allen Lane The Penguin Press.

Lindsay, Timothy C. (1993), Concrete Ideology: Taste, Tradition, and the Javanese Past in the New Order Public Space. In V. Matheson Hooker (ed.), *Culture and Society in New Order Indonesia*. Kuala Lumpur: Oxford University Press, 166-182.

Linenthal, Ed (2001), *The Unfinished Bombing: Oklahoma City in American Memory*. New York: Oxford University Press.

Lippard, L. (1999), *Off the Beaten Track: Tourism, Art, and Place*. New York: The New Press.

Lipsitz, George (1990), *Time Passages: Collective Memory and American Popular Culture*. Minneapolis: University of Minnesota Press.

Lloyd, David W. (1998), *Battlefield Tourism: Pilgrimage and the Commemoration of the Great War in Britain, Australia and Canada, 1919-1939*. Oxford: Berg.

Lopez, Ian F. (1996), *White By Law: The Legal Construction of Race*. New York: New York University Press.

Lott, Eric (1993), *Love and Theft: Blackface Minstrelsy and the American Working Class*. New York: Oxford University Press.

Lubis, Mochtar (1969), Mysticism in Indonesian Politics. In Robert O. Tilman (ed.), *Man, State, and Society in Contemporary Southeast Asia*. New York: Praeger Publishers.

Luckmann, Thomas (1967), *The Invisible Religion: The Problem of Religion in Modern Society*. New York: Macmillan.

Luckmann, Thomas (1990), Shrinking Transcendence, Expanding Religion? *Sociological Analysis* 50(2), 127-138.

Lukken, Gerard (2005), *Rituals in Abundance. Critical Reflections on the Place, Form, and Identity of Christian Rituals in our Culture*. Leuven: Peeters.

Mitchell, N. (1995), Emerging Ritual in Contemporary Culture. *Concilium* 31(3), 121-129.

Lupo, Salvatore (1999), *Histoire de la mafia des origines à nos jours*, Paris: Flammarion.

Lyon, David (2000), *Jesus in Disneyland. Religion in Postmodern Times*. Cambridge: Polity Press.

Macioti, Maria I. (2002), Pilgrimages of Yesterday, Jubilees of Today. In William H. Swatos Jr. and Luigi Tomasi (eds), *From Medieval Pilgrimage to Religious Tourism: The Social and Cultural Economics of Piety*. Westport CT: Praeger, 75-90.

Macwilliams, Mark W. (2002), Virtual Pilgrimages on the Internet. *Religion* 32, 315-335.

Macwilliams, Mark W. (2004), Virtual Pilgrimage to Ireland's Croagh Patrick. In Lorne L. Dawson, and Douglas E. Cowan (eds), *Religion Online. Finding Faith on the Internet*. London: Routledge, 223-238.

Maffesoli, Michel (1996), *The Time of the Tribes: The Decline of Individualism in Mass Society*. Transl. D. Smith. London: Sage.

Mailer, Norman (1957) The White Negro. *Dissent* 4 (Spring), 311-331.

Malkki, L. (1997), Speechless Emissaries: Refugees, Humanitarianism, and Dehistoricization. In Karen F. Olwig and Kirsten Hastrup (eds), *Siting Culture: The Shifting Anthropological Object*. London: Routledge, 223-252.

Maltwood, Katharine E. (1964 [orig. 1929]), *A Guide to Glastonbury's Temple of the Stars: Their Giant Effigies Described from Air Views, Maps, and from 'The High History of the Holy Grail.'* 16th ed. London: James Clarke & Co.

Margry, Peter Jan (2000), *Teedere Quaesties: religieuze rituelen in conflict. Confrontaties tussen katholieken en protestanten rond de processiecultuur in 19e-eeuws Nederland*. Hilversum: Verloren.

Margry, Peter Jan (2003), The Murder of Pim Fortuyn and Collective Emotions. Hype, Hysteria and Holiness in The Netherlands? *Etnofoor* 16(2), 102-127.

Margry, Peter Jan (2004a), New Transnational Religious Cultures: The Networks and Strategies of Modern Devotions in Contemporary Europe. In Attila Paládi-Kovács (ed.), *Times, Places, Passages. Ethnological Approaches in the New Millennium*. Budapest: Akadémiai Kiadó, 205-213.

Margry, Peter Jan (2004b), Global Network of Divergent Marian Devotion. In Christopher Partridge (ed.), *Encyclopedia of New Religions: New Religious Movements, Sects and Alternative Spiritualities*. Oxford: Lion Publishing, 98-102.

Margry, Peter Jan (2007), Performative Memorials: Arenas of Political Resentment in Dutch Society. In Peter Jan Margry and Herman Roodenburg (eds), *Reframing Dutch Culture: Between Otherness and Authenticity*. Aldershot: Ashgate, 109-133.

Margry, Peter Jan, and Cristina Sánchez-Carretero (2007), Memorializing traumatic death. *Anthropology Today* 23, no 3: 1-2.

Margry, Peter Jan, and Charles Caspers (eds) (1997-2004), *Bedevaartplaatsen in Nederland*, 4 vol. Hilversum: Verloren.

Margry, Peter Jan, and Paul Post (1998), The 'Places of Pilgrimage in the Netherlands' Project. An Orientation. In Paul Post, Jos Pieper and Marinus van Uden, *The Modern Pilgrim: Multidisciplinary Explorations of Christian Pilgrimage*. Leuven: Peeters, 49-88.

Martikainen, Tuomas (2001), Religion and Consumer Culture. *Tidsskrift for kirke, religion og samfunn* 14(2), 111-125.

Mathiesen Hjemdahl, Kirsti (2006), Slijedeći neke od Titovih putešestvija. Interpretacije transformacija. In Kirsti Mathiesen Hjemdahl and Nevena Škrbić Alempijević (eds), *O Titu kao mitu. Proslava Dana mladosti u Kumrovcu*. Zagreb: FF Press & Srednja Europa, 49-74.

McChesney, Bill (1981), Stories of Steve Prefontaine: The 'Legend' of Tracktown, U.S.A. Randall V. Mills Archive of Northwest Folklore, University of Oregon (Spring).

McKevitt, Christopher (1991), San Giovanni Rotondo and the Shrine of Padre Pio. In John Eade and Michael J. Sallnow (eds), *Contesting the Sacred: The Anthropology of Christian Pilgrimage*. London and New York: Routledge, 77-97.

Meunié, Eric (2005), Résurrection de Jim Morrison. *La Revue Littéraire* 2, July/August, no. 16.

Michalowski, Raymond, and Jill Dubisch (2001), *Run for the Wall: Remembering Vietnam on a Motorcycle Pilgrimage*. New Brunswick, NJ: Rutgers University Press.

Michell, John (1973), *The View Over Atlantis*. London: Abacus

Miller, Shawn (2006), A Larger-than-Life Legacy (*Oregon Daily Emerald*, 12 May). http://www.dailyemerald.com/home/index.cfm?event=displayArticl e&ustory_id=7a4edf76-80bc-4078-bcb7-0938a49f7a26.

Moddemann, Rainer (2003), *Jim Morrison. Paris – Führer*. Kreutzfeldt Electronic Publishing. www:kreutzfeldt.de

Moore, Kenny (2006), *Bowerman and the Men of Oregon: The Story of Oregon's Legendary Coach and Nike's Cofounder*. New York: Rodale.

Morinis, Alan (ed.) (1992), *Sacred Journeys: The Anthropology of Pilgrimage*. Westport: Greenwood.

Morinis, Alan (1992) Introduction: The Territory of the Anthropology of Pilgrimage. In Alan Morinis (ed.), *Sacred Journeys. The Anthropology of Pilgrimage*. Westport: Greenwood, 1-28.

Morrison, Jim (1970), *The Lords and the New Creatures. Poems*. New York: Simon & Schuster.

Morrison, Jim (1985), *The Only Published Poetry of Jim Morrison*. London: Omnibus Press.

Newnham, Blaine (1975), Apologies, Apple Pies. *The Register Guard* (Eugene, Oregon, 20 April), B1.

Nolan, Mary Lee, and Sidney Nolan (1989), *Christian Pilgrimage in Modern Western Europe*. Chapel Hill: University of North Carolina Press.

O'Connor, Mary (1999), The Pilgrimage to Magdalena. In S. D. Glazier (ed.), *Anthropology of Religion. A Handbook*, Westport: Praeger, 369-389.

Orsi, Robert (1991) The Center Out There, In Here, and Everywhere Else: The Nature of Pilgrimage to the Shrine of Saint Jude, 1929-1965. *Journal of Social History* 25(2) (Winter), 213-232.

Ortíz, Ricardo L. (1998), L.A. Woman: Jim Morrison with John Rechy. *Literature and Psychology*, 44, 41-77.

Pahl, Jon (2003), *Shopping Malls and Other Sacred Places. Putting God in Place*. Grand Rapids: Brazos Press.

Passariello, Phyllis (2005), Desperately Seeking Something: Che Guevara as Secular Saint. In James F. Hopgood (ed.), *The Making of Saints: Contesting Sacred Ground*. Tuscaloosa: University of Alabama Press, 75-89.

Pastoureau, Michel (1993), Introduction à la symbolique médiévale du bois. In *L'arbre, histoire naturelle et symbolique de l'arbre, du bois et du fruit au Moyen Age*. Paris: Cahiers du Léopard d'or, 25-40.

Patterson, J. (2002), A New Generation Keeps Elvis A Pop-Culture Icon, 25 Years After His Death. *The San Diego Union-Tribune* (15 August), M-13.

Penders, C.L.M (1974), *The Life and Times of Sukarno*. London: Sidgwick & Jackson.

Pichaske, David (1979), *A Generation in Motion: Popular Music and Culture in the Sixties*. New York: Schirmer Books.

Pierce, Patricia J. (1994), *The Ultimate Elvis*. New York: Simon and Schuster.

Pierce III, Marshal (2003), *The Lost Diaries of Jim Morrison*. Louisville: Wasteland Press.

Pierson, Melissa H. (1997), *The Perfect Vehicle: What Is It About Motorcycles*. New York: Norton.

Piette, Albert (2003), *Le fait religieux. Une théorie de la religion ordinaire*. Paris Economica.

Piquet, Cheryn, and Reba A. Best (1986), *Post-traumatic Stress Disorder, Rape Trauma, Delayed Stress, and Related Conditions: A Bibliography*. Jefferson, N.C.: McFarland.

Plasketes, George (1997), *Images of Elvis Presley in American Culture, 1977-1997*. Birmingham, New York: Harrington Park Press.

Ponisch, Gabriele (2003), 'Du weisst, was ich meine!.' Zur Konstruktion Sozialer Sicherheit im Anliegenbuch. In Gábor Barna (ed.), *Ritualisierung, Zeit, Kommunikation*. Budapest: Akadémiai Kiadó, 19-29.

Porter, Jennifer E. (2004), Pilgrimage and the IDIC Ethic: Exploring *Star Trek* Convention Attendance as Pilgrimage. In Ellen Badone and Sharon R. Roseman (eds), *Intersecting Journeys: The Anthropology of Pilgrimage and Tourism*. Chicago: University of Illinois Press, 160-179.

Post, Paul (1995), *Ritueel landschap: over liturgie-buiten. Processie, pausbezoek, danken voor de oogst, plotselinge dood.* Hilversum: Gooi en Sticht.

Post, Paul (1996), Paysage rituel: la liturgie en plein air (1). *Questions liturgiques / Studies in Liturgy* 77, 174-190, 240-256.

Post, Paul (2000), *Het wonder van Dokkum. Verkenningen van populair religieus ritueel.* Nijmegen: Valkhof Pers.

Post, Paul (2004a), Een ideaal bevraagd: actuele kritische notities bij het adagium van bewuste actieve deelname van de gemeenschap in de liturgie. *Tijdschrift voor liturgie* 88, 2-14.

Post, Paul (2004b), Panorama of Current Ritual-Liturgical Inculturation and Participation in the Netherlands: Sketch and Perspective. In Jozef Lamberts (ed.), *The Active Participation Revisited/La participation active 100 ans après Pie X et 40 ans après vatican II.* Leuven: Acco, 32-69.

Post, Paul (2005), The Trees for Life day in the Netherlands and the Ritual Reference of Pilgrimage. *Mortality* 10(4), 251-261.

Post, Paul, Albertina Nugteren and Hessel Zondag (2003), *Disaster Ritual. Explorations of an Emerging Ritual Repertoire.* Leuven: Peeters.

Post, Paul, Jos Pieper and Marinus van Uden (1998), *The Modern Pilgrim: Multidisciplinary Explorations of Christian Pilgrimage.* Leuven: Peeters.

Post, Paul, and Louis van Tongeren (eds) (2001), *Devotioneel ritueel. Heiligen en wonderen, bedevaarten en pelgrimages in verleden en heden.* Kampen: Gooi en Sticht.

Price, Joseph L. (2000), An American Apotheosis: Sports as Popular Religion. In Bruce David Forbes and Jeffrey H. Mahan (eds), *Religion and Popular Culture in America.* Berkeley: University of California Press, 201-218.

Primiano, Leonard Norman (1995), Vernacular Religion and the Search for a Method in Religious Folklife. *Western Folklore* 54, 37-56.

Prince, Ruth, and David Riches (2000), *The New Age in Glastonbury: The Construction of Religious Movements.* New York and Oxford: Berghahn Books.

Prins, Maerten H. (2006), *The Fragmentization of Youth.* Nijmegen: s.n.

Puccio, Deborah (2001), L'ethnologue et le juge. L'enquête de Giovanni Falcone sur la mafia en Sicile. *Ethnologie française,* 31(1), 15-27.

Puccio, Deborah (2002), Mieux vaux habiller les saints que déshabiller les ivrognes. *Terrain* 38, 141-152.

Puccio-Den, Deborah (2006), Sainte Rosalie de Palerme, entre politique et religieux. *Etudes Corses* [issue'Le fait religieux en Méditerranée'], 62, 145-160.

Puccio-Den, Deborah (2007a), De la sainte pèlerine au saint martyr. Les parcours de l'antimafia en Sicile. *Politix*, 77, 105-128.

Puccio-Den, Deborah (2007b), Mafia: stato di violenza o violenza dello stato? In Tommaso Vitale (ed.), *Alla prova della violenza. Introduzione alla sociologia pragmatica dello stato*. Rome: Riuniti.

Puccio-Den, Deborah (2007c), Sainte Rosalie, les Maures et les mafieux: imageries religieuses et imaginaires politiques. In Jean-Daniel Dubois (ed.), *Visions, images et communautés religieuses*. Turnhout: Brepols.

Puccio-Den, Deborah (forthcoming), *Guerres et conversions. Anthropologie des conflits entre 'Maures et Chrétiens.'* Turnhout: Brepols.

Quain, Kevin (1992), *The Elvis Reader: Texts and Sources on the King of Rock'N'Roll*. New York: St. Martin's Press.

Ragland, Lord Fitzroy (1956 [1936]), *The Hero: A Study in Tradition, Myth, and Drama*. Westport, CN: Greenwood.

Reader, Ian, and Tony Walter (eds) (1993), *Pilgrimage in Popular Culture*. Basingstoke: Palgrave Macmillan.

Rebić, Adalbert (ed.) (2002), *Opći religijski leksikon.* Zagreb: Leksikografski zavod Miroslav Krleža.

Reed, J.D., and Maddy Miller (2005), *Stairway to heaven. The Final Resting Places of Rock's Legends*. New York: Wenner Books.

Reid, J., and Reid, C. (2001), A Cross Marks the Spot: A Study of Roadside Death Memorials in Texas and Oklahoma. *Death Studies* 25(4), 341–356.

Ricœur, Paul (2000), *La mémoire, l'histoire, l'oubli*. Paris: Le Seuil.

Rijff, Ger (1987), *Long Lonely Highway: A 1950s Elvis Scrapbook*. Ann Arbor: The Pierian Press.

Rinschede, G., and S.M. Bhardwaj (eds) (1990), *Pilgrimage in the United States*. Berlin: Dietrich Reimer Verlag.

Riordan, James, and Jerry Prochnicky (1991), *Break on through. The life and death of Jim Morrison*. New York: W. Morrow & Co.

Rodenberg, Hans-Peter (1983), *Subversive Phantasie. Untersuchungen zur Lyrik der amerikanischen Gegenkultur 1960-1975*. Giessen: Focus-Verlag.

Rodman, Gilbert (1996), *Elvis After Elvis: The Posthumous Career of a Living Legend*. New York: Routledge.

Roediger, David R. (1991), *The Wages of Whiteness: Race and the Making of the American Working Class*. New York: Verso.

Rojek, Chris (2001), *Celebrity*. London: Reaktion Books.

Roof, Wade C. (1993), *A Generation of Seekers: The Spiritual Journeys of the Baby Boom Generation*. New York: Harper.

Rosenbaum, R. (1995), Among the Believers. *New York Times Magazine* (24 September 24), 50-57, 62, 64.

Rowbottom, Anne (2002), Subject Positions and 'Real Royalists': Monarchy and Vernacular Civil Religion in Great Britain. In Nigel Rapport (ed.), *British Subjects: An Anthropology of Britain*. Oxford: Berg, 31-47.

Rowlands, M. (1999), Remembering to Forget: Sublimation as Sacrifice in War Memorials. In Adrian Forty and Susanne Kuchler (eds), *The Art of Forgetting*. Oxford: Berg.

Sallnow, Michael J. (1981), Communitas Reconsidered. The Sociology of Andean Pilgrimage. *Man* 16, 163-183.

Schreiner, Klaus H. (2002), 'National Ancestors': The Ritual Construction of Nationhood. In Henri Chambert-Loir and Anthony Reid (eds), *The Potent Dead: Ancestors, Saints and Heroes in Contemporary Indonesia*. Honolulu: Allen & Unwin / University of Hawai'i Press, 183-204.

Schwarze, Bernd (1997), *Die Religion der Rock- und Popmusik. Analysen und Interpretationen*. Stuttgart: Kohlhammer.

Scott, J. (1991), The Evidence of Experience. *Critical Inquiry* 17, no. 4 (Summer), 773-797.

Seay, David, and Mary Neely (1986), *Stairway to Heaven. The Spiritual Roots of Rock 'n' Roll – From the King and Little Richard to Prince and Amy Grand*. New York: Ballatine Books.

Serwer, A. (2005) The Man Who Bought Elvis. *Fortune* (12 December).

Seymore, Bob (1991), *The End. The Death of Jim Morrison*. New York: Omnibus Press.

Soeharto (1989), *Pikiran, ucapan, dan tindakan saya. Otobiografi.* Jakarta: Citra Lamtoro Gung Persada.

Spencer, J. M. (1997), A Revolutionary Sexual Persona: Elvis Presley and the White Acquiescence of Black Rhythms. In Vernon Chadwick (ed.), *In Search of Elvis: Music, Race, Art, Religion.* Boulder: Westview Press.

Spera, Enzo (1977), Ex-voto fotografici e oggettuali. In Emmanuela Angiuli (ed.), *Puglia ex-voto.* Bari: Congedo.

Stoddard, Robert H., and Alan Morinis (1997), *Sacred Places, Sacred Spaces. The Geography of Pilgrimages.* Baton Rouge: Geoscience Publications.

Stromberg, Peter (1990), Elvis Alive? The Ideology of American Consumerism. *Journal of Popular Culture* 24, no. 3 (Winter), 11-19 .

Swatos Jr., William H., and Luigi Tomasi (eds) (2002), *From Medieval Pilgrimage to Religious Tourism: The Social and Cultural Economics of Piety.* Westport CT: Praeger.

Syariffudin, Amak (2001), *Hari-hari terakhir Bung Karno.* S.l.: Guyup Rukun Ing Panguripan.

Sánchez-Carretero, Cristina (2006), Trains of Workers, Trains of Death: Some Reflections after the March 11 Attacks in Madrid. In Jack Santino (ed.), *Spontaneous Shrines and the Public Memorialization of Death.* New York: Palgrave, 333-347.

Santino, Jack (1992), 'Not An Unimportant Failure': Rituals of Death and Politics in Northern Ireland. In Michael McCaughan (ed.), *Displayed in Mortal Light,* Antrim, Northern Ireland: Antrim Arts Council.

Santino, Jack (2001), *Signs of War and Peace: Social Conflict and the Use of Public Symbols in Northern Ireland.* New York: Palgrave.

Santino, Jack (ed.) (2006a), *Spontaneous Shrines and the Public Memorialization of Death.* New York: Palgrave.

Santino, Jack (2006b), Performative Commemoratives: Spontaneous Shrines and the Public Memorialization of Death. In Jack Santino (ed.), *Spontaneous Shrines and the Public Memorialization of Death.* New York: Palgrave, 5-15.

Scruggs, Jan C., and J. Swerdlow (1985), *To Heal a Nation: The Vietnam Veterans Memorial.* New York: Harper and Row.

Sellers, Richard W., and Tony Walter (1993), From Custer to Kent State: Heroes, Martyrs, and the Evolution of Popular Shrines in the U.S.A. In Ian Reader and Tony Walter (eds), *Pilgrimage in Popular Culture*. Basingstoke, England: MacMillan.

Shay, Jonathan (1994), *Achilles in Vietnam: Combat Trauma and the Undoing of Character*. New York: Atheneum.

Sheehan, George A. (1978), *Running and Being: The Total Experience*. New York: Simon and Schuster.

Socolov, Emily (1997), Pilgrimage. In Thomas A. Green (ed.), *Folklore: An Encyclopedia of Beliefs, Customs, Tales, Music, and Art*. Santa Barbara: ABC-CLIO, 647-649.

Söderholm, Stig (1990), *Liskokuninkaan mytologia. Rituaali ja rocksankarin kuolema: Jim Morrison-kultin etnografinen tulkinta*. Helsinki: Suomalaisen Kirjallisuuden Seura.

Stater, Susan (2007), Pre's Rock File. Randall V. Mills Archive of Northwest Folklore, University of Oregon (Summer).

Stengs, Irene (2003), Ephemeral Memorials against 'Senseless Violence.' Materialisations of Public Outcry. *Etnofoor* 16(2), 26-40.

Strete, Craig (1982), *Dreams that Burn down the Night*. New York: Doubleday.

Sugerman, Danny, and Benjamin Edmonds (eds) (1983), *The Doors. The illustrated history*. London: Vermillion.

Tambiah, S.J. (1976), *World Conqueror & World Renouncer. A Study of Buddhism and Polity in Thailand against a Historical Background*. Cambridge: Cambridge University Press.

Thomas, Jeannie Banks (2006), Communicative Commemoration and Graveside Shrines: Princess Diana, Jim Morrison, My 'Bro' Max, and Boogs the Cat. In Jack Santino (ed.), *Spontaneous Shrines and the Public Memorialization of Death*. New York: Palgrave, 17-40.

Tick, Ed (2005), *The Golden Tortoise. Journeys in Viet Nam*. Granada Hills: Red Hen Press.

Timothy, Dallen J., and Daniel H. Olsen (eds) (2006), *Tourism, Religion and Spiritual Journeys*. London: Routledge.

Tomasi, Luigi (2002), Homo Viator: From Pilgrimage to Religious Tourism via the Journey. In William H. Swatos Jr. and Luigi Tomasi (eds), *From Medieval Pilgrimage to Religious Tourism: The Social and Cultural Economics of Piety.* Westport, CN: Praeger, 1-24.

TRE: *Theologische Realenzyklopädie* XXXV (2003) 408-432: 'Wallfahrt / Wallfahrtswesen' I-VI, esp. VI 'Praktisch-theologisch' (A. Gerhards), 431-435.

Trwoga, Chris (2001), *Grail Quest in the Vales of Avalon* Glastonbury: Speaking Tree

Tumarkin, Nina (1997), *Lenin Lives! The Lenin cult in Soviet Russia.* Harvard University Press, Cambridge, Massachusetts.

Turner, Victor W. (1969), *Ritual Process: Structure and Anti-Structure.* Chicago: Aldine.

Turner, Victor W., and Edith Turner (1978), *Image and Pilgrimage in Christian Culture. Anthropological Perspectives.* New York/Oxford: Columbia UP/ Blackwell.

Urry, John (2002), Mobility and proximity. *Sociology* 46 (2), 255-274.

Van Ede, Yolanda et al. (eds) (1999), Editorial [special issue Personality Cults]. *Etnofoor* 12,2: 3-5.

Van Alphen, Jim (1980), *Slotakkoord.* Amsterdam: P. van der Velden.

Van de Bles, C., and L. Hollander (2000), *In het bos voor 't leven. Opdracht Staatsbosbeheer regio Flevoland/Overijssel, Opleiding Tuin- en Landschapsinrichting.* Velp: Internationale Agrarische Hogeschool Larenstein te Velp (final thesis).

Van der Veer, Peter (1994), *Religious Nationalism: Hindus and Muslims in India.* Berkeley: University of California Press.

Van Eijnatten, Joris, Fred van Lieburg and Hans de Waardt (eds) (2007), *Heiligen of Helden. Opstellen voor Willem Frijhoff.* Amsterdam: Bert Bakker.

Van Gennep, Arnold (1909), *Les rites de passage.* Paris: Nourry.

Van Gennep, Arnold (1960 [1909]), *The Rites of Passage.* Transl. Monika B. Vizedom and Gabrielle L. Caffee. Chicago: University of Chicago Press.

Van Tongeren, Louis (2004), Individualizing Ritual: The Personal Dimension in Funeral Liturgy. In *Worship* 78(2), 117-138.

Vanreusel, Bart (2003), Elite Sports as a Catwalk. The Culture of the Body and the Normalization of Excess. In: Robert Burggraeve et al. (eds) (2003), *Desirable God? Our Fascination with Images, Idols and New Deities*. Leuven: Peeters, 199-209.

Verdery, Katherine (1999), *The Political Lives of Dead Bodies*. Columbia University Press, New York.

Verheul, Ineke (1999), *The tenth Life of Jim Morrison*. Utrecht: private press.

Vikan, Gary (1994) Graceland as *Locus Santos.* In Geri DePaoli (ed.), *Elvis + Marilyn 2 x Immortal*. New York: Rizzoli.

Walter, Tony (1993), War Grave Pilgrimage. In Ian Reader and Tony Walter (eds), *Pilgrimage in Popular Culture*. Basingstoke: MacMillan, 29-62.

Walter, Tony (ed.) (1999), *The Mourning for Diana*. Oxford and New York: Berg.

Walton, Theresa A. (2004), Steve Prefontaine: From Rebel with a Cause to Hero with a Swoosh. *Sociology of Sport Journal* 21, 61-83.

Wessing, Robert (2003), The Kraton-City and the Realm: Sources and Movement of Power in Java. In Peter Nas, Gerard Persoon and Rivke Jaffe (eds), *Framing Indonesian Realities. Essays in Symbolic Anthropology in Honour of Reimar Schefold*. Leiden: KITLV Press, 199-250.

Wilson, Stephen (ed.) (1983), *Saints and Their Cults: Studies in Religious Sociology, Folklore, and History*. Cambridge, MA: Cambridge University Press.

Windsor, J. (1992), Faith and the State of Graceland Enterprises. *The Independent* (15 August), 33.

Winkelman, Michael, and Jill Dubisch (2005), Introduction: The Anthropology of Pilgrimage. In Jill Dubisch and Michael Winkelman (eds), *Pilgrimage and Healing*. Tucson: University of Arizona Press, ix-xxxvi.

Wojcik, Daniel (1996), Polaroids from Heaven: Photography, Folk Religion, and the Miraculous Image Tradition at a Marian Apparition Site. *Journal of American Folklore* 109, 129-148.

Wojcik, Daniel (1997), *The End of the World As We Know It: Faith, Fatalism, and Apocalypse in America*. New York and London: New York University Press.

Wojcik, Daniel (2008), Outsider Art, Vernacular Traditions, Trauma, and Creativity. *Western Folklore* 66, 11-35.

Wolf, Daniel R. (1991), *The Rebels: A Brotherhood of Outlaw Bikers*. Toronto: University of Toronto Press.

Wood, Nancy (1999), *Vectors of Memory: Legacies of Trauma in Postwar Europe*. Oxford: Berg.

Wuthnow, Robert (1992), *Rediscovering the Sacred: Perspectives on Religion in Contemporary Society*. Grand Rapids: W.B. Eerdmans.

Yoder, Don (1974), Toward a Definition of Folk Religion. *Western Folklore* 33, 2-15.

York, Michael (2002), Contemporary Pagan Pilgrimages. In William H. Swatos, Jr., and Luigi Tomasi (eds), *From Medieval Pilgrimage to Religious Tourism: The Social and Cultural Economics of Piety*. Westport, CN: Praeger, 137-158.

Young, Allan (1995), *The Harmony of Illusions: Inventing Post Traumatic Stress Disorder*. Princeton, NJ: Princeton University Press.

Zelinsky, Wilbur (1990), Nationalistic Pilgrimages in the United States. In G. Rinschede and S.M. Bhardwaj (eds), *Pilgrimage in the United States*. Berlin: Dietrich Reimer Verlag, 253-267.

Zimdars-Swartz, Sandra L. (1991), *Encountering Mary. Visions of Mary from La Salette to Medjugorje*. Princeton: Princeton University Press.

Index